SWITCHING MACHINES

VOLUME 1

J.-P. PERRIN, M. DENOUETTE, AND E. DACLIN

SWITCHING MACHINES

VOLUME 1

COMBINATIONAL SYSTEMS

INTRODUCTION TO SEQUENTIAL SYSTEMS

D. REIDEL PUBLISHING COMPANY/DORDRECHT-HOLLAND

SYSTÈMES LOGIQUES, TOME 1
First published by Dunod, Paris, 1967
Translated from the French

Library of Congress Catalog Card Number 70–118379

ISBN-13:978-94-010-2866-0   e-ISBN-13:978-94-010-2864-6
DOI: 10.1007/978-94-010-2864-6

INTRODUCTION

We shall begin this brief section with what we consider to be its objective. It will be followed by the main outline and then concluded by a few notes as to how this work should be used.

Although logical systems have been manufactured for some time, the theory behind them is quite recent. Without going into historical digressions, we simply remark that the first comprehensive ideas on the application of Boolean algebra to logical systems appeared in the 1930's. These systems appeared in telephone exchanges and were realized with relays. It is only around 1955 that many articles and books trying to systematize the study of such automata, appeared. Since then, the theory has advanced regularly, but not in a way which satisfies those concerned with practical applications. What is serious, is that aside the books by Caldwell (which dates already from 1958), Marcus, and P. Naslin (in France), few works have been published which try to gather and unify results which can be used by the practising engineer; this is the objective of the present volumes.

The reader of this work (whom we wish will be rather a user) must therefore not expect to find revelations and discoveries in the theory of logical automata. We are much more modest than that; we have tried to put forth in as directly applicable a fashion as we could, the results obtained by research workers in this field. This goal was, however, coupled with that of trying to indicate to those who feel oriented towards research, what paths seem most fruitful for the practical application of this young science.

The main outline we have followed seemed to stem naturally from the orientation which we have tried to give to this work. The first two chapters introduce the essential instruments used in the rest of the book: Boolean algebra, the theoretical tool, and the diverse technological components known at present, the practical tool.

Chapter 1 contains notions of Boolean algebra with a rather original discussion of the use of Boolean matrices in problems of Boolean function decomposition. Chapter 2 deals with the study of components. We have tried to give as complete a picture as possible of the subject by including a discussion of fluidic components. Chapter 3 is an application of the first two chapters. Analysis and synthesis of combinational electronic or relay systems are developed.

The seven chapters which follow cover sequential systems. Chapter 4 is an introductory chapter bringing to light the fact that a sequential system's structure is characterized by the presence of loops in the diagrams. This introduces the concept of internal variables. Chapter 5 puts sequential machines into two different classes depending on the nature of the outputs and inputs. We then apply these tools to the analysis of sequential systems, particularly to the determination of different types of hazards (Chapter 6).

Chapters 7, 8, 9, and 10 treat the synthesis of sequential systems in three steps:

(1) We go from a correspondence between a certain number of input sequences and output sequences to the table of the system under study (Chapter 7).

(2) We reduce this table (Chapter 8).

(3) We assign states to the table. This is done in two different ways depending on whether we deal with an asynchronous sequential system (Chapter 9) or a synchronous sequential system (Chapter 10).

In Chapter 11 we have tried to show with real examples what applications of the theories can be envisaged. Exercises are composed in each of the first ten chapters.

As far as Chapters 12 and 13 are concerned, the study of linear sequential systems and many-valued algebras are to indicate in a more precise fashion than what preceeded them, which paths of theoretical research must be taken today to bear fruit.

Having exposed the objective sought and the main outline followed, we now try to complete this panorama of our work. We wish our work, addressed to the practising engineer, not to be a book of recipes. This led to a rigorous discussion of all theoretical results. Proofs which were too involved, were put in the appendices at the end of the chapters. Further, each chapter has a scrupulous list of bibliographical references. Finally, exercises at the end of the chapter allow the reader to tackle problems himself and hence provides him with the means of verifying his knowledge.

We have also tried to give a glimpse of all the present-day methods of study. For this reason, the reader will find a good number of methods and names from Eastern Europe and the Soviet Union. We believe this to be one of the innovations of our book: the proportion of Russian authors whose works have been used as the basis of different chapters is higher than in other works by French authors dealing with this subject.

Finally, always faithful to the task we have choosen, every time that it was possible, we have indicated which of the methods discussed could be used by numerical computer, since this tool is becoming more and more important in applications.

In conclusion, all critical comments and suggestions from the reader will be more than welcome, for it is a collaboration between users of these methods and those who try to perfect them, which really should lead to processes still more efficient for the study of logical systems.

This work was carried out at the Centre d'Études et de Recherches en Automatismes (C.E.R.A.) as a contract with the Direction des Recherches and Moyens d'Essais (D.R.M.E.).

The authors are particularly grateful to J. C. Gille, M. Pelegrin and N. Mignot for their encouragements. They also wish to thank many of their colleagues at C.E.R.A., particularly J. Delisle, Y. Joffrin and J. Chinal, with whom the authors have had many enriching discussions during the course of this work.

ACKNOWLEDGEMENTS

We want to thank a lot Mrs. Zaidman, who has translated the bigger part of this book into English, P. Stern who has helped us also and Mrs. Delacourt, who has typed the French manuscript, as well as Mrs. Meulin, who did the same for a part of the English one.

FOREWORD

The past thirty years have allowed the technical construction of many finite state automata. Abstract algebra has been enriched by the new chapter of their study, work upon Boolean algebras has been continued by new problems and new results, work upon Lukasiewicz's algebras has found a physical justification; Galois fields and semi-groups have offered a growing interest for technicians; strong connections have been established between these studies and those referring to finite state grammars.

This field of research (narrowly bound to a technical point of view) has been the first to show that a larger concept of 'technique' has been brought to light by the emergence of logic and algebra as the leaders of modern mathematics. Today, an engineer has not only to calculate some pieces for a mechanism, but also to assemble them in structures, not only to deal with energy and its transformations, but also with information and its treatment.

Historically, algebraic theory of finite state automata began quite modestly with the works of Nakashima and Hanzawa (Japan), V. I. Shestakov (U.S.S.R.), Cl. Shannon (U.S.A.). The main problem was then a reduction in the number of relays or tubes. In algebraic terms this was the problem of the simplification of a Boolean function and Quine's method was the main goal for research. Fifteen to ten years ago, attention began to be focused on finite sequential automata. S. C. Kleene gave a clear answer to the question "What can an automaton do?" D. A. Huffman showed which way should be taken when an automaton was wanted for a special job.

From this time, two distinct ways appeared. On one hand, the idea of an abstract automaton has been quickly outlined. A theory of abstract automata (specially of finite ones) has been quickly built: homomorphisms, isomorphisms, congruence relations, factorization relations, decomposition. Sequential automata are a category, the properties of which are beginning to be well known. Relations between automata and grammars have been classified. Among many proposed generalizations, one must emphasize the notion of stochastic automaton which has as great an importance from a theoretical as from a practical point of view.

On the other hand, the 'handwidth' of the ordinary concept of an automaton has been explored. One can not now study completely automata with delays. But, one knows that circuits using electronic tubes or transistors, cryotons or magnetic rings, step by step selecting devices or polarized relays, pneumatic or fluid components are finite automata. Does this fact mean that we have no problem with them, and, in consequence, that no further study is necessary? In fact, two classes of phenomena have caught the attention of people for a long time. The first one we call change-over hazard. It is well known that the sequence of states for the components of a circuit is not the same when two or more 'relays' change state simultaneously as when only one change at a time is allowed. This type of hazard can be brought about by assignment. In the ensemble of internal states for a relay circuit we can find allowed and forbidden sequences. The same is true when contacts are taken from selecting devices. A second class of hazard is due to the fact that contacts from a same relay change state not all at once, but one by one, or two by two, and so on. The classical static hazard is due to the fact that the excitation of the relay happens before make-contacts are closed. Study of speed-independent and hazard-free circuits is of great practical importance.

I consider this book quite characteristic of this third step in the history of algebraic theory of automata with contacts and relays or electronic components. Not a quarter of this book deals with combinational circuits, while an important part of the rest deals with hazards.

Among the most interesting points in this work, I would like to emphasize the following. There is the research for a clear introduction to sequential systems, with an interesting synthesis of results established in the U.S.A. about the assignment problem. Chapter 11 gives a good illustration for the application of theories to real problems. Chapter 12 is an original presentation of the study of linear automata (introduced by D. A. Huffman). Chapter 13 is a good introduction to the use of Lukasiewicz's algebras, not forgetting the application in this algebra of the Quine-McCluskey method.

I have been quite interested by reading the manuscript, and I have no doubt that the future readers of this book will be equally interested.

University of Bucarest   GR. C. MOISIL

CONTENTS

CHAPTER 2/PRACTICAL REALIZATION
OF LOGICAL FUNCTIONS

CHAPTER 3/COMBINATIONAL SYSTEMS

CHAPTER 4/INTRODUCTION TO SEQUENTIAL SYSTEMS

CHAPTER 5/REPRESENTATION AND CLASSIFICATION
OF SEQUENTIAL SYSTEMS

CHAPTER 1

BOOLEAN ALGEBRA

1.1. INTRODUCTION

In control research, two large classes can be distinguished. In one we deal with quantities which can take an infinity of values such as servomechanisms (linear, non-linear or sampled). The classical example of a servomechanism is an automatic airplane pilot. The input signals are the different parameters of the airplane and the exterior parameters. Their variations, for the most part, are continuous. The output signals are, for example, the airplane's speed and direction which also vary continuously within a certain domain of values.

In the other class we deal with quantities which can take only a finite number of values. Here the main element is sequential automata; the classical example of which is a telephone circuit. The input signal of a telephone circuit is a series of pulses identical in intensity and duration; the output signal is a sound signal indicating that connection has been made between two telephones. In this case, we may consider the output signal to be two-valued: the connection can or cannot be fully completed depending upon the presence or absence of a person to receive the call.

This very schematic example shows how important it is to have an algebraic language for 'sequential systems' study which expresses, without ambiguity, the properties of variables having a finite number of values. In most cases met with in practise, this finite number is two, which corresponds to the number of stable equilibrium positions in a classical relay (energized or deenergized), a transistor (conducting or nonconducting), or a diode. In the present work, we shall limit ourselves to two-valued systems. We shall use Boolean algebra as our language and therefore list its essential properties. We wish to make it clear that we have no intention of presenting a mathematical 'exposé,' but shall simply give basic postulates, axioms and short proofs of fundamental theorems necessary for the comprehension of that which follows. We refer the reader desiring a rigorous formulation to the bibliography at the end of this chapter.

On the other hand, we shall insist as much as possible on the passage, often necessary in practise, from one operator type logic to another. We shall then discuss simplification and factorization methods for Boolean functions.

1.2. BINARY NUMBER SYSTEMS–CODES

We know that in a number system of base n, an array of numbers $abcd$ has the value

$$d \cdot n^0 + c \cdot n^1 + b \cdot n^2 + a \cdot n^3.$$

Hence, in a system of base 10, the array 1865 has the value $5 \cdot 10^0 + 6 \cdot 10^1 + 8 \cdot 10^2 + 1 \cdot 10^3$, and in the octal system (base 8), 2735 has the value $5 + 3 \cdot 8 + 7 \cdot 64 + 2 \cdot 512$ (1501 in decimals). In the binary system, that is of base 2, there are only two numbers, called digits, 0 and 1. The array 1 0 1 1 therefore has the value $1 \cdot 1 + 1 \cdot 2 + 0 \cdot 4 + 1 \cdot 8 = 11$ (in decimals).

The last digit in the array, to the right, is called the digit of least weight, and the first digit in the array the digit of greatest weight. A digit has less weight than the preceeding and more weight than the following.

For example, if we write the binary equivalent of the ten decimal numbers, we obtain Figure 1.1. The sequence of binary numbers thus obtained constitutes the translation of the decimal numbers into *pure binary code*.

Decimal number	Pure binary code	Decimal number	Reflected binary code
0	0 0 0 0	0	0 0 0 0
1	0 0 0 1	1	0 0 0 1
2	0 0 1 0	2	0 0 1 1
3	0 0 1 1	3	0 0 1 0
4	0 1 0 0	4	0 1 1 0
5	0 1 0 1	5	0 1 1 1
6	0 1 1 0	6	0 1 0 1
7	0 1 1 1	7	0 1 0 0
8	1 0 0 0	8	1 1 0 0
9	1 0 0 1	9	1 1 0 1

FIG. 1.1.   FIG. 1.2.

From a technological point of view, it is more interesting to relate the ten decimal numbers to other digital combinations, rather than their strict binary equivalents. This is done with the condition that only one binary 'word' corresponds to a decimal number and vice-versa.

In this way, we can obtain a code having certain useful properties in applications. Thus, we often use codes called *reflected binary codes* an example of which is shown in Figure 1.2) having the following property: the passage from the binary equivalent of a number n to the binary equivalent of $n + 1$ is done by changing the value of only 1 digit.

It is also possible to construct a code, the *binary coded decimal*, in which each decimal number is coded by four binary numbers (Figure 1.3). We must note, however, that here it is no longer a question of a

1 is written	0000	0001
9 is written	0000	1001
10 is written	0001	0000
11 is written	0001	0001
20 is written	0010	0000
50 is written	0101	0000
51 is written	0101	0001
99 is written	1001	1001

FIG. 1.3.

number system as was the pure binary code, but rather a simple translation of 'words' written in decimals into 'words' written in binary. Note, that instead of coding numbers we can code any objects. Thus, if the choice of a work tool depends upon weight (good or bad), form (good or bad), and size (good or bad), a correspondence can be made by associating a digit to each of these qualities (weight, size, form). For example, a tool coded 0 1 1 would be good with respect to its size and form, but bad with respect to its weight. The correspondence could also be made by attributing 2 digits to each quality, which would distinguish $2^2 = 4$ classes for each quality. In this way, 'weight' could be coded:

11	good weight
01	too light
10	10 grams or less too heavy
00	more than 10 grams overweight.

If the digits characterizing a tool are written in the same order (weight size, form) as above, we see that the 2 digits of least weight characterize the form and those of greatest weight characterize the mass of he tool.

We remark that a cyclic code in Figure 1.2 is obtained by coding 9 by 1000.

Numbers from 0 to 99 can be represented by using two decimal blocks as in Figure 1.3.

1.3. POSTULATES AND THEOREMS OF BOOLEAN ALGEBRA

1.3.1. *Postulates*

A Boolean algebra is a nonempty set of elements E on which two binary laws of composition $+$ (or $\vee$), called Boolean addition, $\cdot$ (or $\wedge$), called Boolean multiplication, and a unary law $-$, called negation, are defined. The elements of this set satisfy the following properties:

Idempotence

P_1 $A + A = A$

P_1' $A \cdot A = A$

Commutativity

P_2 $A + B = B + A$

P_2' $A \cdot B = B \cdot A$

Associativity

P_3 $A + (B + C) = (A + B) + C = A + B + C$

P_3' $A \cdot (B \cdot C) = (A \cdot B) \cdot C = A \cdot B \cdot C$

Distributivity

P_4 $A \cdot (B + C) = A \cdot B + A \cdot C$

P_4' $A + (B \cdot C) = (A + B) \cdot (A + C)$

P_5 Existence of a neutral element denoted '0' for addition

$$A + 0 = A$$

P_5' Existence of a neutral element denoted '1' for multiplication

$$A \cdot 1 = A$$

P_6 Definition of the complementary element

$$A + \bar{A} = 1$$

P_6' $A \cdot \bar{A} = 0$

P_7 Involution
$$\bar{\bar{A}} = A$$

De Morgan's laws
$P_8 \qquad \overline{A+B} = \bar{A} \cdot \bar{B}$
$P_8' \qquad \overline{A \cdot B} = \bar{A} + \bar{B}$

These laws show the duality between the two operations. They can be generalised to include cases of more than two variables.

The operation $(+)$ will be called OR; the operation $(\cdot)$ will be called AND. As in ordinary arithmetic multiplication we shall almost always leave out the sign $(\cdot):A \cdot B \cdot C$ will be written ABC. The associativity and commutativity of the laws permit the suppression of many parentheses: $A(B+C)(D \cdot E) = ADE(B+C)$. The generalized De Morgan's laws permit us to simplify formulas. The complement of a function of many variables is equal to the same function in which the variables have been replaced by their complements and the two fundamental operations are exchanged.

Example:

$$\overline{(\bar{A} + BC)} = A(\bar{B} + \bar{C})$$

We note it

$$\bar{F}(X_1, X_2, \ldots, X_n, +, \cdot) = F(\bar{X}_1, \bar{X}_2, \ldots, \bar{X}_n, \cdot, +).$$

1.3.2. *Other relations*
The following theorems can be proven:

$T_1 \quad A + 1 = 1$
      $(A+1)(1) = (A+1)(A+\bar{A})$ (from P_5' and P_6). Hence
      $A+1 = A+1 \cdot \bar{A}$ (from P_4') $= (A+\bar{A})$ (from P_5') $= 1$
      (from P_6).

$T_1' \quad A \cdot 0 = 0$
      $A \cdot 0 = A \cdot 0 + 0 = A \cdot 0 + A \cdot \bar{A}$ by analogy with T_1.

$T_2 \quad 1$ *is a unique element.*
      Suppose that another such element $1'$ existed:
      $A+1 = 1$
      $A+1' = 1'.$

Letting $A = 1'$ in the first equation and $A = 1$ in the second we have

$$1' + 1 = 1 \qquad 1 + 1' = 1' \quad \text{that is} \quad 1 = 1'.$$

T_2' 0 *is a unique element:* this is seen by duality.

T_3 The absorption law: $A + AB = A$
From P_5': $A + AB = A \cdot 1 + A \cdot B$
From P_4 $= A(1 + B)$
From T_1 $= A \cdot 1 = A$ (from P_5')

T_3' $A(A + B) = A$

This is the dual of the preceding. The proof is immediate

T_4 $A + \bar{A}B = A + B$
Since $A + \bar{A}B = (A + \bar{A})(A + B)$

T_4' $A(\bar{A} + B) = AB$

The reader can prove the following theorems as an exercise if he wishes:

T_5 $AB + \bar{A}C + BC = AB + \bar{A}C = (\bar{A} + B)(A + C)$
T_6 $\overline{AC + B\bar{C}} = \bar{A}C + B\bar{C}$
T_6' $\overline{(A + C)(B + \bar{C})} = (\bar{A} + C)(\bar{B} + \bar{C})$

Note: In the following we shall consider the particular case in which the set E consists of two elements 0 and 1. This particular Boolean algebra is often mistakenly called the Algebra of Boole. A variable defined in this set will be called a *Boolean variable.*

1.4.   BOOLEAN FUNCTIONS

In Section 1.3.2 we proved different theorems relative to Boolean variables. However, these variables do not generally appear alone. We are thus led to study the functions of Boolean variables; that is, the quantities, also Boolean, whose values depend, in a more or less simple way, upon the values of a certain number of Boolean variables. We give an example.

Consider a series of three lamps L_1, L_2, L_3. A Boolean variable X_i is associated with each lamp: X_i equals 1 if the lamp L_i is on and 0 if it is off. We also define a quantity 'illumination of a room' E. The illumination is 'sufficient' $(E = 1)$ if at least 2 of the 3 lamps are on. E is a function of x_1, x_2, and x_3. In the same way as in classical algebra where we are concerned with the value of a function $y(x)$, we shall be interested in the value of E. But in contrast with function theory where we express a relation between y and x, for example, we shall study Boolean functions as being characterized by the points at which they equal 1. This is possible since we know that Boolean functions can take only 2 values, 0 and 1. It is consequently of no interest to have a more complicated formulation.

Returning to our example of a Boolean function $E(x_1, x_2, x_3)$, we see that E takes the value 1 in the following cases: when $x_1 = 1$ and $x_2 = 1$, or $x_1 = 1$ and $x_3 = 1$, or $x_2 = 1$ and $x_3 = 1$, or $x_1 = 1$, and $x_2 = 1$, and $x_3 = 1$, which is expressed in Boolean language by the relation

$$E = x_1 x_2 + x_2 x_3 + x_3 x_1 + x_1 x_2 x_3.$$

We shall now study diverse ways of representing Boolean functions, then discuss certain Boolean functions commonly met with in practise.

1.4.1. *Truth tables*

1.4.1.1. *Generalities*
Let $f(A, B)$ be a Boolean function of the variables A and B, defined by $f(A, B) = \bar{A} + \bar{B}$. This means that $f(A, B) = 1$ if $\bar{A} = 1$, if $\bar{B} = 1$, or if $\bar{A} = \bar{B} = 1$. We know that there are four possible combinations for the values of $\bar{A}$ and $\bar{B}$. They are:

$$\bar{A} = 0 \quad \text{and} \quad \bar{B} = 0$$
$$\bar{A} = 0 \quad \text{and} \quad \bar{B} = 1$$
$$\bar{A} = 1 \quad \text{and} \quad \bar{B} = 0$$
$$\bar{A} = 1 \quad \text{and} \quad \bar{B} = 1$$

These conditions can be put in the form of a three-column table in which, from left to right, we read:
– The different values of $\bar{A}$ ⎫ Repeated so as to obtain
– The different values of $\bar{B}$ ⎭ all possible combinations
– The values of F corresponding to each possible combination of $\bar{A}$ and $\bar{B}$ (Figure 1.4).

It can be imagined that this process is hardly practicable if a minimum number of conventions are not imposed. In fact, by De Morgan's relation, it is possible to write $f(A, B) = \overline{A \cdot B}$. If we draw a table of f using this equivalent definition, it would not be the same as the first.

$\bar{A}$	$\bar{B}$	$f(A, B)$
0	0	0
0	1	1
1	0	1
1	1	1

B	A	f
0	0	1
0	1	1
1	0	1
1	1	0

FIG. 1.4.   FIG. 1.5.

The first two columns would be the values of A and B instead of $\bar{A}$ and $\bar{B}$, even though the function and conditions are the same. In order to avoid this difficulty, we shall always write the combinations taken with unbarred variables and opposite them the values of f. Thus, the table of $f(A, B)$ which has just served as example will be as indicated in Figure 1.5 and will be called the truth table of the function f.

We examine its construction.

The different combinations of A and B are taken from top to bottom in the order of a pure binary number system. The value of A (first letter in alphabetical order) corresponds to the digit of least weight in the envisaged binary sequence.

First row $\begin{cases} A = 0 & \bar{A} = 1 \\ B = 0 & \bar{B} = 1 \end{cases}$ $\bar{A} + \bar{B} = 1 = f$

Second row $\begin{cases} A = 1 & \bar{A} = 0 \\ B = 0 & \bar{B} = 1 \end{cases}$ $\bar{A} + \bar{B} = 1 = f$

Third row $\begin{cases} A = 0 & \bar{A} = 1 \\ B = 1 & \bar{B} = 0 \end{cases}$ $\bar{A} + \bar{B} = 1 = f$

Fourth row $\begin{cases} A = 1 & \bar{A} = 0 \\ B = 1 & \bar{B} = 0 \end{cases}$ $\bar{A} + \bar{B} = 0 = f.$

With the help of truth tables, all the theorems and relations preceedingly announced can be 'proven' (or more precisely verified) by identification. For example, we verify De Morgan's first relation $\overline{(A + B)} = \bar{A} \cdot \bar{B}$.

Let $f_1 = \overline{(A + B)}$ and $f_2 = \bar{A} \cdot \bar{B}$. We write the truth tables of f_1 (Figure 1.6a) and f_2 (Figure 1.6b), then the table comparing them (Figure 1.6c).

B	A	$\bar{f}_1$	f_1
0	0	0	1
0	1	1	0
1	0	1	0
1	1	1	0

B	A	f_2
0	0	1
0	1	0
1	0	0
1	1	0

B	A	f_1	f_2
0	0	1	1
0	1	0	0
1	0	0	0
1	1	0	0

FIG. 1.6(a). FIG. 1.6(b). FIG. 1.6(c).

Examination of Figure 1.6c shows that $f_1 = f_2$. f_1 and f_2 have in fact been studied for all combinations of A and B. As these two functions take the same value at each point, they are identical.

1.4.1.2. *Some particular functions*

We shall now give truth tables of several classical functions, or operators, frequently used in Boolean calculation and technology.

(a) *Dilemma function* (also called exclusive OR, or addition modulo two): $f(A, B) = A\bar{B} + \bar{A}B$. This function has the value 1 if and only if A or B (but not both) equals 1. This function is ordinarily symbolized by the sign $\oplus$. Thus $f(A, B) = A \oplus B$. (truth table Figure 1.7).

The reader may use such tables to show that:

$$A \oplus 1 = \bar{A}$$
$$A \oplus \bar{A} = 1.$$

(b) *Implication function*: $f(A, B) = \bar{A} + B$. We say that A implies B (notation $A \subseteq B$) if $f = 1$ (truth table, Figure 1.8). Implication behaves like inequality: $A \leq B$ signifies: if $B = 0$, then $A = 0$; if $B = 1$, then $A = 1$ or $A = 0$.

(c) *NOR function* (also called Peirce's function): $f(A, B) = \bar{A} \cdot \bar{B}$ (2 variables) of $f(A, B, C) = \bar{A} \cdot \bar{B} \cdot \bar{C}$ (3 variables). f takes the value 1 if all the variables are 0. This function is noted $\downarrow$:

$$f(A, B, C) = A \downarrow B \downarrow C$$

(truth table Figures 1.9a, b).

(d) *NAND function* (also called Sheffer's function): $f(A, B) = \bar{A} + \bar{B}$ (2 variables) or $f(A, B, C) = \bar{A} + \bar{B} + \bar{C}$ (3 variables). f takes the value 1 if A, B, or C or two of the three or all three are 0. The function is noted $/$ (truth table Figures 1.10a, b): $f(A, B, C) = A / B / C$.

B	A	f
0	0	0
0	1	1
1	0	1
1	1	0

$f(A,B) = A \oplus B$

B	A	f
0	0	1
0	1	0
1	0	1
1	1	1

$A \subseteq B$ if $f = 1$

C	B	A	f
0	0	0	1
0	0	1	0
0	1	0	0
0	1	1	0
1	0	0	0
1	0	1	0
1	1	0	0
1	1	1	0

$f(A,B,C) = A \downarrow B \downarrow C$

B	A	f
0	0	1
0	1	0
1	0	0
1	1	0

$f(A,B) = A \downarrow B$

FIG. 1.7.   FIG. 1.8.   FIG. 1.9(a).   FIG. 1.9(b).

In the following chapters we shall use some properties of NOR and NAND functions which we state here.

(1) Both operators are commutative: $A \downarrow B = B \downarrow A$; in fact we have $A \downarrow B = \bar{A}\bar{B} = \bar{B}\bar{A} = B \downarrow A$; in the same way we find, $A \mid B = B \mid A$.

(2) On the other hand, they are not associative.
Example:

$$A \downarrow (B \downarrow C) = \bar{A}(B + C) \quad \text{while} \quad (A \downarrow B) \downarrow C = (A + B)\bar{C}.$$

The non-associativity of the NAND operation is seen in the same way:

$$A \mid (B \mid C) = \bar{A} + BC \quad \text{while} \quad (A \mid B) \mid C = \bar{C} + AB$$

(3) Note that

$$A \downarrow 1 = 0 \quad \text{and} \quad A \mid 1 = \bar{A}$$
$$A \downarrow 0 = \bar{A} \quad \text{and} \quad A \mid 0 = 1$$
$$(A \downarrow B) \downarrow (C \downarrow D) = (A + B)(C + D) \quad \text{and}$$
$$(A \mid B) \mid (C \mid D) = AB + CD.$$

The NOR and NAND operations are widely used in practise. The reason for this is that all Boolean algebra operations can be derived from only one of them. Thus, Boolean multiplication of two variables $P = A \cdot B$ can be written in terms of the NOR operator as $P = \bar{A} \downarrow \bar{B}$ or $(A \downarrow 0) \downarrow (B \downarrow 0)$ and addition as $S = (A \downarrow B) \downarrow 0$, and $\bar{A} = A \downarrow 0$. Analogous calculations can be redone with the NAND operator;

$$P = (A \mid B) \mid 1 \qquad \bar{A} = A \mid 1 \qquad S = (A \mid 1) \mid (B \mid 1).$$

Table 1.1 lists the properties and formulas pertinent to the NOR and NAND functions. In order to familiarize himself with them, the reader should derive these properties as we have just done for the formulas established above.

TABLE 1.1.

Property	Function: NOR	Function: NAND
Idempotence	$A \downarrow A \downarrow B = A \downarrow B$	$A \mid A \mid B = A \mid B$
Absorption	$A \downarrow (A \downarrow B) = A \downarrow \bar{B}$ $A \downarrow (A \downarrow B \downarrow C) = A \downarrow (B \downarrow C)$ $(A \downarrow B) \downarrow (A \downarrow B \downarrow C)$ $\quad = (A \downarrow B) \downarrow 0$ $(A \downarrow B) \downarrow (A \downarrow B \downarrow C) \downarrow D$ $\quad = (A \downarrow B) \downarrow D$	$A \mid (A \mid B) = A \mid \bar{B}$ $A \mid (A \mid B \mid C) = A \mid (B \mid C)$ $(A \mid B) \mid (A \mid B \mid C)$ $\quad = (A \mid B) \mid 1$ $(A \mid B) \mid (A \mid B \mid C) \mid D$ $\quad = (A \mid B) \mid D$
Pseudo-distributivity	$(A \downarrow B) \downarrow (A \downarrow C)$ $\quad = [A \downarrow (\bar{B} \downarrow \bar{C})] \downarrow 0$ $(A \downarrow B) \downarrow (A \downarrow C) \downarrow D$ $\quad = [A \downarrow (\bar{B} \downarrow \bar{C})] \downarrow D$ $(A \downarrow B \downarrow C) \downarrow (A \downarrow D \downarrow E) \downarrow F$ $\quad = \{A \downarrow [(B \downarrow C) \downarrow (D \downarrow E)]\} F$	$(A \mid B) \mid (A \mid C)$ $\quad = [A \mid (\bar{B} \mid \bar{C})] \mid 0$ $(A \mid B) \mid (A \mid C) \mid D$ $\quad = [A \mid (\bar{B} \mid \bar{C})] \mid D$ $(A \mid B \mid C) \mid (A \mid D \mid E) \mid F$ $\quad = \{A \mid [(B \mid C) \mid (D \mid E)]\} \mid F$
Excluded middle	$(A \downarrow B) \downarrow (A \downarrow \bar{B}) = A$ $(A \downarrow B) \downarrow (A \downarrow \bar{B}) \downarrow C$ $\quad = (A \downarrow 0) \downarrow C$ $(A \downarrow B \downarrow C) \downarrow (A \downarrow B \downarrow \bar{C}) \downarrow D$ $\quad = (A \downarrow B) \downarrow D$	$(A \mid B) \mid (A \mid \bar{B}) = A$ $(A \mid B) \mid (A \mid \bar{B}) \mid C$ $\quad = (A \mid 1) \mid C$ $(A \mid B \mid C) \mid (A \mid B \mid \bar{C}) \mid D$ $\quad = (A \mid B) \mid D$

C	B	A	f
0	0	0	1
0	0	1	1
0	1	0	1
0	1	1	1
1	0	0	1
1	0	1	1
1	1	0	1
1	1	1	0

(a) $f(A, B, C) = A/B/C$

Fig. 1.10.

B	A	f
0	0	1
0	1	1
1	0	1
1	1	0

(b) $f(A, B) = A/B$

C	B	A	f
0	0	0	0
0	0	1	0
0	1	0	0
0	1	1	1
1	0	0	0
1	0	1	1
1	1	0	1
1	1	1	1

$f(A, B, C) = \text{maj}(A, B, C)$

Fig. 1.11.

(e) *Majority function*: $f(A, B, C) = AB + BC + CA$; $f = 1$ if at least two of the three variables are equal to 1. Notation:

$$f(A, B, C) = \text{maj}(A, B, C)$$

(truth table Figure 1.11).

1.4.2. *The designation number of a Boolean function*
Introduction

In the preceeding section we represented a Boolean function of n variables $f(x_1, ..., x_n)$ by a 2^n row (as many as there are possible combinations of the variables) and $(n + 1)$ column (n variables plus the function) table. In reality, only one of these columns interests us: the column giving the values of f. The first n columns of two truth tables T_1 and T_2 defining the Boolean functions f_1 and f_2 are exactly the same; only the columns concerning the values of f_1 and f_2 differ.

In order not to repeat these first n columns, we shall decide a fixed order for them and the 2^n rows that they generate (standard base); this is what we actually started to do in Section 1.4.1. From now on we shall use the following conventions:

(a) The variables of least weight (those appearing at the end of the sequence) will be either the lowest in alphabetical order (A will be placed after B, Q after R, etc.) or the lowest in index (x_1 will be placed after x_2, x_{64} after x_{65} etc.).

(b) The order of the combinations (order of the rows) will be that of the pure binary code, increasing from top to bottom. Thus, the row of $f(x_1, x_2\ x_3, x_4)$ corresponding to $x_1 = 0$, $x_2 = 1$, $x_3 = 0$, $x_4 = 0$ will be above the row $x_1 = 1$, $x_2 = 1$, $x_3 = 0$, $x_4 = 0$.

In this system the Boolean function $f(x_1, \ldots, x_n)$ can be represented by a single column of zeros and ones with no other specifications.

Example: $f(x_1, x_2, x_3) = \text{maj}\ (x_1, x_2, x_3)$ will be represented by the column appearing in Figure 1.12a.

To economize space, we prefer to represent the functions by a row instead of a column; we shall do this by simply transposing the column. Thus the column in Figure 1.12a becomes the row in Figure 1.12b.

$$
\begin{array}{l}
0 \\
0 \\
0 \\
1 \\
0 \\
1 \\
1 \\
1
\end{array}
$$

0 0 0 1   0 1 1 1

FIG. 1.12(a).   FIG. 1.12(b).

This representation is called the *designation number* of the function and is noted $\div f$. We therefore have two equivalent notations:

$$f(x_1, x_2, x_3) = \text{maj}(x_1, x_2, x_3)$$
$$\div f(x_1, x_2, x_3) = 0\ 0\ 0\ 1\quad 0\ 1\ 1\ 1$$

Designation number of the sum or product of Boolean functions
Given two Boolean functions of the n variables $x_1, \ldots, x_n$ the designation number of their sum (resp. product) is the sum (resp. product) of their designation numbers, digit by digit.

In order to obtain the different values of the sum (resp. product) of the two functions, we must study the expression of every possible n-tuple in $x_1, \ldots, x_n$; that is, for each digit of the same order as the designation numbers of the two functions.

Consider the two functions:

$$f_1 = x_1x_2 + x_2\bar{x}_3 \quad \text{or} \quad \div f_1 = 0\ 0\ 1\ 1 \quad 0\ 0\ 0\ 1$$
$$f_2 = x_1\bar{x}_3 + x_2x_3 \quad \text{or} \quad \div f_2 = 0\ 1\ 0\ 1 \quad 0\ 0\ 1\ 1$$
$$\div (f_1 \cdot f_2) = (\div f_1)(\div f_2) = 0\ 0\ 0\ 1 \quad 0\ 0\ 0\ 1$$
$$\div (f_1 + f_2) = (\div f_1) + (\div f_2) = 0\ 1\ 1\ 1 \quad 0\ 0\ 1\ 1$$

Remark. The order in which the variables are taken is called the *base* with respect to which the designation number is obtained. It is important always to specify with respect to which base the designation number of a function is obtained. If, for example, we take $f = x_2x_3 + x_1x_2$ with respect to base (x_3, x_1, x_2) we have $\div f = 0\ 0\ 1\ 0\ \ 0\ 0\ 1\ 1$ while $\div f = 0001\ \ 0101$ with respect to the normal base (x_1, x_2, x_3).

Some rules, permitting one to pass from the designation number of a function with respect to a given base to its designation number with respect to another base are given in an appendix.

The table in Figure 1.13 contains the designation numbers of the functions defined in Section 4.1. These designation numbers are taken with respect to the usual bases. The reader may verify these results as an exercise.

$f(x_1, x_2, x_3)$	$\div f$	
$A \oplus B \oplus C$	0 1 1 0	1 0 0 1
$A \downarrow B \downarrow C$	1 0 0 0	0 0 0 0
$A \mid B \mid C$	1 1 1 1	1 1 1 0

FIG. 1.13.

An important remark concerning notation.

$$f(x_1, x_2, x_3) = \text{maj}\ (x_1, x_2, x_3)$$

is such that $\div f = 0\ 0\ 0\ 1\ \ 0\ 1\ 1\ 1$. By referring to the truth table of this function, we see that the ones of f (or of $\div f$) correspond to the numbers 3, 5, 6, 7 (given in the table by their decimal equivalents). That is maj$(x_1, x_2, x_3) = 1$ if the combinations $3(x_1 = 1, x_2 = 1, x_3 = 0)$, 5, 6, or 7 take the value 1. We agree to represent f as $R(3, 5, 6, 7)$ under the following rules:

(a) The letter R means that we consider a Boolean sum or 'reunion'.

(b) The decimal numbers indicate which decimals corresponding to the combinations of variables should equal 1 in order that $f = 1$.

For example: $f = R(3, 7, 11, 15)$ means that

$$f = \bar{x}_4\bar{x}_3x_2x_1 + \bar{x}_4x_3x_2x_1 + x_4\bar{x}_3x_2x_1 + x_4x_3x_2x_1.$$

This in fact is the reunion of the binary terms 0 0 1 1, 0 1 1 1, 1 0 1 1, and 1 1 1 1.

This notation is simply a matter of facilitating the writing of formulas. In contrast with the idea of designation number, which is an algebraic notion, the use of the symbol $R(i, j, ..., f)$ simply makes the writing of a function of many variables easier, especially when there are many terms.

1.5. REDUCTION OF BOOLEAN FUNCTIONS–MAP REPRESENTATION

1.5.1. *Veitch maps*

(a) It is useful in many applications, such as the reduction (or simplification) of Boolean functions, to have a type of representation which is more compact than that of the truth table or designation number.

Consider, for example, $\div f = 0001 \quad 0111$. By simple inspection of the designation number, we have $R(3, 5, 6, 7) = f$ and

$$f = x_1 x_2 \bar{x}_3 + x_1 \bar{x}_2 x_3 + \bar{x}_1 x_2 x_3 + x_1 x_2 x_3.$$

Since $\div f$ is nothing but $\div \mathrm{maj}(x_1, x_2, x_3)$ we can write it more simply as $f = x_1 x_2 + x_2 x_3 + x_1 x_3$. The representation which we shall introduce in this section will give a simple process for determining this kind of reduction.

(b) By recalling the way in which $\div f$ was determined, we note that in the example given above, the first group of four digits corresponds to $x_3 = 0$ and the second to $x_3 = 1$. In fact, all the terms of the four digit first group include $\bar{x}_3$ and all the terms of the second include x_3. We therefore associate f with a four column and two row table obtained by superposing the left part of f onto its right part. We obtain the table in Figure 1.14.

A *partition* of the set of variables (x_1, x_2, x_3) is said to be realized. The associated table is denoted $F_{x_3; x_1 x_2}$. The variable x_3 represents the

| 0 | 0 | 0 | 1 |
| 0 | 1 | 1 | 1 |

FIG. 1.14.

row index, and the variables (x_1, x_2) represent the column indices. Indeed we can see that the columns in the table are marked from left to right according to the combinations of $x_1 x_2$ taken in an increasing binary order (x_1 is always the least weight digit).

The first column, starting from the left, corresponds to 0 0, the second to 0 1. Similarly, the first row is defined by 0 and the second by 1. (The variable x_3 serves as a reference point for them. $x_3 = \bar{x}_3$ for all the terms in the first row and equals x_3 for the terms in the second row.)

This notation can evidently be generalized. As another example, we consider:

$$f(x_1, x_2, x_3, x_4) = R(0, 1, 3, 4, 7, 8, 11, 12, 13, 15).$$

We immediately find

$$\div f = 1\ 1\ 0\ 1 \quad 1\ 0\ 0\ 1 \quad 1\ 0\ 0\ 1 \quad 1\ 1\ 0\ 1.$$

We seek, for example, $F_{x_4; x_1 x_2 x_3}$; here the first eight digits correspond to x_4 (x_4 figures in the first eight terms, x_4 in the last eight terms). In order to obtain $F_{x_4; x_1 x_2 x_3}$, it is sufficient to repeat the same operation as above. The table is shown in Figure 1.15.

1	1	0	1	1	0	0	1
1	0	0	1	1	1	0	1

FIG. 1.15.

We can make other partitions, $F_{x_3 x_4; x_1 x_2}$. The term $\bar{x}_3 \bar{x}_4$ will appear in the first four digits (always starting from the left) of $\div f$, $x_3 \bar{x}_4$ in the next four digits, etc. It is therefore sufficient, in this case, to superpose, by groups of four digits, the 'pieces' of $\div f$. We have the table in Figure 1.16. Similarly, we obtain $F_{x_2 x_3 x_4; x_1}$ (Figure 1.17). $F_{x_1 x_2 x_3; x_4}$ can be found, for example, by remarking that the first term of $\div f$ corresponds to the combination $\bar{x}_1 \bar{x}_2 \bar{x}_3 \bar{x}_4$ (0 0 0 0) and the ninth to $x_1 \bar{x}_2 \bar{x}_3 \bar{x}_4$ (1 0 0 0), etc. Since the row indices here are $x_1 x_2 x_3$, we see that the first column of $F_{x_4; x_1 x_2 x_3}$ will be the first row of $F_{x_1 x_2 x_3; x_4}$, etc.

In other words, the table of $F_{x_1 x_2 x_3; x_4}$ is found by 'rotating' the $F_{x_4; x_1 x_2 x_3}$ table 90 degrees. The first row of this last matrix becomes the first column of the other and so on, as illustrated in Figure 1.18.

1	1	0	1
1	0	0	1
1	0	0	1
1	1	0	1

1	1
0	1
1	0
0	1
1	0
0	1
1	1
0	1

1	1
1	0
0	0
1	1
1	1
0	1
0	0
1	1

FIG. 1.16.   FIG. 1.17.   FIG. 1.18.

It is extremely important to be careful as to which partition is being manipulated when using this notation. As a general rule, there are two ways to operate (and we shall use them indifferently in that which follows):

Either the corresponding partition is indicated under each table; i.e. $F_{X,Y}$ marked under a table means that the row indices are the variables in set Y and the column indices those of set X; or the column indices appear above and the row indices below an oblique line drawn in the left hand corner (such as in Figure 1.19).

The order of the variables will always be such that the letter to the extreme right (of set X or set Y) is that of least weight in the set under consideration.

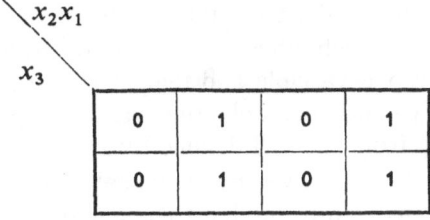

FIG. 1.19.

1.5.2. *Karnaugh maps*

The representation of f which we have just given is particularly rich in algebraic implications (especially in the field of Boolean function factorization). In their present form the Veitch maps do not provide an approach to the problem posed at the beginning of this section, i.e., the problem of Boolean function simplification. We, therefore, seek to perfect this tool in order to give it the supplementary properties necessary for the solution of our problem. As before, we begin with an example.

Consider the Boolean function of three variables:

$$f(x_1, x_2, x_3) = R(1, 3, 5, 7).$$

We deduce

$$\div f = 0\ 1\ 0\ 1\ \ 0\ 1\ 0\ 1.$$

$F_{x_3, x_1 x_2}$ is represented in Figure 1.19.

By inverting the 3rd and 4th columns of this map we obtain Figure 1.20. Each square is referred to as a cell and we define adjacent cells as those being such that we can move from one to the other by changing a single variable the same as in the passage from a number n to $n-1$ or $n+1$ in a reflected binary code.

x_3 \ $x_2 x_1$	00	01	11	10
0	0	1	1	0
1	0	1	1	0

FIG. 1.20.

Examining Figure 1.20 we see that the two end columns ($\bar{x}_1 \bar{x}_2$ and $\bar{x}_1 x_2$) are adjacent to each other, since we move from one to the other by changing only one variable and that, if we go from one cell to a geometrically adjacent one, only one variable changes value. For example, starting from the cell defined by $x_1 = 1$, $x_2 = 1$, $x_3 = 0$ (cell which we shall call 0 1 1), we move one cell to the right by changing $x_1 = 1$ to $x_1 = 0$, one cell to the left by changing $x_2 = 1$ to $x_2 = 0$ and one cell below by changing the variable x_3 from 0 to 1. Thus we see that any two *geographically adjacent* cells in the map we have just described are *adjacent in the Boolean sense*; that is, *we move from one to the other by changing one and only one variable.*

These maps are known as *Karnaugh maps.*

With this in mind, let us write the logical sum of terms in two adjacent cells in a Karnaugh map. Let x_i be the variable that changes when passing from one cell to another, and A the set (unchanged) of the other variables. We may then write the sum

$$A \cdot x_i + A \cdot \bar{x}_i.$$

By (P'_5) we have

$$A(x_i + \bar{x}_i) = Ax_i + A\bar{x}_i$$

and (P_6) gives

$$x_i + \bar{x}_i = 1.$$

Therefore,

$$Ax_i + A\bar{x}_i = A.$$

In other words, the logical sum of terms of two adjacent cells of a Karnaugh map eliminates the variable which changes value when we go from one cell to the other.

In the example being considered, if we perform the reunion of the 1's in the cells 0 1 1 and 0 0 1, we see that only x_2 varies and consequently the resulting term is $\bar{x}_3\bar{x}_1$. Similarly, the sum of cells 1 1 1 and 1 0 1 is x_3x_1. Note that we have not been concerned with the four other cells of the Karnaugh map since they correspond to $f = 0$, that is, to the terms which do not figure in the explicit expression of f.

We observe that, in the same way, the reunion of the terms contained in four adjacent cells of the Karnaugh map which are such that each of them is adjacent to two cells of the reunion, eliminates the two variables which change value in the passage across all the cells. The same reasoning as above can be applied.

A one-to-one correspondence associates each of the four cells to one of the following combinations

$$B\bar{x}_i\bar{x}_j, \quad Bx_i\bar{x}_j, \quad B\bar{x}_jx_i, \quad Bx_ix_j,$$

that is, the resulting term can be written

$$B(x_i + \bar{x}_i)(x_j + \bar{x}_j) = B \cdot 1 \cdot 1 = B.$$

In the example being considered, if we take the reunion of the 1's in the four cells (this is possible since they are adjacent in the Boolean sense) we see that this reunion operation comes down to $f = x_3 x_1 + \bar{x}_3 x_1$ (since x_2 has already been eliminated), from which we have $f = x_1$.

We return to the example of Figures 1.15, 1.16, 1.17, and 1.18

$$\div f = 1 \ 1 \ 0 \ 1 \quad 1 \ 0 \ 0 \ 1 \quad 1 \ 0 \ 0 \ 1 \quad 1 \ 1 \ 0 \ 1.$$

To plot the partition $F_{x_3 x_4; x_1 x_2}$ onto a Karnaugh map, it is sufficient to invert the third and fourth columns in Figure 1.16, then the third and fourth rows. The result is shown in Figure 1.21.

$x_4 x_3$ \ $x_2 x_1$	00	01	11	10
00	1	1	1	0
01	1	0	1	0
11	1	1	1	0
10	1	0	1	0

FIG. 1.21. $f_{x_3 x_4; x_1 x_2}$.

In order to avoid confusion (which is always possible, for example, in the case of partitions having sub-sets of three or more variables), the corresponding combinations of variables are indicated at the head of each column and to the left of each row.

To obtain the simplest expression for f, we are going to try to group as many 1's as possible since a grouping of 2^k '1' digits eliminates k variables. (It is sufficient to use inductive reasoning given for the elimination of one then two variables.)

Here, as we have four variables and the function is visibly different from 1 ($f = 1$ would suppose that it is composed of $2^4 = 16$ '1' digits) we seek groups (if they exist) which eliminate three variables. It is therefore, necessary to find eight cells, two-by-two adjacents, and such that each of them is adjacent in the Boolean sense, to three other cells of the group.

Figure 1.21 shows that it is impossible to find such a group of 1's. We must, therefore, try to eliminate two variables by looking for groups of $2^2 = 4$ cells. Two exist; they correspond to the terms, $\bar{x}_1 \bar{x}_2$ and $x_1 x_2$. To show that we have used them (we say, 'covered'), we circle them. Two digits remain to be covered in order to express f; one is the cell $x_1 \bar{x}_2 \bar{x}_3 \bar{x}_4$ (0 0 0 1) and the other is in cell 1 1 0 1. As we know from Theorem 1 that $A + A = A$, the terms of f already covered can be associated to these 1's.

For example, we can re-group the first with its adjacent to the right or left, and cover the second in the same way. Grouping these two 1 digits with the terms of column 1 1, we have

$$f = \bar{x}_1 \bar{x}_2 + x_1 x_2 + \bar{x}_3 \bar{x}_4 x_1 + x_3 x_4 x_1.$$

Grouping these 1 digits with the terms of column 0 0, we have

$$f = \bar{x}_1 \bar{x}_2 + x_1 x_2 + \bar{x}_3 \bar{x}_4 \bar{x}_2 + x_3 x_4 \bar{x}_2.$$

Grouping the first with its adjacent to the right and the second with its adjacent to the left gives:

$$f = \bar{x}_1 \bar{x}_2 + x_1 x_2 + \bar{x}_3 \bar{x}_4 x_1 + x_3 x_4 \bar{x}_2.$$

The inverse grouping gives

$$f = \bar{x}_1 \bar{x}_2 + x_1 x_2 + \bar{x}_3 \bar{x}_4 \bar{x}_2 + x_3 x_4 x_1.$$

This shows an interesting property of Boolean functions: the designation number, with respect to a fixed base (also called standard base), of a function is unique; this is not necessarily so for the reduced forms of the function.

When the function is given by simple transcription of its designation number (as the Boolean sum of Boolean products of variables), its form is unique; we call it the *disjunctive canonical form* of f. If it is a function of n variables, each of its terms is a Boolean product of the n variables, some of which are barred and others non-barred.

These Boolean products are called *minterms* of the disjunctive canonical form. Several disjunctive reduced forms obtained by simplification correspond to the same disjunctive canonical form. The Boolean products figuring in a disjunctive reduced form are called *prime implicants* of the disjunctive reduced form.

Certain of these prime implicants are necessary in the expression of the reduced form of f ($x_1 x_2$ and $\bar{x}_1 \bar{x}_2$ in our example): we call them *essential prime implicants*.

A conjunctive canonical form can also be defined as the Boolean product of Boolean sums of variables (these terms are referred to as *maxterms*). This form is easily obtained from the disjunctive canonical form by using De Morgan's theorem and remarking that $f = (\bar{\bar{f}})$ and $\bar{f}$ can be calculated by using all the 0's of $\div f$.

1.6. REDUCTION OF BOOLEAN FUNCTIONS (continued) – MCCLUSKEY-QUINE METHOD

In the preceeding section we obtained the reduced formulas of a Boolean function by making the terms Ax_i and $A\bar{x}_i$ figure on the maps, then re-grouping them so as to eliminate the variables x_i. During the entire procedure of reduction, we have used only Postulate P_5 $(A + \bar{A} = 1)$ and Theorem 1 $(A + A = A)$. This avoided long and tedious algebraic manipulations which often cause error. We shall now describe another method for reducing Boolean functions. This new method is based on the same principles but has the advantage of being more systematic and thus easier to program.

The principle is the following: try to group all the minterms of the function in pairs. This leads to a first reduced form; we then try to reduce this first form (always by applying $A + \bar{A} = 1$) and so on. As in Karnaugh's method, the same term can be re-grouped several times with different terms (by using the postulate $A + A = A$).

We begin by defining our vocabulary:

DEFINITION 1. The binary equivalent of a minterm is obtained by replacing all the letters $\bar{x}_k$ by 0 and all the letters x_j by 1.

DEFINITION 2. The weight of a minterm is the weight of its binary equivalent.

DEFINITION 3. The weight of a binary number is the total number of 1's it contains.

This map, unlike Karnaugh's representation, is constructed by placing the minterms of the function above each of their binary equivalents in the following way: suppose, for example, that Ax_i and $A\bar{x}_i$ can be combined. The weight of the first is $P_1 = P(A) + 1$ (weight of the 1st term A plus the weight of the variable x_i, i.e. 1) and that of the second is $P_2 = P(A)$, $(P(\bar{x}_i) = 0)$. Thus, we see that the weights of two minterms which can be combined, necessarily differ by 1. Consequently, a minterm M_c of weight P can be combined with a minterm M'_c of weight P' where $P' = P - 1$ and a term M''_c of weight P'' where $P'' = P + 1$ (notice that combination with all terms of weights P' and

P'', is not a priori possible. We leave to the reader the task of finding the rule of combination.)

We shall now try to solve a problem.

Consider the function $f(x_1, x_2, x_3, x_4)$ already studied and such that

$$f = R(0, 1, 3, 4, 7, 8, 11, 12, 13, 15).$$

We divide the binary equivalents of the function's minterms into several groups; each group is characterized by the number of '1' digits that the numbers figuring in it contain. We have

weight $0 = 0$
weight $1 = 1, 4, 8$
weight $2 = 3, 12$
weight $3 = 7, 11, 13$
weight $4 = 15.$

Hence in binary we have Table 1.2.

TABLE 1.2.

Weight 0	0 0 0 0	0
Weight 1	0 0 0 1	1
	0 1 0 0	4
	1 0 0 0	8
Weight 2	0 0 1 1	3
	1 1 0 0	12
Weight 3	0 1 1 1	7
	1 0 1 1	11
	1 1 0 1	13
Weight 4	1 1 1 1	15

We proceed with a comparison of the terms 0 0 0 0 $(\bar{x}_1, \bar{x}_2, \bar{x}_3, \bar{x}_4)$ and 0 0 0 1 $(x_1, \bar{x}_2, \bar{x}_3, \bar{x}_4)$. The Boolean sum of these two terms is $\bar{x}_2\bar{x}_3\bar{x}_4$ which we write 0 0 0 –. The dash – appearing after the three zeros signifies that the variable x_1 plays no part in the term. Similarly the Boolean sum of 0 0 0 0 and 0 1 0 0 is 0 – 0 0 $(\bar{x}_1\bar{x}_2\bar{x}_4)$ and so on.

The Boolean sum of 0 0 0 0 and 0 0 1 1 and its reduction are impossible operations because these two terms are not adjacent, (since their weights differ by two unities which means that two of the variables, at least, differ in these two terms). Comparison of 0 0 0 1 and 1 1 0 0 shows that their Boolean sum cannot be reduced, since, although their weights differ by only 1 unity, three variables x_1, x_2, and x_3 change value when we go from one minterm to the other. Another comparison shows that the Boolean sum of 0 0 0 1 and 0 1 0 0 is impossible to reduce since both x_1 and x_3 change value between the first and second minterms. We can therefore announce the following rule (answer to the problem posed to the reader):

RULE. The Boolean sum of two minterms can be reduced if their weights differ by one unity and their decimal equivalents differ by a power of 2 (the term of the group having more weight is greater than the one having less weight).

With this rule in mind, we reconsider our example. We systematically compare each term of each group with each term of the group next in order of increasing weight. When the sum of two terms, thus compared, is reduced, these two terms are followed by a cross in the map to show that they are covered. The result of the reduction is recorded on a second map. We obtain the maps in Figure 1.22.

This first series of comparisons is equivalent to associating the terms grouped in two adjacent cells of the Karnaugh map; i.e., each new group contains only one variable less than its predecessor. We must now see if more variables can be eliminated in the implicants.

It is necessary that the two terms to be combined have the dash of their binary equivalent in the same place; i.e., the variable, in each term to be combined, which was eliminated by the first series of comparisons must be the same. Consequently, only comparison of the groups $R(i,j)$ and $R(k,l)$ (i, j, k, l are the decimal equivalents of the minterms under consideration) where $j - i = l - k = 2^p$ and $k - i = 2^m$, will give interesting results in the second series of comparisons.

Figure 1.23 shows the maps resulting from this second series of reunions.

The terms giving reducible Boolean sums are followed by a cross. The other terms are followed by a capital letter, which, in a way, is a name given to these irreducible groups. In this case, they are the

Decimal
equivalent

0 0 0 0	×	0
0 0 0 1	×	1
0 1 0 0	×	4
1 0 0 0	×	8
0 0 1 1	×	3
1 1 0 0	×	12
0 1 1 1	×	7
1 0 1 1	×	11
1 1 0 1	×	13
1 1 1 1	×	15

Canonical form

0 0 0 –	from	R (0,1)
0 – 0 0	from	R (0,4)
– 0 0 0	from	R (0,8)
0 0 – 1	from	R (1,3)
– 1 0 0	from	R (4,12)
1 – 0 0	from	R (8,12)
0 – 1 1	from	R (3,7)
– 0 1 1	from	R (3,11)
1 1 0 –	from	R (12,13)
– 1 1 1	from	R (7,15)
1 – 1 1	from	R (11,15)
1 1 – 1	from	R (13,15)

Result of the first
step in comparisons

Fig. 1.22.

0 0 0 –	A	R (0,1)
0 – 0 0	×	R (0,4)
– 0 0 0	×	R (0,8)
0 0 – 1	B	R (1,3)
– 1 0 0	×	R (4,12)
1 – 0 0	×	R (8,12)
0 – 1 1	×	R (3,7)
– 0 1 1	×	R (3,11)
1 1 0 –	C	R (12,13)
– 1 1 1	×	R (7,15)
1 – 1 1	×	R (11,15)
1 1 – 1	D	R (13,15)

Result of the first
step in comparisons

– – 0 0 E R (0, 4, 8, 12)

– – 1 1 F R (3, 7, 11, 15)

Result of the second step
in comparisons

Fig. 1.23.

groups A, B, C, D. They are employed in the final reduced expression of f if they are essential.

It is clear in the example given, that a third series of comparisons would shed no new light. We, therefore, call E and F the two implicants found from the second series of comparisons and try to represent f in its reduced form.

When we used Karnaugh's map method to study the problem, we sought the prime implicants which covered the largest possible number of 1 digits of the function and we continued the covering by decreasing the number of minterms regrouped in a same prime implicant. This led, in the same example, to four possible solutions.

Taking into account the difference in the formulation of the two methods, the path we intend to follow is rather close to the preceeding method. The representative map, called prime implicant chart (Figure 1.24) is composed of ten vertical lines corresponding to the ten minterms of f, indicated at the top by their decimal equivalent, and six horizontal lines corresponding to the six prime implicants indicated by their names from A to F, in the reduction of f.

An intersection marked with a cross signifies that the prime implicant represented by this row covers the minterm represented by the corresponding column. Thus, we see that A covers 0 and 1, is noted by

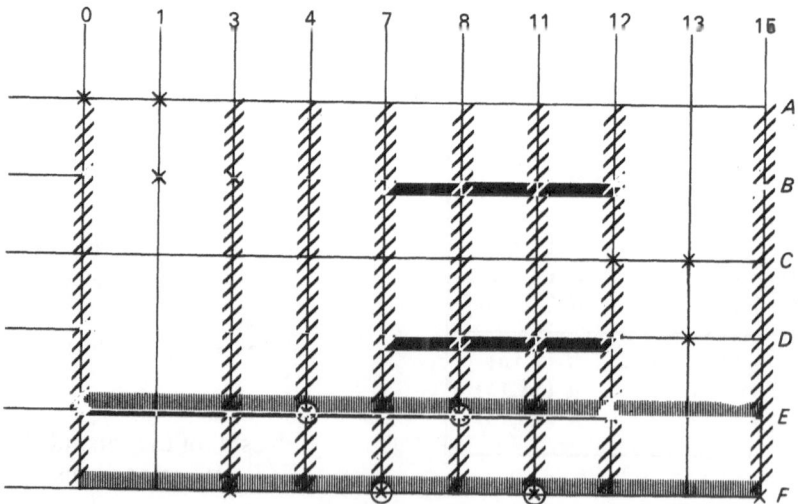

FIG. 1.24.

a cross at the intersection of row A and column 0 and another cross at the intersection of row A and column 1.

We circle the crosses which are unique in a column (here 4, 7, 8, 11). Each of these minterms is covered by only one prime implicant. Consequently, this means that these prime implicants necessarily appear in the final reduced form if we wish a complete covering of f. In other words, these prime implicants are essential. The rows corresponding to the essential prime implicants are indicated by a heavier line. In the example being studied, we see that there are only two essential prime implicants, E and F, and that they cover 0, 3, 12 and 15. We bar the columns 0, 3, 4, 7, 8, 11, 12, and 15 to show that the corresponding minterms have been covered. The minterms 1 and 13 remain to be covered. We can use the prime implicants A or B to cover 1, and C or D to cover 13. We find the same solutions as in the Karnaugh map.

$$F = E + F + A + C = E + F + B + D = E + F + A + D$$
$$= E + F + B + C,$$

with

$$A = \bar{x}_4 \bar{x}_3 \bar{x}_2 \quad B = \bar{x}_4 \bar{x}_3 x_1 \quad C = x_4 x_3 \bar{x}_2 \quad D = x_4 x_3 x_1$$
$$E = \bar{x}_2 \bar{x}_1 \quad F = x_1 x_2.$$

1.7 REDUCTION OF FUNCTIONS CONTAINING 'DON'T CARE' TERMS

Until now, we have studied Boolean functions which had their designation numbers composed of only 1's or 0's. We can, however, come across functions which are not completely defined; i.e. certain minterms can make f take the value 0 or 1 as we wish. This is the case, for example, when the minterms represent combinations of variables which are not physically real. In the Karnaugh map of the function or its designation number, we shall use the symbol $\emptyset$ (obtained by superposing 0 and 1) to signify that the corresponding minterm is unspecified (we say a 'don't care'); $\emptyset$ corresponds to minterms which are never physically real. The presence of such terms in the reduction of the Boolean function adds a supplementary degree of freedom as shown by the following example. Let

$$f(x_1, x_2, x_3, x_4) = \bar{x}_1 \bar{x}_2 \bar{x}_3 \bar{x}_4 + \bar{x}_1 x_2 \bar{x}_3 \bar{x}_4 + \bar{x}_1 \bar{x}_2 \bar{x}_3 x_4$$
$$+ \bar{x}_1 \bar{x}_2 x_3 x_4 + x_1 \bar{x}_2 x_3 x_4.$$

The value of f is indifferent for:

$$x_1\bar{x}_2\bar{x}_3\bar{x}_4, \quad \bar{x}_1\bar{x}_2x_3\bar{x}_4, \quad x_1\bar{x}_2x_3\bar{x}_4, \quad \bar{x}_1x_2x_3\bar{x}_4, \quad \bar{x}_1x_2x_3x_4.$$

We can express f; $\quad f = R(0, 2, 8, 12, 13) + R_\emptyset(1, 4, 5, 6, 14)$.

$R_\emptyset$ indicates that the terms in parentheses following the symbol are 'don't cares'. We can write the designation number of f

$$\div f = 1 \; \emptyset \; 1 \; 0 \quad \emptyset \; \emptyset \; \emptyset \; 0 \quad 1 \; 0 \; 0 \; 0 \quad 1 \; 1 \; \emptyset \; 0.$$

Figure 1.25 is the Karnaugh map of this function.

If we do not take into account the 'don't cares' (that is, if we let 0 take the place of $\emptyset$), the function becomes, for example,

$$f = \bar{x}_1\bar{x}_3\bar{x}_4 + \bar{x}_2x_3x_4 + \bar{x}_1\bar{x}_2x_4$$

or

$$f = \bar{x}_1\bar{x}_3\bar{x}_4 + \bar{x}_2x_3x_4 + \bar{x}_1\bar{x}_2\bar{x}_3.$$

To use the 'don't cares', we seek, as in the method described in Section 1.5, the largest possible groups obtained by the least possible number of transformations of 0 into 1. Here we have three 1's in the 00 column. By transforming the $\emptyset$ of the cell indicated by an asterisk, we re-group a maximum of four 1's which generate the term $\bar{x}_1\bar{x}_2$. If the 0 of cell 0 1 0 1 (indicated by two asterisks in the map) is transformed into 1, we are able to determine a group which covers the 1 in cell 1 1 0 1 and gives a two-variable term $(\bar{x}_2x_3)$. The term 1 in cell 0 0 1 0 remains to be covered. The most economic covering is to transform the 0 of cell 0 1 1 0 into 1. We find, with the groups indicated in Figure 1.26, the term $\bar{x}_1\bar{x}_4$.

	00	01	11	10
00	1	$\emptyset$	0	1
01	$\emptyset$	$\emptyset$	0	$\emptyset$
11	1	1	0	$\emptyset$
10	1	0	0	0

FIG. 1.25. Partition $f_{x_3x_4; x_1x_2}$.

	00	01	11	10
00	1	0	0	1
01	1	1	0	1
11	1	1	0	0
10	1	0	0	0

FIG. 1.26. Partition $f_{x_3x_4; x_1x_2}$.

We note here that *once a term $\emptyset$ is transformed into 0 or 1, it can never again change value.*

Finally, we find

$$f = \bar{x}_1 \bar{x}_2 + \bar{x}_1 \bar{x}_4 + \bar{x}_2 \bar{x}_3.$$

It is evident that in the general case, there are many ways in which the $\emptyset$ can be transformed into 1, all of which lead to solutions differing in their formulation, but equivalent from the point of view of the realization of the function. We give an example. Let

$$\div f = \emptyset \; 1 \; 0 \; 0 \quad 1 \; 1 \; 0 \; \emptyset \quad 0 \; 1 \; 0 \; 0 \quad \emptyset \; 1 \; 0 \; 1.$$

Figure 1.27a is the Karnaugh map of f. Figures 1.27b and c show two possible coverings of f which give two equivalent solutions.

$$f = x_1 \bar{x}_2 + x_1 x_3 + \bar{x}_2 x_3 \qquad \text{(c)}$$
$$f = x_1 \bar{x}_2 + x_1 x_3 + \bar{x}_2 \bar{x}_4. \qquad \text{(b)}$$

We can also use the Quine-McCluskey method. Here we assign the value 1 to the indifferent terms and reduce the function in the usual way. But, when we come to the covering of the function by prime implicants, we consider only the minterms for which it is imperative that $f = 1$ as those which should be covered. We examine this more closely by two examples already treated by the Karnaugh method.

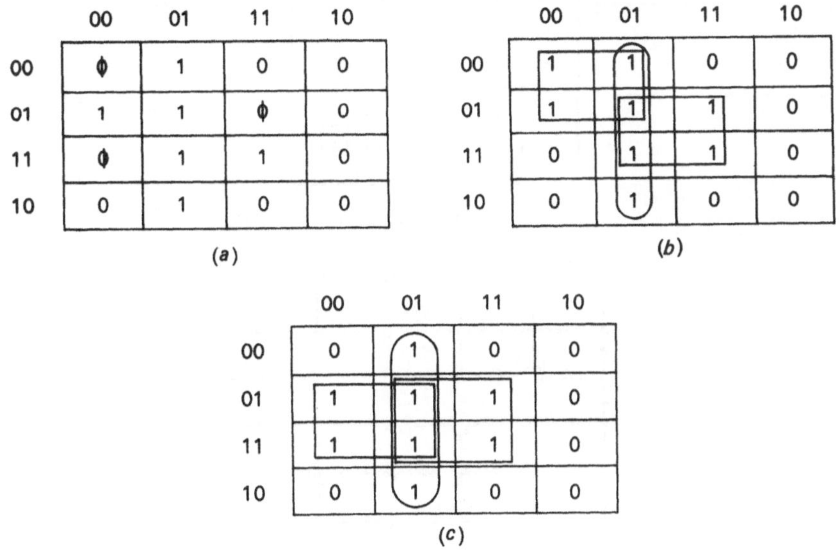

(a)

(b)

(c)

FIG. 1.27. Partition $f_{x_3 x_4; x_1 x_2}$.

First example. We have reduced the function as indicated in Figure 1.28. To cover f, we shall have a five-row (prime implicants), five-column (f has five minterms, which are not indifferent, to cover) map. We see that B, C, and D are essential and we once again find

$$f = \bar{x}_1\bar{x}_2 + \bar{x}_1\bar{x}_4 + \bar{x}_2x_3 \quad \text{(Figure 1.29)}.$$

Second example. The reduction and covering of f require no further comment. We find the same choice given by the Karnaugh maps (Figures 1.30 and 1.31)

$$f = A + B + D \quad \text{or} \quad f = C + B + D.$$

0	0 0 0 0	×

1	0 0 0 1	×
2	0 0 1 0	×
4	0 1 0 0	×
8	1 0 0 0	×

5	0 1 0 1	×
6	0 1 1 0	×
12	1 1 0 0	×

13	1 1 0 1	×
14	1 1 1 0	)(

0 0 0 −	×	(0,1)
0 0 − 0	×	(0,2)
0 − 0 0	×	(0,4)
− 0 0 0	×	(0,8)

0 − 0 1	×	(1,5)
0 − 1 0	×	(2,6)
0 1 0 −	×	(4,5)
0 1 − 0	×	(4,6)
− 1 0 0	×	(4,12)
1 − 0 0	×	(8,12)

1 0 1	×	(5,10)
− 1 1 0	×	(6,14)
1 1 0 −	×	(12,13)
1 1 − 0	×	(12,14)

0 − 0 −	(0,1,4,5) A
0 − − 0	(0,2,4,6) B
− − 0 0	(0,4,8,12) C

− 1 0 −	(4,5,12,13) D
− 1 − 0	(4,6,12,14) E

Fig. 1.28.

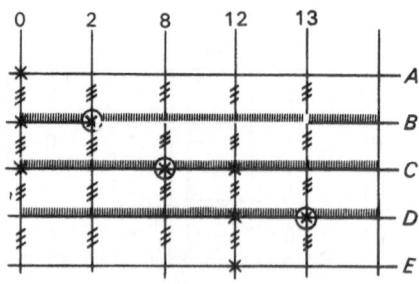

Fig. 1.29.

0	0 0 0 0	×	(0,1)	0 0 0 –	×	(0,1,4,5)	0 – 0 – A	
			(0,4)	0 – 0 0	×			
1	0 0 0 1	×				(1,5,9,13)	– – 0 1 B	
4	0 1 0 0	×	(1,5)	0 – 0 1	×	(4,5,12,13)	– 1 0 – C	
			(1,9)	– 0 0 1	×			
5	0 1 0 1	×	(4,5)	0 1 0 –	×	(5,7,13,15)	– 1 – 1 D	
9	1 0 0 1	×	(4,12)	– 1 0 0	×			
12	1 1 0 0	×						
			(5,7)	0 1 – 1	×			
7	0 1 1 1	×	(5,13)	– 1 0 1	×			
13	1 1 0 1	×	(9,13)	1 – 0 1	×			
			(12,13)	1 1 0 –	×			
15	1 1 1 1	×						
			(7,15)	– 1 1 1	×			
			(13,15)	1 1 – 1	×			

Fig. 1.30.

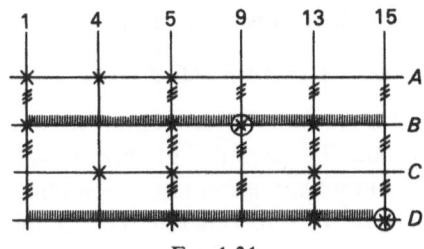

Fig. 1.31.

Important comments

(1) What has just been done brings out the fact that the two methods of reduction just exposed are complementary rather than equivalent. In fact, the Karnaugh map method is very easy to handle up to five variables; but, from five on, the problem of adjacent cells becomes complicated since two adjacent cells in the Boolean sense are not necessarily geometrically adjacent in a planar representation. This situation leads to tedious computational manipulations which can quickly become a source of error.

Although it is in our interest to seek the reduction of a function by the Quine-McCluskey method whenever we can (and certainly as soon as the number of variables used is more than five or six), especially since there exist programs permitting the solution of this problem by digital computer, at least up to the point of covering. We shall, however, see that in the study of sequential systems the nature of the problems encountered implies the use of Karnaugh maps.

(2) There exists a method for covering a reduced function by a set of prime implicants, which is more systematic than the one we have described. We give an example of its application.

Consider the function f which we reduced in Section 1.6. The reduced function has six prime implicants (A to F) and its disjunctive canonical form counted ten minterms (0, 1, 3, 4, 7, 8, 11, 12, 13, 15). We may therefore put the problem in the following form: we must cover the minterms $0, 1, 3, ..., 15$. 0 can be covered by either the prime implicant A or B, 1 by A or B, etc. In other words, we can express this by the relation

$$1 = (A+E)(A+B)(B+F) \cdot E \cdot F \cdot E \cdot F(C+E)$$
$$\cdot (C+D)(D+F).$$

The essential prime implicants are E and F; we therefore, keep them and suppress all the terms in the parentheses containing them:

$$(A \not{+} E)(A+B)(B \not{+} F)(C \not{+} E)(C+D)(C \not{+} F).$$

Thus we see that once E and F are taken, we can take either A and C or A and D or B and D or B and C to finish covering the function.

Let's consider the first example studied in Section 1.7. The essential prime implicants are B (the only one to cover the minterm represented by 6), C (which covers 8), and D (which covers 13). The covering equation is therefore

$$1 = (A+B+C)(C+D+E).$$

Each of the two parentheses contains at least one essential prime implicant. Therefore, f does not need them, and is entirely covered by B, C, and D.

In the second example of the same section, B and D are the essential prime implicants. Therefore, we have:

$$1 = (A+B)(A+C)(A+B+C+D)(B+C+D),$$

we may make the following cancellations

$$(A \not{+} B)(A+C)(A \not{+} B \not{+} C \not{+} D)(B \not{+} C \not{+} D).$$

We therefore, see the necessity of B and D and A, or B and D and C to cover f.

(3) These methods of simplification are interesting when we dispose of independent logical circuits realising simple functions (AND, OR, NOR, NAND) for the realization of the functions under consideration. In the computer industry (in particular) we most often use modules realizing more elaborate logical functions (generally Boolean sums and products). The Quine-McCluskey and Karnaugh methods are no longer applicable when we factorize the function f in terms of the existing modules. Thus it is more interesting to try to apply the factorization methods of Boolean functions which we discuss in the following section.

1.8. FACTORIZATION OF BOOLEAN FUNCTIONS*

We have just studied (1.5 to 1.7) the minimization of Boolean functions given by a product of Boolean sums or a sum of Boolean products. As interesting as this aspect of the problem may be, it is not always the most useful. In fact, the realization of the minimal form as a product of sums (or sum of products) can be more expensive or weaker than that of a sum of products of sums or a product of sums of products. But in this last case, there are no existing adequate algorithms. Thus we seek a factorization of $f(x_1, x_2, ..., x_n)$ expressed by a function of functions.

From another point of view, it can be interesting in many applications to see if a function factorizes in terms of several given Boolean functions. Such is the case of logical circuits which we wish to realize with the aid of previously built functions (modules). Here again, the two-level minimization theorem offers no solution.

The study of Boolean function factorization (or decomposition) has been developing for some years. In the following we shall expose the principal results obtained at the present time. Before discussing the Boolean factorization theory itself, we must have some notion of Boolean matrices, which are the subject of the next section. After defining two principal types of problems, we shall apply ourselves to the task of solving them.

Limiting ourselves to a brief review, we shall expose the theoretical concepts necessary to understand factorization. The reader can find

* The principal results of this article are due to M. E. Pandeff, mathematical engineer at the Société Européenne pour le traitement de l'Information, whom the authors would like to thank for permitting them to use his work in this book.

more elaborate proofs in the works cited in the bibliography, particularly in Ledley[16] and the proceedings of the colloquium on Boolean algebra held at Grenoble, 1965.

1.8.1. *Basic notions of Boolean matrices*

DEFINITION. We call by *Boolean matrix* a two-dimensional rectangular table whose elements are 0, 1 or binary variables.

Operations on Boolean Matrices

Transposition. Given an m by n (m rows, n columns) Boolean matrix A, in which the general element is a_{ij}, the transposed matrix t_a is of dimension $n \times m$ and its general element is $t_{ij} = a_{ji}$.

Complementation. Given an $m \times n$ Boolean matrix A, a_{ij}, its complement, noted $\bar{A}$, is an $m \times n$ Boolean matrix with entries c_{ij} such that $(\bar{a}_{ij}) = c_{ij}$ defines it.

Sum. The sum $A + B$ (or $A \lor B$) of two $m \times n$ Boolean matrices A, defined by a_{ij}, and B, defined by b_{ij}, is the $m \times n$ Boolean matrix $a_{ij} + b_{ij}$ (or $a_{ij} \lor b_{ij}$).

Logical product. Let a_{ij} and b_{ij} be two $m \times n$ Boolean matrices. Their logical product $A \cdot B$, is an $m \times n$ Boolean matrix $a_{ij} \cdot b_{ij}$.

Matrix product. If a_{ik} is an $m \times p$ Boolean matrix, A, and b_{ij} a $p \times n$ Boolean matrix B, then

$$p_{ij} = \sum_k a_{ik} b_{kj}$$

is the $m \times n$ Boolean matrix $A \otimes B$ called the matrix product of A and B.

Examples. Let

$$A = \begin{bmatrix} a & 1 & 1 & 0 \\ b & 1 & 0 & 1 \\ 1 & 0 & 1 & c \end{bmatrix} \qquad B_1 = \begin{bmatrix} 1 & \bar{a} & 1 & 0 \\ 1 & 0 & \bar{b} & 0 \\ 0 & 1 & 0 & 1 \end{bmatrix} \qquad B_2 = \begin{bmatrix} 1 & 0 \\ c & 1 \\ 1 & c \\ 1 & 0 \end{bmatrix}.$$

We have

$$t_a = \begin{bmatrix} a & b & 1 \\ 1 & 1 & 0 \\ 1 & 0 & 1 \\ 0 & 1 & c \end{bmatrix} \quad \text{The first row of } A \text{ becomes the first column of } t_a, \text{ etc.}$$

$$\bar{A} = \begin{bmatrix} \bar{a} & 0 & 0 & 1 \\ \bar{b} & 0 & 1 & 0 \\ 0 & 1 & 0 & \bar{c} \end{bmatrix} \quad \text{Each element of } \bar{A} \text{ is the complement, in the Boolean sense, of the corresponding element of } A.$$

$$A + B_1 = S = \begin{bmatrix} 1 & 1 & 1 & 0 \\ 1 & 1 & \bar{b} & 1 \\ 1 & 1 & 1 & 1 \end{bmatrix}$$ Each element of S is the sum of the corresponding elements of A and B_1.

$$A \cdot B_1 = P_1 = \begin{bmatrix} a & \bar{a} & 1 & 0 \\ b & 0 & 0 & 0 \\ 0 & 0 & 0 & c \end{bmatrix}$$ Each element of P_1 is the algebraic product of the corresponding elements of A and B_1.

$$A \otimes B_2 = P_2 = \begin{bmatrix} 1 & 1 \\ 1 & 1 \\ 1 & c \end{bmatrix}$$ Each element of P_2 is obtained by logical multiplication of the i row in A by the j column of B_2.

Comments

(1) In order to perform their sum or logical product, it is necessary that two matrices have the same dimensions. On the contrary, the matrix product operation is performed only when the number of columns of the matrix appearing on the left of the product equals the number of rows of the matrix appearing on the right.

(2) We can also define the implication of two matrices. We shall say that A implies B (A and B being of the same dimensions $m \times n$ and defined by a_{ij} and b_{ij}) $A \rightarrow B$ if $a_{ij} \subseteq b_{ij}$ which means $a_{ij} \cdot \bar{b}_{ij} = 0$ or $A \cdot \bar{B} = 0$. Thus if

$$B_3 = \begin{bmatrix} 1 & 1 & 1 & 0 \\ 1 & 1 & 0 & 1 \\ 1 & 0 & 1 & 1 \end{bmatrix}$$

we have $A \subseteq B_3$.

1.8.2. *Matrix representation of a Boolean function*

Let $\div F$ be the designation number of the Boolean function F of variables $x_1, x_2, \ldots, x_p$.

Let X be the column vector of the respective combinations of these variables arranged from top to bottom in ascending order of their corresponding decimal values.

Now each digit of $\div F$ indicates whether the corresponding combination of X belongs to the function or not: the latter can be expressed as a Boolean sum of these different combinations. The disjunctive canonical form of F is thus obtained.

Written in a matrix form this relation is:

$$F = [\div F] \otimes [X] \tag{1}$$

Let us consider the case of a function F_1, whose image is given in Figure 1.32. Referring to Figure 1.33 we write

$$F = [\div F] \otimes [X] = \bar{x}_3\bar{x}_2x_1 + x_3\bar{x}_2x_1 + x_3x_2x_1$$
$$F = \bar{x}_2x_1 + x_3x_1.$$

$$\begin{bmatrix} \bar{x}_3 & \bar{x}_2 & \bar{x}_1 \\ \bar{x}_3 & \bar{x}_2 & x_1 \\ \bar{x}_3 & x_2 & \bar{x}_1 \\ \bar{x}_3 & x_2 & \text{-}x_1 \\ x_3 & \bar{x}_2 & \bar{x}_1 \\ x_3 & \bar{x}_2 & x_1 \\ x_3 & x_2 & \bar{x}_1 \\ x_3 & x_2 & x_1 \end{bmatrix}$$

0 1 0 0 0 1 0 1

FIG. 1.32. Image of F_1.   FIG. 1.33. Matrix X.

Instead of considering the designation number of the function F we could also have divided the set X into 2 subsets X_1, and X_2 from which we could have obtained the Veitch diagram $E_{(X_1,X_2)}$ of the function F from its designation number $\div F$.

If the sets X_1 and X_2 have 2^p and 2^q terms respectively, matrix $E_{(X_1,X_2)}$ will have 2^q rows and 2^p columns. Function F which can be expressed as a Boolean sum of Boolean monomials is thus a matrix of dimension 1×1.

It seems logical then to generalize relation (1) as follows:

$$F = [X_2] \otimes [E_{X_1,X_2}] \otimes [X_1], \tag{2}$$

where $[X_2]$ is the row matrix of the different combinations of the Boolean variables of X_2 taken from left to right in the increasing order of their corresponding decimal values and where $[X_1]$ is the column vector relative to the combinations of X_1.

This matrix product has a 1×1 dimension and is a sum of Boolean monomials. Only the combinations corresponding to a '1' in the Veitch diagram are conserved. This product is, effectively, the expression of the considered function.

Consider the Veitch diagram of Figure 1.34. After simplification we can write:

$$F = (\bar{x}_4\bar{x}_3 + \bar{x}_4x_3 + x_4\bar{x}_3 + x_4x_3)\bar{x}_2x_1 + x_4x_2(\bar{x}_3\bar{x}_1 + \bar{x}_3x_1 \\ + x_3\bar{x}_1 + x_3x_1) + \bar{x}_4\bar{x}_2(\bar{x}_3\bar{x}_1 + \bar{x}_3x_1 + x_3\bar{x}_1 + x_3x_1).$$

Thus

$$F = \bar{x}_2 x_1 + x_4 x_2 + \bar{x}_4 \bar{x}_2.$$

$\diagdown$ $x_2 x_1$ $x_4 x_3$	0 0	0 1	1 0	1 1
00	1	1	0	0
01	1	1	0	0
10	0	1	1	1
11	0	1	1	1

FIG. 1.34. $E_{x_1 x_2 / x_3 x_4}$.

According to Equation (2)

$$[X_2] = [\bar{x}_4 \bar{x}_3 \quad \bar{x}_4 x_3 \quad x_4 \bar{x}_3 \quad x_4 x_3] = [a_1 \; b_1 \; c_1 \; d_1]$$

$$[X_1] = \begin{bmatrix} \bar{x}_2 \; \bar{x}_1 \\ \bar{x}_2 \; x_1 \\ x_2 \; \bar{x}_1 \\ x_2 \; x_1 \end{bmatrix} \quad \begin{bmatrix} a_2 \\ b_2 \\ c_2 \\ d_2 \end{bmatrix}$$

$$F = [X_2] \otimes \begin{bmatrix} 1 & 1 & 0 & 0 \\ 1 & 1 & 0 & 0 \\ 0 & 1 & 1 & 1 \\ 0 & 1 & 1 & 1 \end{bmatrix} \otimes [X_1]$$

with

$$a_1 + b_1 + c_1 + d_1 = 1$$
$$a_2 + b_2 + c_2 + d_2 = 1$$

$$F = [a_1 \; b_1 \; c_1 \; d_1] \otimes \begin{bmatrix} 1 & 1 & 0 & 0 \\ 1 & 1 & 0 & 0 \\ 0 & 1 & 1 & 1 \\ 0 & 1 & 1 & 1 \end{bmatrix} \otimes \begin{bmatrix} a_2 \\ b_2 \\ c_2 \\ d_2 \end{bmatrix}$$

$$F = [a_1 + b_1 \; 1 \; c_1 + d_1 \; c_1 + d_1] \otimes \begin{bmatrix} a_2 \\ b_2 \\ c_2 \\ d_2 \end{bmatrix}$$

$$F = a_2(a_1 + b_1) + b_2 + (c_1 + d_1)(c_2 + d_2)$$
$$F = \bar{x}_2 \bar{x}_1 \bar{x}_4 + \bar{x}_2 x_1 + x_4 x_2.$$

Consequently

$$F = \bar{x}_2\bar{x}_4 + \bar{x}_2x_1 + x_4x_2.$$

Note. As the canonical form of a Boolean function is unique, so is the Veitch diagram associated with it. Consequently, if there are two matrices E_1 and E_2 and a row and a column matrix of the Boolean combinations X_1 and X_2 such that the relation

$$[X_2] \otimes [E_1] \otimes [X_1] = [X_2] \otimes [E_2] \otimes [X_1]$$

is satisfied, then we deduce the equality:

$$[E_1] = [E_2].$$

1.8.3. *Aspect of the problem of decomposition of a Boolean function*

1.8.3.1. *Example of decomposition*

We consider the Boolean function of 5 variables $F(x_1, ..., x_5)$ whose designation number is

$$\div F(x_1, ..., x_5) = 1011 \ 1101 \ 1110 \ 1110 \ 0111 \ 0111 \ 1000 \ 1000 \qquad (3)$$

and the function

$$G(\varphi_1, \varphi_2, x_4, x_5) = \varphi_1\bar{x}_4x_5 + \bar{\varphi}_1\bar{x}_5 + \varphi_2x_4\bar{x}_5 + \bar{\varphi}_2\bar{x}_4 + \bar{\varphi}_1\varphi_2x_4,$$
$$(4)$$

where φ_1 and φ_2 are two functions of the variables x_1, x_2, x_3 defined in the following way:

$$\varphi_1(x_1, x_2, x_3) = x_1\bar{x}_3 + x_2x_3$$
$$\varphi_2(x_1, x_2, x_3) = \bar{x}_1x_3 + \bar{x}_2\bar{x}_3. \qquad (5)$$

We will say that function $F(x_1, ..., x_5)$ can be decomposed with respect to subfunctions $\varphi_1(x_1, x_2, x_3)$ and $\varphi_2(x_1, x_2, x_3)$ if function F can be written in the form of function G with φ_1 and φ_2 defined as above (5). This assumes that the relation

$$G(\varphi_1, \varphi_2, x_4, x_5) = F(x_1, ..., x_5)$$

is satisfied when expressions (5) are substituted for φ_1 and φ_2 in G. According to (5) we can write:

$$\bar{\varphi}_1 = \bar{x}_1\bar{x}_3 + \bar{x}_2x_3$$
$$\bar{\varphi}_2 = x_2\bar{x}_3 + x_1x_3. \qquad (6)$$

We develop G by replacing φ_i and $\bar{\varphi}_i$ ($i = 1$ or 2) by their expressions taken from (5) or (6). Upon simplification the expression for G becomes:

$$G = (x_1\bar{x}_3 + x_2x_3)\bar{x}_4x_5 + \bar{x}_5(\bar{x}_1\bar{x}_3 + \bar{x}_2x_3) + x_4\bar{x}_5(\bar{x}_1x_3 + \bar{x}_2\bar{x}_3) + \\ + \bar{x}_1\bar{x}_2x_4 + \bar{x}_4(x_1x_3 + x_2\bar{x}_3).$$

The Veitch diagram (E_{X_1,X_2}) of function G with respect to variables $x_1, \ldots, x_5$ can immediately be deduced (Figure 1.35). This is the matrix which is associated with the Veitch diagram of function F corresponding to the division of its variable into two subsets $X_1 = (x_1, x_2, x_3)$ and $X_2 = (x_4, x_5)$.

Veitch diagram (E'_{φ,X_2}) of function G with respect to the two sub-sets of variables $\varphi = (\varphi_1, \varphi_2)$, $X_2 = (x_4, x_5)$ is given in Figure 1.36.

x_5x_4 \ $x_3x_2x_1$	000	001	010	011	100	101	110	111
00	1	0	1	1	1	1	0	1
01	1	1	1	0	1	1	1	0
10	0	1	1	1	0	1	1	1
11	1	0	0	0	1	0	0	0

FIG. 1.35. Veitch diagram of $g(x_1, \ldots, x_5)$: E_{X_1/X_2}.

x_5x_4 \ $\varphi_2\varphi_1$	00	01	10	11
00	1	1	1	0
01	1	0	1	1
10	1	1	0	1
11	0	0	1	0

FIG. 1.36. E'_{φ,X_2}.

The problem is to determine under which conditions Veitch diagram E and E' and the two sub-functions φ_1 and φ_2 correspond to a decomposition of function F in the form of function G with φ_1 and φ_2 taken into account. There are two possibilities which we designate by problem of the 1st type and problem of the 2nd type.

Problem of the 1st type. Given the function F of a certain number of variables and of sub-functions $\varphi_1, \ldots, \varphi_k$, can we decompose F with respect to these sub functions?

Problem of the 2nd type. Given a function F of a certain number of variables and of sub-sets $X_1, X_2 \ldots$ of these variables, with respect to which sub-functions of all the variables $X_1, X_2 \ldots$ can we decompose F?

Note. We assume, in all that is to follow, that subsets $X_1, X_2 \ldots$ are disjunctive; that is, there is no variable common to two of them.

1.8.3.2. Matrix analysis of the decomposition

Consider the Boolean function $F(x_1, \ldots, x_n)$. Let X be the alphabet of the inputs: $X = (x_1, \ldots, x_n)$.

We assume that X can be divided into two sub-sets X_1 and X_2 and that the Veitch diagram associated with F is E_{X_1,X_2} (X_1 corresponding to the columns, X_2 to the rows). From (2) it follows that:

$$F = [X_2] \otimes [E] \otimes [X_1]. \qquad (7)$$

We assume, furthermore, that X_1 and X_2 have 9 and $(n-9)$ elements respectively and that there are p sub-functions $\varphi_1, \dots, \varphi_p$ of the variables of the set X_1, such that

$$G(\varphi_1, \dots, \varphi_p, X_2) = F(X_1, X_2) = F(x_1, \dots, x_n).$$

According to (2) this can be stated by the relation (8)

$$G = [X_2] \otimes [E'] \otimes [\varphi], \qquad (8)$$

where E'_{φ,X_2} is the Veitch diagram associated with the function G whose two variable sub-sets are X_2 and φ. $[\varphi]$ is the column matrix of the combination of variables $\varphi_1, \dots, \varphi_p$; it is, thus, a $(2^p \times 1)$ matrix. $[X_1]$ is a $(2^q \times 1)$ matrix. If we want to define G as a function of the variable sub-sets X_1 and X_2 we must define a transformation matrix between $[\varphi]$ and $[X_1]$. This matrix $[T]$ will be of dimensions $(2^p \times 2^q)$ and will satisfy (9).

$$[\varphi] = [T] \otimes [X_1]. \qquad (9)$$

Consequently (8) can be written:

$$G(\varphi, X_2) = [X_2] \otimes [E'] \otimes [T] \otimes [X_1].$$

According to the note at the end of Section 1.8.2 we deduce the fundamental relation

$$[E] = [E'] \otimes [T]. \qquad (10)$$

We must now study the existence of matrix $[T]$, and its properties determination.

1.8.3.3 Determination of matrix T
Matrix $[T]$ gives the relation existing between the column, matrices $[\varphi]$ and $[X_1]$. Functions $\varphi_1, \dots, \varphi_p$ are defined by

$$\varphi_i(X_1) = [\div \varphi_i] \otimes [X_1](\forall_i \in (1, p)).$$

Letting φ_i^* indicate either φ_i or $\bar{\varphi}_i$ we can write

$$\varphi_1^* \varphi_2^* \cdots \varphi_p^* = [\div (\varphi_1^* \cdot \varphi_2^* \cdots \varphi_p^*)] \otimes [X_1].$$

But

$$\div (\varphi_1^* \cdot \varphi_2^* \cdots \varphi_p^*) = (\div \varphi_1^*) \cdot (\div \varphi_2^*) \cdots (\div \varphi_p^*).$$

Consequently

$$[\varphi] = \begin{bmatrix} (\div \bar{\varphi}_p) \cdots (\div \bar{\varphi}_2) \cdot (\div \bar{\varphi}_1) \\ (\div \bar{\varphi}_p) \cdots (\div \bar{\varphi}_2) \cdot (\div \varphi_1) \\ \cdots\cdots\cdots\cdots\cdots\cdots\cdots \\ (\div \varphi_p) \qquad\qquad \cdot (\div \varphi_1) \end{bmatrix} \otimes [X_1]$$

And

$$[T] = \begin{bmatrix} (\div \bar{\varphi}_p) \cdots (\div \bar{\varphi}_2) \cdot (\div \bar{\varphi}_1) \\ (\div \bar{\varphi}_p) \cdots (\div \bar{\varphi}_2) \cdot (\div \varphi_1) \\ \cdots\cdots\cdots\cdots\cdots\cdots\cdots \\ (\div \bar{\varphi}_p) \quad (\div \bar{\varphi}_2) \cdot (\div \bar{\varphi}_1) \end{bmatrix}.$$

We note, by construction, that matrix $[T]$ associated with a set of functions φ_i is unique. We shall first give a practical method of determining $[T]$ and then study its properties.

1.8.4. *Properties of matrix T*

1.8.4.1. *Number of '1's' of matrix T*
For each combination $y_1^*, \ldots, y_q^*$ of the variables of X_1, there exists a corresponding element of $[X_1]$ and a well determined value of the different functions φ_i $(1 \leqslant i \leqslant p)$ and, thus, a single element of the matrix $[\varphi]$ of the combinations of the various functions φ_i.

We are thus led to put in a '1' in matrix $[T]$ in the column associated with the combination of y_j's but only in the row associated with the combination of corresponding φ_i's. (The other rows of this column are filled with 0's.)

Reciprocally for a given combination of the y_j's (which specifies the digit taken in the image of the function φ_i) we know the value of the different φ_i's (since $[T]$ indicates the combination $\varphi_i^*, \ldots, \varphi_q^*$ associated with $y_1, \ldots, y_q$). We can thus construct steps by steps the images of the different functions φ_i. Consequently we deduce Theorem 1.

THEOREM 1. Matrix $[T]$ contains only one '1' per column.

DEFINITION 4. Any matrix having only one '1' per column is called a *pseudo-unitary Boolean matrix*.

Matrix $[T]$ is pseudo-unitary.

1.8.4.2. *Construction of matrix* $[T]$

Given p functions $\varphi_i(X_1)$ of the Boolean variables $y_1, \dots, y_q$ we let $\varphi_{10}, \dots, \varphi_{po}$ be the different values of the function φ_i for a combination of the Boolean variables $y_{10}, \dots, y_{qo}$. (The y_i's are the variables x_i of the set X_1.)

Let N_y and N be the decimal values corresponding to the terms $y_{10}, \dots, y_{qo}$ and $\varphi_{10}, \dots, \varphi_{po}$. In matrix $[T]$ we put a '1' at the intersection of row $(N+1)$ and column (N_y+1) (taken from 1 to 2^p from top to bottom for the rows and from 1 to 2^q from left to right for the columns).

From the preceding example of Section 1.8.3.1 (Equation (5)) we have:

$$\div \varphi_1(x_1, x_2, x_3) = 0\ 1\ 0\ 1\ 0\ 0\ 1\ 1$$
$$\div \varphi_2(x_1, x_2, x_3) = 1\ 1\ 0\ 0\ 1\ 0\ 1\ 0.$$

We take the combination $x_1 = 0$, $x_2 = 1$, $x_3 = 1$ whose decimal value is 6. The corresponding combination of φ is $\varphi_1\varphi_2$ ($\varphi_1 = 1$, $\varphi_2 = 2$) with a decimal value 3.

A '1' is placed in matrix $[T]$ (4×8) at the intersection of row 4 and column 7. Generalizing this operation we get the matrix $[T]$ of Figure 1.37.

$\varphi_2\varphi_1$ ＼ $x_3x_2x_1$	000	001	010	011	100	101	110	111
00	0	0	1	0	0	1	0	0
01	0	0	0	1	0	0	0	1
10	1	0	0	0	1	0	0	0
11	0	1	0	0	0	0	1	0

FIG. 1.37. Matrix $[T]$.

1.8.4.3. *Multiplication of a Boolean matrix on the right by a pseudo-unitary matrix*

Consider an $n \times m$ Boolean matrix A of general term a_{ij} and an $m \times p$ pseudo-unitary matrix α of general term α_{kl}. The product matrix B $(n \times p)$ obtained by multiplication of α on the right by A is:

$$B = A \otimes \alpha.$$

The general term is

$$b_{ij} = \sum_k a_{ik}\alpha_{kj}.$$

We examine the columns of matrix B (j remains constant). Let $\alpha_{k_0 j}$ be the term which is different from 0 in column j of the matrix α

$$b_{ij} = a_{ik_0}.$$

Column j of matrix B is consequently column k_0 of matrix A.

THEOREM 2.   A pseudo-unitary Boolean matrix either permutes, omits or repeats the columns of the matrix that it multiplies on the right.

We assume that the coefficient which is equal to 1 in the j column of matrix α is situated on the kth row; the jth column of B is obtained by recopying the kth column of A.

Application. Consider matrices A and α of Figures 1.39 and 1.40. Matrix B, which is obtained by successively repeating columns 1,2,2,4, 4 of matrix A (column 2 of A is thus omitted) is represented in Figure 1.38.

$$\begin{bmatrix} 1 & 0 & 0 & 1 & 1 \\ 0 & 1 & 1 & 1 & 1 \\ 1 & 1 & 1 & 1 & 1 \\ 1 & 0 & 0 & 0 & 0 \end{bmatrix} \qquad \begin{bmatrix} 1 & 0 & 0 & 1 \\ 0 & 1 & 0 & 1 \\ 1 & 1 & 1 & 1 \\ 1 & 0 & 1 & 0 \end{bmatrix} \qquad \begin{bmatrix} 1 & 0 & 0 & 0 & 0 \\ 0 & 1 & 1 & 0 & 0 \\ 0 & 0 & 0 & 0 & 0 \\ 0 & 0 & 0 & 1 & 1 \end{bmatrix}$$

FIG. 1.38.   M..trix B.   FIG. 1.39.   Matrix A.   FIG. 1.40.   Matrix α.

THEOREM 3.   If α is a pseudo-unitary matrix and if two matrices A and B are related by $B = A \otimes \alpha$, then two identical columns of B will correspond to two identical columns i and j of matrix α. The reciprocal is true if the columns of A are different.

Assume that two columns of matrix (j_1 and j_2) are identical and that only the coefficient of row k_0 is equal to 1

$$\alpha_{k_0 j_1} = \alpha_{k_0 j_2} = 1.$$

Columns j_1 and j_2 of matrix B are given by

$$b_{ij_1} = \sum_k a_{ik}\alpha_{kj_1} = a_{ik_0} \quad (\alpha_{kj_1} = 0 \quad \text{if} \quad k \neq k_0)$$

$$b_{ij_2} = \sum_l a_{il}\alpha_{lj_2} = a_{ik_0} \quad (\alpha_{lj_2} = 0 \quad \text{if} \quad l \neq k_0)$$

Consequently

$$b_{ij_1} = b_{ij_2},$$

and the property is true.

Reciprocally we assume that columns j_1 and j_2 of matrix B are identical. Thus

$$b_{ij_1} = \sum_k a_{ik}\alpha_{kj_1} = a_{ik_0} \quad (\alpha_{kj_1} = 0 \quad \text{if} \quad k \neq k_0)$$

$$b_{ij_2} = \sum_l a_{il}\alpha_{lj_2} = a_{il_0} \quad (\alpha_{lj_2} = 0 \quad \text{if} \quad l \neq l_0)$$

and

$$a_{ik_0} = a_{il_0}. \tag{11}$$

If we assume that the columns of A are distinct then k_0 must equal l_0 and the following relation is true

$$\alpha_{k_0 j_1} = \alpha_{k_0 j_2} = 1.$$

Consequently columns j_1 and j_2 of α are identical. If on the contrary, certain columns of A are identical then two identical columns of α do not necessarily correspond to two identical columns of B. If Equation (11) is satisfied for $k_0 \neq l_0$ then columns k_0 and l_0 of A are identical whereas columns j_1 and j_2 of α are different.

Note

(1) With a pseudo-unitary matrix $(B = A \otimes \alpha)$ if in a column j row k (taken from top to bottom starting with 1) has a 1, column j of B will be column k of A. Consequently we can immediately deduce B from A and α or determine α from A and B; in that case if column j of B is identical to column k of A we put a 1 in matrix α at the intersection of row k and column j.

(2) If the columns of A are all different then a unique matrix α corresponds to matrix B (each column of α is associated with a single column of A to give a column of B).

If, on the contrary, A can have identical columns then there are as many possibilities as there are columns equal to that column of A to establish a column of B. If there are n different columns $1, 2, ..., n$ and if there are p_1 columns identical to column 1, p_2 to column 2, ... and, p_n to column n, then there will be

$$N = 2^{(p_1+1)} \times 2^{(p_2+1)} \times \cdots \times 2^{(p_n+1)}$$

(arithmetic multiplication and addition) possible matrices α to set up B.

Example. In the case of Figures 1.38 to 1.40 matrix α which is obtained is unique as all the columns of A are different. Furthermore, as B does not contain column 3 of A matrix α has only 0's in its 3rd row. In the case of matrices B and A of Figures 1.41 and 1.42 in order to reproduce columns 1 and 3 of B we can choose either column 1 or 3 of A which leads to 4 possible matrices α (Figures 1.43–1.46).

$$\begin{bmatrix} 0 & 1 & 0 & 0 \\ 1 & 1 & 1 & 1 \\ 1 & 0 & 1 & 1 \\ 0 & 0 & 0 & 1 \end{bmatrix}$$

FIG. 1.41. Matrix B.

$$\begin{bmatrix} 0 & 1 & 0 & 0 \\ 1 & 1 & 1 & 1 \\ 1 & 0 & 1 & 1 \\ 0 & 0 & 0 & 1 \end{bmatrix}$$

FIG. 1.42. Matrix A.

$$\begin{bmatrix} 1 & 0 & 1 & 0 \\ 0 & 1 & 0 & 0 \\ 0 & 0 & 0 & 0 \\ 0 & 0 & 0 & 1 \end{bmatrix}$$

FIG. 1.43. Matrix α_1.

$$\begin{bmatrix} 1 & 0 & 0 & 0 \\ 0 & 1 & 0 & 0 \\ 0 & 0 & 1 & 0 \\ 0 & 0 & 0 & 1 \end{bmatrix}$$

FIG. 1.44. Matrix α_2.

$$\begin{bmatrix} 0 & 0 & 0 & 0 \\ 0 & 1 & 0 & 0 \\ 1 & 0 & 1 & 0 \\ 0 & 0 & 0 & 1 \end{bmatrix}$$

FIG. 1.45. Matrix α_3.

$$\begin{bmatrix} 0 & 0 & 1 & 0 \\ 0 & 1 & 0 & 0 \\ 1 & 0 & 0 & 0 \\ 0 & 0 & 0 & 1 \end{bmatrix}$$

FIG. 1.46. Matrix α_4.

1.8.5. *Application to the solution of the two types of decomposition problems*

1.8.5.1. *Problem of the 1st type*

We assume that the following are known: function F of 2 disjointed sub-sets of variables X_1 and X_2, the set of sub-functions φ of the variables of X_1, and the expression G of F as a function of X_1 and φ.

Let $E_{X_1X_2}$ and $E'_{\varphi X_2}$ be the Veitch diagrams associated with F and G. Matrix $[T]$ is related to the sub-function φ. The following fundamental relation exists between $[E]$, $[E']$ and $[T]$

$$[E] = [E'] \otimes [T].$$

(a) According to Theorem 2 of Section 1.8.4.3 *each column of E must be a column of E'*. (The reciprocal is not true as certain columns of E' can be omitted in the multiplication on the right by a pseudo-unitary matrix.)

We go back to the example of Section 1.8.3.1. Figures 1.34 and 1.35 represent matrices $E_{X_1X_2}$ and $E'_{\varphi X_2}$ relative to the functions $F(X_1, X_2)$ and $G(\varphi, X_2)$. Each column of E is a column of E'. We can thus write function F in the form of G but we must make sure that the functions φ are appropriate.

(b) According to the note in Section 1.8.4.3 stating that the columns of E' are distinct, if two columns i and j of matrix E are identical, columns i and j of matrix $[T]$ must be also identical. If conditions (a) and (b) are satisfied the decomposition of function F with the help of functions φ_i is possible.

In the example of Section 1.8.4.3 (Figure 1.34) columns 1 and 5, 2 and 7, 3 and 6, and 4 and 8 are identical. Figure 1.36 (matrix $[T]$) has the same identical columns as $[E]$. Consequently decomposition is possible.

1.8.5.2. *Problem of the 2nd type*

Only function $F_{X_1X_2}$ defined by the Veitch diagram $E_{X_1X_2}$ is known. We must define a function G of Veitch diagram E'_{φ,X_2} and a set of functions φ_i such that the matrix relation

$$[E] = [E'] \otimes [T]$$

is satisfied.

We know that each column of E must be a column of E'. Consequently $[E']$ must at least contain all the column of E which are different. The simplest matrix $[E']$ will then have for columns all the different columns of E. The number of columns of matrix $[E']$ will establish the number of elements of the set φ, that is, the number of sub-functions. In effect, each column will be coded by a binary combination of the different sub-functions.

THEOREM 4.   If n is the number of columns of Veitch diagram $E_{X_1X_2}$ of $F(X_1X_2)$ which are different, then the number of sub-functions φ by which the initial function can be decomposed will be equal to p such that

$$2^{p-1} < n \leqslant 2^p.$$

In the example of Section 1.8.4.3 we can, according to Figure 1.35, choose Figure 1.47 as matrix $[E']$. This matrix has only four columns. One may choose two sub-functions (of x_1, x_2, x_3) φ_1 and φ_2. Veitch's map which is related is given on Figure 1.48.

Matrix $[T]$ is computed from Figures 1.35 and 1.47 (matrices $[E]$ and $[E']$). It is shown on Figure 1.49. This matrix allows us to find the designation numbers for φ_1 and φ_2 (Figure 1.50). And so we get

$$\varphi_1 = \bar{x}_3 x_1 + x_3 x_2$$
$$\varphi_2 = \bar{x}_3 x_2 + x_3 x_1. \tag{12}$$

$$\begin{bmatrix} 1 & 0 & 1 & 1 \\ 1 & 1 & 1 & 0 \\ 0 & 1 & 1 & 1 \\ 1 & 0 & 0 & 0 \end{bmatrix}$$

$\diagdown \ \varphi_2\varphi_1$ x_5x_4	00	01	10	11
00	1	0	1	1
01	1	1	1	0
10	0	1	1	1
11	1	0	0	0

FIG. 1.47.   Matrix $[E']$.   FIG. 1.48.   Veitch diagram $E'_{\varphi.x_2}$.

$$\begin{bmatrix} 1 & 0 & 0 & 0 & 1 & 0 & 0 & 0 \\ 0 & 1 & 0 & 0 & 0 & 0 & 1 & 0 \\ 0 & 0 & 1 & 0 & 0 & 1 & 0 & 0 \\ 0 & 0 & 0 & 1 & 0 & 0 & 0 & 1 \end{bmatrix}$$

$\div\varphi_1 = 0\ 1\ 0\ 1\ 0\ 0\ 1\ 1$

$\div\varphi_2 = 0\ 0\ 1\ 1\ 0\ 1\ 0\ 1$

FIG. 1.49.   Matrix $[T]$.   FIG. 1.50.   Image of φ_1 and φ_2.

Note. As we are free to choose the order of the distinct columns of E there are several possible matrices $[T]$ which correspond to the different matrices $[E']$. (One is deduced from the other by permutation of the columns.)

The corresponding functions G are obtained by permuting or complementing the variable φ_i of one of the solutions.

According to Figure 1.47 we can write

$$G' = \bar{\varphi}_1\bar{x}_5 + \varphi_2\bar{x}_4 + \bar{\varphi}_2 x_4\bar{x}_5 + \varphi_1\bar{x}_4 x_5 + \bar{\varphi}_1\bar{\varphi}_2 x_4.$$

Function G of Section 1.8.3.1 is obtained from G' by replacing φ_2 by $\bar{\varphi}_2$ in the latter.

1.8.6. *Case of a non-solvable problem of the 1st type*

1.8.6.1. *Antecedent and consequent solution*

Suppose that we have a function F and thus a Veitch map $E_{x_1x_2}$ and a set of functions φ_i and thus a matrix $[T]$ such that the decomposition of function F is impossible. This means that it is not possible to obtain a function G and Veitch diagram $E'_{\varphi.x_2}$ such that the relation

$$[E] = [E'] \otimes [T]$$

is satisfied. The reason for this is that $[E']$ cannot be constructed from the different columns of $[E]$ such that two identical columns i and j of $[E]$ correspond to two identical columns of $[T]$.

Consider, for example, the function F whose image is

$$\div F = 0101 \quad 0011 \quad 1100 \quad 1010 \quad 0001 \quad 0001 \quad 0010 \quad 0010$$

and whose Veitch map is $E_{x_1 x_2 x_3 / x_4 x_5}$ (Figure 1.51).

$$\begin{bmatrix} 0 & 1 & 0 & 1 & 0 & 0 & 1 & 1 \\ 1 & 1 & 0 & 0 & 1 & 0 & 1 & 0 \\ 0 & 0 & 0 & 1 & 0 & 0 & 0 & 1 \\ 0 & 0 & 1 & 0 & 0 & 0 & 1 & 0 \end{bmatrix}$$

FIG. 1.51.   Matrix E of F.

Suppose that we want to decompose this function by means of sub-functions φ_1 and φ_2 defined by Equations (5) (Section 1.8.3.1). The associated matrix $[T]$ is given in Figure 1.36. Columns 1 and 5, 2 and 7, 3 and 6, and 4 and 8 are identical. The same is not true for E which makes the decomposition impossible. On the other hand it would be possible to replace matrix $[E]$ by matrices $[E_1'']$ and $[E_2'']$ satisfying the inequalities

$$[E_1''] \subset [E] \subset [E_2'']$$

such that a decomposition of the Boolean functions associated with the Veitch map $E_{1(X_1 X_2)}''$ and $E_{2(X_1 X_2)}''$ is possible with respect to function φ_1 and φ_2; that is, identical columns of the same rank in of E_1'' and E_2'' correspond to identical columns of $[T]$.

We are going to show that among all the possible matrices $[E_1'']$ and $[E_2'']$ there are two, $[E_c'']$ and $[E_a'']$, which are respectively the least upper bound and the greatest lower bound. In effect, the $+$ and the $\cdot$ operations in Boolean algebra are lattice operations. By definition, if a and b are Boolean variables $a + b$ and $a \cdot b$ are respectively their least upper bound and greatest lower bound. Consequently we assume that columns k and l of matrix E (column matrices $[N_k]$ and $[N_l]$) are distinct while columns k and l of $[T]$ are identical. The column matrices $[N_k] + [N_l]$ and $[N_k] \cdot [N_l]$, respectively, the logical sum and product of $[N_k]$ and $[N_l]$, are the least upper bound and the greatest lower bound of these matrices. They are unique. We replace $[N_k]$ and $[N_l]$ of E first by $[N_k] \cdot [N_l]$ and then by $[N_k] + [N_l]$. Proceeding in this manner for every column of E by comparison with the columns of $[T]$ we get matrices $[E_a'']$ and $[E_c'']$.

Example. Consider the Veitch map of Figure 1.50 and the matrix $[T]$ of Figure 1.49 in which columns 1 and 5, 2 and 7, 3 and 6, and 4 and 8 are identical. The associated matrices $[E_a'']$ and $[E_c'']$ are obtained as indicated above and are represented by Figures 1.52 and 1.53.

$$\begin{bmatrix} 0 & 1 & 0 & 1 & 0 & 0 & 1 & 1 \\ 1 & 1 & 0 & 0 & 1 & 0 & 1 & 0 \\ 0 & 0 & 0 & 1 & 0 & 0 & 0 & 1 \\ 0 & 0 & 0 & 0 & 0 & 0 & 0 & 0 \end{bmatrix} \qquad \begin{bmatrix} 0 & 1 & 0 & 1 & 0 & 0 & 1 & 1 \\ 1 & 1 & 0 & 0 & 1 & 0 & 1 & 0 \\ 0 & 0 & 0 & 1 & 0 & 0 & 0 & 1 \\ 0 & 1 & 1 & 0 & 0 & 1 & 1 & 0 \end{bmatrix}$$

FIG. 1.52.   Matrix $[E_a'']$.   FIG. 1.53.   Matrix $[E_c'']$.

Let $F_a(x_1, \ldots, x_5)$ and $F_c(x_1, \ldots, x_5)$ be the Boolean function associated with these Veitch maps. They are respectively called the *antecedent solution* and the *consequent solution*.

1.8.6.2. *Decomposition using an antecedent solution*

Given matrices E and E_a'' we can determine a matrix X_a of the same dimensions such that relation (13) is satisfied.

$$[E] = [E_a''] + [X_a]. \tag{13}$$

Let us examine the properties of this matrix $[X_a]$. Let e_{ij}, e_{ij}'' and x_{ij} be the general terms of these three matrices respectively. They must satisfy Equation (14):

$$e_{ij} = e_{ij}'' + x_{ij}. \tag{14}$$

Now the following inequality exists between $[E]$ and $[E_a'']$:

$$[E_a''] \subset [E].$$

Consequently if e_{ij} is equal to 0 then e_{ij}'' is also 0. On the other hand if e_{ij} is equal to 1 then e_{ij}'' can be equal to either 0 or 1. Thus

$$\begin{aligned} &\text{if } \quad e_{ij} = 0 \quad x_{ij} = 0 \\ &\text{if } \quad e_{ij} = 1 \quad x_{ij} = 1 \quad \text{if } \quad e'' = 0 \\ &\phantom{\text{if } \quad e_{ij} = 1 \quad} x_{ij} = \emptyset^* \quad \text{if } \quad e_{ij}'' = 1. \end{aligned}$$

We then deduce that the matrix solution $[X_a]$ of (13) is not unique. Assume that the Veitch diagram E corresponds to the set of row and column variables X_2 and X_1. We can write

$$F = [X_2] \otimes [E] \otimes [X_1].$$

---

* $\emptyset$ indicates 0 or 1 ('don't care' term).

Taking into account (13) we can write

$$F = [X_2] \otimes ([E_a''] + [X_a]) \otimes [X_2].$$

Referring to Equation (19) of the appendix

$$F = ([X_2] \otimes [E_a''] \otimes [X_1]) + ([X_2] \otimes [X_a] \otimes [X_1]).$$

But E_a'' is the Veitch diagram of a function which is decomposable with respect to the function φ_i to which is associated matrix $[T]$. Let $[E_a'']$ be the matrix of the different columns of $[E_a'']$ taking into account $[T]$. We can write

$$[X_2] \otimes [E_a''] \otimes [X_1] = [X_2] \otimes [E_a'] \otimes [T] \otimes [X_1].$$

But

$$[\varphi] = [T] \otimes [X_1] \quad \text{(according to Equation (10)).}$$

Consequently

$$F = ([X_2] \otimes [E_a'] \otimes [\varphi]) + ([X_2] \otimes [X_a] \otimes [X_1]). \quad (15)$$

Let $G_a(X_2, \varphi)$ and $H_a(X_1, X_2)$ be the Boolean functions associated with Veitch diagram E_a' and X_a. From (15) we deduce:

$$F = G_a(X_2, \varphi) + H_a(X_1, X_2)$$

with the functions φ_i that we choose.

Application

Consider matrices $[T]$ and $[E]$ of Figures 1.49 and 1.51. Figure 1.52 gives matrix $[E_a'']$. Matrix X_a obtained as indicated above is represented by Figure 1.54 and matrix $[E_a']$ which is related to $[E_a'']$ and $[T]$ is given in Figure 1.53.

The reader may verify that the functions G_a and H_a obtained from Veitch maps E_a' and X_a (deduced from Figures 1.54 and 1.55) have the following expressions

$$G_a(X_2, \varphi) = \bar{x}_5 x_4 \bar{\varphi}_2 + \bar{x}_5 \bar{x}_4 \varphi_1 + \bar{x}_4 \varphi_1 \varphi_2$$
$$X_a(X_1, X_2) = x_5 x_4 x_2 \bar{x}_1$$
$$F = G_a + X_a.$$

$$\begin{bmatrix} 0 & 1 & 0 & 1 \\ 1 & 1 & 0 & 0 \\ 0 & 0 & 0 & 1 \\ 0 & 0 & 0 & 0 \end{bmatrix}$$

FIG. 1.54.   Matrix $[E_a']$.

$$\begin{bmatrix} 0 & - & 0 & - & 0 & 0 & - & - \\ - & - & 0 & 0 & - & 0 & - & 0 \\ 0 & 0 & 0 & - & 0 & 0 & 0 & - \\ 0 & 0 & 1 & 0 & 0 & 0 & 1 & 0 \end{bmatrix}$$

FIG. 1.55.   Matrix $[X_a]$.

Functions φ_1 and φ_2 are defined in Figure 1.50.

1.8.6.3. *Decomposition using the consequent solution*

Given matrices $[E]$ and $[E''_a]$ we can determine a matrix $[X_c]$ of the same dimension such that Equation (16) is satisfied.

$$[E] = [E''_c] \cdot [X_c]. \tag{16}$$

In order to examine the properties of matrix $[X_c]$ we let e_{ij}, e''_{ij} and x_{ij} be the general terms of these 3 matrices. They must satisfy Equation (17)

$$e_{ij} = e''_{ij} \cdot x_{ij}. \tag{17}$$

But $[E]$ and $[E''_c]$ are related by the inequality

$$[E] \subset [E''_c].$$

Consequently if e_{ij} is equal to 1, e''_{ij} is also equal to 1. If, on the other hand, e_{ij} is equal to 0, e''_{ij} is equal to either 0 or 1.

Then

$$\begin{array}{ll} \text{if} \quad e_{ij} = 1 & x_{ij} = 1 \\ \text{if} \quad e_{ij} = 0 & \begin{cases} x_{ij} = 0 & \text{if} \quad e''_{ij} = 1 \\ x_{ij} = \emptyset & \text{if} \quad e''_{ij} = 0. \end{cases} \end{array}$$

We deduce that matrix $[X_c]$, solution of (16), is not unique. Assume that Veitch map E corresponds to the sets of row and column variables X_2 and X_1. We can write

$$F = [X_2] \otimes [E] \otimes [X_1].$$

Taking (16) into account we have

$$F = [X_2] \otimes ([E''_c] \cdot [X_c]) \otimes [X_1].$$

And according to §1.8.7 we can write

$$F = ([X_2] \otimes [E''_c] \otimes [X_1]) \cdot ([X_2] \otimes [X_c] \otimes [X_1]).$$

But $[E''_c]$ is the Veitch map of a function decomposable with respect to functions φ (Figure 1.49) to which is associated the matrix $[T]$. Let $[E'_c]$ be the matrix of the different columns of $[E''_c]$ taking into account $[T]$. We can write

$$[X_2] \otimes [E''_c] \otimes [X_1] = [X_2] \otimes [E'_c] \otimes [T] \otimes [X_1],$$

but

$$[\varphi] = [T] \otimes [X_1]$$

according to Equation (10). Consequently

$$F = ([X_2] \otimes [E'_c] \otimes [\varphi]) \cdot ([X_2] \otimes [X_c] \otimes [X_1]). \quad (18)$$

Let $G_c(X_2, \varphi)$ and $H_c(X_1, X_2)$ be the Boolean functions associated with the Veitch map E'_c and X_c. From (18) we deduce

$$F = G_c(X_2, \varphi) \cdot H_c(X_1, X_2)$$

with the functions φ that we choose.

Application

Consider matrices $[T]$ and $[E]$ of Figures 1.49 and 1.51. Figure 1.53 gives matrix $[E''_c]$. Matrix $[X_c]$ obtained as indicated above is represented by Figure 1.57 and matrix E'_c which is related to $[E''_c]$ and $[T]$ is given in Figure 1.56.

The reader may verify that functions G_c and H_c obtained from Veitch maps E'_c and X_c (deduced from Figures 1.56 and 1.57) have the following expressions

$$G_c(X_2, \varphi) = \bar{x}_2 \bar{x}_5 \varphi_1 + x_4 \bar{x}_5 \bar{\varphi}_2 + x_4 \varphi_1 \bar{\varphi}_2 + \bar{x}_4 \varphi_1 \varphi_2 + x_4 x_5 \bar{\varphi}_1 \varphi_2$$
$$X_c(X_1, X_2) = (x_2 + \bar{x}_5)$$
$$F = G_c \cdot X_c$$

where functions φ_1 and φ_2 are defined by Figure 1.50.

$$\begin{bmatrix} 0 & 1 & 0 & 1 \\ 1 & 1 & 0 & 0 \\ 0 & 0 & 0 & 1 \\ 0 & 1 & 1 & 0 \end{bmatrix}$$

FIG. 1.56. Matrix $[E'_c]$.

$$\begin{bmatrix} - & 1 & - & 1 & - & - & 1 & 1 \\ 1 & 1 & - & - & 1 & - & 1 & - \\ - & - & - & 1 & - & - & - & 1 \\ - & 0 & 1 & - & - & 0 & 1 & - \end{bmatrix}$$

FIG. 1.57. Matrix $[X_c]$.

1.8.7. *Theoretical justifications*

Let $A(m, n)$, $B(n, p)$, $C(n, p)$ and $D(p, q)$ be four Boolean matrices. We are going to set up the following relations among them.

$$A \otimes (B + C) \otimes D = (A \otimes B \otimes D) + (A \otimes C \otimes D) \quad (19)$$
$$A \otimes (B \cdot C) \otimes D \subseteq (A \otimes B \otimes D) \cdot (A \otimes C \otimes D). \quad (20)$$

Let us examine the general term x_{ij} of the matrix of the left hand side of Equation (19).

$$x_{ij} = \sum_k \sum_l a_{ik}(b_{kl} + c_{kl}) d_{lj}.$$

Now taking into account the distributivity of the product with respect to the Boolean sum we deduce

$$x_{ij} = \sum_k \sum_l a_{ik} b_{kl} d_{lj} + \sum_k \sum_l a_{ik} c_{kl} d_{lj}.$$

In this form x_{ij} is the general term of the right hand side of Equation (19) which justifies Equation (19). Now consider the right hand side of Equation (20); its general term x_{ij} is given by

$$x_{ij} = \left(\sum_{k'} \sum_{l'} a_{ik'} b_{k'l'} d_{l'j} \right) \left(\sum_{k''} \sum_{l''} a_{ik''} c_{k''l''} d_{l''j} \right).$$

We can write

$$x_{ij} = \sum_{k'} \sum_{l'} a_{ik'} b_{k'l'} c_{l'j} d_{l'j}$$
$$+ \sum_{k'} \sum_{l'} \sum_{(k'' \neq k')} \sum_{\cup (l'' \neq l')} a_{ik'} a_{ik''} b_{k'l'} c_{k''l''} d_{l'j} d_{l''j}.$$

But the term

$$y_{ij} = \sum_k \sum_l a_{ik} (b_{kl} \cdot c_{kl}) d_{lj}$$

is the left hand side of Equation (20).

There is equality only if the second term of x_{ij} is identical to zero as in the case, for example, when the following relations are satisfied

$$a_{ik'} a_{ik''} = 0 \quad \forall i, k' \neq k''$$

or

$$d_{l'j} d_{l''j} = 0 \quad \forall j, l' \neq l''.$$

(We assume $b_{k'l'} c_{k''l''} \neq 0$).

We now apply (19) and (20) to the case of Boolean functions. If $[X_1]$ and $[X_2]$ are the matrices of the combinations of the variables associated with the rows and columns of Veitch map of a Boolean function we can write:

$$F = [X_1] \otimes ([E_1] + [E_2]) \otimes [X_2] = [X_1] \otimes [E_1] \otimes [X_2]$$
$$+ [X_1] \otimes [E_2] \otimes [X_2]$$

if F_1 and F_2 are the Boolean functions associated with Veitch maps E_1 and E_2.

Similarly,

$$F = [X_1] \otimes ([E_1] \cdot [E_2]) \otimes [X_2]$$
$$= ([X_1] \otimes [E_1] \otimes [X_2]) \cdot ([X_1] \otimes [E_2] \otimes [X_2]).$$

The products of the different terms of the matrix combinations X_1 and X_2 of the Boolean variables taken two by two are, in effect, equal to zero.

1.9. CONCLUSIONS

We shall again discuss these simplification and factorization methods of Boolean functions in the chapter dealing with the synthesis of combinational systems. For the moment, we should only like to point out two or three important things.

First of all, these two methods (simplification and decomposition) are not too similar, but even less opposed. It is better to say that they are complementary. In fact, the last step of decomposition is always a simplification step. We, therefore, cannot say that one method is better than another.

As far as simplification methods, which are of particular interest to us, are concerned, we seem to have reached the most advanced point of our discussion in light of present day knowledge. As long as the problem of choosing prime implicants remains to be solved in a systematic way, it is rather illusory to look for new simplification methods. All existing methods in this field (we have only given two, but the reader can find references to others' at the end of this chapter) are equivalent in practice (here we are thinking particularly of the different improvements of the Quine-McCluskey type methods); that is, essentially in the facility and rapidity of programming.

There is, to our knowledge, no existing procedure, which provides a completely systematic way of covering a Boolean function.

Finally, in what concerns decomposition methods (where we seem as yet to be at the infant stage) a very important problem arises: that of the choice of possible decompositions. We have noted this in the decomposition of the first example of the second type problem, where we had a choice of 24 possible solutions. We can, for example, imagine the case of a matrix E_{YX} of a function having 5 different columns. The matrix $E'_{Y;\varphi_1\varphi_2\varphi_3}$ could be chosen with complete freedom ... a very annoying situation to say the least.

Other than the 120 possible permutations of the imposed columns, there would still be a totally indifferent choice of the three arbitrarily remaining columns, since their place and structure are arbitrary.

In order to see if there is a possibility of finding rigorous criteria for decreasing the number of possible choices within the factorization of a function, we must see the birth of an enormous collaboration among mathematicians working in the field of Boolean Algebra, technicians building the circuits, and experts in reliability.

APPENDIXES

1.A.1. TRANSPOSITION OF TWO VARIABLES IN THE DESIGNATION NUMBER OF A FUNCTION

There is a strict analogy between this problem and that of changing the base in the expression of the designation number of a Boolean function $f(x_1, ..., x_n)$. As a matter of fact, the transposition of two variables x_i and x_j comes down to searching $\div f$ with respect to base $(x_1 \cdots x_i \cdots x_j \cdots x_n)$ instead of to base $(x_1 \cdots x_j \cdots x_i \cdots x_n)$.

We can announce the following rule with respect to this subject: we divide the designation number of f into P packages of 2^{j-i} elements (we suppose $i < j$) then into P' packages of 2^{i-1} elements. Within each of the P packages, we number the P' packages from 0 to $2^{j-i}-1$. We finish with the operation schematized in Figure 1.58.

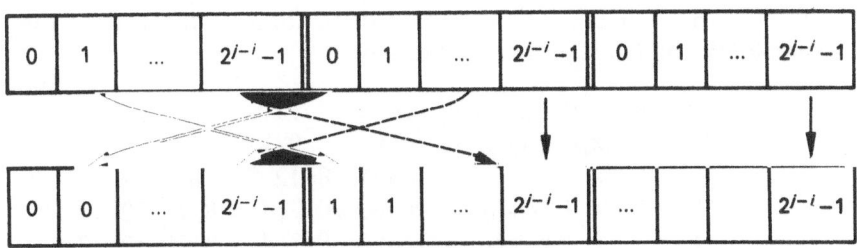

FIG. 1.58.

We give a simple example to illustrate this rule:

$$\div f(x_1, x_2, x_3, x_4) = 1\ 0\ 1\ 1 \quad 1\ 1\ 0\ 1 \quad 1\ 1\ 1\ 0 \quad 1\ 0\ 0\ 0.$$

We transpose x_1 and x_3; $i = 1$, $j = 3$, $2^{j-i} = 4$, $2^{j-i}-1 = 3$, $2^{i-1} = 1$

gives the division:

$$\div f = \begin{array}{|c|c|c|c|} 1 & 0 & 1 & 1 \\ \hline 0 & 1 & 2 & 3 \end{array} \quad \begin{array}{|c|c|c|c|} 1 & 1 & 0 & 1 \\ \hline 0 & 1 & 2 & 3 \end{array} \quad \begin{array}{|c|c|c|c|} 1 & 1 & 1 & 0 \\ \hline 0 & 1 & 2 & 3 \end{array} \quad \begin{array}{|c|c|c|c|} 1 & 0 & 0 & 0 \\ \hline 0 & 1 & 2 & 3 \end{array}.$$

$$\underbrace{}_{a} \qquad \underbrace{}_{b} \qquad \underbrace{}_{c} \qquad \underbrace{}_{d}$$

Hence, if we transpose:

$$\div f(x_3 x_2 x_1 x_4) = \begin{array}{|c|c|c|c|} 1 & 1 & 1 & 0 \\ \hline 0 & 0 & 2 & 2 \end{array} \quad \begin{array}{|c|c|c|c|} 0 & 1 & 1 & 1 \\ \hline 1 & 1 & 3 & 3 \end{array} \quad \begin{array}{|c|c|c|c|} 1 & 1 & 1 & 0 \\ \hline 0 & 0 & 2 & 2 \end{array} \quad \begin{array}{|c|c|c|c|} 1 & 0 & 0 & 0 \\ \hline 1 & 1 & 3 & 3 \end{array}.$$

$$a\,b\,a\,b \qquad a\,b\,a\,b \qquad c\,d\,c\,d \qquad c\,d\,c\,d$$

Other examples:

$$\div f(x_1 x_2 x_4 x_3) = 1\ 0\ 1\ 1 \quad 1\ 1\ 1\ 0 \quad 1\ 1\ 0\ 1 \quad 1\ 0\ 0\ 0$$

$$\div f(x_3 x_2 x_4 x_1) = 1\ 1\ 1\ 0 \quad 1\ 1\ 1\ 0 \quad 0\ 1\ 1\ 1 \quad 1\ 0\ 0\ 0.$$

1.A.2.

Verification of Exercise 1 Section 1.8.4. The given function is:
$f(x_5 x_4 x_3 x_2 x_1) = R(0, 2, 3, 4, 5, 7, 8, 9, 10, 12, 13, 14, 17, 18, 19, 21, 22, 23, 24, 28)$. The result has 10 terms in φ_1, φ_2, x_4, x_5 which we reduce by the Quine-McCluskey method (Case: $\varphi_1 \varphi_2 x_4 x_5$).

$F = A + B + C + D + E$ is the developed form at the end of the example. We find the following coverings:

$$\begin{array}{ll} A = x_1 \bar{x}_3 \bar{x}_4 x_5 + x_2 x_3 \bar{x}_4 x_5 & \text{covers } 17, 19, 21, 23 \\ B = \bar{x}_1 x_3 x_4 \bar{x}_5 + \bar{x}_2 \bar{x}_3 x_4 \bar{x}_5 & \text{covers } 8, 9, 12, 13 \\ C = \bar{x}_1 \bar{x}_2 x_4 & \text{covers } 8, 12, 24, 28 \\ D = \bar{x}_2 \bar{x}_3 \bar{x}_5 + \bar{x}_1 \bar{x}_3 \bar{x}_5 & \text{covers } 0, 2, 4, 5, 8, 10, 12, 13 \\ E = x_1 x_3 \bar{x}_4 + x_2 \bar{x}_3 \bar{x}_4 & \text{covers } 0, 2, 4, 5, 8, 10, 12, 13. \end{array}$$

We verify that all the given terms are covered.

1.A.3. CONSENSUS METHOD

There exists another method for the reduction of Boolean functions called the consensus method [12, 13, 14, and 22]. It was first exposed by Bartee then improved and restated in more detail by Tison. It is based on the 'consensus' operation. If we have two Boolean monomials A_1 and A_2, such that $A_1 = \alpha a_1$ and $A_2 = \bar{\alpha} a_2$, then we call con-

sensus of A_1 and A_2 the product a_1a_2 carried out according to the rules of Boolean algebra. If we let $C = a_1a_2$ then we see that $C \subseteq A_1 + A_2$.
Example.

$$A_1 = a\bar{b}c \quad A_2 = \bar{a}bd$$
$$a_1 = \bar{b}c \quad a_2 = \bar{b}d \quad a_1a_2 = C = \bar{b}cd.$$

To verify that $C \subseteq A_1 + A_2$, we compute the designation numbers corresponding to C and $(A_1 + A_2)$. (a always corresponds to the least weight variable and d to the variable of most weight.)

$$\div (A_1 + A_2) = 0\ 0\ 0\ 0 \quad 0\ 1\ 0\ 0 \quad 1\ 0\ 0\ 0 \quad 1\ 1\ 0\ 0$$
$$\div C = 0\ 0\ 0\ 0 \quad 0\ 0\ 0\ 0 \quad 0\ 0\ 0\ 0 \quad 1\ 1\ 0\ 0$$
$$\div (\bar{C} + A_1 + A_2) = 1\ 1\ 1\ 1 \quad 1\ 1\ 1\ 1 \quad 1\ 1\ 1\ 1 \quad 1\ 1\ 1\ 1.$$

Therefore, $C \subseteq A_1 + A_2$.

The following procedure can be deduced from this property: Let A and B be two terms of a Boolean function F which has been put in the form of a sum of products. The consensus of A and B is C. Nothing in the expression changes if we add C to it because $C \subseteq A + B \subseteq F$. Therefore, $F = F + C$. But, $F + C$ can be reduced because it is possible that C covers terms which already exist in F and consequently, allows us to eliminate them.

We see that it is possible to find the prime implicants of a function f by using iteration to form all possible consensus and by suppressing the redundant terms one by one as we come across them. We finish with a set of prime implicants from which we take the essential implicants by one of the methods discussed in the chapter. We give two examples illustrating the search for prime implicants.

Example 1. $f = (a, b, c, d) = R(1, 2, 3, 4, 5, 6, 8, 10, 12)$ ($d =$ digit of least weight) (Figure 1.59).

The sign / indicates a covering by consensus starting from a. The sign × indicates a covering by consensus starting from b. The sign − indicates a covering by consensus starting from c. The terms which are not marked are the essential terms.

Example 2. $f(a, b, c, d, e, f) = R(0, 1, 12, 13, 37, 39, 45, 47, 49, 51, 53, 55)$ (f is the least weight digit) (Figure 1.60).

The computation of the consensus, starting from a and b, is left to the reader (none and $a\bar{c}df$).

Function

$\bar{a}\,\bar{b}\,\bar{c}\,d$ ×
$\bar{a}\,\bar{b}\,c\,\bar{d}$ /
$\bar{a}\,\bar{b}\,c\,d$ —
$\bar{a}\,b\,\bar{c}\,\bar{d}$ /
$\bar{a}\,b\,\bar{c}\,d$ ×
$\bar{a}\,b\,c\,\bar{d}$ ×
$a\,\bar{b}\,\bar{c}\,d$ ×
$a\,\bar{b}\,c\,\bar{d}$ /
$a\,b\,\bar{c}\,\bar{d}$ /
_____
$b\,\bar{c}\,\bar{d}$
$\bar{b}\,c\,\bar{d}$
_____
$a\quad\bar{c}\,\bar{d}$
$\bar{a}\quad c\,\bar{d}$
$\bar{a}\quad\bar{c}\,d$
_____
$\bar{a}\,b\quad\bar{d}$
$a\,\bar{b}\quad\bar{d}$
$\bar{a}\,\bar{b}\quad d$
_____
$\bar{a}\,\bar{b}\,c$
$\bar{a}\,b\,\bar{c}$

Residues

with respect to $\bar{a}$
$\begin{cases}\bar{b}\,\bar{c}\,d\\ \bar{b}\,c\,\bar{d}\\ \bar{b}\,c\,d\\ b\,\bar{c}\,\bar{d}\\ b\,\bar{c}\,d\\ b\,c\,\bar{d}\end{cases}$

with respect to a
$\begin{cases}\bar{b}\,\bar{c}\,\bar{d}\\ \bar{b}\,c\,\bar{d}\\ b\,\bar{c}\,\bar{d}\end{cases}$

with respect to $\bar{b}$
$\begin{cases}\bar{a}\,\bar{c}\,d\\ \bar{a}\,c\,d\\ a\,\bar{c}\,\bar{d}\\ c\,\bar{d}\end{cases}$

with respect to b
$\begin{cases}\bar{a}\,\bar{c}\,d\\ \bar{a}\,c\,d\\ \bar{c}\,\bar{d}\end{cases}$

with respect to $\bar{c}$
$\begin{cases}b\,\bar{d}\\ a\,\bar{d}\\ \bar{a}\,d\end{cases}$

with respect to c
$\begin{cases}\bar{a}\,\bar{b}\,d\\ \bar{b}\,\bar{d}\\ \bar{a}\,\bar{d}\end{cases}$

with respect to $\bar{d}$
$\begin{cases}b\,\bar{c}\\ \bar{b}\,c\\ a\,\bar{c}\\ \bar{a}\,c\\ a\,\bar{b}\\ \bar{a}\,b\end{cases}$

with respect to d
$\begin{cases}\bar{a}\,\bar{c}\\ \bar{a}\,\bar{b}\end{cases}$

FIG. 1.59.

Eq.

d^{al}	Function		Residues

Left table — Eq. number, d^{al} index, Function:

Eq.	d^{al}	Function	
0	1	$\bar{a}\,\bar{b}\,\bar{c}\,\bar{d}\,\bar{e}\,\bar{f}$	X
1	2	$\bar{a}\,\bar{b}\,\bar{c}\,\bar{d}\,\bar{e}\,f$	X
12	3	$\bar{a}\,\bar{b}\,c\,d\,\bar{e}\,\bar{f}$	X
13	4	$\bar{a}\,\bar{b}\,c\,d\,\bar{e}\,f$	X
37	5	$a\,\bar{b}\,\bar{c}\,d\,\bar{e}\,\bar{f}$	X
39	6	$a\,\bar{b}\,\bar{c}\,d\,e\,f$	X
45	7	$a\,\bar{b}\,c\,d\,\bar{e}\,f$	X
47	8	$a\,\bar{b}\,c\,d\,e\,f$	X
49	9	$a\,b\,\bar{c}\,\bar{d}\,\bar{e}\,f$	X
51	10	$a\,b\,\bar{c}\,\bar{d}\,e\,f$	X
53	11	$a\,b\,\bar{c}\,d\,\bar{e}\,f$	X
55	12	$a\,b\,\bar{c}\,d\,e\,f$	X

———

$\bar{a}\,\bar{b}\,\bar{c}\,\bar{d}\,\bar{e}$ 1,2
$\bar{a}\,\bar{b}\,c\,d\,\bar{e}$ 3,4

———

$a\,\bar{b}\,\bar{c}\,d\,f$ + 5,6
$a\,\bar{b}\,c\,d\,f$ + 7,8
$a\,b\,\bar{c}\,\bar{d}\,f$ × 9,10
$a\,b\,\bar{c}\,d\,f$ × 11,12

———

$a\,b\,\bar{c}\,f$ 9,10,11,12

———

$a\,\bar{b}\,d\,f$ 5,6,7,8

———

$a\,\bar{c}\,d\,f$ 5,6,7,8,9,10,11,12

———

Residues (middle and right):

$\bar{f}$
$\bar{a}\,\bar{b}\,\bar{c}\,\bar{d}\,\bar{e}$ 1
$\bar{a}\,\bar{b}\,c\,d\,\bar{e}$ 3

f
$\bar{a}\,\bar{b}\,\bar{c}\,\bar{d}\,\bar{e}$ 2
$\bar{a}\,\bar{b}\,c\,d\,\bar{e}$ 4
$a\,\bar{b}\,\bar{c}\,\bar{d}\,\bar{e}$ 5
$a\,\bar{b}\,\bar{c}\,d\,e$ 6
$a\,\bar{b}\,c\,d\,\bar{e}$ 7
$a\,\bar{b}\,c\,d\,e$ 8
$a\,b\,\bar{c}\,\bar{d}\,\bar{e}$ 9
$a\,b\,\bar{c}\,\bar{d}\,e$ 10
$a\,b\,\bar{c}\,d\,\bar{e}$ 11
$a\,b\,\bar{c}\,d\,e$ 12

$\bar{e}$
$a\,\bar{b}\,\bar{c}\,d\,f$ 5
$a\,\bar{b}\,c\,d\,f$ 7
$a\,b\,\bar{c}\,\bar{d}\,f$ 9
$a\,b\,\bar{c}\,d\,f$ 11
$\bar{a}\,\bar{b}\,\bar{c}\,\bar{d}$ 1,2
$\bar{a}\,\bar{b}\,c\,d$ 3,4

e
$a\,\bar{b}\,\bar{c}\,d\,f$ 6
$a\,\bar{b}\,c\,d\,f$ 8
$a\,b\,\bar{c}\,\bar{d}\,f$ 10
$a\,b\,\bar{c}\,d\,f$ 12

$\bar{d}$
$\bar{a}\,\bar{b}\,\bar{c}\,\bar{e}$ 1,2
$a\,b\,\bar{c}\,f$ 9,10

d
$\bar{a}\,\bar{b}\,c\,\bar{e}$ 3,4
$a\,\bar{b}\,\bar{c}\,f$ 5,6
$a\,\bar{b}\,c\,f$ 7,8
$a\,b\,\bar{c}\,f$ 11,12

$\bar{c}$
$\bar{a}\,\bar{b}\,d\,\bar{e}$ 1,2
$a\,\bar{b}\,d\,f$ 5,6
$a\,b\,f$ 9,10,11,12

c
$\bar{a}\,\bar{b}\,d\,\bar{e}$ 3,4
$a\,\bar{b}\,d\,f$ 7,8

Fig. 1.60.

1.A.4. MINIMAL CONJUNCTIVE FORM–MINIMAL DISJUNCTIVE FORM

THEOREM. A minimal conjunctive form of a Boolean function f is obtained by negation of a minimal disjunctive form of its complementary.

In other words, we first determine the complement $\bar{f}$, of f, then search a minimal disjunctive expression for $\bar{f}$. The complement of this form is one of the minimal conjunctive forms of f.

Before proving this theorem, we are going to give another definition of the conjunctive or disjunctive prime implicants of a Boolean function. Let (f_a) be a disjunctive and (f_b) a conjunctive form of a Boolean function of n variables $(x_1, \ldots, x_n)$.

$$f_a = A + B + \cdots + L \quad f_b = A'B' \cdots L'.$$

Let K be a term of f_a and K' a term of f_b.

$$K = x_{a_1}^* \cdots x_{a_p}^*$$

($x_{a_i}^*$ is one of the variables $x_1, \ldots, x_n$, barred or unbarred); $a_1, \ldots, a_p$ can take the values $1, \ldots, n$; $a_i \neq a_j$ $(i \neq j)$,

$$K' = x_{b_1}^* + \cdots + x_{b_q}^*$$

In the same way $b_1, \ldots, b_q$ can take the values $1, \ldots, n$ and verify $b_i \neq b_j$ $(i \neq j)$.

The expression of K shows that $f_a = 1$ if the $x_{a_i}^*$ verify: $x_{a_1}^* = 1, \ldots, x_{a_p}^* = 1$. From the definition of K' we have $f_b = 0$ if $x_{b_1}^* = 0, \ldots, x_{b_q}^* = 0$.

DEFINITION 1. K is a disjunctive prime implicant of f if no term K_1 containing K is at the same time contained in f_a.

DEFINITION 2. K' is a conjunctive prime implicant of f if no term K_2 is simultaneously contained in K' and f.

This means that no subset of relations of the $x_{b_j}^*$ can make $f_b = 0$. In the same way no subset of relations of the $x_{a_i}^*$ can make $f_a = 1$.

Suppose that we have the following minimal disjunctive form of $\bar{f}$:

$$\bar{f} = A_1 + B_1 + \cdots + L_1,$$

$A_1, B_1, ..., L_1$ are the disjunctive prime implicants of $\bar{f}$. Let K_1 be one of them,

$$K_1 = x_{a_1}^*, x_{a_2}^*, ..., x_{a_p}^*.$$

The relations $x_{a_1}^* = 1, ..., x_{a_p}^* = 1$ imply $\bar{f} = 1$. Therefore, we shall have $f = 0$.

We may write:

$$f = \bar{A}_1 \cdots \bar{L}_1; \quad \bar{K}_1 = \bar{x}_{a_1}^* + \cdots + \bar{x}_{a_p}^*.$$

From the definition we see that the $x_{a_i}^*$ are the least number of variables which, if they are all 0, can make $f = 0$; all these terms are conjunctive prime implicants of f.

Furthermore, if a relation of consensus existed between two elements of f, M_1 and N_1, for example, we could write:

$$M_1 + N_1 = M_1 + N_1 + C_{M_1 N_1}$$

$C_{M_1 N_1}$ = consensus of M_1 and N_1.

The complement of this expression is:

$$\bar{M}_1 \bar{N}_1 = \bar{M}_1 \bar{N}_1 \overline{C_{M_1 N_1}}.$$

There is also an operation of consensus between $\bar{M}_1$ and $\bar{N}_1$. If the prime implicants M_1 and N_1 correspond to a minimal form of $\bar{f}$ no other prime implicant of this form corresponds to a consensus operation between M_1 and N_1. Consequently, the same goes for $\bar{M}_1$, $\bar{N}_1$ and $\bar{f}$. The expression $\bar{A}_1 \cdots \bar{L}_1$ is hence a minimal form.

ab \ cd	00	01	11	10
00	1	1	0	1
01	0	—	0	0
11	0	—	0	1
10	1	1	—	1

FIG. 1.61. Function f.

ab \ cd	00	01	11	10
00	0	0	1	0
01	1	—	1	1
11	1	—	1	0
10	0	0	—	0

FIG. 1.62. Function $\bar{f}$.

Example. Let f be defined by the Karnaugh map in Figure 1.61 and its complement by Figure 1.62. Figure 1.62 permits us to write the minimal form of $\bar{f}$:

$$\bar{f} = ab + \bar{a}d + \bar{c}d.$$

We deduce the minimal conjunctive form of the initial function:

$$f = (\bar{a} + \bar{b})(a + \bar{d})(c + \bar{d}).$$

1.A.5. QUINE-MCCLUSKEY ALGORITHM–GENERALIZATIONS

We introduced the Quine-McCluskey minimization method for Boolean functions expressed in their normal disjunctive form. The function was initially expressed as a sum of minterms, each minterm being the Boolean product of binary variables. We shall now apply the Quine-McCluskey method to functions expressed by relations of other operators.

1.A.5.1. *Lagrange's function*

Given a set of integers M $(0, 1, ..., m-1)$, a, an element of M, x, a variable which can take values in M, we call a function $L_a(x)$ defined on M, taking its values in $(0, 1)$ according to the relations (A.1), Lagrange's function.

$$
\begin{aligned}
L_a(x) &= 0 \quad \text{if} \quad x \neq a \\
L_a(x) &= 1 \quad \text{if} \quad x = a.
\end{aligned}
\qquad (A.1)
$$

In the particular case of Boolean algebra where M consists of the two integers 0 and 1, Lagrange's functions are:

$$
\begin{aligned}
L_0(x) &= \bar{x} \quad (\text{function} = 1 \text{ if } x = 0) \\
L_1(x) &= x \quad (\text{function} = 1 \text{ if } x = 1).
\end{aligned}
\qquad (A.2)
$$

1.A.5.2. *Canonical forms of a Boolean function of n variables**

a. *Normal disjunctive form*

Given a Boolean function of n Boolean variables $x_1, ..., x_n$ (the variables x_i can take only the values 0 or 1), the normal (or canonical)

---

* The terms 'canonical form' and 'normal form' are used indiscriminately.

disjunctive form can be written according to the relation (A.2):

$$f(x_1, \ldots, x_n) = \bigcup_{a_i = 0 \text{ or } 1} f(a_1, \ldots, a_n) L_{a_1}(x_1) \cdots L_{a_n}(x_n)$$

$$1 \leqslant i \leqslant n. \qquad (A.3)$$

In fact, if we have the conditions

$$x_1 = a_1, \ldots, \quad x_n = a_n$$

the first term of (A.3) becomes $f(a_1, \ldots, a_n)$.

All the minterms of the second member are zero since they all differ by at least one of the $L_{a_i}(x_i)$ except the term:

$$f(a_1, \ldots, a_n) L_{a_1}(a_1) \cdots L_{a_n}(a_n)$$

which takes the value $f(a_1, \ldots, a_n)$.

Consider, for example, the following function f:

$$f = x_1 \bar{x}_2 x_3 + x_1 x_2 \bar{x}_3 + \bar{x}_1 \bar{x}_2 x_3 + x_1 x_2 x_3.$$

We can write:

$$\begin{aligned} f = & f(0\ 0\ 0) \bar{x}_1 \bar{x}_2 \bar{x}_3 + f(0\ 0\ 1) \bar{x}_1 \bar{x}_2 x_3 + f(0\ 1\ 1) \bar{x}_1 x_2 x_3 \\ & + f(0\ 1\ 0) \bar{x}_1 x_2 \bar{x}_3 + f(1\ 1\ 0) x_1 x_2 \bar{x}_3 + f(1\ 1\ 1) x_1 x_2 x_3 \\ & + f(1\ 0\ 0) x_1 \bar{x}_2 \bar{x}_3 + f(1\ 0\ 1) x_1 \bar{x}_2 x_3. \end{aligned}$$

In fact,

$$\begin{aligned} f(0\ 0\ 0) &= f(1\ 0\ 0) = f(0\ 1\ 0) = f(0\ 1\ 1) = 0 \\ f(1\ 0\ 1) &= f(1\ 1\ 0) = f(0\ 0\ 1) = f(1\ 1\ 1) = 1. \end{aligned}$$

With the notation:

$$L_0(x_i) = \bar{x}_i$$

$$L_1(x_i) = x_i.$$

We can write:

$$\begin{aligned} f = & f(0\ 0\ 0) L_0(x_1) L_0(x_2) L_0(x_3) \\ & + f(0\ 0\ 1) L_0(x_1) L_0(x_2) L_1(x_3) + f(0\ 1\ 1) L_0(x_1) L_1(x_2) L_1(x_3) \\ & + f(0\ 1\ 0) L_0(x_1) L_1(x_2) L_0(x_3) + f(1\ 1\ 0) L_1(x_1) L_1(x_2) L_0(x_3) \\ & + f(1\ 1\ 1) L_1(x_1) L_1(x_2) L_1(x_3) + f(1\ 0\ 1) L_1(x_1) L_0(x_2) L_1(x_3) \\ & + f(1\ 0\ 0) L_1(x_1) L_0(x_2) L_0(x_3), \end{aligned}$$

which corresponds to relation (A.3).

b. *Other normal forms*

The normal conjunctive form (product of maxterms) is written:

$$f(x_1, \ldots, x_n) \prod_{a_i = 0 \ r1} [f(\bar{a}_1, \ldots, \bar{a}_n)$$

$$+ L_{a_1}(x_1) + \cdots + L_{a_n}(x_n)]. \qquad (A.4)$$

We see that if we let

$$x_1 = \bar{a}_1, \ldots, x_n = \bar{a}_n$$

the first member is written $f(\bar{a}_1, \ldots, \bar{a}_n)$. All the factors of the second member are equal to 1 except the factor

$$f(\bar{a}_1, \ldots, \bar{a}_n) + L_{a_1}(\bar{a}_1) + \cdots + L_{a_n}(\bar{a}_n)$$

which takes the value $f(\bar{a}_1, \ldots, \bar{a}_n)$.

Note that we could express Equations (A.3) and (A.4) in a different way by using operators $\otimes$ (or Σ), $+$ (or $\cup$), $\cdot$ (or Π), $\downarrow$, $/$. These relations are the following:

$$f(x_1, \ldots, x_n) = \sum_{a_i = 0 \ or \ 1} \ '[f(a_1, \ldots, a_n) L_{a_1}(x_1) \cdots L_{an}(x_n)]$$

$$(A.5)$$

$$f(x_1, \ldots, x_n) = \bigcup_{a_i = 0 \ or \ 1} [\bar{f}(\bar{a}_1, \ldots, \bar{a}_n) \downarrow L_{a_1}(x_1) \downarrow \cdots \downarrow L_{a_n}(x_n)]$$

$$(A.6)$$

$$f(x_1, \ldots, x_n) = \prod_{a_i = 0 \ or \ 1} [\bar{f}(\bar{a}_1, \ldots, \bar{a}_n) \ / \ L_{a_1}(x_1) \ / \cdots \ / \ L_{an}(x_n)]$$

$$(A.7)$$

$$f(x_1, \ldots, x_n) = \mathop{/}_{a_i = 0 \ or \ 1} [\bar{f}(\bar{a}_1, \ldots, \bar{a}_n) + L_{a_1}(x_1) + \cdots + L_{a_n}(x_n)]$$

$$(A.8)$$

$$f(x_1, \ldots, x_n) = \mathop{\downarrow}_{a_i = 0 \ or \ 1} [\bar{f}(\bar{a}_1, \ldots, a_n) \cdot L_{a_1}(x_1) \cdot \cdots \cdot L_{a_n}(x_n)]$$

$$(A.9)$$

$$f(x_1, \ldots, x_n) = \mathop{/}_{a_i = 0 \ or \ 1} [f(a_1, \ldots, a_n) \ / \ L_{a_1}(x_1) \ / \cdots \ / \ L_{a_n}(x_n)]$$

$$(A.10)$$

$$f(x_1, \ldots, x_n) = \mathop{\downarrow}_{a_i = 0 \ or \ 1} [f(\bar{a}_1, \ldots, \bar{a}_n) \downarrow L_{a_1}(x_1) \downarrow \cdots \downarrow L_{a_n}(x_n)]$$

$$(A.11)$$

Since the normal conjunctive and disjunctive forms are unique, the other forms are also unique.

We shall now prove relation (A.8). If we let $x_1 = a_1, ..., x_n = a_n$ in both members of Equation (A.8), then the first member of the equation takes the value $f(a_1, ..., a_n)$. All the terms of the second member equal 1 except for:

$$\bar{f}(a_1, ..., a_n) + L_{\bar{a}_1}(a_1) + \cdots + L_{\bar{a}_n}(a_n),$$

which takes the value $\bar{f}(a_1, ..., a_n)$. The relation (A.8) is therefore verified.

1.A.5.3. General expression for the normal form of a Boolean function

The relations (A.2 – A.11) show that every normal form of a Boolean function can be written in the following way:

$$f(x_1, ..., x_n) = \mathop{\mathsf{T}}_{a_i = 0 \text{ or } 1} [f^*(a_1^*, ..., a_n^*)$$
$$\omega L_{a_1}(x_1) \omega \cdots \omega L_{a_n}(x_n) \quad \text{(A.12)}$$

or

$$f(x_1, ..., x_n) = (x_{11}^* \omega x_{12}^* \omega \cdots \omega x_{1n}^*) \mathsf{T} \cdots \mathsf{T} (x_{m_1}^* \omega \cdots \omega x_{m_n}^*)$$
$$\text{(A.13)}$$

The symbol * represents the variables a_i or their complements:

$$f^* = f \quad \text{or} \quad \bar{f}; \qquad x_i^* = x_i \quad \text{or} \quad \bar{x}_i.$$

The symbol x_{ij}^* represents x_j or $\bar{x}_j$ in the i-term of the development of the function. Consider, for example, the following function represented in its (A.13) form:

$$f = abc + \bar{a}bc + ab\bar{c} + \bar{a}b\bar{c}$$

with the equivalence $\mathsf{T} = +, \omega = \cdot$.
It is written in its (A.12) form

$$f = f(0\ 0\ 0)\bar{a}\bar{b}\bar{c} + f(0\ 0\ 1)\bar{a}\bar{b}c + f(0\ 1\ 1)\bar{a}bc +$$
$$+ f(1\ 0\ 0)a\bar{b}\bar{c} + f(1\ 0\ 1)a\bar{b}c + f(1\ 1\ 0)ab\bar{c}$$
$$+ f(1\ 1\ 1)abc$$

with the conditions:

$$f(0\ 0\ 0) = f(0\ 1\ 1) = f(1\ 1\ 0) = f(1\ 1\ 1) = 1$$
$$f(0\ 0\ 1) = f(0\ 1\ 0) = f(1\ 0\ 0) = f(1\ 0\ 1) = 0.$$

Note that only combinations of the table in Figure 1.63 are possible.

The reader can verify, as an exercise, that the other combinations of the operators $\cup, \Pi, \downarrow, /$, do not give a normal form.

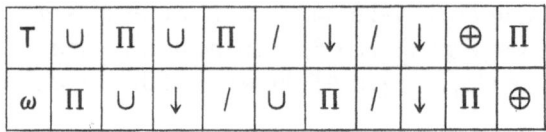

T	∪	Π	∪	Π	/	↓	/	↓	⊕	Π
ω	Π	∪	↓	/	∪	Π	/	↓	Π	⊕

FIG. 1.63.

1.A.5.4. *Quine-McCluskey minimization algorithm*

We shall study some properties of the operators T and ω in order to apply the Quine-McCluskey minimization algorithm to normal forms of a Boolean function. We shall show that the minimization operations are established in the same way for all normal forms and lead to a 2 level minimal system. We shall then derive a practical method of minimization.

a. *Level of a system*

DEFINITION 1. A system will be called two-leveled if its functioning is represented by a Boolean equation analogous to Equation (A.14):

$$f = A_1 \, \mathsf{T} \cdots \mathsf{T} \, A_n, \tag{A.14}$$

where the terms A_i are of the form:

$$A_i = a_{i1} \, \omega \cdots \omega \, a_{ip}, \tag{A.15}$$

a_{ij} is a Boolean variable.

The function $f = (a+b)(\bar{a}+\bar{c})(\bar{b}+d)$ is a two-leveled function.

DEFINITION 2.   A system will be called three-leveled if its functioning is represented by an equation of the form:

$$f = A_1 \mathsf{T} \cdots \mathsf{T} A_n, \tag{A.16}$$

where at least one of the A_i terms is defined in the following way:

$$A_i = a_{i1}\omega \cdots \omega a_{ik}\omega (a_{ik+1} \mathsf{T} \cdots \mathsf{T} a_{ik+q})\omega \cdots \omega a_{ip}, \tag{A.17}$$

a_{ij} is a Boolean variable.

The function $f = a(b+\bar{c}) + bc$ is a three-leveled function; the corresponding two-leveled system is $f = ab + a\bar{c} + bc$.

These two definitions could be generalized to p-leveled systems.

b. *Commutativity of the T and ω functions*

Consider the functions $+, \cdot, \oplus, \downarrow, /$. They are all commutative.

$$a + b = b + a \qquad a \downarrow b = b \downarrow a$$

$$ab = ba$$
$$a \oplus b = b \oplus a \qquad a \mid b = b \mid a.$$

a and b can be Boolean variables or Boolean functions. In general, if ϵ is a certain permutation of the indices $1, \ldots, n$, then the relations (A.18) hold:

$$a_{\epsilon(1)} \omega \cdots \omega a_{\epsilon(n)} = a_1 \omega \cdots \omega a_n$$
$$a_{\epsilon(1)} \mathsf{T} \cdots \mathsf{T} a_{\epsilon(n)} = a_1 \mathsf{T} \cdots \mathsf{T} a_n. \tag{A.18}$$

c. *Idempotence law*

We shall use the idempotence law in the following form:

$$a_1 + a_1 + a_2 + a_3 + \cdots + a_n = a_1 + a_2 + \cdots + a_n$$
$$a_1 \cdot a_1 \cdot a_2 \cdot a_3 \cdot \cdots \cdot a_n = a_1 \cdot a_2 \cdot \cdots \cdot a_n.$$

Case of the normal disjunctive form. If we consider the normal disjunctive form of a Boolean function of n variables, then application of the idempotence law results in the following relation:

$$a_1 a_1 a_2 a_3 \cdots a_n + b_1 + \cdots + b_m = a_1 a_2 \cdots a_n + b_1 + \cdots + b_m.$$

Case of some general normal form. The relation of idempotence holds for all the operators $\cdot, +, \downarrow, /$ except $\oplus$. We can write:

$$A_1 \mathsf{T} A_1 \mathsf{T} A_2 \mathsf{T} \cdots \mathsf{T} A_p = A_1 \mathsf{T} A_2 \mathsf{T} \cdots \mathsf{T} A_p$$
$$a_1 \omega a_1 \omega a_2 \omega \cdots \omega a_n = a_1 \omega a_2 \omega \cdots \omega a_n,$$

where a_{ij} are Boolean variables, the A_i and B_i Boolean functions. In the case of the normal form, $\mathsf{T}\omega = \downarrow\downarrow$, we can write:

$$A_1 \downarrow A_1 \downarrow A_2 \downarrow \cdots \downarrow A_p = A_1 \downarrow A_2 \downarrow \cdots \downarrow A_p$$

In the same way:

$$(a_1 \downarrow a_1 \downarrow a_2 \downarrow \cdots \downarrow a_n) \downarrow B_1 \downarrow \cdots \downarrow B_q$$
$$= (a_1 + a_1 + \cdots + a_n)\bar{B}_1 \cdot \cdots \cdot \bar{B}_q$$
$$= (a_1 + a_2 + \cdots + a_n)\bar{B}_1 \cdot \cdots \cdot \bar{B}_q$$
$$= (a_1 \downarrow a_2 \downarrow \cdots \downarrow a_n) \downarrow B_1 \downarrow \cdots \downarrow B_q.$$

The idempotence law cannot be applied to the normal form $\mathsf{T}\omega = \oplus$

$$A_1 \oplus A_1 \oplus A_2 \oplus \cdots \oplus A_q = A_2 \oplus \cdots \oplus A_q.$$

d. *Absorption law*

The absorption law can be expressed, for example, by the following relations:

$$a + ab = a \quad a(a+b) = a.$$

Case of the normal disjunctive form. If we consider the normal disjunctive form of a Boolean function of n variables, then application of the absorption law results in the following relation:

$$a_1 a_2 \cdots a_n + a_1 a_2 \cdots a_n b_1 \cdots b_m + C_1 + \cdots + C_p =$$
$$a_1 \cdots a_n + C_1 + \cdots + C_p.$$

Case of some general normal forms. For all operators $+$, $\cdot$, $\downarrow$, $/$, except for $\oplus$, the absorption law is written:

$$(a_1 \omega \cdots \omega a_n) \mathsf{T} (a_1 \omega \cdots \omega a_n \omega b_1 \omega \cdots \omega b_m) \mathsf{T} C_1 \mathsf{T} \cdots \mathsf{T} C_p$$
$$= (a_1 \omega \cdots \omega a_n) \mathsf{T} C_1 \mathsf{T} \cdots \mathsf{T} C_p,$$

a_i and b_j are Boolean variables and C_k Boolean monomials. From the point of view of set theory, we can say that $(a_1 \omega \cdots \omega a_n \omega b_1 \omega \cdots \omega b_m)$ is included in $(a_1 \omega \cdots \omega a_n)$.

In the case of the normal form $\mathsf{T}\omega = \downarrow\downarrow$, we may write

$$(a_1 \downarrow a_2 \downarrow \cdots \downarrow a_n) \downarrow (a_1 \downarrow a_2 \downarrow \cdots \downarrow a_n \downarrow b_1 \downarrow \cdots \downarrow b_m) \downarrow$$
$$C_1 \downarrow \cdots \downarrow C_p$$
$$= (a_1 + \cdots + a_n)(a_1 + \cdots + a_n + b_1 + \cdots + b_m)\bar{C}_1 \cdots \cdot \bar{C}_p$$
$$= (a_1 + \cdots + a_n)\bar{C}_1 \cdots \cdot \bar{C}_p = (a_1 \downarrow \cdots \downarrow a_n) \downarrow C_1 \downarrow \cdots \downarrow C_p.$$

In the case of $\mathsf{T}\omega = \oplus \cdot$ we may write

$$A_1 \oplus A_1 B_1 \oplus C_1 \oplus \cdots \oplus C_p = A_1 \bar{B}_1 \oplus C_1 \oplus \cdots \oplus C_p.$$

e. *Simplification rule*

The simplification rule for a Boolean variable is given by the relation:

$$a + \bar{a} = 1 \quad \text{or} \quad a\bar{a} = 0,$$

where a is a Boolean variable.

Case of the normal disjunctive form. If we consider the normal disjunctive form of a Boolean function of n variables, then the simplification rule gives:

$$f = a_1 a_2 \cdots a_n + \bar{a}_1 a_2 \cdots a_n + B_1 + \cdots + B_p$$
$$= (a_2 \cdots a_n) + B_1 + \cdots + B_p.$$

By the commutativity law we have:

$$f = [a_i \cdots a_{i-1}(a_i + \bar{a}_i)a_{i+1} \cdots a_n] + B_1 + \cdots + B_p$$
$$= a_1 \cdots a_{i-1}a_{i+1} \cdots a_n + B_1 + \cdots + B_p.$$

Case of some general normal form. Consider the expression:

$$f = (a_1 \omega \cdots \omega a_{i-1} \omega a_i \omega a_{i+1} \omega \cdots \omega a_n)$$
$$\mathsf{T} \, (a_1 \omega \cdots \omega a_{i-1} \omega \bar{a}_i \omega a_{i+1} \omega \cdots \omega a_n) \, \mathsf{T} \, B_1 \, \mathsf{T} \cdots \mathsf{T} \, B_p,$$

where the a_i are Boolean variables and the B_j Boolean monomials. Consider the operators $+, \cdot, /, \downarrow$. The function we are studying is written (commutativity law):

$$f = (a_i \omega a_1 \omega \cdots \omega a_n) \, \mathsf{T} \, (\bar{a}_i \omega a_1 \omega \cdots \omega a_n) \, \mathsf{T} \, B_1 \, \mathsf{T} \cdots \mathsf{T} \, B_p.$$

The simplification rule is expressed by the relation:

$$f = (a_1 \omega \cdots \omega a_{i-1} \omega a_{i+1} \omega \cdots \omega a_n) \, \mathsf{T} \, B_1 \, \mathsf{T} \cdots \mathsf{T} \, B_p.$$

In the case of the form $\mathsf{T} \, \omega = \downarrow \downarrow$, we can write:

$$(a_1 \downarrow a_2 \downarrow \cdots \downarrow a_n) \downarrow (\bar{a}_1 \downarrow a_2 \downarrow \cdots \downarrow a_n) \downarrow B_1 \downarrow \cdots \downarrow B_p$$
$$= (a_2 \downarrow \cdots \downarrow a_n) \downarrow B_1 \downarrow \cdots \downarrow B_p.$$

1.A.5.5. *Application of the Quine-McCluskey method*

Consider a Boolean function of n variables represented by a given normal form. Each term is in the form

$$A = x_1^* \, \omega \cdots \omega \, x_n^*,$$

where x_i^* represents x_i or $\bar{x}_i$ and is called the simple term of the function. A general normal form of the Boolean function is written:

$$f = A_1 \, \mathsf{T} \, A_2 \, \mathsf{T} \cdots \mathsf{T} \, A_p.$$

In order to simplify this expression, we seek all pairs of adjacent terms $A_i A_j$; that is, the pairs of simple terms A_i and A_j which differ by *one and only one* of the $x_1, \ldots, x_n$ variables. Application of the idempotence, commutativity, and simplification laws give a certain number of terms having only $(n-1)$ variables:

$$B_1, B_2, \ldots, B_q.$$

Suppose that $A_j \subset B_i$ (from a set theory point of view). The Boolean function is written:

$$f = A_1 \, \mathsf{T} \, A_2 \, \mathsf{T} \cdots \mathsf{T} \, A_n \, \mathsf{T} \, B_1 \, \mathsf{T} \cdots \mathsf{T} \, B_q.$$

By the law of absorption:

$$f = A_{11} \, \mathsf{T} \, A_{12} \, \mathsf{T} \cdots \mathsf{T} \, A_{1k} \, \mathsf{T} \, B_1 \, \mathsf{T} \cdots \mathsf{T} \, B_q.$$

None of the A_{1i} terms of this expression are included in a B_j term. Neither the laws of idempotence, absorption nor the simplification rule can be applied to the A_{1i} terms.

Consider, for example, the following function written in its normal disjunctive form:

$$f = ab\bar{c}d + \bar{a}bcd + abcd + abc\bar{d} + \bar{a}\bar{b}\bar{c}d + ab\bar{c}\bar{d}.$$

We can write:

$$f = ab\bar{c}d + (ab\bar{c}d + abcd) + \bar{a}bcd + (\bar{a}bcd + abcd)$$
$$+ abcd + (abc\bar{d} + abcd) + abcd + \bar{a}\bar{b}\bar{c}d + ab\bar{c}\bar{d}$$

$$f = ab\bar{c}d + \bar{a}bcd + abcd + abc\bar{d} + abd + abc + bcd$$
$$+ \bar{a}\bar{b}\bar{c}d + ab\bar{c}\bar{d}.$$

By the absorption law, we have:

$$f = \underbrace{abd + abc + bcd}_{\text{3 variables}} + \underbrace{\bar{a}\bar{b}\bar{c}d + ab\bar{c}\bar{d}}_{\text{4 variables}}.$$

Among the B_j terms, we seek all pairs of adjacent terms. By application of the laws of absorption, idempotence, commutativity and the simplification rule, we obtain:

$$f = \underbrace{A_{11} \top \cdots \top A_{1k_1}}_{n \text{ variables}} \underbrace{A_{21} \top \cdots \top A_{2k_2}}_{n\text{-1 variables}} \underbrace{C_1 \top \cdots \top C_{q_2} \top \cdots}_{n\text{-2 variables}}.$$

After a finite number (k) of repetitions of the same operations, we could no longer apply the simplification rule.

The A_{ij} obtained in this way are called the *prime implicants* of the Boolean function f. The expression for f is therefore:

$$f = A_{11} \top \cdots \top A_{1k_1} A_{21} \top \cdots \top A_{2k_2} \top \cdots \top A_{l_1} \top \cdots \top A_{lk_l}.$$

Any of the A_{ij} terms has $(n - i)$ letters. The set of the A_{ij} terms is the set of prime implicants of f.

The Quine-McCluskey method can only be applied to normal forms and then only if the operator 'sum modulo 2' is not used, since the idempotence law does not hold for this operator.

1.A.5.6. *Choice of prime implicants*

We obtained an expression for f by application of the absorption law and the simplification rule to all possible adjacent pairs of Boolean monomials. We now propose to solve the following problem: can f be represented with the least possible number of prime implicants by partial application of the simplification rule?

Let p_{ij} $(0 < j < k; 0 < i < n)$ be the set of prime implicants of the function f.

The canonical form can be written:

$$f = A_1 \, \mathsf{T} \cdots \mathsf{T} \, A_q$$

then, if $p_{i1}, \ldots, p_{ik_i}$ is the set of prime implicants containing A_i and if we consider the expression:

$$g = A_1 \, \mathsf{T} \, A_2 \, \mathsf{T} \cdots \mathsf{T} \, A_q \, \mathsf{T} \, p_{11} \cdots \mathsf{T} \, p_{qk_q} \tag{A.19}$$

we have the following: The implicants p_i are obtained from the A_i by successive applications of the simplification rule, the laws of idempotence, commutativity and absorption. Since these operations do not modify the value of f, we conclude that $f = g$ and furthermore by absorption we have:

$$f = g = p_{11} \, \mathsf{T} \cdots \mathsf{T} \, p_{qk_q}. \tag{A.20}$$

Reciprocally, the normal form being unique, we obtain (A.19) from (A.20).

In fact, a Boolean monomial $a_1^* \, \omega \cdots \omega \, a_k^*$ can be written

$$a_1^* \, \omega \cdots \omega \, \alpha_k^* \, \omega \, (a_{k+1}^* \, \mathsf{T}' \, \overline{a_{k+1}^*}) \, \omega \cdots \omega \, (a_n^* \, \mathsf{T}' \, \overline{a_n^*})$$
$$\mathsf{T}' \text{ signifies } \mathsf{T} \text{ or } \tilde{\mathsf{T}}$$

in the expression of the function.

Furthermore, an expression

$$f = [a_1^* \, \omega \cdots \omega a_{n-1}^* \, \omega \, (a_n^* \, \mathsf{T}' \, \overline{a_n^*})] \, \mathsf{T} \, B_1 \, \mathsf{T} \cdots \mathsf{T} \, B_p$$

can be written

$$f = (a_1^* \, \omega \cdots \omega \, a_n^*) \, \mathsf{T} \, (a_1^* \, \omega \cdots \omega \, a_{n-1}^* \, \omega \, \overline{a_n^*}) \, \mathsf{T} \, B_1 \, \mathsf{T} \cdots \mathsf{T} \, B_p.$$

We deduce the following theorem:

THEOREM. Every Boolean function can be represented by a set of prime implicants if all these implicants contain all the Boolean monomials of the initial function.

In practice, the set of all groupings $p_{11}, \ldots, p_{nk_n}$ is obtained as solution of the Boolean equation:

$$(p_{11} + p_{12} + \cdots) \cdots (p_{n1} + p_{n2} + \cdots) = 1.$$

The prime implicant chart process of the Quine-McCluskey method is therefore justified.

1.A.5.7. *Practical application of the Quine-McCluskey method*

If we consider the eight normal forms of a Boolean function expressed in terms of the operators, Π (or $\cdot$), $\cup$ (or $+$), $\downarrow$, $/$ we can divide them into two classes. We designate the first class by the symbol $(+ \cdot)$ and the second by $(\cdot +)$. With respect to this, let us consider the function:

$$f = (a+b+\bar{c})(\bar{a}+b+c)(\bar{a}+\bar{b}+\bar{c}) \tag{A.21}$$

We can write it in the seven following ways (the verification is left to the reader):

$$f = (a \downarrow b \downarrow \bar{c}) \downarrow (\bar{a} \downarrow b \downarrow c) \downarrow (\bar{a} \downarrow \bar{b} \downarrow \bar{c}) \tag{A.22}$$

$$= (\bar{a}bc) \downarrow (a\bar{b}\bar{c}) \downarrow (abc) \tag{A.23}$$

$$= (\bar{a}/\bar{b}/c)(a/\bar{b}/\bar{c})(a/b/c) \tag{A.24}$$

$$f = (\bar{a}b\bar{c}) + (\bar{a}bc) + (ab\bar{c}) + (\bar{a}\bar{b}\bar{c}) + (a\bar{b}c) \tag{A.25}$$

$$= (\bar{a}/b/\bar{c})/(\bar{a}/b/c)/(a/b/\bar{c})/(\bar{a}/\bar{b}/\bar{c})/(a/\bar{b}/c) \tag{A.26}$$

$$= (a+\bar{b}+c)/(a+\bar{b}+\bar{c})/(\bar{a}+\bar{b}+c)/(a+b+c)/ \\ (\bar{a}+b+\bar{c}) \tag{A.27}$$

$$= (a \downarrow \bar{b} \downarrow c) + (a \downarrow \bar{b} \downarrow \bar{c}) + (\bar{a} \downarrow \bar{b} \downarrow c) + (a \downarrow b \downarrow c) + \\ + (\bar{a} \downarrow b \downarrow \bar{c}). \tag{A.28}$$

If we compare relations (A.22), (A.23) and (A.24) with relations (A.21), we notice that each of the Boolean monomials of the first three relations is in one-to-one correspondence with each of the monomials in Equation (A.21). The correspondence is either

$$a^* + b^* + c^* \rightarrow a^* \, \omega \, b^* \, \omega \, c^*$$

or

$$a^* + b^* + c^* \rightarrow \bar{a}^* \, \omega \, \bar{b}^* \, \omega \, \bar{c}^*.$$

a^* signifies a or $\bar{a}$, $\bar{a}^*$ is the complement of a^*.

In the same way we notice that each of the Boolean monomials in equations (A.26), (A.27), and (A.28) is in one-to-one correspondence with each of the monomials of Equation (A.25), the correspondence being the same as the preceeding.

The verification of a one-to-one correspondence between relations (A.4), (A.7), (A.9), (A.11) and relations (A.3), (A.6), (A.8), (A.10), is left to the reader.

The first class $(+, \cdot)$, consists of the normal forms (A.3, A.6, A.8, A.10) and the second class $(\cdot, +)$ of the normal forms (A.4, A.7, A.9, A.11). The term by term correspondence is of the form:

$$a^* + b^* + c^* \rightarrow a^* \,\omega\, b^* \,\omega\, c^* \quad \text{or} \quad \bar{a}^* \,\omega\, \bar{b}^* \,\omega\, \bar{c}^*$$
$$a^* \cdot b^* \cdot c^* \rightarrow a^* \,\omega'\, b^* \,\omega'\, c^* \quad \text{or} \quad \bar{a}^* \,\omega'\, \bar{b}^* \,\omega'\, \bar{c}^*.$$

Two adjacent terms remain adjacent for every other form in the class. The symbol ω represents the operators $\cdot, \downarrow, /$, and the symbol ω' the operators $+, \downarrow\cdot, /$. The minimization operations are the same for every normal form in the same class (simplification rule, commutativity, idempotence, and absorption). The one-to-one correspondence between the forms is kept for each operation. There is therefore a one-to-one correspondence between the prime implicants of the forms in a class and the reduced forms of normal forms of the same class.

Conclusion. This means that when we have a Boolean function expressed in some general form, we must first perform the minimization in the $(+ \cdot)$ or $(\cdot +)$ form, depending on which class the form belongs to, in order to perform a two-leveled minimization of the function. Once the reduced form is obtained, it is sufficient to express it in terms of the initial $\mathsf{T}\omega$ operators.

Comments. There is reason to notice that the Karnaugh reduction is established by the same principles as the Quine-McCluskey method. As a matter of fact, we implicitly apply the simplification rule, commutativity, absorption, and idempotence laws to the tables to find the prime implicants. It could therefore be interesting, especially in the case of incomplete tables, to use the McCluskey covering method to find the minimal form. We note, consequently, that the results obtained for the Quine-McCluskey method are also valid for the Karnaugh map method. This was seen in the examples of Chapter 1.

Example 1. Using the Quine-McCluskey method, reduce the the function:

$$f = (\bar{x} / \bar{y} / \bar{z}) / (\bar{y} / z)/(y / z).$$

This is a first class function, and we can write:

$$f = \bar{x}\bar{y}\bar{z} + \bar{y}z + yz.$$

Reducing this function in its preceeding form, we obtain:

$$f = z + \bar{x}\bar{y}\bar{z} = z + \bar{x}\bar{y}$$

from which we get the 2-leveled minimal form of the initial function:

$$f = \bar{z} \mid (\bar{x} \mid \bar{y})$$

Example 2. Using the Quine-McCluskey method, reduce the function:

$$f = (x \downarrow z \downarrow t) \downarrow (x \downarrow z \downarrow \bar{t}) \downarrow (\bar{x} \downarrow z \downarrow \bar{t}) \downarrow (\bar{x} \downarrow \bar{z} \downarrow \bar{t})$$
$$\downarrow (\bar{x} \downarrow y \downarrow t).$$

Since f is a second class function it can be written:

$$f = (x + z + t)(x + z + \bar{t})(\bar{x} + z + \bar{t})(\bar{x} + \bar{z} + \bar{t})(\bar{x} + y + t).$$

If we study the Karnaugh map of the complementary function (Figure 1.64):

$$\bar{f} = \bar{x}\bar{z}\bar{t} + \bar{x}\bar{z}t + x\bar{z}t + xzt + x\bar{y}\bar{t},$$

$\overset{\displaystyle zt}{xy}$	00	01	11	10
00	1	1	0	0
01	1	1	0	0
11	0	1	1	0
10	1	1	1	1

FIG. 1.64.

we can write:

$$\bar{f} = \bar{x}\bar{z} + xt + x\bar{y} \qquad f = (x + z)(\bar{x} + \bar{t})(\bar{x} + y)$$

from which we can write definitively:

$$f = (x \downarrow y) \downarrow (\bar{x} \downarrow \bar{t}) \downarrow (\bar{x} \downarrow y)$$

the two-leveled minimal expression.

BIBLIOGRAPHY

[1] QUINE, W. V., 'A Way to Simplify Truth Functions', *Am. Math. Monthly* **66** (1955) 627–31.
[2] QUINE, W. V., 'On Cores and Prime Implicants of Truth Functions', *Am. Math. Monthly* **66** (1959) 755–60.
[3] McCLUSKEY, E. J., 'Minimization of Boolean Functions', *Bell System Technical J.* **35** (1956) 1417–44.
[4] Staff of the Harvard Computation Laboratory, *Annals of the Computation Laboratory* in *Synthesis of Electronic Computing and Control Circuits*, vol. 27, Harvard University Press, Cambridge, Mass.
[5] CALDWELL, S. H., *Switching Circuits and Logical Design*, Wiley, New York, 1958.
[6] KARNAUGH, M., 'The Map Method for Synthesis of Combinational Logic Circuits, Communication and Electronic', *Trans. A.I.E.E.* part I, vol. 72, 1953.
[7] VEITCH, E. W., 'Third and Higher Order Minimal Solutions of Logical Equations', in *Symposium d'algèbre des circuits logiques*, I.C.I.P, Paris, 1960.
[8] McCLUSKEY, E. J. and BARTEE, T. C., *A Survey of Switching Circuit Theory*, McGraw-Hill, New York, 1962.
[9] CURTIS, M. A., *A New Approach to the Design of Switching Circuits*, Van Nostrand, 1962.
[10] BOOLE, G., *The Mathematical Analysis of Logic*, Cambridge, 1847.
[11] ASHENHURST, R. L., 'The Decomposition of Switching Functions', Harvard Computation Laboratory, Bell Laboratories' Report No. BL-1 (II), 1952.
[12] TISON, P., 'Recherche de termes premiers d'une fonction booléenne', *Automatisme* **9** (1964) No. 1.
[13] TISON, P., 'Théorie des consensus et algorithmes de recherche des bases premières', in *Colloque d'algèbre de Boole*, Grenoble, 1965.
[14] TISON, P., 'Algèbre booléenne: théorie des consensus. Recherche des bases premières d'une fonction booléenne', *Automatisme* **10** (1965) No. 6.
[15] PANDEFF, E., 'Calcul matriciel booléen', in *Colloque d'algèbre de Boole*, Grenoble, 1965.
[16] LEDLEY, R. S., *Digital Computer and Control Engineering*, McGraw-Hill, New York, 1960.
[17] PHISTER, M., *Logical Design of Digital Computers*, Wiley, New York, 1961.
[18] FLORINE, J., *La synthèse des machines logiques*, Dunod, Paris, et Presses Académiques Européennes, Bruxelles, 1964.
[19] NASLIN, P. and KUNTZMAN, J., *Algèbre de Boole et machines logiques*, Dunod, Paris, 1966.
[20] NASLIN, P., *Circuits logiques et automatismes à séquences*, Dunod, Paris, 1965.

[21] KAUFFMANN, A., DENIS PAPIN, M., and FAURE, R., *Calcul booléen applique*, Albin Michel, Paris, 1962.

[22] BARTEE, T. C., LEBOV, I. L., and REED, I. S., *Theory and Design of Digital Machines*, McGraw-Hill, New York, 1962.

[23] HUMPHREY, W. S., *Switching Circuits with Computer Applications*, McGraw-Hill, New York, 1958.

[24] BRUNIN, J., 'Simplification des fonctions logiques à grand nombre de variables', *Automatisme* 5 (Juillet 1963).

The references [3, 9, 12, 18, 20, 24] are in a way 'historical'; they were the first articles and books to treat the subject of Boolean algebra and the simplification of Boolean functions.

The references [11, 14, 17] are complete works which will be found in the bibliographies of almost all the chapters of the present work.

The references [21, 22, 23] treat a simplification method of Boolean functions by the consensus theory as discussed in [2].

The references [11, 16] are the only ones in which the application of Boolean matrices to the simplification of Boolean functions is discussed. They require (especially [11]) a good knowledge of the algebra of sets.

[1] and [6] treat the same problem but from a slightly different angle. It is to be pointed out that Curtis' book contains an organization allowing the programming of methods detailed by the author.

EXERCISES

Exercises on pure algebra

1.1. Derive $b = c$, from $a + b = a + c$ and $a \cdot b = a \cdot c$.

1.2. Compute a, b, c in function of x, y, z knowing that $x = a, y = b \oplus c, z = a \oplus b$.

1.3. Show by recurrence that a necessary and sufficient condition that

$$f(x_1, x_2, ..., x_n) = x_1 \oplus x_2 \oplus x_3, ..., \oplus x_n = 1$$

is that an odd number of variables $x_1, x_2, ..., x_n$ are 1.

1.4. Express $f(x_1, x_2, x_3) = x_1 \oplus x_2 \oplus x_3$ in terms of operators AND, OR (inclusive), NOT; generalize to n variables and find the result of exercise 2 in this way.

Reduction of functions

1.5. Reduce the following 5 variable function by the Quine-McCluskey method.

$$f(x_1, x_2, x_3, x_5) = R(3, 4, 6, 7, 11, 15, 16, 18, 19, 20, 21, 23, 27, 28, 30)$$
$$+ R_\phi(10, 12, 14, 17, 22, 24, 26, 31).$$

1.6. Reduce the same function by the Karnaugh map method.

1.7. Using one of the preceeding methods, then the other, find the minimal forms in products of sums and sums of products of the following functions:

$$f(x_1, x_2, x_3, x_4) = R(0, 1, 2, 5, 7, 8, 9, 10, 13) + R_\phi(3, 6, 12, 15)$$
$$f(x_1, x_2, x_3, x_4) = R(0, 1, 4, 5, 10, 13, 15) + R_\phi(2, 7, 12, 14)$$
$$f(x_1, x_2, x_3, x_4) = R(3, 4, 6, 11, 13) + R_\phi(5, 7, 8, 12, 15).$$

Use of NOR and NAND operators

1.8. Express the function $f = x_1 \oplus x_2$ in form of a product of sums using the AND, OR and NOT operators; derive an expression in terms of NOR using the minimum of $\downarrow$ symbols.

1.9. Express the functions in exercises 6 and 7 in terms of the NOR operator then in terms of the NAND operator using the minimal number of symbols each time.

Decomposition of Boolean functions

1.10. Find a decomposition of:

$$f(x_1, x_2, x_3, x_4, x_5) = R(2, 4, 6, 7, 9, 13, 15, 17, 21, 23, 25, 29, 31).$$

1.11. Let

$$f(x_1, x_2, x_3, x_4, x_5) = R(1, 2, 4, 7, 8, 11, 13, 14, 16, 18, 21, 23, 28, 30).$$

Find the matrix $E_{Y,X}$ of this function for

$$Y = (x_4, x_5) \text{ and } X = (x_1, x_2, x_3).$$

Find the matrix $E_{Y,X}$ of this function for

$$Y = (x_1, x_4) \text{ and } X = (x_2, x_3, x_5).$$

Letting $\varphi(x_2, x_3, x_5) = x_2 \oplus x_3 \oplus x_5$, seek a decomposition of f according to this function.

1.12. Let

$$f(x_1, x_2, x_3, x_4, x_5) = R(1, 2, 4, 7, 8, 11, 13, 14, 16, 19, 21, 22, 26, 28, 31).$$

Is it possible to put it in the form

$$f = F[\varphi(x_1, x_2, x_3), x_4, x_5)]?$$

Is it possible to put it in the form

$$f = F'(\varphi, x_4, x_5) \cdot H(x_1, x_2, x_3, x_4, x_5)$$

with

$$\varphi = \varphi(x_1, x_2, x_3) = x_1 \oplus x_2 \oplus x_3?$$

Is it possible to put F' in the form

$$F' = F''[\varphi, \psi(x_4, x_5)]?$$

Express ψ.

Miscellaneous subjects

1.13. Consider the 4 digit pure binary code $(D, C, B, A$ in the order of decreasing weight) and the 'excess 3' code in which the digits are, in the same order, Z, Y, X, W. (Figure 1.65.)

	Z	Y	X	W
0	0	0	1	1
1	0	1	0	0
2	0	1	0	1
3	0	1	1	0
4	0	1	1	1
5	1	0	0	0
6	1	0	0	1
7	1	0	1	0
8	1	0	1	1
9	1	1	0	0

FIG. 1.65.

Give the expressions for W, X, Y, Z as a function of A, B, C, D and reduce them.
Give the expression for A, B, C, D as a function of W, X, Y, Z and reduce them.

1.14. Consider the grill in Figure 1.66 in terms of which we wish to design certain letters of the alphabet. Given the letters C, U, T, O and Figures 1.67a to d, express the

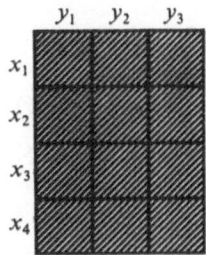

FIG. 1.66.

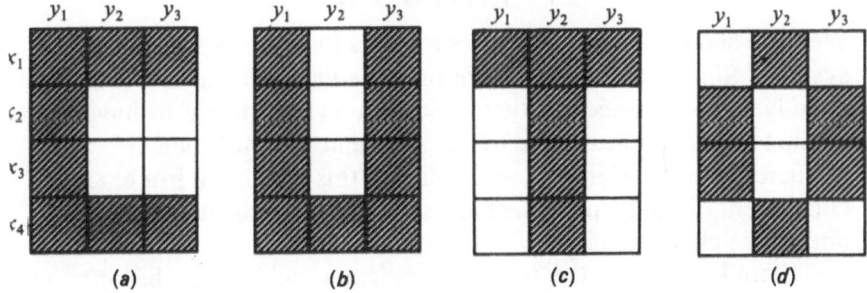

FIG. 1.67.

functions with the following conventions: $y_i = 1$ if at least three cells of the column are black, if not, $y_i = 0$; $x_j = 1$ if at least two cells of the row are black, if not, $x_j = 0$.

What happens to these expressions when we admit the possibility of an error (that is, if one cell can be other than the right colour)?

CHAPTER 2

PRACTICAL REALIZATION OF LOGICAL FUNCTIONS

2.1. INTRODUCTION

We have seen that switching algebra lends itself to the study of logical systems. Since the variables take only the values 0 and 1, it is consequently easy to associate them with any system likely to have two distinct states; 0 is attributed to one state and 1 to the other.

There are many elements which satisfy this condition. For example, components based upon mechanical, electrical, magnetic, and even pneumatic phenomena.

Generally, we are led to consider 'gates' which can be open or closed. That is, a certain electric flux (or some fluid) can be transmitted in a wire (or channel) or, on the contrary, all such propagation can be prevented. To this contradiction ('pass', 'does not pass'), the notion of level (voltage or pressure), high or low, positive or negative, materializing the value of the variable under study, must be added.

As an introduction we give the simplest known example: a light switch which can be actuated by manual or mechanical (cams or levers) means. We shall then successively discuss relays, electronic devices (diode, transistor, tunnel diode), magnetic devices, special cryotron type devices, and pneumatic devices. Finally, we believe it will be useful to give some idea of integrated circuit realizations which are becoming more and more important.

2.2. ELEMENTARY NOTIONS

Consider the example in Figure 2.1a. The battery E produces an input voltage X. Whenever the button A is in 'rest' position, no current can pass in the circuit; the output voltage Y is zero. A lamp under this potential is off. We can say that the binary variable L associated with the lamp is 0 valued.

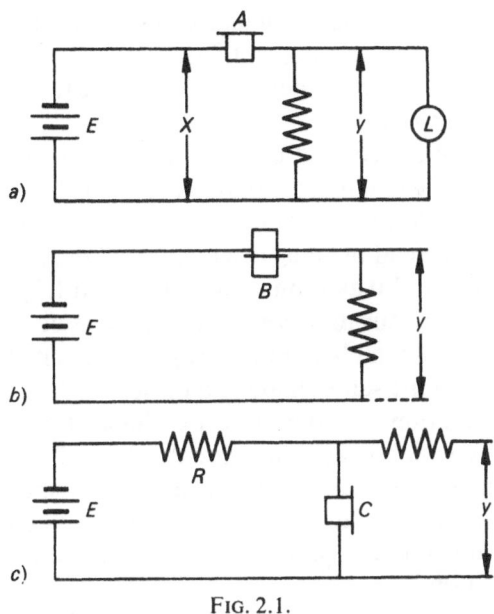

FIG. 2.1.

If we push A (we put the switch in 'work' position) the circuit is supplied with current; the lamp is on and we write $L = 1$.

By associating 0 with the notion of rest, and 1 with the notion of work, we establish the correspondence:

$$A = 0 \quad L = 0$$
$$A = 1 \quad L = 1.$$

We have the Boolean relation $L = A$.

Now let us consider Figure 2.1b. The B contact is of a different nature that the A contact: the rest position closes the circuit while the work position opens it. The correspondance is therefore:

$$B = 0 \quad L = 1$$
$$B = 1 \quad L = 0.$$

That is, $L = \bar{B}$ in Boolean language.

The diagram in Figure 2.1c gives another realization of the preceeding operation using an A type contact. When C is in rest position, a potential appears at Y; when C is in work position, the current passes directly by the contact C, its dissipation being assured by the resistance R.

We note that there is no particular economy to this solution since both configurations lead to a current flow.

Thus we see that a voltage source E, gives rise to a physical expression of a Boolean variable.

The first push of the contact button A induces the passage from the 0 state to the 1 state (Figure 2.2a) the second push provokes the passage from the 1 state to the 0 state (Figure 2.2b). But, if the switch is fixed to a spring instead of being in a fixed position, the level is 1 while it is being pushed and 0 as soon as we let go of it (Figure 2.2c). If we apply pressure only during a very short period of time, we have a limiting condition in which a square wave represents the level variations and has much the same shape as a pulse.

A manual actuation can therefore be simply transformed into an electric quantity which is associated with a logical variable.

We can imagine the same actuation performed mechanically by a cam or any kind of contact which has one end fixed and the other attached to a movable element. The value of the associated variable indicates a position.

In the examples of Figure 2.3, $P = 1$ means that the angle $\alpha = 0$. $Q = 1$ means that the movable part is placed in such a way that the reference system R coincides with r.

In general, we represent contacts in their rest position in circuit diagrams.

We often use double contacts permitting us to have the variable and its complement simultaneously at our disposition. Figure 2.4 gives two schematic representations of this type of contact.

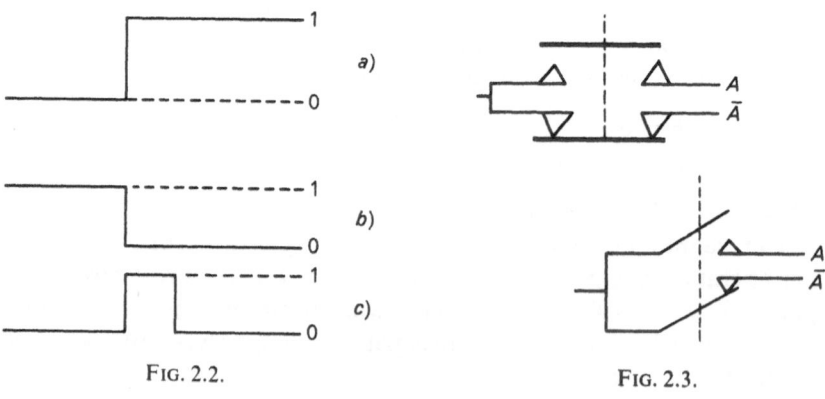

FIG. 2.2.   FIG. 2.3.

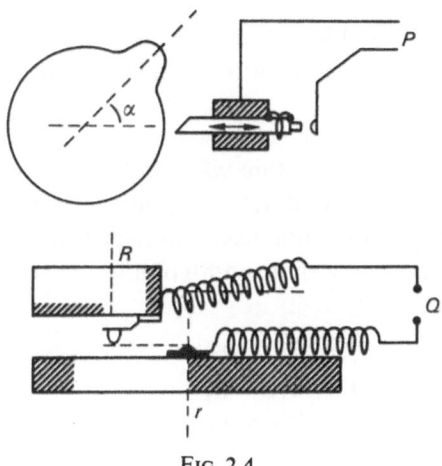

FIG. 2.4.

Generally, particular contacts can be adapted to any system, but we have no need of describing them here.

Series or parallel contact networks can also be imagined. These arrangements will be discussed in the next section which concerns a particular type of contact system: the electromagnetic relay.

2.3.   THE RELAY

In this section we deal with switches which are electromagnetically driven by a winding (Figure 2.5).

Whenever the coil is excited, the movable part pivots about the 0-axis and establishes contact at C.

Here we must separate two different phenomena which occur. We let R be the Boolean variable associated with the coil: $R = 0$ signifies

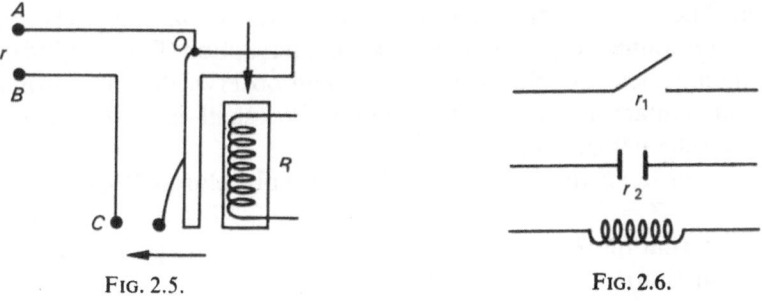

FIG. 2.5.   FIG. 2.6.

that no excitation is produced in the coil; $R = 1$ signifies the contrary. We associate the variable r with the contact. $r = 0$ means that the contact and AB circuit are open; $r = 1$ means that the contact and AB circuit are closed.

The two most common schematic representations are those in Figure 2.6 (r_1 and r_2). Very often we omit the coils in the diagrams.

We can easily imagine that if, for example, R is excited ($R = 1$), the contact spring at C does not react immediately (the acting time of relays is in the order of a thousandth of a second). We may therefore write the sequence:

> initial state ($R = 0, r = 0$)
> excitation ($R = 1, r = 0$)
> final state ($R = 1, r = 1$).

Or:

> initial state ($R = 1, r = 1$)
> non-excitation ($R = 0, r = 1$)
> final state ($R = 0, r = 0$).

This evaluation shows why we prefer to give different names to the two participating components.

There are many types of relays; their difference is in the position of their contacts. Only one, however, generally has several contact springs. These contact springs can be different, but each contact establishes an independent path.

We note:

(1) The normally open contact (make) preceedingly described (Figure 2.7(1)).
(2) The normally closed contact (break), $\bar{r} = R$ (Figure 2.7(2)).
(3) The break-before-make transfer contact. Both contact points are used (Figure 2.7(3)).
(4) The make-before-break contact, makes the bc, then abc, then ab connections. There is no work interruption (Figure 2.7(4)).

Among these simple examples we can observe that the normally closed contact is the NOT function. We shall now describe the circuit schematized in Figure 2.8.

In order to excite the coil Z, x and y must be closed. We may therefore write $Z = x \cdot y$ (AND operator). Figure 2.9 is a diagram in which x or y permit the Z coil to be energized. Here, we may write $Z = x + y$ (OR function).

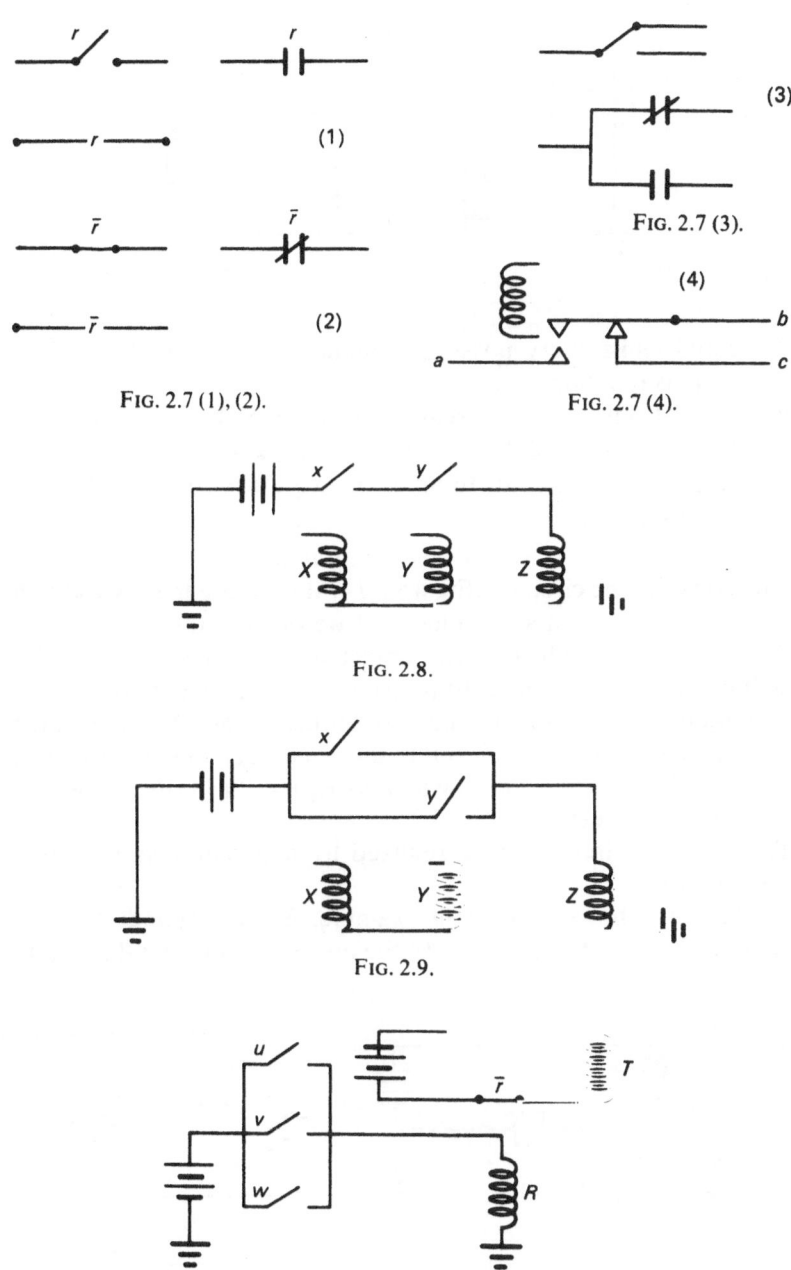

(1)

(2)

FIG. 2.7 (1), (2).

(3)

FIG. 2.7 (3).

(4)

FIG. 2.7 (4).

FIG. 2.8.

FIG. 2.9.

FIG. 2.10(a).

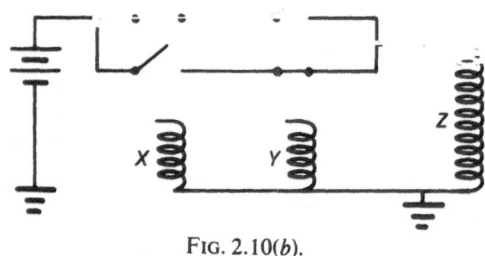

FIG. 2.10(b).

We could make every possible combination of contacts to obtain more complex functions.

Figure 2.10a gives a circuit realization of the NOR function: in fact, $R = u + v + w$ and $T = \bar{r}$; i.e. $T = \bar{u}\bar{v}\bar{w} = u \downarrow v \downarrow w$.

Figure 2.10b corresponds to an exclusive OR or dilemma function $Z = \bar{x}y + x\bar{y} = x \oplus y$.

2.3.1. Memory mounting

Let us consider the circuit in Figure 2.11. If we close the E switch, the coil X receives current and x closes. If we open E, the coil continues to be supplied through its own contact and the normally closed E_0 switch must be open in order to return to the rest state; here X looses its excitation state, x opens, and, by letting E_0 go off, the memory output remains 'no potential'. Only the E contact allows it to be put 'in potential': $x = 1$ as soon as we press E; $x = 0$ as soon as we press E_0 (which we call reset).

This type of circuit can be realized by magnetic components or special relays.

Figure 2.12 shows a two-coil example. B_2 corresponds to E; its excitation touches the contact r. In the absence of current through V_2,

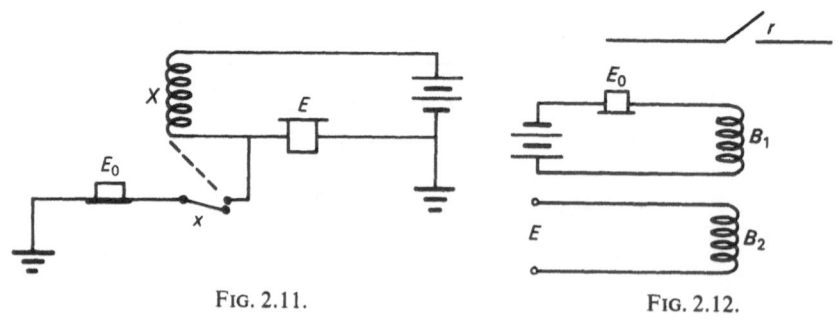

FIG. 2.11.   FIG. 2.12.

the current running through B_1 causes r to remain energized or at rest as it was initially.

This type of system is called a reduced auto-maintenance relay.

In the example of Figure 2.13, the magnetized bar mounted in the pivot O conserves by 'sticking', the position imposed upon it by one of the two windings. Here the magnetic sticking is also very inferior to the electromagnetic attraction of the coils.

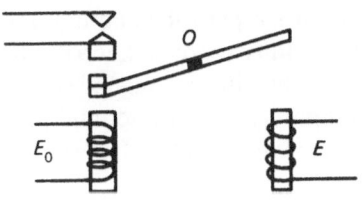

FIG. 2.13.

2.3.2. Special relays

The relay performances which have been described depend on a current running through a winding. We can come across situations which need a different type of relay.

Polarized relays operate only when the current runs through the coil in a certain direction.

The three-position relay is derived from the previously described relays. The positions are: attraction, rest, and reset.

Finally we cite relays containing many windings. Figure 2.14a can represent:

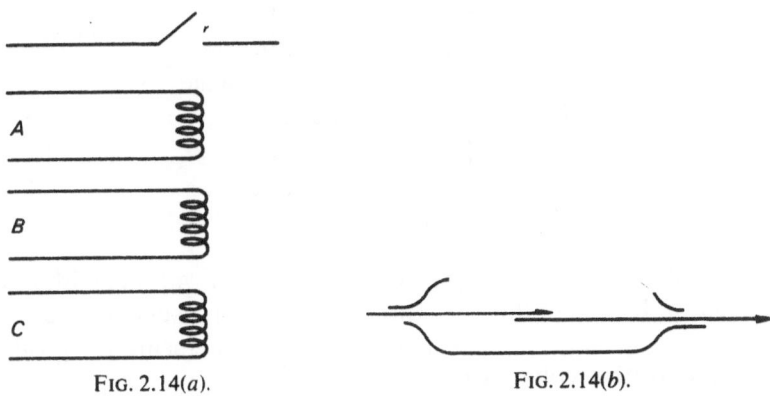

FIG. 2.14(*a*).   FIG. 2.14(*b*).

–an AND operator $(r = ABC)$ if the attraction is sufficient only when the three coils are excited.

–an OR operator $(r = A + B + C)$ if each coil is sufficient to separately attract the r contact.

–a logical operator majority, $r = AB + BC + CA = $ maj. (A, B, C), if at least two of the coils are necessary for attraction.

We see that many combinations are possible.

A new type of relay is being developed by several companies: the reed relay. It consists of simple tubes containing two reeds as shown in Figure 2.14b. Their rigidity tends to keep them separated, but a connection is produced by placing a magnet opposite the contacts. Its main interest is its simplicity, small size, and possibility of supporting relatively high voltage (several volts). The frequency used can exceed the kHz.

2.4. ELECTRONIC CIRCUITS–POSITIVE AND NEGATIVE LOGICS

We mentioned that in electronics, the two logical states, 0 and 1, are associated with two voltage levels. Generally, we use the ground potential and a positive or negative voltage.

We say that we deal with positive logic whenever the voltage representing '1' is higher than the voltage representing '0' (Figure 2.15a).

For example, $18 V = 1$, $0 V = 0$; $-18 V = 0$, $0 V = 1$. Contrary to this, negative logic attributes 0 to the higher voltage (Figure 2.15b).

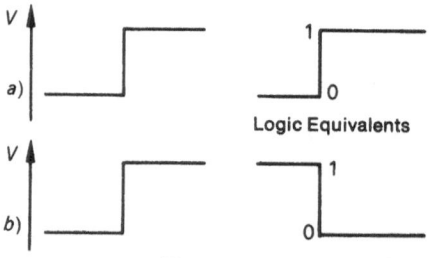

FIG. 2.15.

We shall often adopt this second solution when working with negative voltage levels. In this case the 0 potential represents the value 0, which is completely without ambiguity. (It is the same for positive logic and positive voltages.)

In circuit realization, we could indifferently use the two logics: permutation of barred and unbarred variables permits us to go from one representation to the other in a simple way.

The most commonly used levels are 3 V, 6 V, 18 V, and 24 V.

2.5. DIODE CIRCUITS

Semiconductor diodes (and vacuum diodes) are passive components (i.e. energy consumers) which, if suitably used, behave like relays.

In fact, if we polarize a diode in the 'forward' sense (Figure 2.16a), it presents a few ohm of resistance; if we polarize it in the opposite sense the resistance can reach several hundred kilo-ohm, even mega-ohm. The inverse current which runs through the diode is very weak. Thus, for example, we could use a diode to produce a given voltage level.

Figure 2.17 shows a 10 V amplitude input being converted into 6 V output, because the diode is polarized in the backward direction (we say 'blocked'). Generally, diodes support inverse voltages in the order of 100 V.

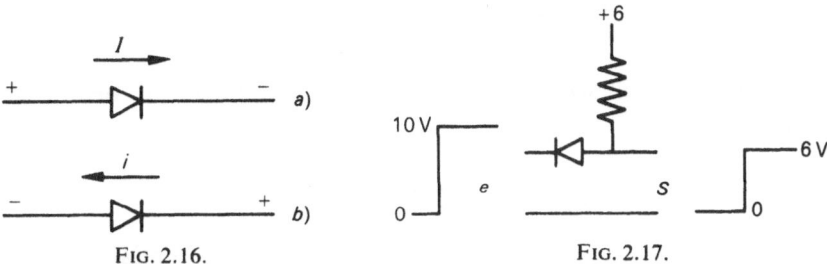

FIG. 2.16.   FIG. 2.17.

2.5.1 *Diode gates*

Let us consider the circuit in Figure 2.18. The signals are arranged so that the 0 volt level corresponds to the logical value 0, and the 18 volt level to the value 1. (We are therefore using positive logic.)

Assume that a, b, and c are at 0 potential; the diodes therefore permit passage and offer a low resistance r. The voltage V at S is:

$$I = \frac{18-V}{R} = I_a + I_b + I_c = \frac{3V}{r},$$

that is, $V = 18r/(3R+r)$ is in the neighbourhood of 0 since r is very small (especially compared to R).

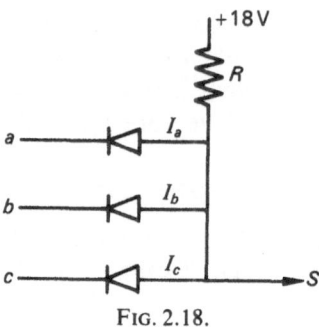

Fig. 2.18.

If we now assume that only a is at a 18 volt potential, it is clear that V will have a value of less than 18 V. Consequently, the diode will be polarized in the backward sense and have a very high resistance R':

$$I = \frac{18 - V}{R} = \frac{2V}{r} - \frac{18 - V}{R'}.$$

That is,

$$V = \frac{18}{1 + 2RR'/(2R + R')}$$

is still a potential in the neighbourhood of zero.

A similar result will be found if we assumed a and b to be at a 18 volt potential:

$$V = \frac{18}{1 + RR' / (r(2R + R'))}.$$

If we assume the three inputs to be at a 18 volt potential the three diodes are blocked. No current flows and the voltage at S is 18 volt. We therefore, have the following result: There is an 18 volt output if and only if an 18 volt potential is applied at all three levels. In logical language we write: $abc = S$. A three-input AND operator is realized.

When we try to increase the number of components at this gate, we find a limiting condition: Whenever, among n diodes, mounted as in Figure 2.18, $n-1$ are blocked, the conducting diode receives all the current being supplied (bias and reverse current). The corresponding input must, therefore, have sufficient energy. We shall generally limit ourselves to three-input systems in order to avoid such inconveniences.

Let us now study the diagram in Figure 2.19. As before, systematic examination shows that the output voltage will be approximately

S
−u

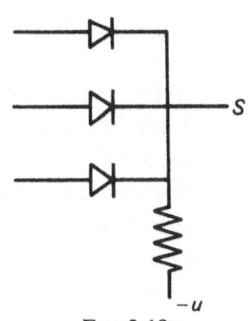

FIG. 2.19.

TABLE 2.1.
Diode circuits

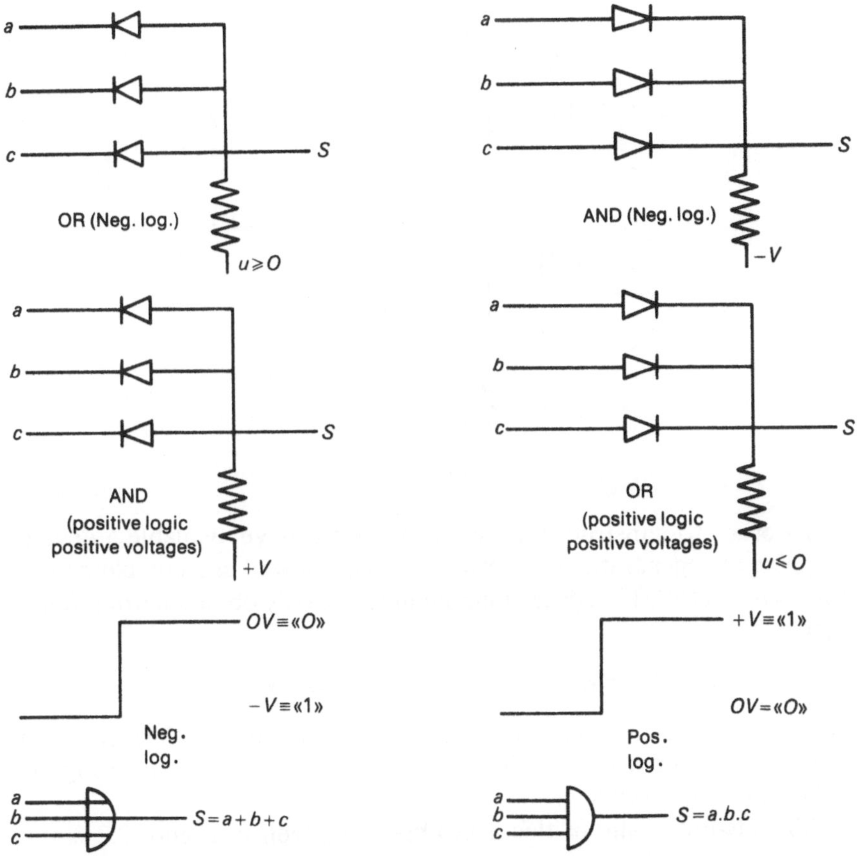

a
b
c
S
OR (Neg. log.)
u⩾O
a
b
c
S
AND (Neg. log.)
−V
a
b
c
S
AND
(positive logic
positive voltages)
+V
a
b
c
S
OR
(positive logic
positive voltages)
u⩽O
OV≡«O»
−V≡«1»
Neg.
log.
+V≡«1»
OV=«O»
Pos.
log.
a
b
c
S=a+b+c
a
b
c
S=a.b.c

equal to 18 volts if this potential is applied to one or both inputs. This circuit realizes the OR function.

Table 2.1 shows four possible arrangements which depend upon whether positive or negative logic is used. In the same table, we also find the symbolic representation used for AND and OR gates.

From the basic operators which we have defined, a great number of logical functions can be realized. It must be carefully noted that these gates consume power and consequently, it will be impossible to couple a large number of these circuit stages.

As an example, we give, in Figure 2.20, a circuit realization in negative logic such that $S = a\bar{b} + \bar{a}b$, that is $S = a \oplus b$, addition modulo 2 (or exclusive OR). The possibility of using barred variables is assumed.

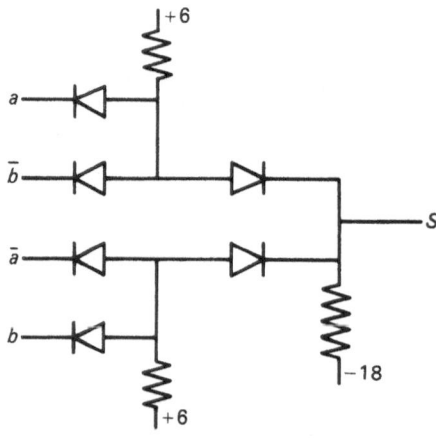

Fig. 2.20.

In order to construct a network, we must have available a device capable of regenerating power to the signal as well as a complementation system (NOT). These components are easily obtained from transistors.

2.6. TRANSISTOR CIRCUITS

Let us consider an p-n-p transistor. The collector is polarized at $-v$ volt through a resistor R. The base is polarized at $+v$ volt through r. The emitter is grounded.

The characteristic of this assemblage is given in Figure 2.21. We

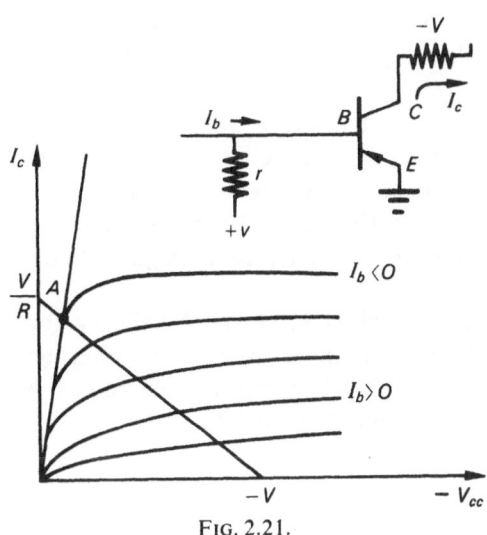

FIG. 2.21.

draw the load line of slope $-1/R$. Whenever the base current is positive, the collector current is sensibly zero and the collector voltage is in the neighbourhood of $-v$. If, on the contrary, we make I_b negative (we move along the load line to the saturation point A for which the collector voltage is in the neighbourhood of zero and a collector current is maximal), the transistor becomes a saturated conductor in contrast with the first case in which it was blocked.

If, we apply a 0 potential to the input e, the output potential is $-v$; if we then apply a $-v$ potential to e, the output potential is 0. Figure 2.22 represents a NOT operator; its logical function is written $s = \bar{e}$.

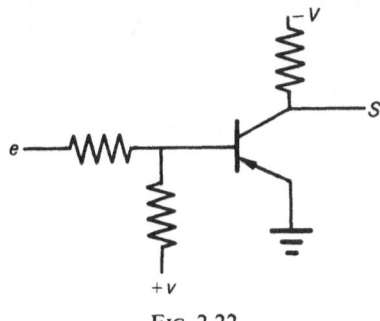

FIG. 2.22.

Sometimes we prefer to use a '$-w$' bias, with $w > v$, and place a '$-v$' polarized blocking diode at the terminal in order to obtain higher output.

If the signals use positive voltage, an n-p-n transistor can be employed. Generally, we shall give p-n-p realizations. They are the most common and best adapted to commutation.

The arrangement in Figure 2.22 is interesting (as we have already mentioned) because it gives back to the signal the energy lost through passive elements.

The role of the amplifier is shown by the symbol used in Figure 2.23. If we wish to obtain the exact input regenerated into power, it is sufficient that a NOT-NOT circuit be realized by putting two transistors in series as shown in Figure 2.24.

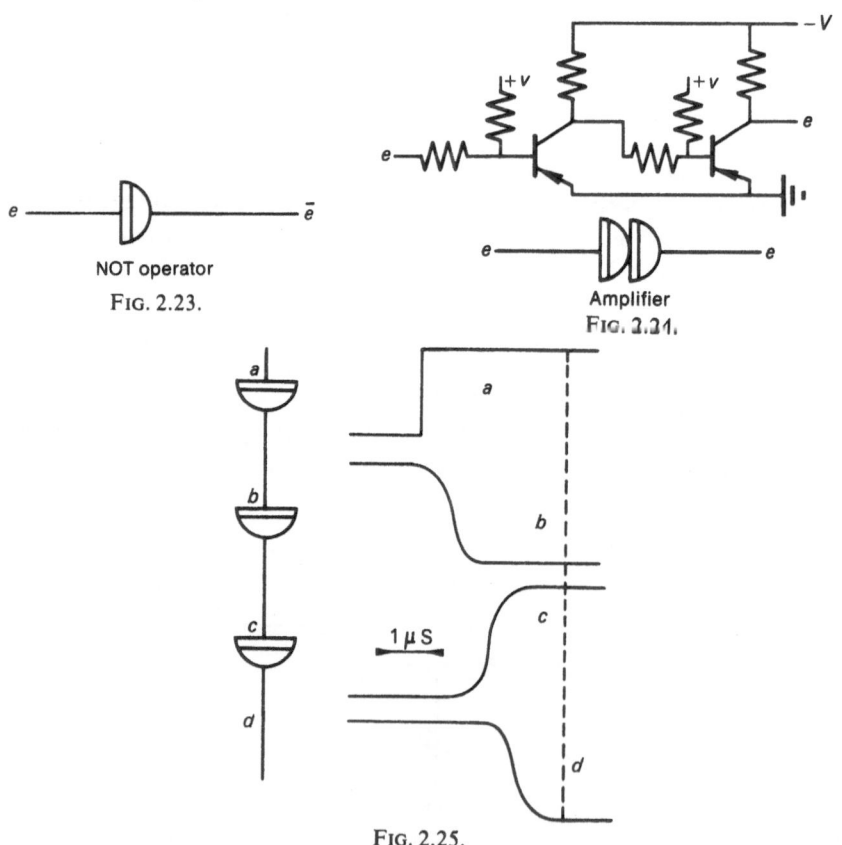

NOT operator

FIG. 2.23.

Amplifier

FIG. 2.24.

FIG. 2.25.

However, the delay attached to each element must not be neglected. The response time of transistors is in the order of a microsecond and the voltage wave forms are effected by these transistors.

Figure 2.25 gives an example of the deformations and delays of a step when it goes through a series of several NOT operators.

These delays impose a frequency functioning limit which is not ordinarily annoying, but can become so when, for example, dealing with computers. In order that certain wave forms appear simultaneously, it can be necessary to reset.

2.6.1. *Transistor-resistor gates*

If we add other inputs to the NOT circuit already defined (Figure 2.26), the base current becomes sufficiently negative as soon as a −18 volt potential is applied to at least one of the inputs, a, b, or c. The logical representation (in negative logic) is therefore:

$$e = a + b + c$$
$$S = \bar{e},$$

i.e. $S = \bar{a}\bar{b}\bar{c} = a \downarrow b \downarrow c$. Therefore, Figure 2.26 corresponds to a NOR circuit.

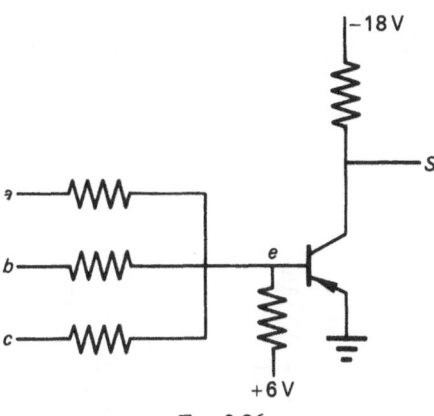

FIG. 2.26.

To represent such circuits, we use the symbol in Figure 2.27 which expresses NOR = OR − NOT. If we keep the same diagram, but use positive logic, we obtain:

$$e = abc$$
$$S = \bar{e},$$

i.e. $S = \bar{a} + \bar{b} + \bar{c} = a \mid b \mid c$. Therefore, Figure 2.26 corresponds to a NAND circuit in this case (we are dealing with a logic defined by $-18\,\text{V} = 0$ and $0\,\text{V} = 1$).

The symbol retained for the NAND circuit, by analogy with the preceding, is shown in Figure 2.28. We can obtain similar results using an p-n-p transistor (Table 2.2).

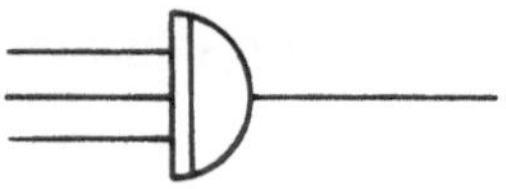

| FIG. 2.27. | FIG. 2.28. |

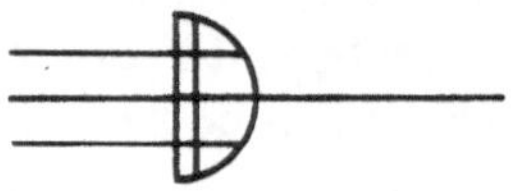

Table 2.2

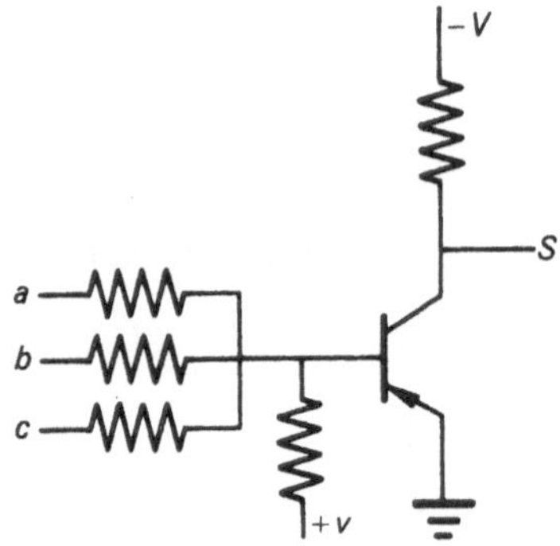

NOR – negative logic   (Resistances)   NOR – positive logic

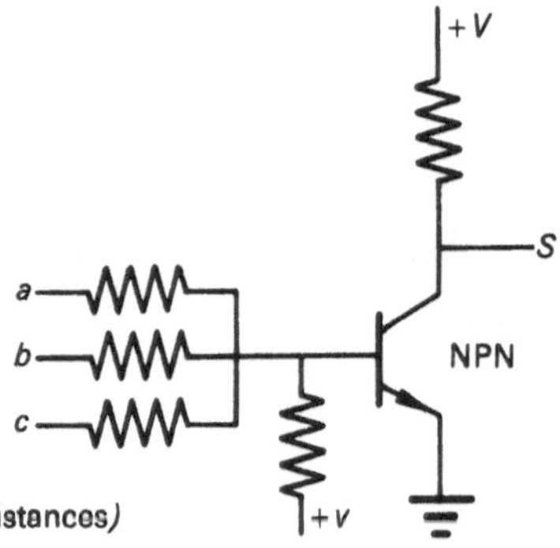

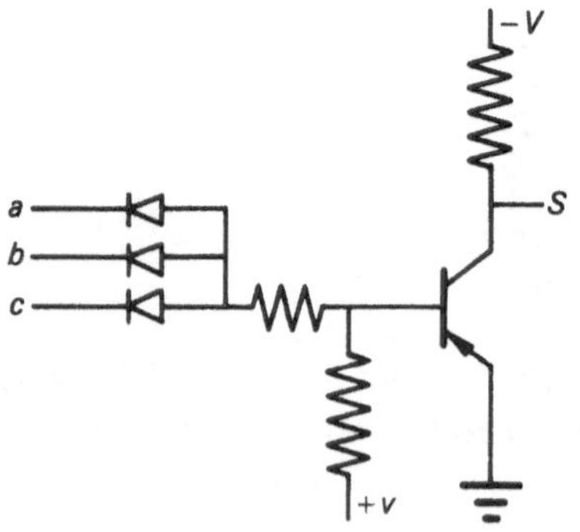

NOR – negative logic   (Diodes)   NAND – negative logic

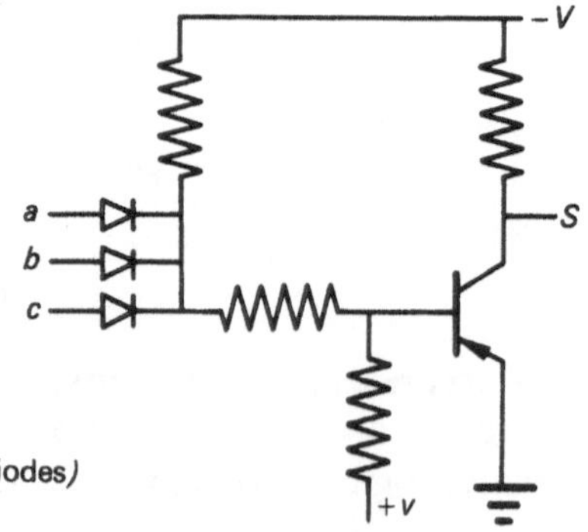

2.6.2. *Transistor-diode gates*

Using the same analogies which led to the symbols just described, we can combine the diode gates of the preceding section with an amplifier transistor inverter in a simple way and we immediately obtain the circuits in Table 2.2.

The advantage of this solution is that a higher charge can thus be applied to the input operators (fan-in). In fact, a diode gate can be placed at each transistor-resistor operator input. Simple operators are obtained if all the gates are identical and complex operators if they are different.

Figure 2.29 shows a mounting which realizes

$$\bar{a}\bar{b}\bar{c}\bar{d}(\bar{e}+\bar{f}+g) = S \quad \text{(negative logic)}$$

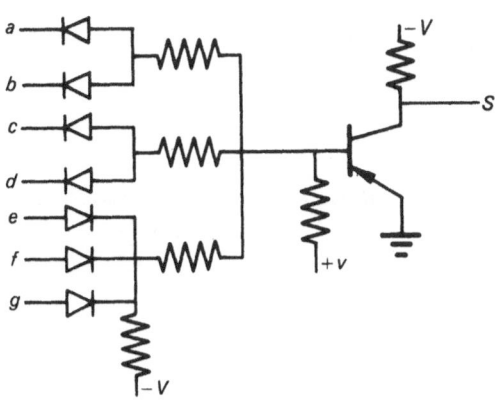

FIG. 2.29.

2.6.3. *Directly coupled transistors*

A third solution is to use directly coupled transistors. Its advantage is that it increases power and therefore permits a greater charge (fan-out).

Series or parallel transistors behave exactly like switches; they are followed by an inverter. It is therefore easy to obtain the NOR and NAND operations.

Table 2.3 shows a few possible realizations with p-n-p in negative logic and n-p-n in positive logic.

We sometimes use direct coupling type mountings. The transistor emitter follower gives high signal amplitude.

TABLE 2.3.

Directly coupled transistors

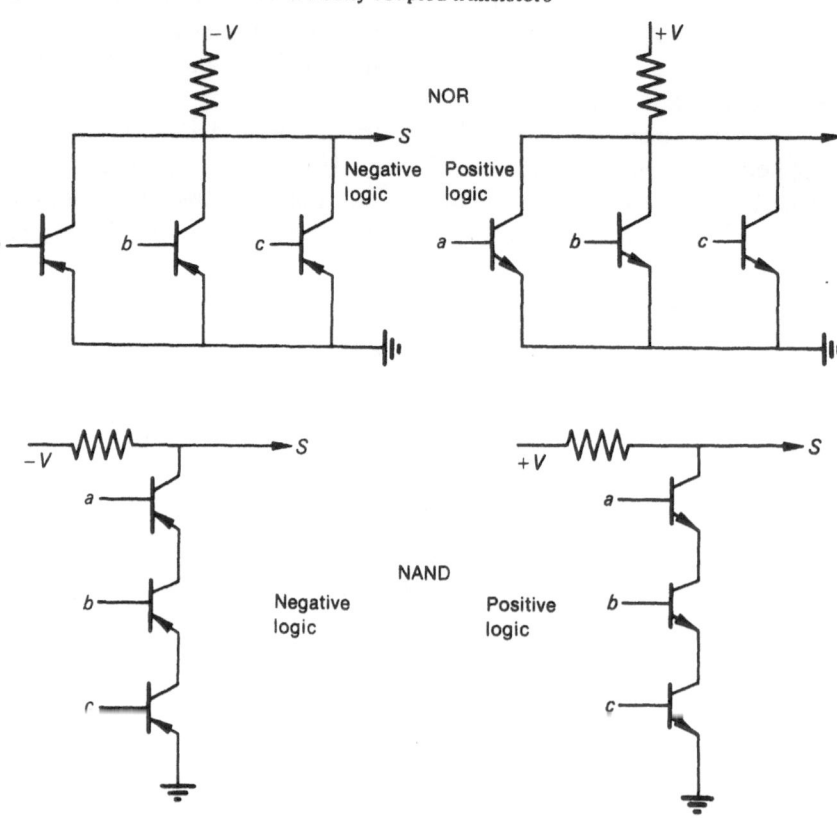

We shall not detail this subject as the object of this chapter is only to familiarize the reader with fundamental circuits.

2.6.4. *Note on vacuum tube circuits*

All the preceding examples have been taken from a semiconductor viewpoint since they are very important in modern circuits. As a matter of fact, the mountings are to a large extent derived from vacuum tube diagrams. A transistor is, in a certain sense, equivalent to a classical triode.

We cite some particular examples.

The double triode (or multi-triode) realizes the NOR function. The inputs are made at the different grids, the outputs on the set of plates.

The pentode (Figure 2.30) realizes the NAND function $(S = \bar{a} + \bar{b})$ since it conducts only if a and b are at a positive potential.

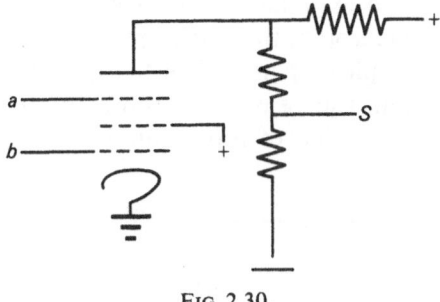

FIG. 2.30.

2.7. FLIP-FLOP AND MEMORY TRANSISTORIZED LOGICS

2.7.1. *Utilization of pulses*

In the preceeding section we presented a certain number of circuits which realized the main logical functions relative to voltage levels.

These levels can rise to a more or less high frequency, giving more or less square waves. At the limit, the signal can behave like a pulse causing several problems in its utilization (particularly synchronization). Later, we shall describe networks which permit the transformation of these pulses into levels; inversely, we can transform voltage variation into pulses.

A simple RC circuit of which the response is in the form $U \cdot e^{-t/RC}$, corresponds a pulse type voltage point to a step arriving at instant 0 (Figure 2.31).

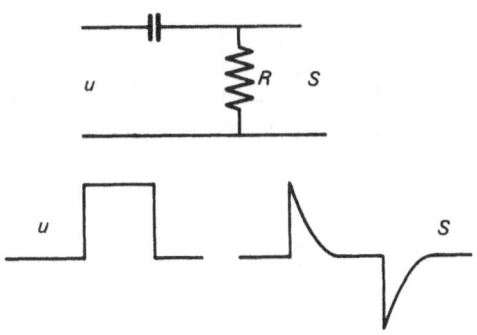

FIG. 2.31.

If a properly placed diode is added to the system, it is possible to
conserve just one pulse corresponding to a square wave and consider
either the rise or the fall of the voltage (Figure 2.32).

Another aspect is to sometimes let a clock control a logical network.
It is sufficient to synchronize the clock's pulse rate with the levels. We
can obtain, for example, a pulse when the level is valued at '1'. We
could use the different square waves to represent the '0' and '1' logics.
Figure 2.33 gives this kind of representation as well as the signals
obtained.

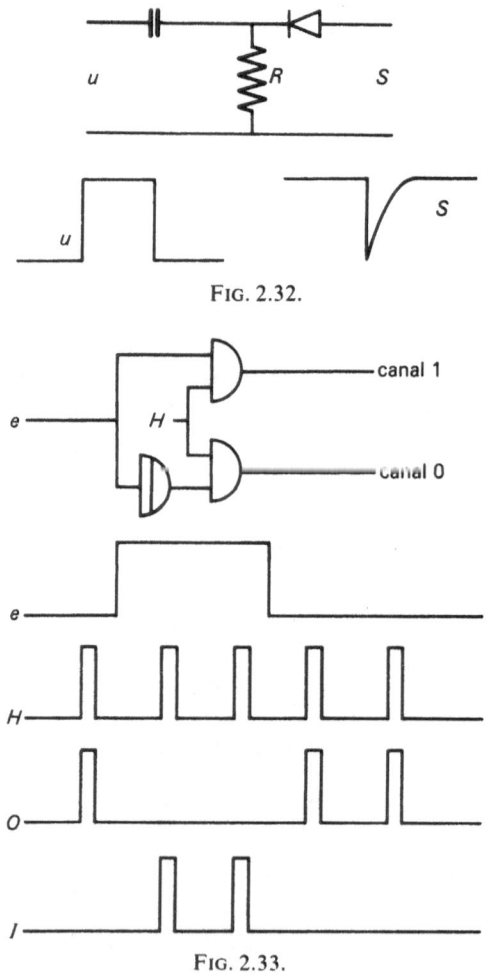

FIG. 2.32.

FIG. 2.33.

Note that the clock could be replaced by a transmission of pulses, and it is not absolutely necessary that these pulses arrive at a set frequency.

2.7.2. *Memory*

In Section 2.2 we showed how, starting from relays, we can create a network which stores the last signal received (E corresponds to 1, E_0 to 0). A similar circuit, based on NOR operators, can be realized. Consider the logical diagram in Figure 2.34; its circuit diagram is given in Figure 2.35b.

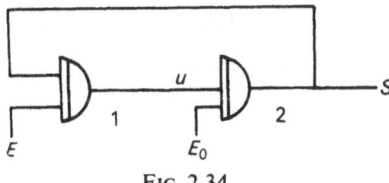

FIG. 2.34.

Let the initial state be, $S = 0$, $E = 0$, $E_0 = 0$. The operator 1 output, $\bar{S} \cdot \bar{E} = 1$ which is compatible with the operator 2 state.

If we let $E = 1$, the operator 1 output becomes 0, and the operator 2 output 1: $S = 1$ which is compatible with the operator 1 state ($\bar{S} \cdot \bar{E} = 0$) and nothing changes if E returns to a 0 value.

If, in this last configuration, we let $E_0 = 1$, operator 2 having a 1 input, gives $S = 0$ which produces $\bar{S} \cdot \bar{E} = 1$ and nothing changes if E_0 returns to 0.

The table in Figure 2.35a shows these results. We observe in

E_0	E	u	S
0	0	1	0
0	1	0	1
0	0	0	1
1	0	1	0

FIG. 2.35(a).

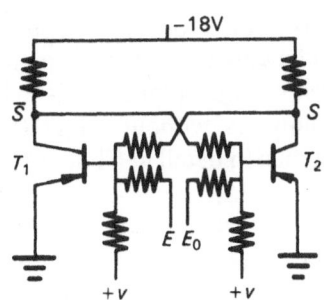

FIG. 2.35(b).

particular, that $u = \bar{S}$ and that this circuit reacts to the logic level rise (passage of E or E_0 from 0 to 1) while the drop of level has no effect on it.

Simultaneous presence of E_0 and E is excluded; in spite of the fact that it would mean $u = S = 0$, which is derived from the condition $\bar{E} \cdot \bar{S} = 0, \bar{E}_0 \cdot \bar{u} = 0$ as soon as $E_0 = E = 1$.

2.7.3. *Application to input-output rectification*

Whenever we let a switch simulate a logical variable a rebound problem can occur. In fact, whenever a contact spring no longer touches the contact point, the rupture is clean, but when it sticks we can get a jerky transition flow (Figure 2.36a).

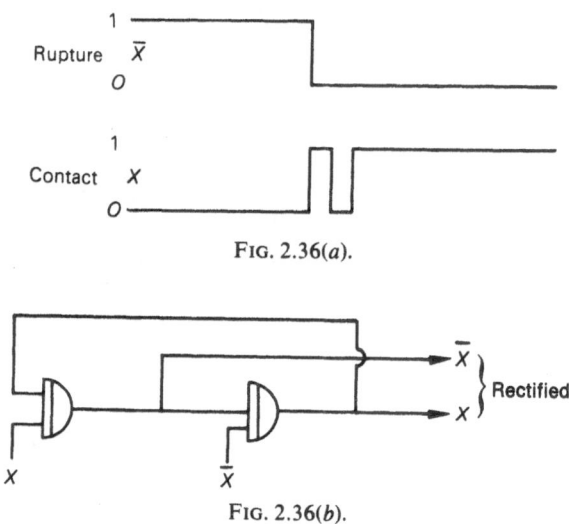

FIG. 2.36(*a*).

FIG. 2.36(*b*).

We can avoid this inconvenience by simultaneous use of a rupture and a contact level in a memory circuit (transistors, for example). The first voltage point established activates the circuit. The variation which follows is without effect (Figure 2.36b). This phenomenon will be studied in detail in Chapter 6 (Section 6.34).

2.7.4. *Flip-flops*

Pulse inputs or level variation inputs are possible in the mountings shown in Table 2.4. In practise, however, the mountings used are slightly more complex. The double input flip-flop is obtained directly

TABLE 2.4.

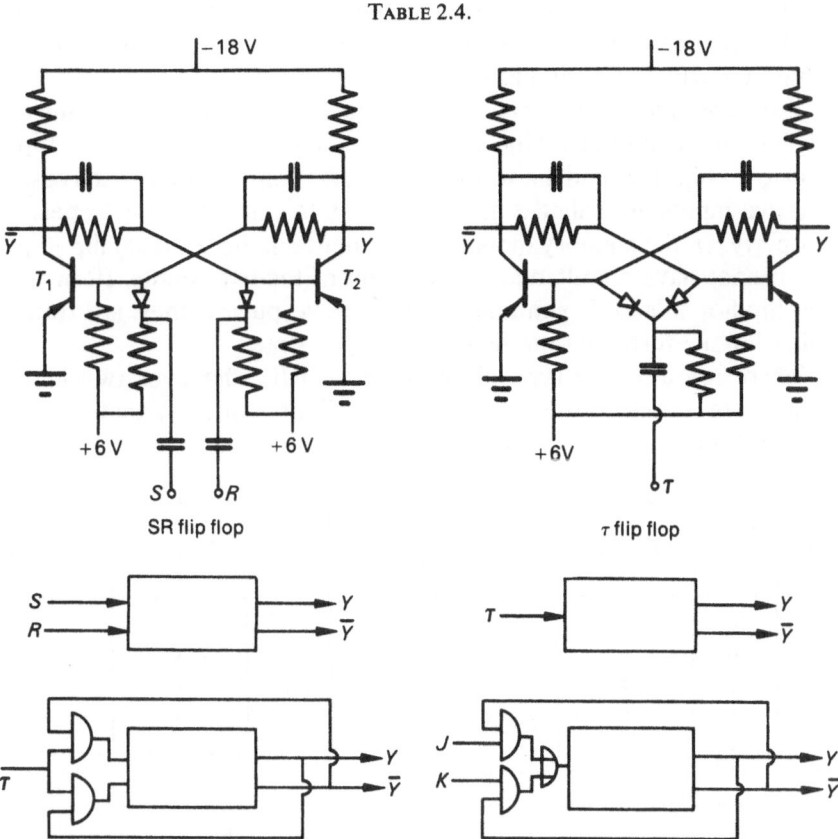

from the memory circuit in Figure 2.35b. Its functioning is bi-stable; that is, there are only two possible configurations:

$$\text{saturated } T_1 \text{ transistor} - \text{blocked } T_2 \text{ transistor} \quad y = 1$$
$$\text{blocked } T_1 \text{ transistor} - \text{saturated } T_2 \text{ transistor} \quad y = 0.$$

In the first case, if R receives a negative pulse (or a level drop cf. Figure 2.32), a negative base current appears at T_2 giving $y = 0$. The T_1 base voltage becomes positive thus blocking T_1 and the network is stabilized. A pulse at S resets it. This is called the set-reset flip-flop (SR).

The single input or τ flip-flop (also called symmetrical) is shown in the same Table 2.4. It is another version of the network which changes state with each pulse received at the unique input τ. The diodes placed at the access to each base allow the signal to be oriented towards the transistor which was blocked.

We have given a schematic representation of these two systems as well as two mountings. One shows the conversion of a set-reset flip-flop to a τ flip-flop; and the second the inverse conversion. In each case, the two inputs are called J and K because this network has a special property. In the memory mounting, and hence in the set-reset flip-flop, we cannot have simultaneous excitation of the two inputs. If, in the JK flip-flop J and K simultaneously receive pulses, they are transmitted in a τ form and the flip-flop changes state.

There are also PQ type flip-flops, in which, whenever two input pulses are simultaneously produced, inhibition occurs; that is, the network does not change state.

R	S	Y_{initial}	Y_{final}
0	0	0	0
0	0	1	1
0	1	0	1
0	1	1	1
1	0	0	0
1	0	1	0

FIG. 2.37(a).

τ	Y_{initial}	Y_{final}
0	0	0
0	1	1
1	0	1
1	1	0

FIG. 2.37(b).

J	K	Y_{initial}	Y_{final}
0	0	0	0
0	0	1	1
0	1	0	0
0	1	1	0
1	0	0	1
1	0	1	1
1	1	0	1
1	1	1	0

FIG. 2.37(c).

P	Q	Y_{initial}	Y_{final}
0	0	0	0
0	0	1	1
0	1	0	0
0	1	1	0
1	0	0	1
1	0	1	1
1	1	0	0
1	1	1	1

FIG. 2.37(d).

The preceding results are shown in Figure 2.37.

The *RC* circuits which figure at the collector connection of one transistor, but base of the second and reciprocally, are very often used for the coupling of transistorized logical elements. They permit an improved commutation whenever abrupt level changes occur.

The reader may find it useful to refer to books dealing with electronic circuit which are listed in the bibliography at the end of this chapter. They discuss in detail the different possibilities of transistors.

2.8. TUNNEL DIODES

Figure 2.38 represents the characteristic of a semi-conductor dipole called the tunnel diode (due to the Japanese inventor Esaki, about 1958). The load line (R, V_t) cuts this characteristic at two stable points A and B. If, starting at A, we move the load line upwards, the figurative point (intersection at load line and curve) reaches M_a and jumps to the BB' branch. It stabilizes itself at B when we return to the initial conditions. The same phenomenon is symmetrically produced if we move the figurative point from B downward; it reaches M_b, then jumps to the AA' branch and stabilizes itself at A. Thus, if we displace V_t on one side and then the other of its basic value, we obtain the two states A and B.

The tunnel diode, a relatively expensive component, can become a

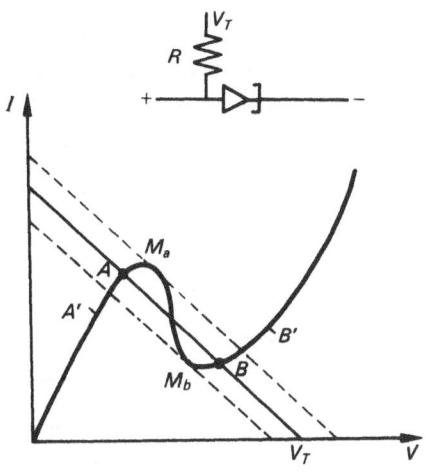

Fig. 2.38.

very important logical element, especially because of its high switching speed (in the order of the nanosecond, 10^{-9} s).

Figure 2.39a gives an example of a τ flip-flop. $D_1 D_2$ are alternatively in the A and B or B and A states.

The basic logical circuits are simply realized. It is sufficient to build the inputs in such a way as to cause the displacement necessary to change the stable state. Suppose that one of the three inputs is sufficient to produce the current necessary for the flip-flop. We have an OR circuit (Figure 2.39b). In this case the bias intensity must be such that the point is at $A'M_a$. If several inputs are necessary to put the load line above M_a and switch to $M_b B'$, we have a threshold logic, and at the limit (all three inputs) an AND operator.

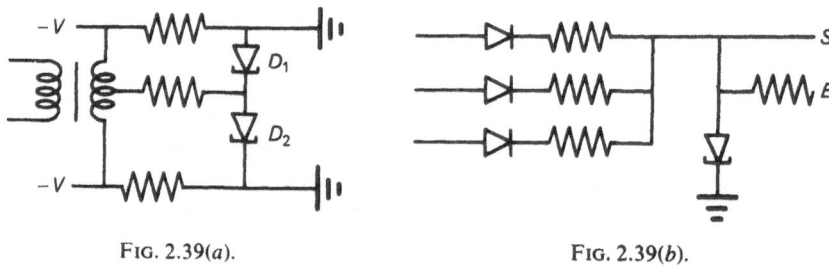

FIG. 2.39(a).   FIG. 2.39(b).

2.9. MAGNETIC CIRCUITS

Figure 2.40 represents magnetic core hysteresis cycles. We observe that there are two zones, $P'P''$ and $Q'Q''$, in which there is little variation of the B induction. But, there are two regions, $P'Q$ and $Q'P$, in

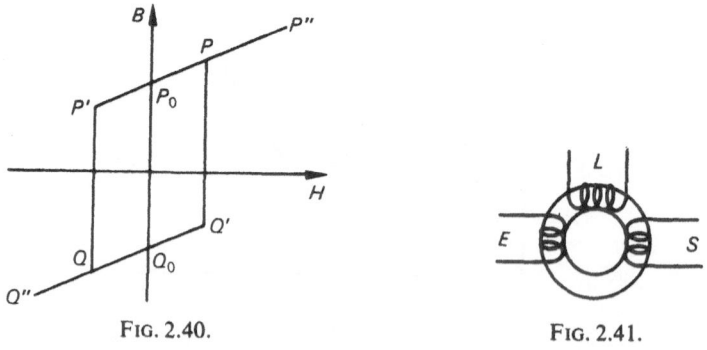

FIG. 2.40.   FIG. 2.41.

which there is a rapid B variation for a weak H variation. If the starting point is Q_0, an H increase would have little effect until a certain threshold (H_Q), then, abruptly, we move to P and section $P_0 P''$. When H returns to 0, the point P_0 is reached. Only the inverse process (H negative) permits us to return to the initial state. If we send a positive pulse on a winding, we can get to P_0; a negative pulse leads to Q_0.

The magnetic core used is a small toroid (Figure 2.41). There is a readout process which tells us the state of this core, but in doing so, it destroys this state. For example, if we send a positive pulse to L the core changes state if it was in Q_0 ($E = 0$) and a pulse is discharged at S; but, if it was in P_0 nothing changes and $S = \bar{E}$ is realized after a delay in L's transmission.

We can also consider E and L as two inputs. In this way, S realizes the operation $\bar{E}L = S$; but, a reset by negative pulse is necessary.

By combining several windings, logical functions can be realized, particularly threshold or majority functions, according to a principle similar to that of the multiple winding relays.

We use a negative readout pulse which induces current in the output circuit if the preceding input was a pulse; the diode placed at the output allows only the P_0 to Q_0 passage and not the inverse.

In order to avoid the destruction due to the readout process, we sometimes use a second core which has a coil to receive current (if it exists) induced by the readout pulse. An instant after a readout pulse appears on the second core, the information which was stored in the main core is replaced. Other methods permit readout without erasing the information.

We observe the interest in having the most rectangular hysteresis cycle possible.

More complex magnetic networks use cores having several apertures (transfluxor). Here we must keep in mind the flux surrounding the apertures.*

Figure 2.42 gives an example from Braun[4]. Passages 1, 2, 3, 4 are in the Q_0 situation after a strong enough negative erasing pulse. The 2, 3 and 3, 4 openings are blocked because the paths on either side are each saturated in one direction. B and C are without effect. Only A can reverse the flux around aperture 1, 2, but not beyond; which gives the possibility of the B operation, then C delivers an output. We can write

---

* Certain networks called 'mad' for 'multiple-aperture devices'.

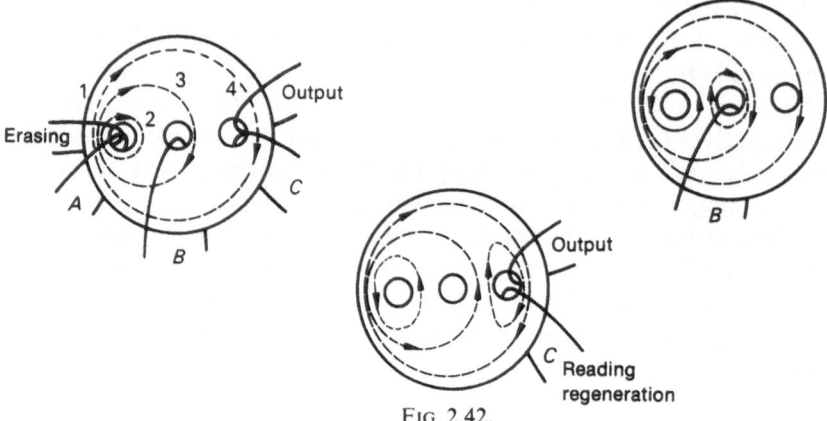

FIG. 2.42.

$C = A$ then B which is an AND type logical function, but with priority. We could send successively positive and negative pulses in C giving readout and regeneration. Thin 'layer film circuits' can also be realized.

Generally a rather particular network layout is needed for magnetic circuits (LOGIMAG, for example): their basic usage remains rapid memory realization for computers.

2.10. CRYOTRONS

These switching devices have the advantage of superconductivity. If we bring an appropriate metal conductor to a very low temperature, near absolute zero, by means of liquid helium, it suddenly loses all resistance as soon as the temperature falls below a certain critical point, and thus constitutes a direct passage for current. Creation of a magnetic field around the conductor (by a winding, for example) switches it back to a non zero resistance. In this way, we define a critical field which varies in function of the temperature.

The functioning of such a network is therefore, exactly analogous to that of the diode.

As an example let us consider the circuit in Figure 2.43(a). Whenever the coil E is excited, without E_0 being excited, the conductor C_1 shows a resistance but C_0 does not. A current circulates exciting C_3 and therefore making C_3 resistant and slowing down the current in the other loop. A current I_1 circulates while I_0 is negligible. If we suppress

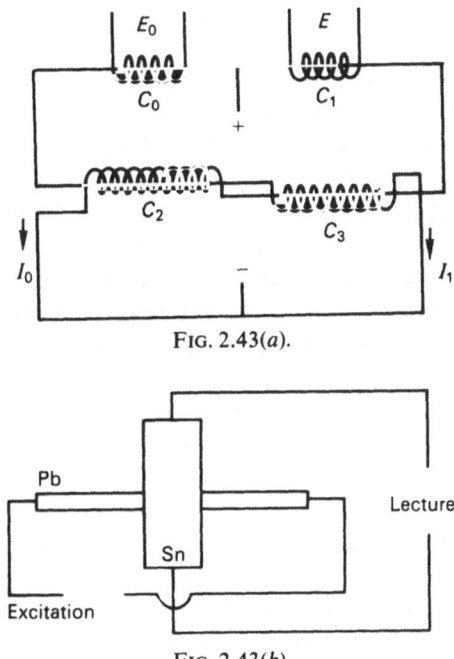

FIG. 2.43(a).

FIG. 2.43(b).

the excitation in E_1, I_0 increases a little but nevertheless remains very weak compared to I_1. If we excite E_0, the inverse phenomenon occurs; thus, E_1 tends to create a current I_1, E_0 a current I_0, and a memory circuit or two input flip-flop is realized.

I_1 and I_0 can be exploited by means of output cryotrons analogous to inputs C_1 and C_0. Six cryotrons realize a flip-flop.

Note that, since these switching devices operate in liquid gas, it is necessary to avoid all heat dissipation. Therefore, the passage of a current in a resistor cannot be permitted. At least one of the two paths necessary to foresee, must be a superconductor. This necessity results in more complex logical design when using cryotrons.

In practice, a cryotron is realized by using two different kinds of wires: a band (of tin, for example) is the conductor, and a second band (of lead) is the magnetic excitation wire placed perpendicularly to the first as shown in Figure 2.43b. Their width varies from about a hundredth of a micron to some hundreds of Ångströms. There is also need for a support. Nevertheless we can hope to put more than 10 000 points by cm³.

2.11. FLUIDIC LOGIC

The fluidic (or hydraulic) to electric analogy is generally well known by cyberneticists. It is also true that in our particular case, control of some fluid permits the realization of basic logical functions.

Fluidic circuits give rise to some very interesting realizations: they are simple and rugged (especially static circuits). They are not sensible to many parameters such as temperature, electromagnetic phenomena, radiations, and vibrations; and they are not costly.

But they have the inconvenience of being slow to propagate signals and difficult to construct because they call for complicated aero-dynamic considerations.

Their industrial advantages, however, are often more important than their disadvantages since their response time is sufficient in most cases.

Several types of circuits exist or are under study. There are two large classes; the devices using mechanical displacement (contact springs, balls, diaphragms) and devices without mechanical displacement which thus avoids mechanical restraint such as friction and dilatation; they make direct use of the flowing properties of liquids (particularly the phenomena of boundary layer).

2.11.1. *Fluidic logical devices using mechanical displacement*

a. *Flapper valve obturation networks*

Consider the network schematized in Figure 2.44. At the input there is a supply button P connected to base B through a throttling. A flapper valve L permits us to seal B. Pressure can be applied at S. Whenever L is not applied in B, there is a direct flow of current. If, on the contrary, L is stuck, the pressure is found at S. We see at this early stage, that $S = \bar{E}$ is realized if E is the variable attributed to the L position. (L = stuck, $d = 0$, $E = 0$.)

If we consider the curve giving the output pressure P_s as a function

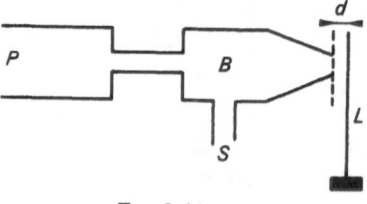

FIG. 2.44.

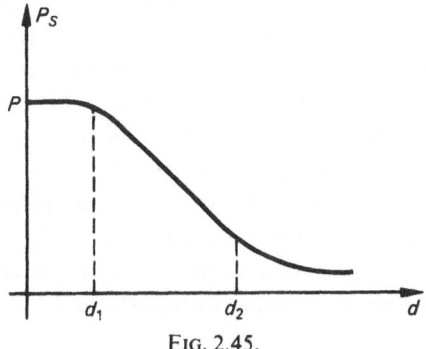

FIG. 2.45.

of d (0 or very weak output flow the same as we consider electronic circuits as being connected to load of large impedance), we see that (Figure 2.45) d can vary between a very small value and a very large value d_2, the output pressure varying from a value near P to a value near 0. This device can therefore play the part of an amplifier in the way that a transistor does. Furthermore, by attributing a logical value to the position of L (or to d) opposite of that defined in Figure 2.44, we obtain an output equivalent to the power of the amplified input.

Figure 2.46 shows the practical realization of the input of this kind

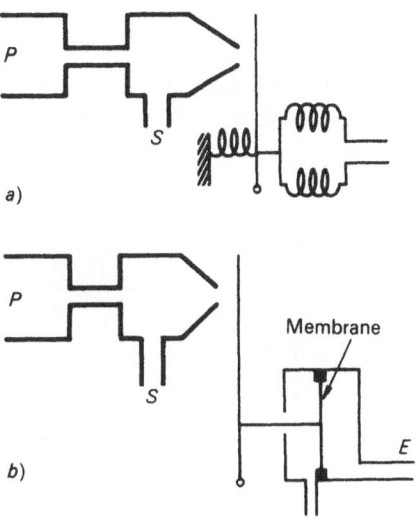

FIG. 2.46.

of network. The valve's moves are directed by a diaphragm in a capsule as in Figure 2.46b or simply by a barometric capsule (Figure 2.46a). If, instead of supplying a base pressure P, we use this base as input, an AND circuit is realized since $S = E \cdot P$; if, instead of applying a force from the capsule on the valve, we apply several forces from several input capsules, we obtain the operation $S = P(E_1 + E_2 + \cdots)$.

A diagram of this type of realization is given in Figure 2.47. The use of P as a constant power source leads to $S = E_1 + E_2$; that is, to the OR operator. The major inconvenient of these components is the lengthy response time (the bandwidth is about 1 Hz.).

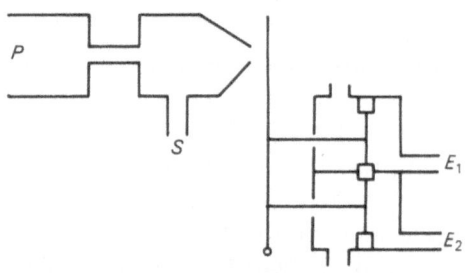

FIG. 2.47.

We must mention here that networks which directly use diaphragm effects also exist.

b. *Spool valve networks*

Consider the diagram in Figure 2.48 (included is a simplified representation in which the two possible paths are shown, the heavier line is the rest state).

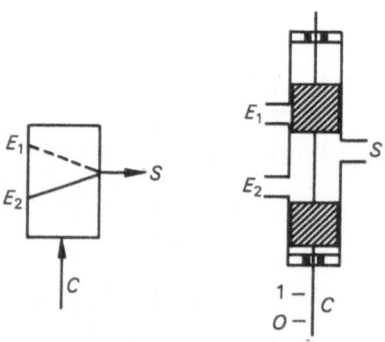

FIG. 2.48.

If we associate the variable C with the spool valve position, we see that for $C = 0$ the flux goes from E_2 to S, for $C = 1$, it goes from E_1 to S, that is $S = E_1C + E_2\bar{C}$. Under these conditions E_1 and E_2 are bias pressures.

By letting $E_1 = 1$ and $E_2 = 0$ (1 signifies that we apply pressure) we obtain an amplifier $S = C$. By letting $E_1 = 0$ and $E_2 = 1$ we obtain a NOT circuit, $S = \bar{C}$. The spool valve can be handled in different ways as the contact spring in the preceding section.

Starting with this basic element, several arrangements are possible. We mention two interesting examples here.

In the diagram in Figure 2.49, operator 1 realizes $\bar{A}$, operator 2 realizes $\bar{A}B + A\bar{B}$. The output therefore, represents the dilemma function $S = A \oplus B$. An auxiliary pressure should be applied at input E_2 of the first operator.

Figure 2.50 represents a memory device with inscription input (I) and reading input (L). Suppose that $E = 0$ and we apply pressure at I. Operator 2 receives the command E; that is 0; the output is therefore

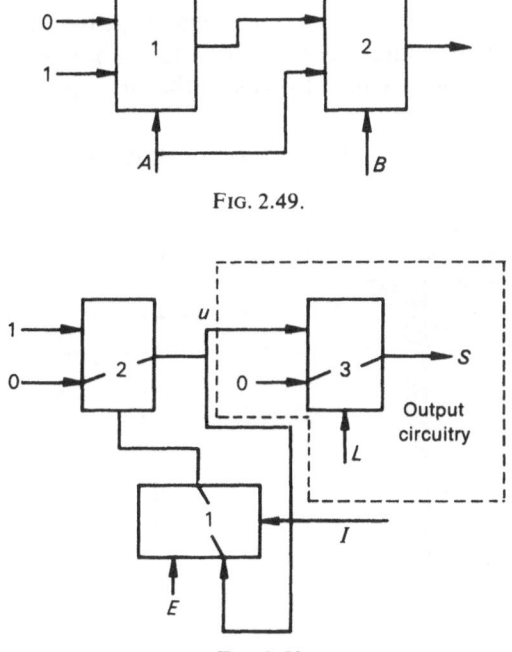

FIG. 2.49.

FIG. 2.50.

$U = 0$ and a readout signal gives $S = 0$. If $E = 1$, we have, $U = 1$ and $S = 1$. If the writing signal disappears, the information is stored, since U is looped onto the second 1 input. Here we are sure that we have a memory circuit.

Our last observation is that the AND and OR functions are realized by the basic element in a simple fashion. If, in fact, $E_2 = 0$ the general output expression is $S = E_1C$, if $E_1 = 1$ the general output expression is $C + E_2\bar{C}$ which after logical simplification is equivalent to $S = C + E_2$.

There exists variations of these spool valves which permit the realization of more complicated functions.

The switching speed of such devices is relatively low but at least as rapid as the precedingly described devices. They are small in size and printed type circuits, blocks in which connections channels are cut and folders in which the spool valves are introduced can be realized.

c. *Ball systems*

Here a ball plays the part of obturator; it moves freely in a cylinder between two entries 1 and 2 as a function of command inputs 3 and 4 (Figure 2.51). Two equilibrium positions of the ball (up and down) are defined. Channels 1 and 2 are attached to the pressure supply P. We also use a 5th channel which figures on the simplified diagram given in Figure 2.52.

At rest 3, 4, and 5 are attached to the atmosphere; the ball is in the

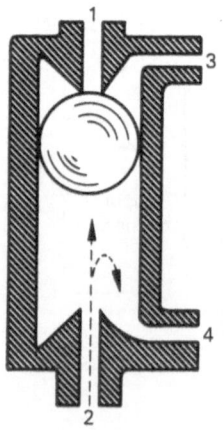

FIG. 2.51.

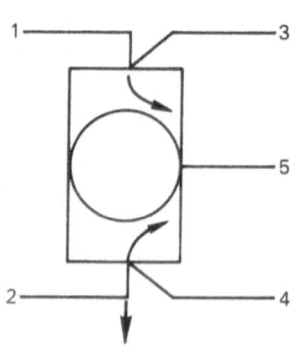

FIG. 2.52.

center of the cylinder. Application of a pressure step at 3 disturbs equilibrium; the ball seals the lower base and, with input 4, the upper base.

By taking the output at 2, an amplification signal introduced at 3 is realized since if the ball is stuck, a signal at 3 makes all the supply pressure available at this output.

Diverse arrangements permit us to obtain AND and OR operators. By placing two elementary cells in series as in Figure 2.53 we obtain an AND circuit operating in the following way:

The inputs are apertures 3a and 3b. The apertures 4 and 5 of the 2 elements are grounded (atmospheric pressure). Apertures 1 and 3 are supplied by pressure P. The output is taken at aperture 2b. When there is no input, the balls are in equilibrium and the flux flows directly from 2b to 4b: $S = 0$. When there is input only at E_b, the ball B cannot stick to the lower base because the flux finds a path towards 4a. But, if E_a is also excited, the output conditions at level are realized: $S = E_a \cdot E_b$. The reader can use similar reasoning to study the OR circuit in Figure 2.54 which uses a modified form of the base cell (2 supplementary apertures). The caliber of the constrictions which can be observed, makes the functioning of these operators more or less convenient.

We mention in passing that the network in Figure 2.52 behaves like a dull element because whenever the ball is caught in the flux 1-5 and 2-5, it remains in equilibrium in the center. The practical realization of

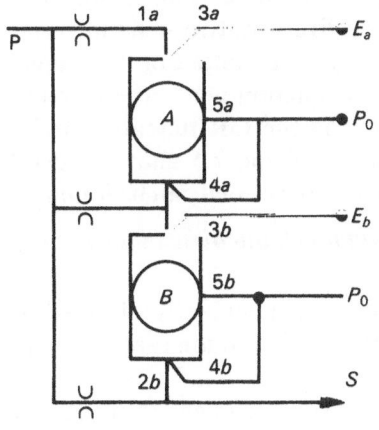

Fig. 2.53.

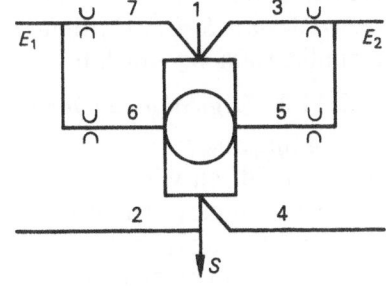

Fig. 2.54.

this device leads to enormous technical problems, but there are very few existing networks which can simulate three-value logic.

The study of miniaturization for ball networks is practically exhausted. By using balls of diameter less than a millimeter and pressure in the order of 10 atmospheres, we have obtained a flip-flop frequency in the order of 100 kHz. It is not cumbersome and the functioning conditions are wide.

An example of a particular realization is the logical transiflux cell (copyright Ugine/CPOAC). It employs three balls of different diameters, placed in a complicated metal or plastic container. Its exterior form is that of a cylinder with four apertures: two inputs; one output, and an exhaust (this last aperture is not represented in the diagram of Figure 2.55).

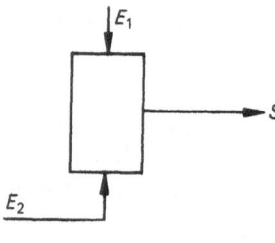

Fig. 2.55.

If pressure is constantly applied at E_1 ($E_1 = 1$) we obtain $S = \bar{E}_2$; if E_1 is considered as an input, $S = E_1\bar{E}_2$ is realized. This is the basic cell function. Amplification is readily realized by two cells in series making $S = \bar{E}_2$ and $S' = \bar{S}$; that is $S' = E_2$ at the output of the second cell for which we let $E' = S'$. The AND function needs the E_2 complementation, therefore also two cells, and the OR function can be realized with $S = \bar{\bar{E}_1\bar{E}_2}$, that is three cells. Table 2.5 shows several mountings among which those we have just described can be found.

2.11.2. *Logical fluidic devices without mechanical displacement*

a. *Amplifiers*

Jets of fluid, on which there are other jets conveniently directed or dosed, are employed in this type of device. Two solutions are possible:

(a) Either simply create a jet interaction as shown in Figure 2.56 by means of a jet command at C. The absence or presence of pressure at C is characterized by the possibility of recovering the main jet going

TABLE 2.5.

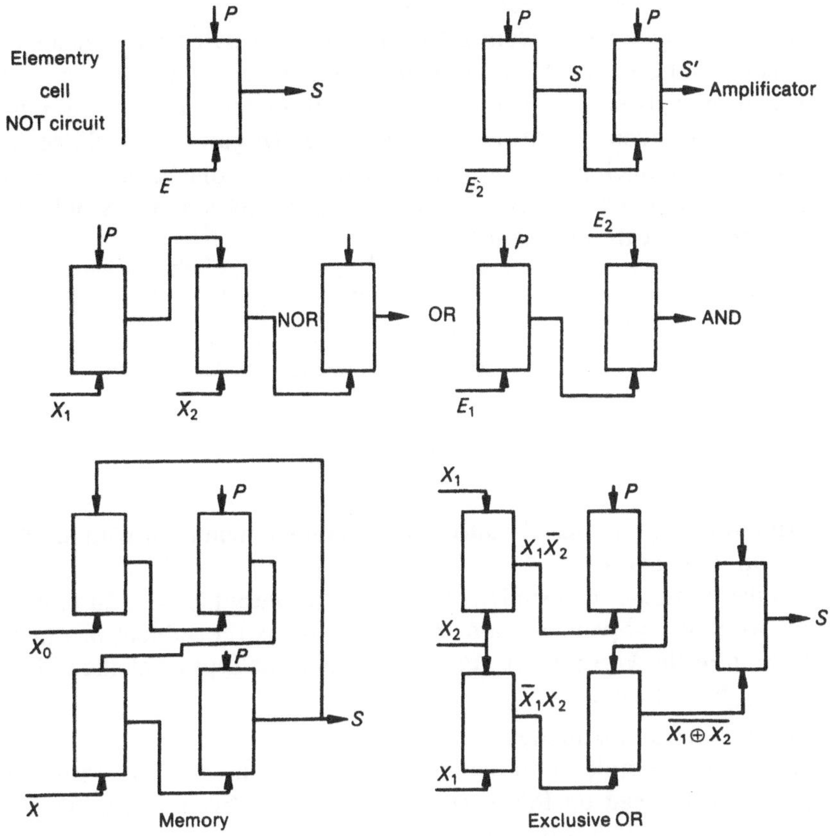

Elementry cell NOT circuit

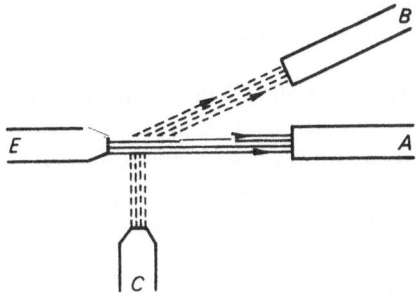

FIG. 2.56.

from E to A or B. The pressure change at A (for example) is generally much higher than that needed in the control tube.

(b) Use a laminar jet from E to A to create turbulence by means of C. This solution exploits aerodynamic phenomena which we shall not explain here. It should be remembered that under certain conditions the jet can become perturbed and diverges (Figure 2.57). Since its section has a much larger surface, we can recover only a small part of the flux coming from E at A and a weak transmission at C would be sufficient to create turbulence.

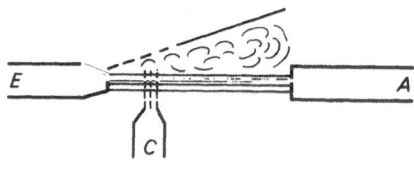

FIG. 2.57.

In both cases, a logical equivalent of complementation with amplification is recovered at A.

In the first case, it is sufficient to take B as output to have amplification without complementation. This network is the subject of much research in the U.S.S.R. A computer, using this type of element, has already been realized.

b. *Jet interaction networks*

We give an example of an operator realized by this process. Multiple applications based on this system have already been studied in the U.S.A. and the U.S.S.R. Printed circuit techniques are used for their fabrication. Sheets cut out according to special patterns are piled one on another forming 'walls' between which the liquid flows. (Figure 2.58). These networks are quite rugged and have wide tolerance specifications.

In Figure 2.59 we have an OR circuit in which the flux flow comes from U and, in the absence of a jet arriving from E_1 or E_2, is indifferently distributed to S_1 and S_2. A weak pressure P directs it towards S_2. If on the contrary there is pressure applied at E_1 or E_2, the flux is directed toward S_1 the principal output of the network. An AND circuit is better realized by dosing E_1 and E_2. Figure 2.59 also gives a schematic representation.

If we consider the U pressure as an input, the output S_1 realizes

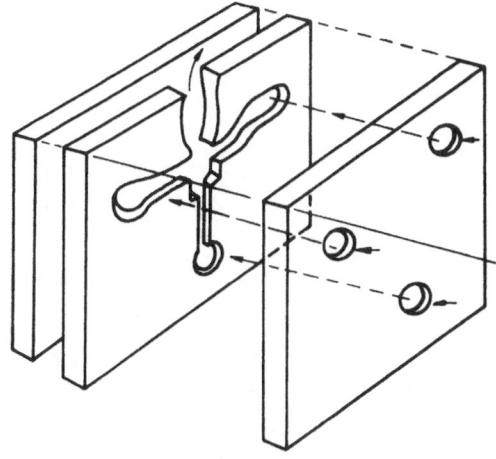

FIG. 2.58.

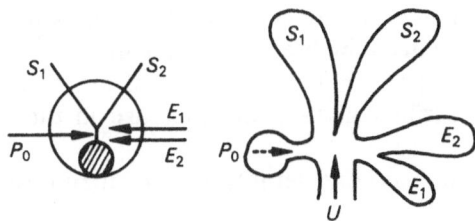

FIG. 2.59.

$U(E_1 + E_2)$, the output S_2 realizes $U\bar{E}_1\bar{E}_2$. Instead of injection, suction study for the inputs at P_0 is being done on these networks. If we let '1' be the logical symbol for the absence of suction we see that the flux is directed toward S_2 as soon as one of the inputs is at 0, that is $S_2 = U(\bar{E}_1 + \bar{E}_2)$ and $S_1 = UE_1E_2$.

Letting $U = 1$ we find once again the OR, NOR, NAND, and AND circuits because of the two functionings.

Starting from a neighbouring cell to that described here, a memory circuit can be realized (Figure 2.60). The direction of the jet determined by one of the inputs is preserved by a loop of samples brought from the outputs to the inputs.

c. *Boundary layer control*
Here the phenomena of the boundary layer are used. A command

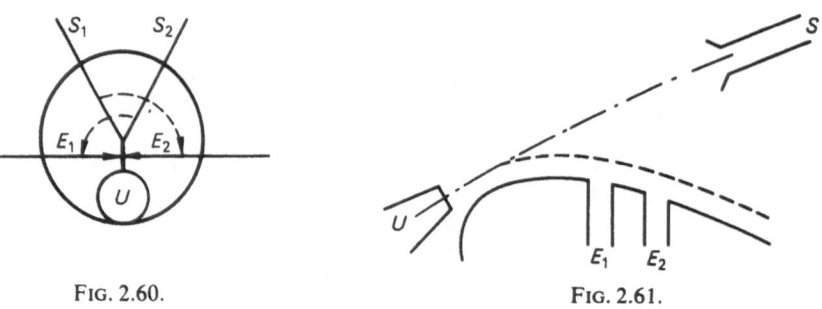

FIG. 2.60.   FIG. 2.61.

pressure arriving at the middle of the 'wall' followed by the flux in absence of command releases the layer.

In the diagram in Figure 2.61, the surface is viewed so that the original flux U follows the wall. If one of the inputs, E_1 or E_2 (or both depending on the intensity), supplies a release flux, a certain magnitude is recovered at S. An OR circuit is realized (or an AND circuit in the case in which both inputs are used). Loops can also be realized by making S arrive in a tube branched to the input.

Note, in conclusion, that the absence of mechanical parts in the systems just described gives a net increase in their reliability and response speed.

Mass production has considerably lowered their cost.

2.12. INTEGRATED CIRCUITS

The past few years have brought much progress in the field of semi-conductors. This has led to the realization of circuits in which the components are now practically microscopic. The different over-lapping layers of semiconductors give more or less complicated and microminiatured operators.

Thus, series of transistors and diodes appear as multiple junctions between the P and N stages. Capacity is established by dielectric layers. Bands of material are needed for the resistors. Numerous problems arise in the logical realization of these circuits: in fact, in these conditions, the diode is the most elementary part and the resistors the most expensive. Direct coupling is therefore particularly interesting.

Among the advantages, other than their being compact, we mention that they generally function at high speeds. Figures 2.62 and 2.63

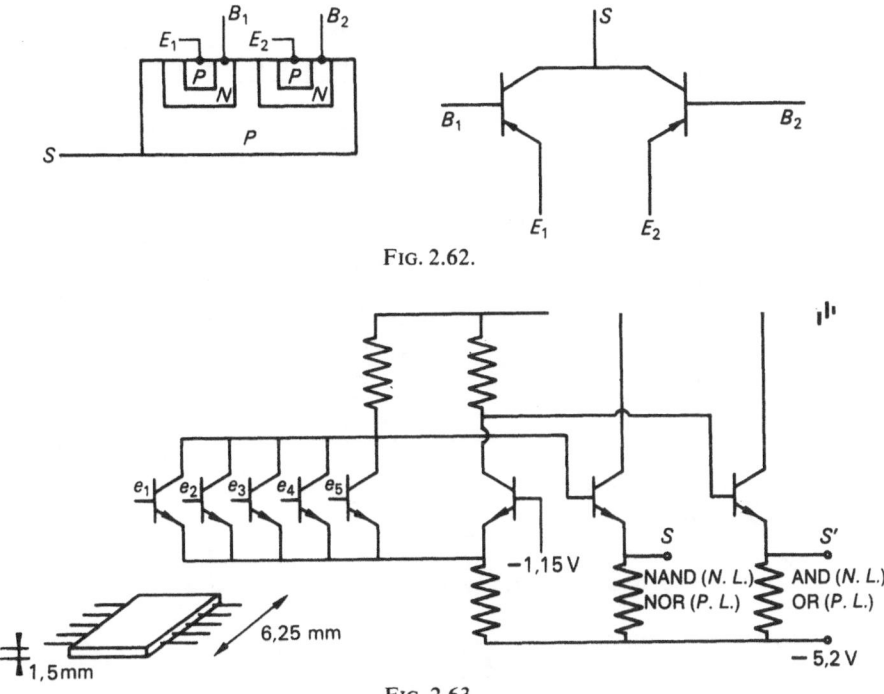

FIG. 2.62.

FIG. 2.63.

show a practical realization of a simple circuit and an example of standard multiple function circuit (Motorola 301): this circuit allows the realization of NAND, AND, NOR, or OR functions depending upon the logic used.

In the first case, the '1' level is 0.75 V, and the '0' level is 1.15 V. In the second case the levels are reversed. The response time is in the order of 10 ns (10^{-8} sec). More than 20 outputs can be used (fan-out) making it smaller than a dime.

2.13. LOGICAL SIMULATORS

Digital training devices have been realized by different companies for university and industrial research. Some use contact relays (Delle simulator verificator-CGE) but most are based on static relays and diodes: Logistor (Alsthom), Logimors (Mors), Logimag (Merlin and Gérin). They are in the form of a device onto which circuits can be wired.

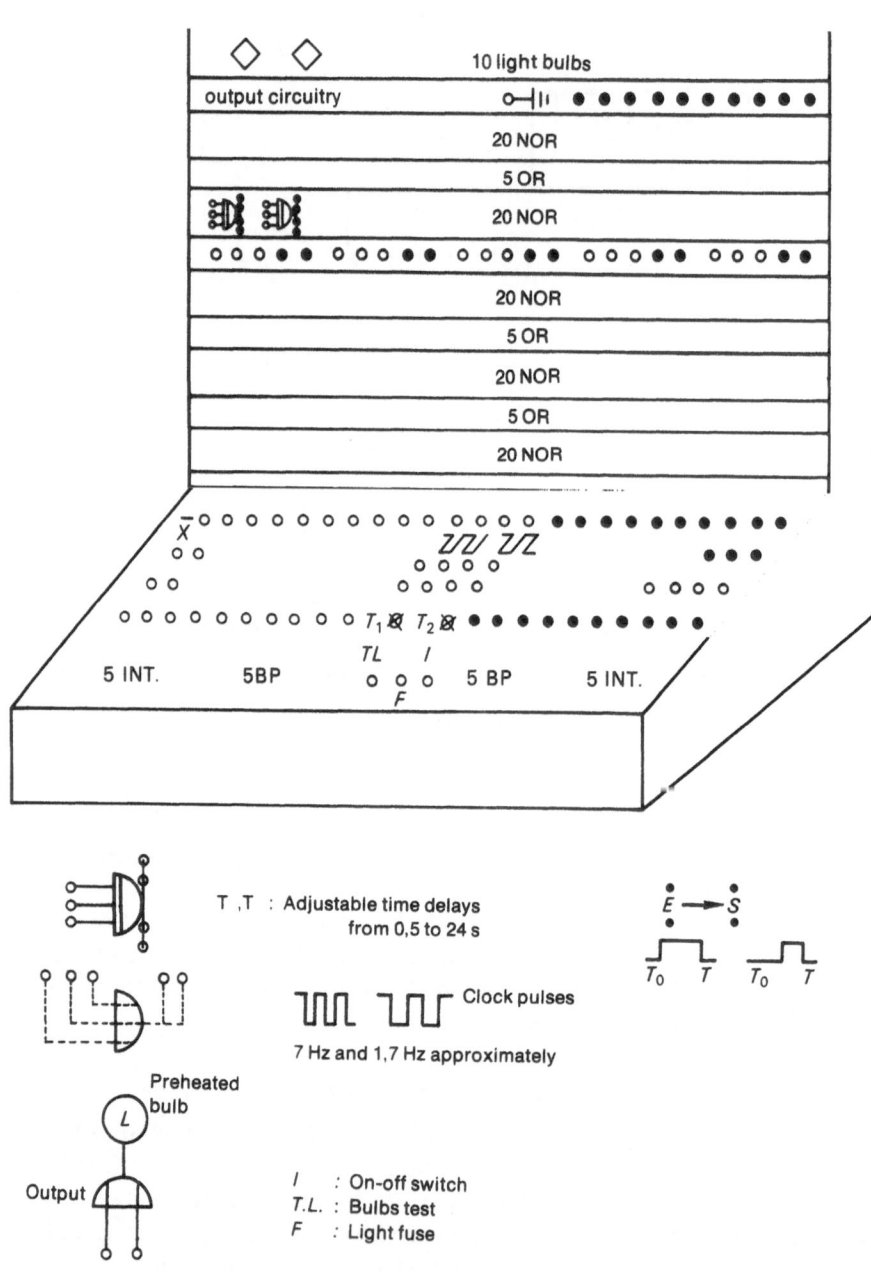

10 light bulbs

output circuitry

20 NOR

5 OR

20 NOR

20 NOR

5 OR

20 NOR

5 OR

20 NOR

5 INT.   5 BP T_1 T_2 5 BP   5 INT.

TL   I

F

T ,T : Adjustable time delays
       from 0,5 to 24 s

Clock pulses

7 Hz and 1,7 Hz approximately

Preheated bulb

Output

$E \longrightarrow S$

T_0 T T_0 T

I   : On-off switch
T.L. : Bulbs test
F   : Light fuse

FIG. 2.64.

Switches or push buttons permit input variable simulation and a series of lights form the output elements. Variable delay elements assure delays up to a few seconds.

More complicated systems use modular blocks already cabled and wired to a given network: Logispace (Socap electric), Digithom (Alsthom).

Generally it is possible to add sets of printed circuits to the digital training device.

Industrial application is made possible by using input elements which permit the reception of high level signals (the most common voltages used in this circuit do not exceed 24 V).

We give a diagram (Figure 2.64) of Logimors digital training device as an example. A fluidic type of simulator has been realized by the 'Conservatoire National des Arts et Métiers' in Paris, France, the connections are made by fitting tubes together, Transiflux type elements are used.

We have mentioned some of the digital training devices made in France. There are, of course, many similar systems made all over the world, they are all based on the same principles.

BIBLIOGRAPHY

[1] MILLMAN. J. and TAUB. H., *Pulse and Digital Circuits* McGraw-Hill, New York, 1956.

[2] CATTERMOLE. K. W., *Circuits à transistors*, Dunod, Paris, 1963 (original in English, 1961).

[3] PRESSMAN. A. I., *Circuits à transistors pour calculateurs numériques*, Dunod, Paris, 1963 (original in English 1961).

[4] BRAUN, E. L., *Digital Computers Design*, Academic Press, New York, 1963.

[5] KHAMBATA, A. J., *Introduction to Integrated Semi-conductor Circuits*, Wiley, New York, 1963.

[6] ALT. F. L., and RUBINOFF, M., *Advances in Computers* – Vol. IV, Academic Press, New York, 1963.

[7] KNOOP, A. R., *Fundamental of Relay Circuit Design*, Reinhold, New York, 1963.

[8] NASLIN. P., *Circuits logiques et automatismes à séquences*, Dunod, Paris, 1965.

[9] PIQUET, P. and PRUDHOMME, R., 'La logique pneumatique. Méthode simple de détermination des circuits logiques pneumatiques utilisant la cellule transiflux', *Automatisme*, (1964) No. 12, 519, 529–31.

[10] WARNER, Jr., R. M., *Integrated Circuits Design. Principles and Fabrication*, McGraw-Hill, New York, 1965.

[11] CARROLL. J. M., *Microelectronic Circuits and Applications*, McGraw-Hill, New York, 1965.

EXERCISES

2.1. What logical operation is realized with the circuit in Figure 2.65? (In positive logic; then in negative logic.)

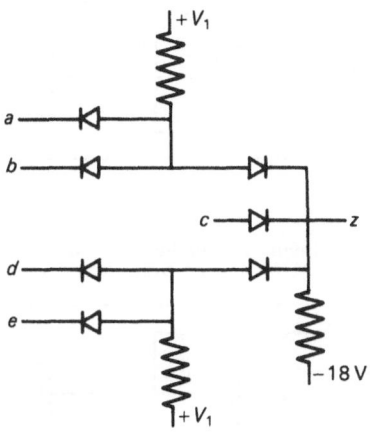

FIG. 2.65.

2.2. What logical operations are performed at the terminals V and W of the circuit in Figure 2.66? (Motorola circuit MC 356/MC 357.)

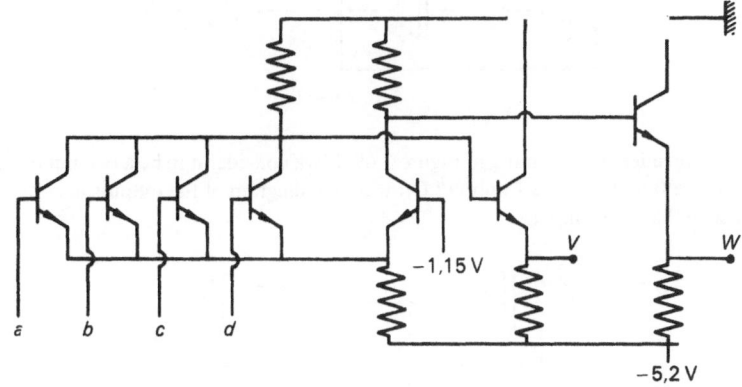

FIG. 2.66.

2.3. Consider the logical flip-flop in Figure 2.67. The uncomplemented output is indicated by y and the complemented output by $\bar{y}$. When a series of commands τ is sent: How does the transistor 1 output vary? Transistor 2? etc. Draw a unique time diagram of the functions $Z_1(t), \ldots, Z_6(t)$ which represents the quantities. Represent $\tau(t)$.

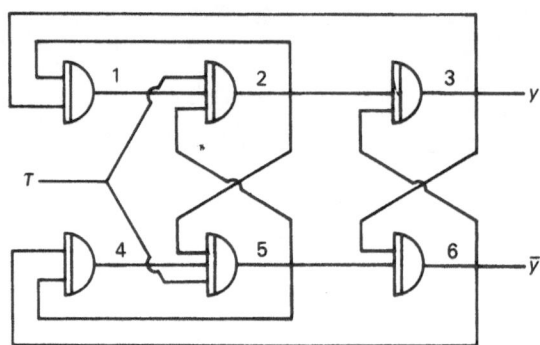

FIG. 2.67.

2.4. Study the flip-flop in Figure 2.68 in the same way.

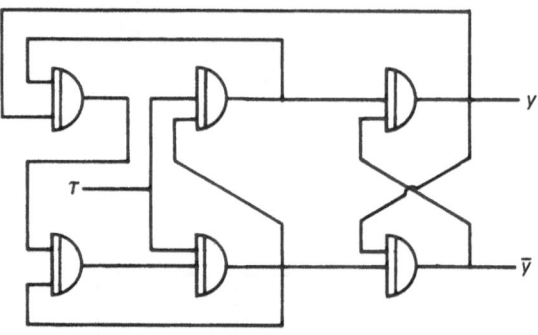

FIG. 2.68.

2.5. Consider the mounting in Figure 2.69. If we consider it to be a two input flip-flop what is the 0 output? The 1 output? Draw a time diagram of the outputs in correspondence with that of the inputs.

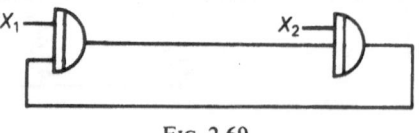

FIG. 2.69.

2.6. Is there a difference in the way in which the flip-flops react to the commands? From this, does the Figure 2.69 mounting seem valid? Why?

2.7. Study the Figure 2.70 circuit in the same way. Does the mounting seem more or less satisfactory? Why?

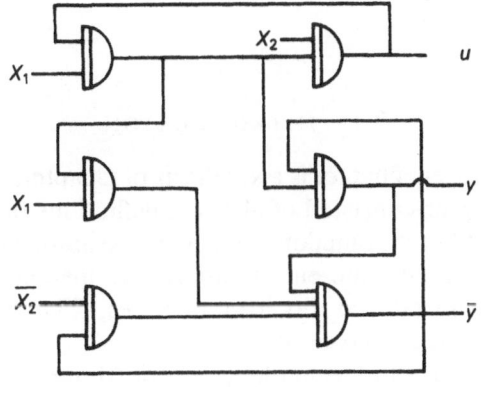

FIG. 2.70.

CHAPTER 3

COMBINATIONAL SYSTEMS

3.1. INTRODUCTION

In a way, the present chapter is a synthesis of Chapters 1 and 2.

The first chapter consisted of abstract definitions of the algebra of Boole and the different functions which can be associated with the set (0,1). We discussed different minimization methods for Boolean functions and introduced Boolean matrices. The second chapter outlined different technologies used.

Now we shall use the technology described in Chapter 2 to apply the methods of Chapter 1 to circuits.

3.2. BOOLEAN ALGEBRA AND TECHNOLOGY

Although diodes can be used both as rectifiers and logical devices, we shall, for the moment, consider only their latter function. We intend to show how the use of functions defined on the set (0, 1), which were discussed in Chapter 1, explains how a relay, diode, or transistor circuit operates.

3.2.1. *The algebra of relay circuits*

Let the binary variable x denote a normally open contact and $\bar{x}$ a normally closed contact of a relay X. If the relay X is operated $(X = 1)$, the normally open contact is closed $(x = 1)$ while the normally closed contact is open $(\bar{x} = 0)$ and vice-versa.

In Chapter 2, we showed that the conductibility of these contacts, when mounted in series, is the Boolean product of their individual conductibilities; whereas, if mounted in parallel, it is the reunion (Boolean sum, disjunction) of their conductibilities.

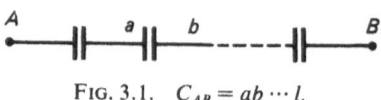

FIG. 3.1. $C_{AB} = ab \cdots l.$

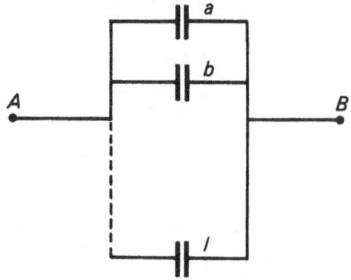

FIG. 3.2. $C_{AB} = a + b + \cdots l.$

We shall show that the algebra which describes how relays operate is the algebra of Boole. The results are indicated in Table 3.1.

3.2.2. *Diode circuit algebra*

Consider the diagrams in Figures 3.3 and 3.4 (positive logic).

$$z = a + b + \cdots + 1 \quad \text{(Figure 3.3)}$$
$$z = a \cdot b \cdot \cdots + 1 \quad \text{(Figure 3.4)}.$$

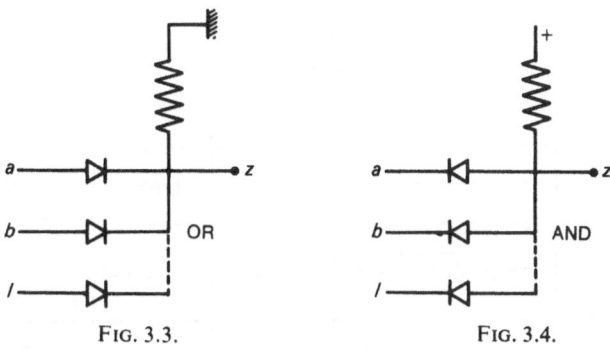

FIG. 3.3.   FIG. 3.4.

In the same way it can be shown that diode circuit algebra is Boolean algebra.

3.2.3. *Transistor circuit algebra*

Every transistor realizes the NOR (Figure 3.5a) or NAND functions (Figure 3.5b) and every combination of transistors leads to circuits which have their conductibility function expressed only by the NOR or NAND functions.

TABLE 3.1.

Type of the contact	Circuit	Associated Boolean expression	Equivalent	Equivalent circuit
Parallel connections of contacts		$a+a$	a	
		$a+b$	$b+a$	
		$a+1$	1	
		$a+b+c$	$(a+b)+c$	
Series connection of contacts		$a \cdot a$	a	
		$a \cdot 0$	0	
		$a \cdot b$	$b \cdot a$	
		$a \cdot b \cdot c$	$(ab) \cdot c$	
Parallel-series connection of contacts		$ab+ac$	$a \cdot (b+c)$	
		$a+bc$	$(a+b)(a+c)$	
Connection of the two complementary contacts of the same relay		$a+\bar{a}$	1	
		$a \cdot \bar{a}$	0	

FIG. 3.5(a). $z = a \downarrow b \downarrow \cdots \downarrow l = \bar{a}\bar{b} \cdots \bar{l}.$ FIG. 3.5(b). $z = a/b \cdots /l = \bar{a} + \bar{b} + \cdots + \bar{l}.$

3.3.   COMBINATIONAL SYSTEMS

DEFINITION.   Given a circuit with binary switching elements, we say that it is combinational if at any given instant the outputs are expressed as a function of the inputs only, at the same instant.

In other words, if there are $x_1, ..., x_p$ possible inputs, the system is combinational if the z_i output at the instant considered, is expressed as a function of the inputs,

$$z_i = f_i(x_1, ..., x_p) \tag{3.1}$$

and is not modified unless the inputs change.

A combinational system is therefore defined by a truth table or a relation analogous to (3.1).

From a technological point of view, we shall only consider the following combination systems:

(a) relay systems formed by series-parallel mountings of relay contacts or switches.

(b) diode systems formed by combination of the circuits in Figures 3.3 and 3.4.

(c) transistor (p-n-p or n-p-n) systems formed by combining the same or different type transistors.

There will be occasion to consider combinational dipoles with one or more inputs and a single output, and combinational multipoles with one or more inputs and several outputs.

3.4.   COMBINATIONAL DIPOLES

We shall successively study the analysis then the synthesis of combinational dipoles. In synthesis study, we shall try to represent the system with a minimum of switching elements in order to cut cost.

3.4.1. *Combinational dipole analysis*
In order to know how a combinational system functions, given its circuit diagram, the Boolean output equation which gives the truth table must be formed.

The Boolean function is first written in terms of the operators corresponding to the circuit's switching elements. Then we search the equivalent function expressed in terms of the AND, OR, NOT operators. We shall consider three cases:

(1) a relay system;
(2) a diode system;
(3) a transistor system.

Relay systems

We consider the dipole relay in Figure 3.6. By Kirchhoff's laws, we have the Boolean function representing the output value:

$$z = d(ab + \bar{a}c) + a\bar{d}$$

from which we deduce the Karnaugh map in Figure 3.9.

This map gives every value of the variables a, b, c and d; thus, it gives the output value from the state of the different contacts.

Diode systems

Operators 1, 2, 3, 4, 5, 6 in the circuit in Figure 3.7 are those in Figures 3.3 and 3.4. 1, 2, 4, 5 are AND circuits; 3 and 6 are OR circuits.

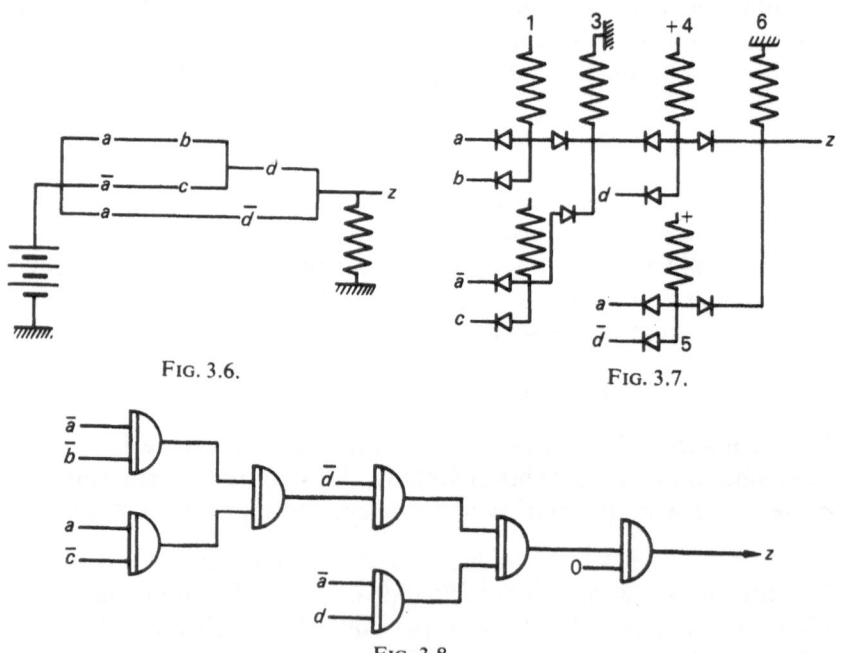

FIG. 3.6.

FIG. 3.7.

FIG. 3.8.

ab cd	00	01	11	10
00	0	0	1	1
01	0	0	1	0
11	1	1	1	0
10	0	0	1	1

FIG. 3.9.

The output expression is therefore:

$$z = (ab + \bar{a}c)d + ad.$$

Figure 3.9 is the corresponding Karnaugh map.

Transistor systems

The output expression of the circuit in Figure 3.8 is:

$$z = [(((\bar{a} \downarrow \bar{b}) \downarrow (a \downarrow \bar{c})) \downarrow \bar{d}) \downarrow (\bar{a} \downarrow d)] \downarrow 0.$$

Its development in terms of AND, OR, NOT is

$$z = (ab + \bar{a}c)d + a\bar{d},$$

expression which we have already encountered in the first two examples.

General technological systems

It is sometimes important to know if switching elements have bilateral conduction or not, because we generally do not combine relays and unilateral conduction electronic devices.

The output is known by application of Kirchhoff's laws. Consider the circuit in Figure 3.10. Assuming all elements to be of unilateral conduction, we may write:

$$z = \overline{(\text{maj } (a, b, c) \downarrow (b \,/\, \bar{c}))} \,/\, \text{maj } (\bar{a}, b, d)$$
$$z = \overline{(\text{maj } (a, b, c) \downarrow (\bar{b} + c))} + \text{maj } (\bar{a}, b, d)$$
$$= \text{maj } (a, b, c) + \bar{b} + c + \text{maj } (\bar{a}, b, d)$$
$$z = ab + bc + ca + \overline{(\bar{a}b + \bar{a}d + bd)} + \bar{b} + c$$
$$= a + \bar{b} + c + (a + \bar{b})(a + \bar{d})(\bar{b} + \bar{d})$$
$$= a + \bar{b} + c + a\bar{b} + a\bar{d} + \bar{b}\bar{d} = a + \bar{b} + c$$

from which we derive the corresponding Karnaugh map in Figure 3.11.

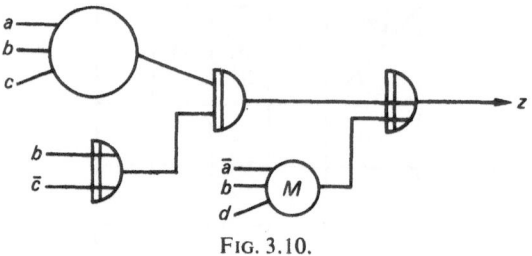

FIG. 3.10.

ab cd	00	01	11	10
00	1	0	1	1
01	1	0	1	1
11	1	1	1	1
10	1	1	1	1

FIG. 3.11.

3.4.2. *Combinational dipole synthesis*

The problem is the realization, in one of the three preceding technologies, of a circuit which operates according to a given truth table at minimal cost.

First we must define what we mean by the 'cost' of a circuit, then search the minimal cost circuit.

3.4.2.1. *Cost of a circuit*

DEFINITION. The cost of a circuit is the number of switching elements necessary for its realization.

Cost therefore depends upon technology. At present, we intend to consider only the three technologies already mentioned.

(a) *Relay circuits*. The operating function of a relay circuit can be expressed as a sum of products or a product of sums. For example, the expression

$$z = ab + \bar{c}d + a\bar{c} \quad \text{(form 1)}$$

can be written

$$z = (a + \bar{c})(a + d)(b + \bar{c}) \quad \text{(form 2)}$$

by applying the distributivity laws to the '+' and '·' operations.

The cost of a relay network is the number of contacts used, therefore the number of letters in the corresponding Boolean function.

In the present example, forms 1 and 2, need 6 contacts.

(b) *Diode circuits*. Here we need only consider the AND and OR circuits. If an AND (or OR) circuit has k $(k > 1)$ inputs, its cost is k (k diodes are necessary for its realization). If $k = 1$, the cost is 0 because no diodes are needed.

Consider the Boolean output function

$$z = a(b + cd) + bde + c.$$

Let $m_1 = a(b + cd)$, $m_2 = bde$, $m_3 = c$. The cost of the circuit, $z = m_1 + m_2 + m_3$ is three. We compute the individual costs of the m_1, m_2, and m_3 circuits: the cost of m_3 is zero, the cost of m_2 is three (three input AND circuit). To compute the cost of m_1, we proceed in the following way: two diodes are necessary for the realization of cd, two diodes for $b + cd$ and two for $a(b + cd)$, that is 6 diodes. The cost of the output circuit is therefore 12 diodes.

Transistor circuits. If we consider a Boolean function for which the only operator is NOR, the evaluation of its cost is very simple since its cost is the number of transistors used to represent this circuit.

Since the NOR function is not associative, the circuit's various transistors correspond to the parentheses in the output function.

$(a \downarrow b \downarrow c)$ corresponds to one transistor.

$((a \downarrow b \downarrow c) \downarrow (c \downarrow d))$ corresponds to 3 transistors.

We notice that generally the number of transistors corresponding to a Boolean function expressed in terms of the NOR operator, equals the number of left (or right) parentheses in the expression.

As an example consider:

$$z = ((((a \downarrow b \downarrow c) \downarrow d) \downarrow e) \downarrow (f \downarrow (g \downarrow h) \downarrow d) \downarrow e).$$

The system is realized with 6 transistors (there are 6 left parentheses and therefore 6 right parentheses).

Realization of a minimal system. In Chapter 1, we explained three minimization methods for Boolean functions. The Quine-McCluskey and Karnaugh map methods are two different ways of applying the same minimization method, (see the note at the end of Appendix 5, Chapter 1), but Boolean function decomposition is based on an entirely different principle.

3.4.2.2. *Karnaugh and Quine-McCluskey methods*

In both these methods, we look for the prime implicants. The final expression for the initial function f is of the form (see Appendix A, Chapter 1):

$$f = A_1 \mathsf{T} \cdots \mathsf{T} A_n \quad \text{with} \quad A_i = (a_{i_1} \omega \cdots \omega \, a_{i_{q_i}}).$$

Four observations can be made:

(1) The number of terms, n, chosen to represent the function is minimal.

(2) Each term is a prime implicant.

(3) This is a two-level representation.

(4) If a Boolean function is expressed in terms of one of the eight possible pairs of $(\mathsf{T}\omega)$ operators, its two-level minimization is performed by first expressing the function as $(\mathsf{T}, \omega) = (+, \cdot)$ or $(\mathsf{T}, \omega) = (\cdot, +)$ (depending on which class the initial function belongs to) and minimizing this form. The reduced form thus obtained is then expressed in terms of the initial operators which gives the desired minimal form.

Transistor circuits. The Boolean function which is the expression for the circuit's output, belongs to the second class. To minimize the function expressed as a pɪoduct of sums $(\mathsf{T}, \omega = \cdot, +)$ the complementary function is used (Appendix 4, Chapter 1).

The two-level minimal form obtained by the Karnaugh and Quine-McCluskey methods, is written:

$$f = A_1 \downarrow \cdots \downarrow A_n, \qquad A_i = (a_{i_1} \downarrow \cdots \downarrow a_{i_{q_i}}).$$

Each A_i term and the combination of the A_i needs a transistor for its realization. The two stage minimal transistorized circuit is therefore realized by the minimal form obtained by either of the methods with n chosen minimum.

Example. Find, if it exists, a two-level circuit simpler than the one in Figure 3.12.

We can write:

$$f = [(\bar{b} \downarrow c) \downarrow (\bar{a} \downarrow b) \downarrow (\bar{a} \downarrow \bar{c}) \downarrow (\bar{c} \downarrow d)].$$

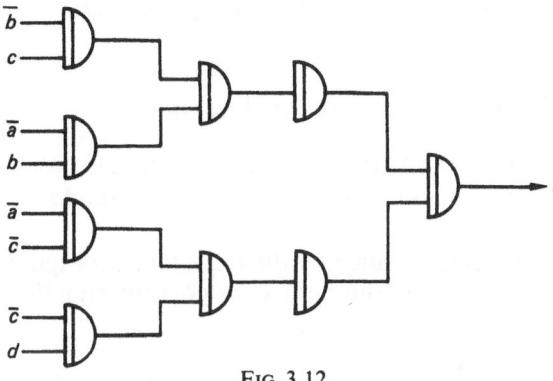

FIG. 3.12.

Furthermore, the NOR series-circuits have no influence:

$$(a \downarrow 0) \downarrow 0 = a.$$

We may write:

$$f = (\bar{b} + c)(\bar{a} + b)(\bar{a} + \bar{c})(\bar{c} + d).$$

By Appendix 1.A.4 we shall study the complementary function:

$$\bar{f} = b\bar{c} + a\bar{b} + ac + c\bar{d}.$$

Figure 3.13 is the Karnaugh map of $\bar{f}$. We may write:

$$\bar{f} = a + c\bar{d} + b\bar{c}$$
$$f = \bar{a}(\bar{c} + d)(\bar{b} + c).$$

ab \ cd	00	01	11	10
00	0	1	1	1
01	0	1	1	1
11	0	0	1	1
10	1	1	1	1

FIG. 3.13.

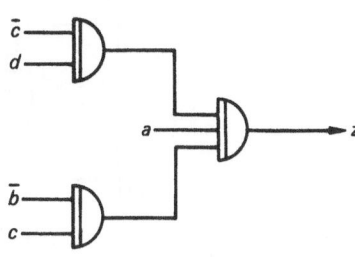

FIG. 3.14.

The two-level minimal form of f in terms of the NOR operator is:

$$f = a \downarrow (\bar{c} \downarrow d) \downarrow (\bar{b} \downarrow c).$$

Figure 3.14 represents the corresponding circuit.

Note. Starting with a two-level NOR circuit, it is possible to build a three- (or more) level circuit by applying the pseudo-distributive or absorption laws.

Consider the circuit defined by the truth table in Figure 3.15. If we use the Karnaugh map method, the only possible simplification is:

$$f = (a \downarrow b \downarrow \bar{c}) \downarrow (\bar{a} \downarrow \bar{b} \downarrow c)$$
$$= ((a \downarrow b) \downarrow (c \downarrow 0)) \downarrow ((a \downarrow 0)(b \downarrow 0) \downarrow c)),$$

which shows the need of six transistors for the realization of this circuit (Figure 3.16); but by using the absorption law (Section 1.4.1) for the NOR circuits, $a \downarrow (a \downarrow b) \downarrow c = a \downarrow \bar{b} \downarrow c$, we may write,

$$f = [a \downarrow b \downarrow (b \downarrow c)] \downarrow [\bar{a} \downarrow b \downarrow (b \downarrow c)]$$

and the corresponding circuit needs only five transistors (Figure 3.17).

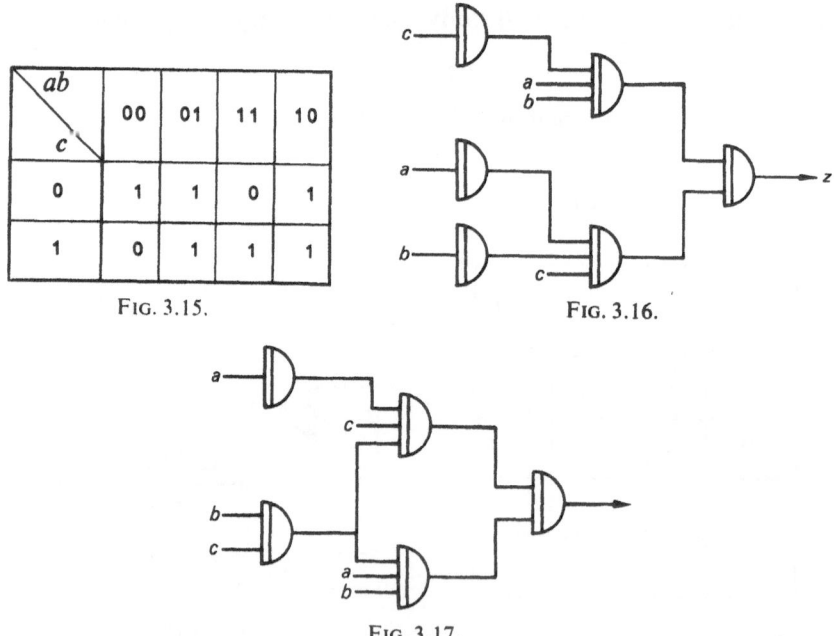

ab c	00	01	11	10
0	1	1	0	1
1	0	1	1	1

Fig. 3.15.   Fig. 3.16.

Fig. 3.17.

This is no practical method for obtaining a minimal circuit because we cannot affirm that it simplifies the circuit.

The reader interested in this question can refer to Maley and Earle [4], who give some interesting ideas for problems involving not more than four variables, but deduces no systematic approach.

Relay circuits. For relay circuits, the Karnaugh and Quine-McCluskey methods lead to one of the two following forms:

$$f = m_1 + \cdots + m_p \qquad m_i = (a_{i_1} \cdots a_{i_{q_i}})$$
$$f = M_1 \cdots M_q \qquad M_j = b_{j_1} + \cdots + b_{j_{q_j}}.$$

The m_i and M_j are prime implicants.

Both forms (conjunctive and disjunctive) contain a minimal number of prime implicants for the reduction of the function. However, in order to obtain the minimal circuit (the circuit having the least number of contacts), all the conjunctive and disjunctive reduced minimal forms must be compared.

Example. Consider the following function:

$$f(d, c, b, a) = R(2, 4, 5, 7, 8, 13) + R_\phi(0, 1, 6, 9, 10, 15).$$

We apply the Quine-McCluskey method (Figure 3.18); f has seven prime implicants

$$
\begin{aligned}
&A = \bar{a}\bar{c} \quad && D = \bar{b}\bar{d} \quad && G = bd \\
&B = \bar{b}\bar{c} \quad && E = \bar{a}b \\
&C = \bar{a}\bar{d} \quad && F = \bar{c}d.
\end{aligned}
$$

Figure 3.19 is the prime implicant chart showing the coverings of the necessary terms, from which we deduce the relation:

$$(C+D)(A+C+E)(A+E+F+G)(E+G)(B+D)(F+G) = 1$$
$$(C+D)(A+C+E)(E+G)(B+D)(F+G) = 1$$
$$(G+EF)(D+BC)(A+C+E) = 1$$
$$(G+EF)(BC+DA+DE+DC) = 1.$$

The solutions are therefore:

$$(GBC), \quad (GDA), \quad (GDC), \quad (GDE), \quad (DEF).$$

The cost for all these solutions is six since each prime implicant has a cost of two.

0	0, 1	0, 1, 4, 5	A
	0, 2	0, 1, 8, 9	B
1	0, 4	0, 2, 4, 6	C
2	0, 8	0, 2, 8, 10	D
4			
8	1, 5	4, 5, 6, 7	E
	1, 9	1, 5, 9, 13	F
5	2, 6		
6	2, 10	5, 7, 13, 15	G
9	4, 5		
10	4, 6		
	8, 9		
7	8, 10		
13			
	5, 7		
15	5, 13		
	6, 7		
	9, 13		
	7, 15		
	13, 15		

FIG. 3.18.

	2	4	5	7	8	13
A		×	×			
B					×	
C	×	×				
D	×					×
E		×	×	×		
F			×			×
G			×	×		×

FIG. 3.19.

Now consider the complementary function:

$$\bar{f}(a, b, c, d) = R(3, 11, 12, 14) + R_\phi(0, 1, 6, 9, 10, 15).$$

We apply the Quine-McCluskey method (Figure 3.20).
$\bar{f}$ has five prime implicants:

$$A = \bar{a}\bar{b}\bar{c} \qquad C = ab\bar{d} \qquad E = ac$$
$$B = bc\bar{d} \qquad D = \bar{b}d.$$

Figure 3.21 is the prime implicant chart of $\bar{f}$. C and D are essential. We may therefore write:

$$\bar{f} = \bar{b}d + ab\bar{d}$$
$$f = (b + \bar{d})(\bar{a} + \bar{b} + d).$$

The circuit has only five contacts and is therefore minimum.

Diode circuits. The process is identical to that of relays but cost evaluation is different. In the preceding example, in the case of the disjunctive form, each minimal form needed two diodes per prime

0	(0 1) A	1, 3, 9, 11 D
1	1,3	10, 11, 14, 15 E
3	1,9	
6	3,11	
9	(6,14) B	
10	9,11	
12	10,11	
11	10,14	
14	(12,14) C	
	11,15	
15	14,15	

FIG. 3.20.

	3	11	12	14
A				
B				×
C			×	×
D	×	×		
E		×		×

FIG. 3.21.

implicant and three diodes to cover the function, therefore nine diodes. The cost was seven for the normal disjunctive form.

Note. It is possible, using the Karnaugh map, to obtain multi-level realizations which use fewer implicants than two-level circuits.

Let $f = ab + bc + c\bar{a}$. This function has six contacts (or nine diodes). We may express it as $f = b(a + c) + \bar{a}c$, and the corresponding circuit has five contacts (or eight diodes). There is a one-contact or one-diode profit.

In the case of transistor circuits, we have already mentioned the book of Maley and Earle. The method for diodes and relays is the following:

Suppose that in a Karnaugh map, a rectangle of 1 (*A*) contains an enclave of 0 (*B*) as in Figure 3.22.

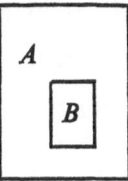

FIG. 3.22.

We may say that the corresponding function f must have points which are simultaneously interior to A and exterior to B.

Therefore, $f = A \cdot \bar{B}$ (the complement in a set theory sense). This method gives a multi-level representation of a circuit.

Example. Consider the Karnaugh map Figures 3.23 and 3.24 (order: c, d, a, b).

$$f = R(1, 3, 5, 8, 9, 13, 14, 15).$$

cd \ ab	00	01	11	10
00	0	1	1	0
01	0	1	0	0
11	0	1	1	1
10	1	1	0	0

FIG. 3.23.

cd \ ab	00	01	11	10
00	0	1	1	0
01	0	1	0	0
11	0	1	1	1
10	1	1	0	0

FIG. 3.24.

If we consider the points 8, 9, 13, 14, 15, we can take (8, 9, 10, 11, 12, 13, 14, 15) for A and (2, 3, 4, 5, 10, 11, 12, 13) for B. In Figure 3.23, A is represented by dashed lines and B by full lines.

In a similar way, consider the points (1, 3, 5, 9, 13, 15). We may take (1, 3, 5, 7, 9, 11, 13, 15) for A and (6, 7, 10, 11, 14, 15) for B. In Figure 3.24 the dashed line contains A and the full line B.

The function can therefore be written:

$$f = c\overline{(\bar{a}d + a\bar{d})} + \overline{ba(c + d)}$$
$$f = c(a + \bar{d})(\bar{a} + d) + b(\bar{a} + \bar{c}\bar{d}),$$

which needs nine relay contacts or 15 diodes. The function corresponding to a two-level circuit would be written:

$$f = \bar{a}b + \bar{a}c\bar{d} + b\bar{c}\bar{d} + acd,$$

which would need 11 relay contacts or 15 diodes.

The three-level realization therefore minimizes the number of relay contacts. In the same way, we could operate on the function's zeros to obtain a three-level conjunctive form of f.

Reconsider the preceding example. Figure 3.25 and Figure 3.26 are the Karnaugh maps of $\bar{f}$.

$$\bar{f} = R(0, 2, 4, 6, 7, 10, 11, 12).$$

$\begin{matrix}ab\\cd\end{matrix}$	00	01	11	10
00	1	0	0	1
01	1	0	1	1
11	1	0	0	0
10	0	0	1	1

$\begin{matrix}ab\\cd\end{matrix}$	00	01	11	10
00	1	0	0	1
01	1	0	1	1
11	1	0	0	0
10	0	0	1	1

FIG. 3.25.   FIG. 3.26.

Consider the points 0, 2, 4, 6, 12. We can take (0, 2, 4, 6, 8, 10, 12, 14) for A and (8, 9, 10, 11, 14, 15) for B as in Figure 3.25.

Consider the points (7, 10, 11). We can take (2, 3, 6, 7, 10, 11, 14, 14) for A and (0, 1, 2, 3, 12, 13, 14, 15) for B as in Figure 3.26. We deduce the expression for $\bar{f}$.

$$\bar{f} = \bar{b}\overline{c(a+\bar{d})} + a\bar{c}(\bar{d} + cd)$$

$$\bar{f} = \bar{b}(\bar{c} + \bar{a}d) + a(c+d)(\bar{c}+\bar{d}) = \bar{b}(\bar{c}+\bar{a}d) + a(c\bar{d}+\bar{c}d)$$

$$f = [b + c(a+\bar{d})](\bar{a} + \bar{c}\bar{d} + cd).$$

This circuit needs nine relay contacts or 15 diodes. The expression of f corresponding to a two-level circuit would be:

$$\bar{f} = \bar{b}\bar{c} + \bar{a}\bar{b}d + a\bar{c}d + ac\bar{d}$$

$$f = (b+c)(a+b+\bar{d})(\bar{a}+c+\bar{d})(\bar{a}+\bar{c}+d),$$

and the corresponding circuit would need 11 relay contacts or 15 diodes. The three-level realization minimizes the number of relay contacts. This method can be used for maps containing 'don't cares'. It is possible to seek circuits having more than three levels, but the method is very complicated.

3.4.2.3. *Utilization of Boolean matrices for the realization of dipoles*

In combinational circuit synthesis considerations, Boolean matrices can be employed with two different objectives. We can use them to see if the envisaged function is decomposable then express it in terms of subfunctions, but we can also use them to see if the function to be realized is decomposable in terms of a certain number of given subfunctions.

The second approach to the problem is particularly adapted to the case in which we use circuits which have already realized complete functions (for example Boolean sums of Boolean products), instead of elementary circuits for the synthesis of a combinational system.

We shall examine these two methods of employing Boolean matrices by studying examples.

a. *Research of the possible decompositions of a Boolean function.* Let

$$f(a, b, c, d, e) = (0, 3, 5, 6, 9, 10, 12, 14, 15, 16, 17, 18, 19, 21, 22, 30).$$

Consider the matrix $E_{Y,X}$, where

$$X = (a, b, c) \qquad Y = (d, e).$$

We observe that this matrix has only four different columns which are grouped in the following way:

$$
\begin{bmatrix}
1 & 0 & 0 & 1 & 0 & 1 & 1 & 0 \\
0 & 1 & 1 & 0 & 1 & 0 & 1 & 1 \\
1 & 1 & 1 & 1 & 0 & 1 & 1 & 0 \\
0 & 0 & 0 & 0 & 0 & 0 & 1 & 0
\end{bmatrix}
\qquad
\begin{matrix}
-(0, 3, 5) \\
-(1, 2) \\
-(4, 7) \\
-(6).
\end{matrix}
$$

Matrix $E_{Y,X}$

We see that we could put f in the form:

$$f = F[\varphi_1(a, b, c), \varphi_2(a, b, c), d, e].$$

The matrix F will be, for example, $E'_{de, \varphi_1 \varphi_2}$ (below). But in fact, $4! = 24$ matrices are possible since we are free to arrange the order of the columns. Here we have reproduced them in the same order as in the initial $E_{Y,X}$ matrix. We therefore find:

$$F = \bar{\varphi}_1\bar{\varphi}_2\bar{d} + \varphi_1\varphi_2 + (\varphi_1 + \varphi_2)d\bar{e} + \varphi_1\bar{d}e$$
$$F = \bar{\varphi}_1\bar{\varphi}_2 d + \varphi_1\varphi_2 + (\varphi_1 + \varphi_2)d\bar{e} + \bar{\varphi}_2 de.$$

We must now determine the matrix T_{JI} such that $E' \otimes T_{JI} = E$, which gives the values of the functions φ_1 and φ_2.

From Chapter 1, we know that row No. 0 of T will have ones in columns No. 0, 3 and 5 (as columns 0, 3 and 5 are identical in E). In the same way, line No. 1 will have ones in columns 1 and 2, line No. 2 will have ones in columns 4 and 7, line No. 3 in column No. 7. This allows us to draw directly the following matrix T:

$$T = \begin{bmatrix} 1 & 0 & 0 & 1 & 0 & 1 & 0 & 0 \\ 0 & 1 & 1 & 0 & 0 & 0 & 0 & 0 \\ 0 & 0 & 0 & 0 & 1 & 0 & 0 & 1 \\ 0 & 0 & 0 & 0 & 0 & 0 & 1 & 0 \end{bmatrix}.$$

Hence.

$$\div \varphi_1 = 0\ 1\ 1\ 0\ 0\ 0\ 1\ 0$$
$$\div \varphi_2 = 0\ 0\ 0\ 0\ 1\ 0\ 1\ 1$$

Finally, we find the expression:

$$\varphi_1 = a\bar{b}\bar{c} + \bar{a}b$$
$$\varphi_2 = bc + \bar{a}c.$$

That is to say:

$$F = \varphi_2(d\bar{e} + \varphi_1) + \varphi_2\bar{d}(\bar{\varphi}_1 + e) + \varphi_1 d\bar{e}.$$

A circuit using AND, OR, and NOT operators can easily be derived from the last expressions.

b. *Research of the decomposition in terms of given subfunctions.* Consider the function $f(a, b, c, d, e)$ (with the same weight conventions as in Chapter 1) such that

$$f = R(3, 7, 8, 10, 18, 19, 21, 23, 25, 27, 31).$$

We wish to express f in terms of $\varphi_1 = ab + a\bar{c}$ and $\varphi_2 = ac + b\bar{c}$. We shall therefore take the $(abc; de)$ partition of f; that is, we write the

$E_{Y,X}$ matrix (below) as well as the T_{JI} matrix corresponding to φ_1 and φ_2.

$$
\begin{bmatrix}
0 & 0 & 0 & 1 & 0 & 0 & 0 & 1 \\
1 & 0 & 1 & 0 & 0 & 0 & 0 & 0 \\
0 & 0 & 1 & 1 & 0 & 1 & 0 & 1 \\
0 & 1 & 0 & 1 & 0 & 0 & 0 & 1
\end{bmatrix}
\qquad
\begin{bmatrix}
1 & 0 & 0 & 0 & 1 & 0 & 1 & 0 \\
0 & 1 & 0 & 0 & 0 & 0 & 0 & 0 \\
0 & 0 & 1 & 0 & 0 & 1 & 0 & 0 \\
0 & 0 & 0 & 1 & 0 & 0 & 0 & 1
\end{bmatrix}
$$
$$
\qquad\qquad E_{Y,X} \qquad\qquad\qquad\qquad\qquad\qquad T_{JI}
$$

$X = (a, b, c), Y = (d, e)$.

The process is the converse of that which has been employed just before.

We find the matrix

$$
E' =
\begin{bmatrix}
0 & 0 & 0 & 1 \\
1 & 0 & 1 & 0 \\
0 & 0 & 1 & 1 \\
0 & 1 & 0 & 1
\end{bmatrix}.
$$

which leads to:

$$
f = F(\varphi_1, \varphi_2, d, e) = \varphi_1 de + \varphi_2 \bar{d} e + \bar{\varphi}_1 \bar{d}\bar{e} + \varphi_1 \varphi_2 \bar{d}\bar{e}
$$

or

$$
F = \varphi_1 de + \varphi_2 \bar{d}(e + \varphi_1) + \bar{\varphi}_1 d\bar{e}.
$$

That is, for f we obtain the realization in AND, OR, NOT circuits of Figure 3.27.

c. *Conclusion.* The great interest of these methods appears when we have electronic computers at our disposal. Under these circumstances, the computation of the different matrices needed is done very rapidly. We can therefore imagine the following process: Given a function f to be realized in terms of diverse existing subfunctions $(\varphi_1, \ldots, \varphi_p)$, it is necessary to set a criterion for the choice of the partitions to be made. In fact, as soon as there are a large number of variables, the number of possible partitions also becomes very large. The choice must therefore be limited (by a technological choice for example) to two or three possible partitions.

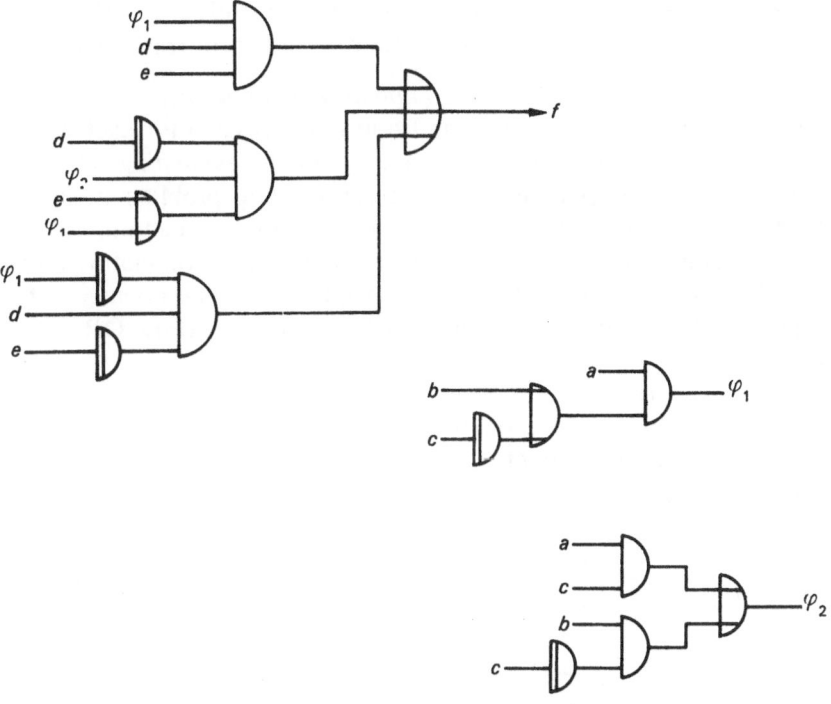

FIG. 3.27.

When this is done, the matrix corresponding to this partition is obtained and its distinct columns counted. The number of subfunctions to be studied is thus set at n $(n \leqslant p)$. These subfunctions are grouped n by n which leads to $\binom{n}{p}$ possible R_{JI} matrices for which X_a and X_c are computed then verified to see if they lead to a solution.

We mention (relative to what was said at the end of the first chapter) that his method is *not a reduction method* for Boolean functions. Its object is simply to *factorize* the functions so that their realization in circuits already manufactured or manufactured from complex functions is readily possible.

3.5. STUDY OF COMBINATIONAL MULTIPOLES

DEFINITION. A multipole is a network having one or more input terminals and several output terminals.

We shall, as we did for dipoles, successively study the analysis and synthesis of multipole relays and multipole diodes or transistors.

3.5.1. *Analysis of combinational multipoles*

The problem is to determine the Boolean expression for each of the circuit's outputs. It is therefore a question of evaluating all paths leading to the output under consideration. The problem is simple when the switching elements have an unilateral conduction, but becomes complicated when elements having bilateral conduction (such as relays) are involved. We shall proceed in the same manner as for dipoles, that is, we express outputs in terms of the AND, OR, NOT operators.

Relay systems

Consider the relay multipole in Figure 3.28. From Kirchhoff's laws, we have the Boolean expressions for z_1, z_2, z_3. We explain the computation of z_1.

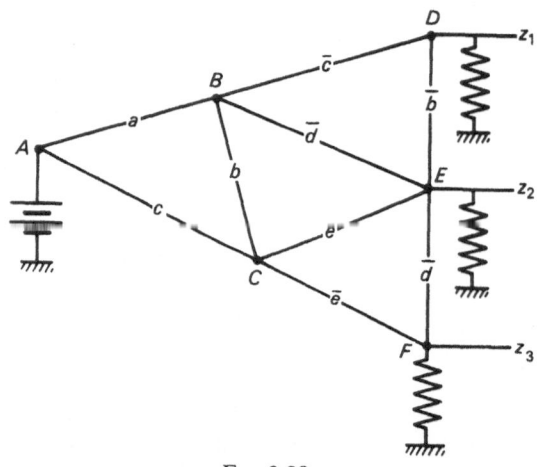

FIG. 3.28.

Computation of z_1

We seek all electric paths joining the point A to the point D.

(a) Paths containing AB. These paths can either go directly to $D(ABD)$ or pass $E(ABED)$, $CE(ABCED)$, $CFE(ABCFED)$; their expression is written:

$$a(\bar{c} + \bar{d}b + be\bar{b} + b\bar{e}\bar{d}b).$$

(b) Paths containing AC. We may write the conductibility of all these paths in the same way:

$$c(b\bar{c} + bd\bar{b} + e\bar{b} + \bar{e}\bar{d}b).$$

(c) Expression of z_1. The final expression of the z_1 output is therefore:

$$z_1 = a(\bar{c} + \bar{b} \cdot \bar{d}) + c(e\bar{b} + \bar{e}\bar{b}\bar{d}) = a(\bar{c} + \bar{b}\bar{d}) + \bar{b}c(e + \bar{d}).$$

In the same way, we can determine the expressions of z_2 and z_3.

$$z_2 = a\bar{d} + a\bar{b}\bar{c} + abe + ce + c\bar{e}\bar{d} + cb\bar{d} = a\bar{d} + a\bar{b}\bar{c} + abe$$
$$+ ce + c\bar{d}$$
$$z_3 = c\bar{e} + ce\bar{d} + cb\bar{d} + ab\bar{e} + abe\bar{d} + a\bar{d} + a\bar{c}\bar{b}\bar{d} = c\bar{e} + c\bar{d}$$
$$+ a\bar{d} + ab\bar{e}$$

The Boolean equations of z_1, z_2, z_3 give the truth table.

Diode systems

Consider the circuit in Figure 3.29. The elements 2, 3, 5, 7, 8, 9, 11 are AND circuits; 1, 4, 6, 10 are OR circuits; 1, 2, 3, 4, 5 define z_1; 5, 6, 7, 8, 9, 10, and 11 define z_2. The expressions are written:

$$z_1 = (b + \bar{c})(\bar{a}\bar{b} + \bar{a}\bar{c})$$
$$z_2 = (\bar{a}\bar{c} + \bar{c}\bar{d})(a\bar{b} + a\bar{c}).$$

Transistor systems

Consider the circuit in Figure 3.30. The transistors 1, 2, 3, 4, 5 intervene in the definition of z_1; the transistors 5, 6, 7, 8, 9, 10, 11 figure in the definition of z_2. We may write:

$$z_1 = [((a \downarrow b) \downarrow (a \downarrow c)) \downarrow (b \downarrow \bar{c})]$$
$$= \overline{(a + b)(a + c)}(b + \bar{c})$$
$$= (\bar{a}\bar{b} + \bar{a}\bar{c})(b + \bar{c})$$
$$z_2 = [((a \downarrow c) \downarrow (c \downarrow d)) \downarrow ((\bar{a} \downarrow b) \downarrow (\bar{a} \downarrow c))]$$
$$= [((a + c)(c + d)) \downarrow ((\bar{a} + b)(\bar{a} + c))]$$
$$= (\bar{a}\bar{c} + \bar{c}\bar{d})(a\bar{b} + a\bar{c}).$$

Comment. The procedure would be the same if we associated the different technological elements. We would have to distinguish the elements with unilateral conduction from those having bilateral induction in order to make the output clear and evaluate the different paths defining each output.

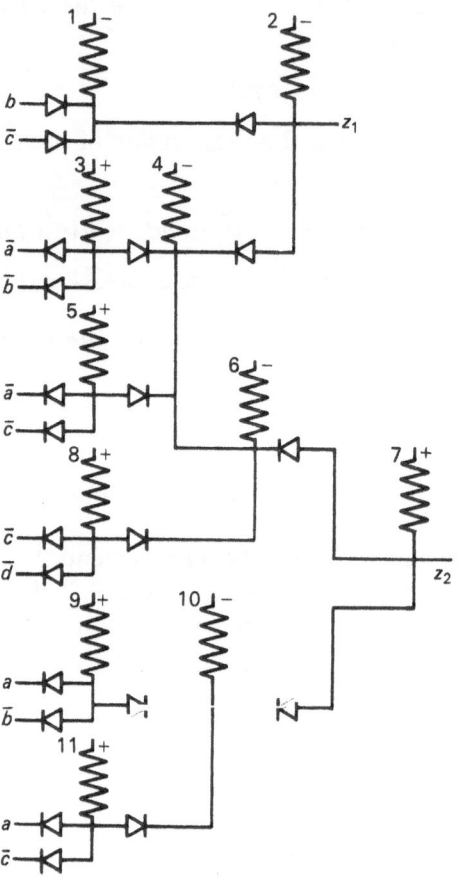

FIG. 3.29.

3.5.2. *Synthesis of a combinational multipole*

Given the truth table of a combinational multipole, we wish to build a circuit with a minimum of elements.

The methods which we shall discuss will be extensions of the methods used for dipoles: McCluskey method and Boolean function decomposition method. We shall show that rectifiers are needed for relays, which are bilateral conduction elements, when the McCluskey method is extended to multipoles.

Nevertheless, there exists a method, for this technology, called

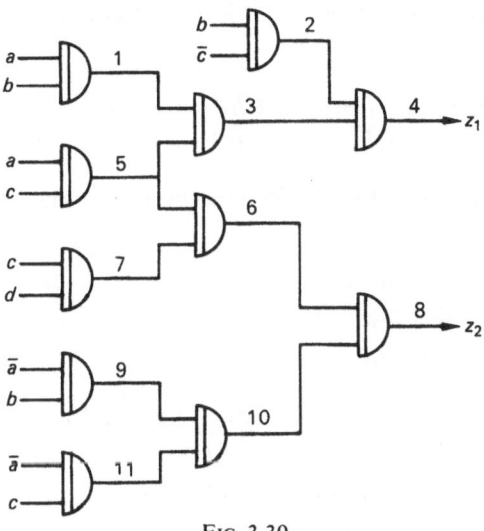

FIG. 3.30.

'matrix method', which gives the solution obtained by the McCluskey method, but without needing rectifiers.

3.5.2.1. *Extension of the McCluskey method*

3.5.2.1.1. *Problem.* As an example, consider the circuit represented by the truth table in Figure 3.31. The output functions z_1 and z_2 are written in their disjunctive forms as:

$$z_1 = \bar{a}\bar{b}\bar{c} + \bar{a}b\bar{c} + ab\bar{c} + abc$$
$$z_2 = \bar{a}bc + ab\bar{c} + abc.$$

a	b	c	z_1	z_2
0	0	0	1	0
0	0	1	0	0
0	1	0	1	0
0	1	1	0	1
1	0	0	0	0
1	0	1	0	0
1	1	0	1	1
1	1	1	1	1

FIG. 3.31.

By using the complementary functions, the conjunctive forms can be obtained:

$$z_1 = (a+b+\bar{c})(a+\bar{b}+\bar{c})(\bar{a}+b+c)(\bar{a}+b+\bar{c})$$
$$z_2 = (a+b+c)(a+b+\bar{c})(a+\bar{b}+c)(\bar{a}+b+c)(\bar{a}+b+\bar{c}).$$

If we apply the Quine-McCluskey method separately to z_1 and z_2, we may write:

$$z_1 = ab + \bar{a}\bar{c}$$
$$z_2 = ab + bc,$$

(3.2)

and in the conjunctive form:

$$z_1 = (a+\bar{c})(\bar{a}+b) = (a \downarrow \bar{c}) \downarrow (\bar{a} \downarrow b)$$
$$z_2 = b(a+c) = \bar{b} \downarrow (a \downarrow c).$$

For the separate realizations of circuits z_1 and z_2, we must have either eight relay contacts or 12 diodes, or five transistors. Figure 3.32 represents the symbolic diagram of Equations (3.2). We observe that the term ab appears in both z_1 and z_2. It is, therefore, sufficient that ab be realized only once and used in the z_1 and z_2 circuits. The corresponding circuit (Figure 3.33) is realized with six relay contacts or 10 diodes. There will always be five transistors because there is no common factor in the conjunctive forms of z_1 and z_2.

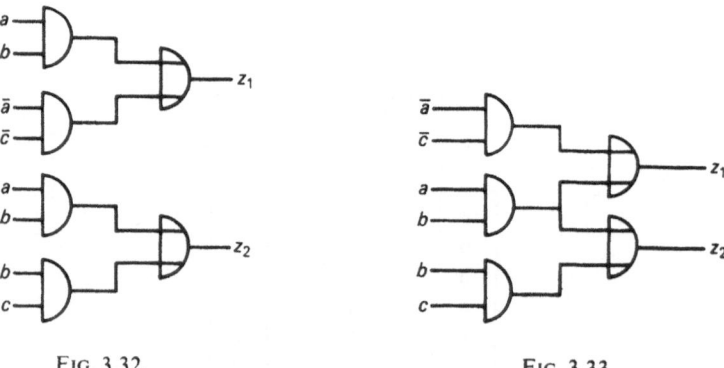

FIG. 3.32.   FIG. 3.33.

It thus appears interesting to look for common factors in the different output functions in order to minimize a combinational multipole.

3.5.2.1.2. *Search for multipole prime implicants.* Given n Boolean output functions expressed in either their disjunctive or conjunctive forms, we first seek their prime implicants in the usual way.

DEFINITION. We call p-order common implicant of n Boolean functions, every term contained in p of the n functions considered.

Given a choice, $f_{m_1}, ..., f_{m_p}$ ($m_1 \neq m_2 ...$; $1 < p \leq n$; $1 \leq (m_1, ..., m_p) \leq n$) the set of all common factors of order p is the function represented by the notation:

$$f_{(m_1, ..., m_p)} \qquad (f_{(m_1, ..., m_p)} = f_{m_1} \cdot f_{m_2} \cdot \cdots \cdot f_{m_p}).$$

Its form is of the same nature as the forms $f_{m_1}, ..., f_{m_p}$. Consider, for example, the three functions f_1, f_2, f_3 of the four variables a, b, c, d:

$$f_1 = R(0, 1, 2, 8, 9, 11, 13, 15)$$
$$f_2 = R(0, 3, 4, 5, 6, 7, 8, 14)$$
$$f_3 = R(0, 4, 5, 6, 7, 8, 9, 10, 11, 12, 13, 15).$$

The set of second-order common implicants is:

$$0, 4, 5, 6, 7, 8, 11, 13, 15..$$

The set of third-order common implicants is: $(0, 8)$. With the preceding conventions, we can write:

$$f_{12} = R(0, 8)$$
$$f_{13} = R(0, 8, 9, 11, 13, 15)$$
$$f_{23} = R(0, 4, 5, 6, 7, 8)$$
$$f_{123} = R(0, 8).$$

DEFINITION. We call common prime implicant, every prime implicant of the function $f_{(m_1, ..., m_j)}$ ($1 < j \leq n$).

The common prime implicant of f_{12} is $(0, 8)$.
The common prime implicants of f_{13} are $(0, 8)$, $(8, 9)$, $(9, 11, 13, 15)$.
The common prime implicant of f_{123} is $(0, 8)$.

DEFINITION. We call multiple prime implicant of a system of several Boolean functions every term which is either a prime implicant or a multiple prime implicant of the functions.

Choice of multiple prime implicants. The problem to be solved is the following: Given the truth table of a combinational multipole, find the minimal cost two-level representation.

We have already discussed two-level representations and know that they correspond to a disjunctive or conjunctive form. We have also defined the cost of diode, relay and transistor circuits. We shall now give another definition pertinent to the solution of the present problem, that of the cost of an element of one of the Boolean output functions.

DEFINITION. The global cost of an element figuring in the expression of output functions is computed in the following way:

(a) In a relay system, it equals the number of letters in the term being considered whether or not the term is a common factor.

(b) In a diode system, it equals the number of letters (if the number is greater than 1, if not it equals 0) in the term being considered, augmented by the number of times the term appears in the set of the system's output functions.

(c) In a transistor system, it equals 0 if the term has only one letter and 1 whether or not it is a comrion factor but has more than one letter.

Consider the two expressions:

$$z_1 = (a \downarrow b) \downarrow (c \downarrow d) = (a+b)(c+d) = ad+bd+ac+bc$$
$$z_2 = (a \downarrow b) \downarrow (d \downarrow e) = (a+b)(d+e) = ad+bd+ae+be.$$

The common factors are $(a+b)$ in the conjunctive form and $(ad+bd)$ in the disjunctive form. The cost of $(a \downarrow b)$ is 1 (transistor technology) The cost for these two equations, of $(a+b)$ is 2 in a relay system and 4 in a diode system.

THEOREM. The Boolean output functions corresponding to a two-stage minimal cost circuit (in one of the technologies considered) are expressed in terms of the multiple prime implicants of the system's output functions.

In fact, the output functions of a combinational multipole have terms which appear in only one function and common terms. The multiple prime implicants have a minimum number of letters. They appear either only in the function being considered, or in several functions. Furthermore, use of multiple prime implicants decreases the number of terms in each function which appear in no other function or the common factors necessary for the representation of the different output functions; that is, the number of input connections in the diode or transistor circuits.

Consequently, after having determined all the multiple prime implicants, we shall choose a certain set of them to represent the function at minimal cost. We are thus led to evaluate the cost of the different sets. We shall therefore form a multiple prime-implicant chart as in the Quine-McCluskey method.

Example. Considering the set of output functions in their disjunctive form, we seek the minimal cost two-level diode or relay circuit.

$$z_1 = abc + \bar{a}bc + \bar{a}\bar{b}c + ab\bar{c} = R(1, 3, 6, 7)$$
$$z_2 = abc + \bar{a}bc + \bar{a}b\bar{c} + \bar{a}\bar{b}\bar{c} = R(0, 2, 3, 7)$$
$$z_3 = \bar{a}\bar{b}\bar{c} + \bar{a}bc + ab\bar{c} + \bar{a}\bar{b}c = R(0, 1, 3, 6).$$

We look for the multiple prime implicants of these functions. We may write:

$$f_1 = bc + ab + \bar{a}c$$
$$f_2 = bc + \bar{a}\bar{c} + \bar{a}b$$
$$f_3 = \bar{a}\bar{b} + \bar{a}c + ab\bar{c}$$
$$f_{12} = bc$$
$$f_{13} = \bar{a}c + ab\bar{c}$$
$$f_{23} = \bar{a}bc + \bar{a}\bar{b}\bar{c}$$
$$f_{123} = \bar{a}bc.$$

For example, the common factors of z_1 and z_3 are 1, 3, 6.

$$f_{13} = \bar{a}\bar{b}c + \bar{a}bc + ab\bar{c} = \bar{a}c + ab\bar{c}.$$

The multiple prime implicant chart is shown in Figure 3.34.

3.5.2.1.3. *Utilization of the multiple prime implicant chart.** The set of multiple prime implicants which cover all the terms in the output functions at minimal cost is the solution to the problem.

Observe that certain are incompatible. Suppose that a term A belongs to two functions $f_{(m_1,...,m_j)}$ and $f_{(m_1,...,m_q)}$. It cannot appear in both these forms in the final expression of the functions $f_1, ..., f_n$; for example, the term $\bar{a}c$ will appear only in one of the forms $f_1, f_2, f_{1,3}$. The multiple prime implicants are represented as in Figure 3.34 by a capital letter.

We shall indicate by the table in Figure 3.35, which multiple prime implicants are incompatible with each other. There exists a particular form of incompatibility: A, belonging to a function $f_{(m_1,...,m_j)}$ is not compatible with B (B belongs to A) figuring in $f_{p_1,...,p_q}$ if certain of the $f_{m_1}, ..., f_{m_j}$ functions are $f_{p_1}, ..., f_{p_q}$ functions.

---

* m.p.i. will signify multiple prime implicant.

		z_1				z_2				z_3				
		1	3	6	7	0	2	3	7	0	1	3	6	
f_1	$b\,c$		×		×									A
	$a\,b$			×	×									B
	$\bar{a}\,c$	×	×											C
f_2	$b\,c$							×	×					D
	$\bar{a}\,\bar{c}$					×	×							E
	$\bar{a}\,b$						×	×						F
f_3	$\bar{a}\,\bar{b}$									×	×			G
	$\bar{a}\,c$										×	×		H
	$a\,b\,\bar{c}$												×	I
f_{12}	$b\,c$		×		×			×	×					J
f_{13}	$\bar{a}\,c$	×	×								×	×		K
	$a\,b\,\bar{c}$			×									×	L
f_{23}	$\bar{a}\,b\,c$							×				×		M
	$\bar{a}\,\bar{b}\,\bar{c}$					×				×				N
f_{123}	$\bar{a}\,b\,c$		×					×				×		O

FIG. 3.34.

    In the first case A is incompatible with D and J. It is impossible to simultaneously have A and J because bc belongs either to f_1 (with A alone) or f_2 (with D alone) or both (with J); as a matter of fact we cannot have either A with J or D with J or A with D for, in this last case,

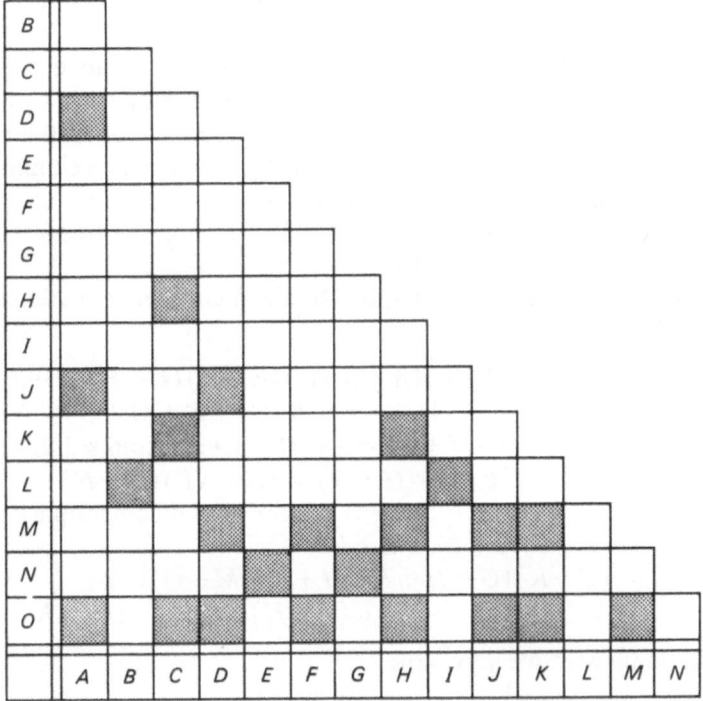

FIG. 3.35.

we would have J. We can, however, have A with M because $\bar{a}bc$ is a common factor of f_2 and f_3 in M, while bc belongs only to f_1 in A.

To represent the second case, note that B and I are compatible, but B and L are not. In fact, f_1 can contain ab and f_3 can contain $ab\bar{c}$. However, ab cannot be contained in f_1 at the same time that $ab\bar{c}$ is contained in f_1 and f_3 because if ab is in f_1, $ab\bar{c}$ becomes a redundant term in f_1 and must be taken out in order to represent the function with the least number of m.p.i. (Figure 3.35).

3.5.2.1.4. *Choice of the minimal covering.* The terms in all three functions, f_1, f_2, f_3 must be covered. The Boolean covering equation is the same as for one output circuits by the classical Quine-McCluskey method:

$$\text{for} f_1: (C+K)(A+C+J+K)(B+L)(A+B+J) = 1$$
$$\text{for} f_2: (E+N)(E+F)(D+F+J+M+O)(D+J) = 1$$
$$\text{for} f_3: (G+N)(G+H+K)(H+K+M+O)(I+L) = 1.$$

Comments. (1) For each function, f_i $(1 < i \le n)$, the operations of the McCluskey method relative to dipoles can be performed. If a function f_i is such that the second of two of its columns in the prime implicant chart has some of its crosses in the same rows as the first column this last column can be eliminated (application of the absorption law). Thus, column 3 in f_1 and column 3 in f_2 can be eliminated.

(2) Several Boolean equations $A = 1$, $B = 1 \ldots L = 1$ can be replaced by a single equation $A \cdot B \ldots L = 1$. The verification of this statement is left to the reader.

In light of these comments, the Boolean covering equation can be written:

$$(C+K)(B+L)(A+B+J)(E+N)(E+F)(D+J)$$
$$\times (G+N)(G+H+K)(H+K+M+O)(I+L) = 1$$
$$(J+A+B)(J+D) = J+BD \quad (A \text{ is incompatible with } D)$$
$$(E+N)(E+F)(G+N) = (E+NF)(G+N)$$
$$= GE+NF(E \text{ is incompatible with } N).$$
$$(B+L)(I+L) = L+BI$$
$$(C+K)(G+H+K)(H+K+M+O)$$
$$= K+C(G+H)(H+M+O) = K+CGM.$$

In the same way, we may write:

$$(J+DB)(L+BI) = (JL+BIJ+BID)$$
$$(GF+NF)(K+CGM) = (KEG+KNF+CGME).$$

The Boolean covering equation is therefore:

$$(JL+BIJ+BID)(KEG+KNF) = 1,$$

because M is incompatible with J and D. The final Boolean equation no longer contains incompatible terms.

We compute the costs, in diodes and relay contacts, of the different terms of the covering equation (Figure 3.36).

The solution $JLKEG$ is therefore minimal in diodes as well as in relays (19 diodes or 11 contacts); the equations of the circuit are:

$$z_1 = bc + ab\bar{c} + \bar{a}c$$
$$z_2 = bc + \bar{a}\bar{c}$$
$$z_3 = b\bar{c} + \bar{a}c + \bar{a}\bar{b}.$$

If we had separately minimized the f_1, f_2, f_3 functions, the output

	I	J	L	B	D	E	G	K	F	N	JL	BIJ	BID	KEG	KNF
Diodes	4	4	5	3	3	3	3	4	3	5	9	11	10	10	12
Contacts	3	2	3	2	2	2	2	2	2	3	5	7	7	6	7

FIG. 3.36.

equations would be:

$$f_1 = \bar{a}c + ab$$
$$f_2 = bc + \bar{a}\bar{c}$$
$$f_3 = \bar{a}\bar{b} + \bar{a}c + ab\bar{c}$$

giving a total of 20 diodes or 13 contacts.

3.5.2.1.5. *Simplified minimization method.* We shall now present a simpler way to solve the problem of covering. When a prime implicant chart is made, if a multiple prime implicant appears in both a term $f_{(m_1,...,m_q)}$ and the next higher term $f_{(m_1,...,m_p)}$, it is kept only in the higher term. Figure 3.34 becomes Figure 3.37.

Comment. The essential difference in the two figures is that Figure 3.34 contains incompatible terms. These must be taken into account when choosing a covering; a choice which must be made by considering the different covering solutions.

Each solution was precisely defined in our preceding discussion. In fact, the $\bar{a}c$ term was represented by 3 possible cases, C, H, or K, which in Figure 3.37 are represented only by I. Therefore, we cannot solve a Boolean covering equation because each term does not play a determined role. The same I can correspond to C, H, or K. Its cost is not defined.

We shall work with each individual function in the following way:

(1) We shall look for the essential terms in each function. For example, G is essential to f_3. In this case the term's cost to create other functions is reduced: it will be 1 for diodes and 0 for relay contacts if we use G to represent f_1. In order to see this, suppose that a multiple prime implicant is necessary to one of the functions. A supplementary diode is needed each time the term is repeated.

(2) For a function f_i, the absorption laws of columns hold; in f_2 column 1 suppresses column 3.

		z_1				z_2				z_3				
		1	3	6	7	0	2	3	7	0	1	3	6	
f_1	$a\,b$			×	×									A
f_2	$\bar{a}\,\bar{c}$					×	×							B
	$\bar{a}\,b$						×	×						C
f_3	$\bar{a}\,\bar{b}$									×	×			D
f_{12}	$b\,c$		×		×			×	×					E
f_{13}	$\bar{a}\,c$	×	×								×	×		F
	$a\,b\,\bar{c}$			×									×	G
f_{23}	$\bar{a}\,\bar{b}\,\bar{c}$					×				×				H
f_{123}	$\bar{a}\,b\,c$		×					×				×		I

FIG. 3.37.

(3) A higher cost row can be suppressed if another row, of minimum cost, has its crosses or a part of its crosses in the same columns.

We apply these rules to the table in Figure 3.37 in the case of a diode circuit.

F is essential to f_1.

E is essential to f_2.

G is essential to f_3.

We suppress columns 1 and 3 in f_1, 3 and 7 in f_2, and 6 in f_3. We obtain the table in Figure 3.38.

The cost of H is 4 or 5 depending upon whether it belongs to f_2, f_3, or both. E and G cover the terms 6 and 7 in f_1 at a cost of 2 instead of 3 which A would have.

We may write:

$$f_1 = F + E + G = bc + \bar{a}c + ab\bar{c}.$$

	f_1		f_2		f_3			
	6	7	0	2	0	1	3	Cost
A	×	×						3
B			×	×				3
C				×				3
D					×	×		3
Ⓔ		×						1
Ⓕ						×	×	1
Ⓖ	×							1
H			×		×			4 or 5
I							×	4

FIG. 3.38.

I costs 4 and *F* costs 1. Therefore, by rule 3, we keep only *F*. *C* can also be eliminated because of *B*. The final table is in Figure 3.39.

The term *F* therefore becomes essential to f_3 eliminating columns 1 and 3 of this function. Terms 0 and 2 in f_2 and 0 in f_3 remain to be covered. *B* and *D* cost 6, while *B* for f_2 and *H* for f_3 cost 7. The minimal solution is written:

$$f_1 = bc + \bar{a}c + ab\bar{c}$$
$$f_2 = bc + \bar{a}\bar{c}$$
$$f_3 = ab\bar{c} + \bar{a}c + \bar{a}\bar{b}.$$

We have already found the same solution by the general method.

3.5.2.1.6. *Transistor circuits*. As already shown, we use normal disjunctive forms and their complements to apply these methods to transistor circuits.

	f_2		f_3			
	0	2	0	1	3	Cost
B	×	×				3
D			×	×		3
(F)				×	×	1
H	×		×			4 or 5

FIG. 3.39.

Consider the three functions f_1, f_2, f_3 to be represented at minimum cost by a 2-level transistor circuit.

$$f_1 = (\bar{a} \downarrow \bar{b} \downarrow \bar{c}) \downarrow (a \downarrow \bar{b} \downarrow \bar{c}) \downarrow (a \downarrow b \downarrow \bar{c}) \downarrow (\bar{a} \downarrow \bar{b} \downarrow c)$$
$$f_2 = (\bar{a} \downarrow \bar{b} \downarrow \bar{c}) \downarrow (a \downarrow \bar{b} \downarrow \bar{c}) \downarrow (a \downarrow \bar{b} \downarrow c) \downarrow (a \downarrow b \downarrow c)$$
$$f_3 = (a \downarrow b \downarrow c) \downarrow (a \downarrow \bar{b} \downarrow \bar{c}) \downarrow (\bar{a} \downarrow \bar{b} \downarrow c) \downarrow (a \downarrow b \downarrow \bar{c}).$$

The corresponding conjunctive forms are:

$$f_1 = (\bar{a} + \bar{b} + \bar{c})(a + \bar{b} + \bar{c})(a + b + \bar{c})(\bar{a} + \bar{b} + c)$$
$$f_2 = (\bar{a} + \bar{b} + \bar{c})(a + \bar{b} + \bar{c})(a + \bar{b} + c)(a + b + c)$$
$$f_3 = (a + b + c)(a + \bar{b} + \bar{c})(\bar{a} + \bar{b} + c)(a + b + \bar{c}).$$

The complementary functions are:

$$\bar{f}_1 = bc + ab + \bar{a}c$$
$$\bar{f}_2 = bc + \bar{a}\bar{c} + \bar{a}b$$
$$\bar{f}_3 = \bar{a}\bar{b} + \bar{a}c + ab\bar{c}.$$

The minimization could be done by attributing a cost of 1 to each implicant whether it appears once or several times.

The Boolean covering equation (see example of the first method) is written:

$$(JL + BIJ + BID)(KEG + KNF) = 1.$$

There are two minimal solutions:

$JLKEG$ and $JLKNF$ (cost of 5 transistors).

The total cost of the 3 functions is 8 transistors. The equations are:

$$\bar{f}_1 = bc + ab\bar{c} + \bar{a}c \qquad f_1 = (\bar{b} \downarrow \bar{c}) \downarrow (\bar{a} \downarrow \bar{b} \downarrow c) \downarrow (a \downarrow \bar{c})$$
$$\bar{f}_2 = bc + \bar{a}\bar{c} \qquad f_2 = (\bar{b} \downarrow \bar{c}) \downarrow (a \downarrow c)$$
$$\bar{f}_3 = ab\bar{c} + \bar{a}c + \bar{a}b \qquad f_3 = (\bar{a} \downarrow \bar{b} \downarrow c) \downarrow (a \downarrow \bar{c}) \downarrow (a \downarrow b).$$

The second solution is:

$$\bar{f}_1 = bc + ab\bar{c} + \bar{a}c$$
$$\bar{f}_2 = bc + \bar{a}\bar{b}\bar{c} + \bar{a}b$$
$$\bar{f}_3 = ab\bar{c} + \bar{a}c + \bar{a}b\bar{c}$$
$$f_1 = (\bar{b} \downarrow \bar{c}) \downarrow (\bar{a} \downarrow \bar{b} \downarrow c) \downarrow (a \downarrow \bar{c})$$
$$f_2 = (\bar{b} \downarrow \bar{c}) \downarrow (a \downarrow b \downarrow c) \downarrow (a \downarrow \bar{b})$$
$$f_3 = (\bar{a} \downarrow \bar{b} \downarrow c) \downarrow (a \downarrow \bar{c}) \downarrow (a \downarrow b \downarrow c).$$

The corresponding circuits are shown in Figures 3.40a and b.

We could reproach ourselves for dealing only with simple and complemented inputs. If we wanted to create the complement of the inputs, it would be sufficient to add 3 supplementary transistors. We could

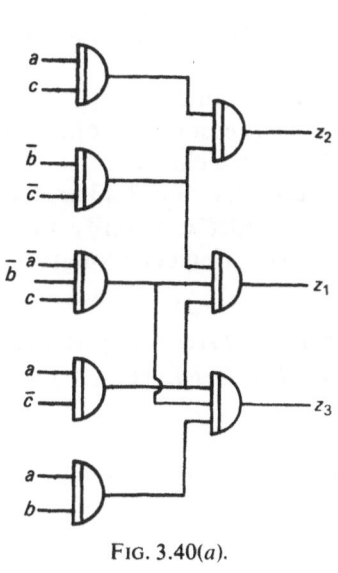

FIG. 3.40(a).

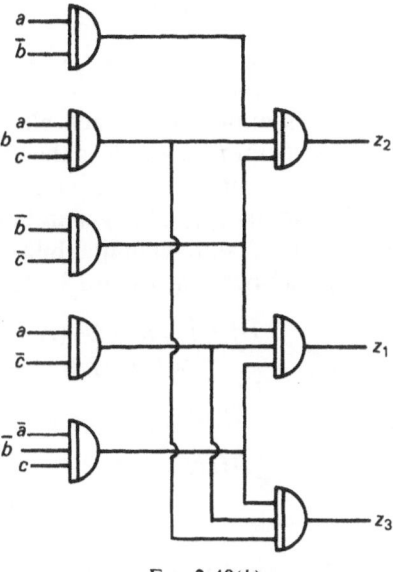

FIG. 3.40(b).

verify that the two minimal solutions in this example would still be minimal solutions. In the general case, it is necessary to study the different covering possibilities and compute their individual costs.

3.5.2.1.7. *Possibilities of the McCluskey approximation method.* Although perhaps easier to handle, the approximation method, due to McCluskey, has several disadvantages: it does not provide a solution in every case; if the final solution is not unique, the evaluation of the different choices is more difficult. In our opinion, this method should be tried first, but if a solution is not readily obtained, we advise use of the general method, certainly more laborous, but completely sure.

We, for example, seek the minimal 2-stage diode circuit realized by the following functions*:

$$f_1 = \bar{a}\bar{c} + \bar{a}b + b\bar{c} = R(0, 2, 3, 6)$$
$$f_2 = \bar{b}\bar{c} + a\bar{b} + a\bar{c} = R(0, 4, 5, 6)$$
$$f_3 = \bar{b} + \bar{a}c = R(0, 1, 3, 4, 5),$$

from which we deduce the multiple functions:

$$f_{12} = \bar{a}\bar{b}\bar{c} + ab\bar{c}$$
$$f_{13} = \bar{a}\bar{b}\bar{c} + \bar{a}bc$$
$$f_{23} = \bar{b}\bar{c} + a\bar{b}$$
$$f_{123} = \bar{a}\bar{b}\bar{c}.$$

Figure 3.41 is the m.p.i chart when McCluskey's approximation method is applied.

J is essential to f_2 which eliminates columns 4 and 5 in f_2; J disappears from f_3, since E is there, which makes E essential. Column 4 of f_3 disappears. It then becomes difficult to make a choice.

Now let us apply the general method. Figures 3.42 and 3.43 are the m.p.i. chart and incompatibility table. The reader can verify that, taking into account Figure 3.41, the Boolean covering equation is:

$$(A + I + K + O)(A + B + C)(B + L)(C + J)$$
$$\times (D + I + M + O)(E + N)(F + J)(G + K + M + O)$$
$$\times (G + H)(H + L)(G + N) = 1$$

Or:

$$[OHN + MNHA + KHND + GE(IH + IL + DAH$$
$$+ DAL)][B + L(A + C)][J + CF] = 1.$$

---

* a is the variable of most weight.

		f_3					f_2				f_1					Function
	Cost	5	4	3	1	0	6	5	4	0	6	3	2	0	Term	
A	3												×	×	$\bar a\ \bar c$	f_1
B	3											×	×		$\bar a\ b$	f_1
C	3										×		×		$b\ \bar c$	f_1
D	3						×		×						$a\ \bar c$	f_2
E	0	×	×		×	×									$\bar b$	f_3
F	3			×	×										$\bar a\ c$	f_{12}
G	4 or 5						×				×				$a\ b\ \bar c$	f_{13}
H	4 or 5			×								×			$\bar a\ b\ c$	f_{13}
I	3 or 4		×			×			×	×					$\bar b\ \bar c$	f_{23}
J	3 or 4	×	×					×	×						$a\ b$	f_{23}
K	4, 5 or 6					×				×				×	$\bar a\ \bar b\ \bar c$	f_{123}

FIG. 3.41.

		f_1				f_2				f_3					
		0	2	3	6	0	4	5	6	0	1	3	4	5	
f_1	$\bar a\,\bar c$	×	×												A
	$\bar a\,b$		×	×											B
	$b\,\bar c$		×		×										C
f_2	$\bar b\,\bar c$					×	×								D
	$a\,\bar b$						×	×							E
	$a\,\bar c$						×		×						F
f_3	$\bar b$									×	×		×	×	G
	$\bar a\,c$										×	×			H
f_{12}	$\bar a\,\bar b\,\bar c$	×				×									I
	$a\,b\,\bar c$			×					×						J
f_{13}	$\bar a\,\bar b\,\bar c$	×								×					K
	$\bar a\,b\,c$			×								×			L
f_{23}	$\bar b\,\bar c$					×	×			×			×		M
	$a\,\bar b$						×	×					×	×	N
f_{123}	$\bar a\,\bar b\,\bar c$	×				×				×					O

Fig. 3.42.

Note that the terms J, C or F appear only in one factor. Furthermore, since the cost of $J(5)$ is less than that of $F(6)$, only J will be kept in the equation.

$$[B+L(A+C)]J = J(B+AL) \quad \text{[according to Figure 3.41].}$$

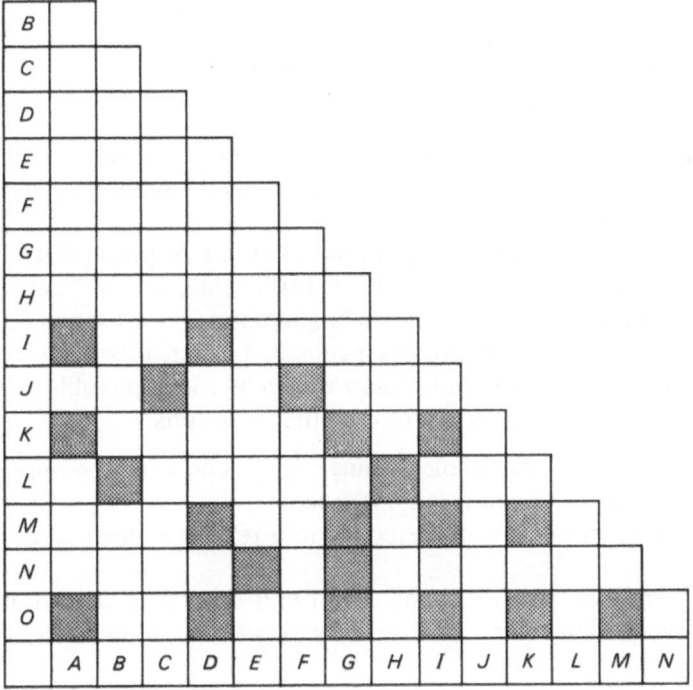

Fig. 3.43.

The Boolean equation is:

$$J[B(OHN + MNHA + KHND + GE(IH + DAH)) + GEDAL] = 1.$$

The costs of the different terms are indicated in the table of Figure 3.44. The minimal solutions are *BEFHIJ* and *ADEGJL* at a cost of

	J	B	OHN	MNHA	KHND	GE	IH	DAH	GEDAL
Cost	5	3	13	14	15	4	8	9	15

Fig. 3.44.

20; they correspond to the equations:

$$f_1 = \bar{a}b + \bar{a}\bar{b}\bar{c} + ab\bar{c} \qquad f_1 = \bar{a}\bar{c} + ab\bar{c} + \bar{a}bc$$
$$f_2 = a\bar{b} + \bar{a}\bar{b}\bar{c} + ab\bar{c} \qquad f_2 = \bar{b}\bar{c} + a\bar{b} + ab\bar{c}$$
$$f_3 = \bar{b} + \bar{a}c \qquad f_3 = \bar{b} + \bar{a}bc.$$

3.5.2.1.8. *Case of incomplete functions.* We shall now show how the preceding methods can be applied when the outputs of a system are not completely defined.

Reduction of the number of output functions. Suppose that several Boolean functions represented by a truth table, are not completely defined. Before applying the preceding methods, we must first find out whether these functions are independent. In fact, if we give certain 'don't cares' a 1 value and others a 0 value, it is possible that the resulting function equals one of the other functions.

DEFINITION. Two Boolean functions f_1 and f_2 are *compatible* if one of the following statements is true:

(a) Every zero of one corresponds to a zero or a 'don't care' of the other.

(b) Every 1 of one corresponds to a 1 or a 'don't care' of the other.

(c) Every 'don't care' of one corresponds to a 'don't care' of the other.

Symbolically $f_1 \simeq f_2$ reads: f_1 is compatible with f_2.

Considering functions f_1, f_2, f_3 in Figure 3.45 we see that f_2 is compatible with f_1 and f_3.

ab	0 0	0 1	1 1	1 0
f_1	0	1	–	1
f_2	–	1	0	–
f_3	1	–	–	1

FIG. 3.45.

Properties of the compatibility relation.

(1) **Reflexive:** f_1 is compatible with f_2 implies f_2 is compatible with f_1.

(2) **Non-transitive:** in the preceeding example, f_2 is compatible with f_1 and f_3, but f_1 and f_3 are not compatible with each other.

In multipole problems, we search for compatible functions. We obtain a certain number of classes of functions to which minimization methods can be applied. For this, we draw a diagram indicating the compatibilities: each point in the diagram corresponds to one of the functions; two points are connected by a line if the two corresponding functions are compatible.

Then we try to regroup the compatible functions to form maximum compatibilities. For this, the compatibility of each pair of functions must be verified, since the relation is not transitive. Three functions, f_1, f_2, f_3 form a compatibility if $f_1 \simeq f_2 . f_1 \simeq f_3 . f_2 \simeq f_3$ is verified.

DEFINITION. A maximal compatibility is one which permits the construction of others, having more terms, from it.

In the example of Figure 3.45 $(f_1 f_2)$ and $(f_2 f_3)$ are maximal compatibilities.

Example. Consider the truth table in Figure 3.46. Figure 3.47 is the compatibility diagram showing that z_1 is compatible with z_2, and z_4 is not compatible with any of the other functions.

Note that groups (13), (15), (16), (23), (25), (26), (34), (35), (46),

	z_1	z_2	z_3	z_4	z_5	z_6
0 0 0	1	1	–	–	–	–
0 0 1	–	–	1	1	1	1
0 1 1	0	0	0	–	–	0
0 1 0	0	0	–	–	1	–
1 1 0	1	–	–	–	–	–
1 1 1	1	1	1	1	1	1
1 0 1	0	0	1	0	0	1
1 0 0	0	0	0	–	1	0

FIG. 3.46.

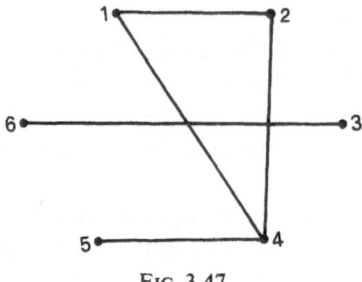

FIG. 3.47.

(56) are not compatible. The term (1 2 3 4 5 6) should be the largest compatibility. If we take into account the impossibilities due to 1, this term will be divided into two parts (the reader will find a more detailed discussion of this technique of reduction of the states of tables in Chapter 8): (1 2 4) (2 3 4 5 6). Taking into account the impossibilities due to 2, we may write: (1 2 4) (2 4) (3 4 5 6). (2 4) is contained in (1 2 4) and therefore can be eliminated. (3 4) and (3 5) impossible imply (1 2 4) (3 6) (4 5) and finally, we obtain (1 2 4) (3 6) (4 5).

The final solution should correspond to a partition of the output set (from a set theory point of view). We draw the m.p.i. chart in Figure 3.48. The three terms are essential.

	1	2	3	4	5	6
124	×	×		×		
36			×			×
45				×	×	

FIG. 3.48.

In order to have a partition of the functions $z_1, ..., z_6$ we can use one of the solutions, (1 2 4) 5(3 6) or (1 2) (3 6) (4 5). We shall consider the solution (1 2) (3 6) (4 5):

$$1 \simeq 2 \qquad 3 \simeq 6 \qquad 4 \simeq 5.$$

Realization of the minimal diode circuit. We employ the simplified McCluskey method. Figure 3.49 is the circuit's truth table. The prime implicants of these different functions are:

$$z_1: \quad ab, \bar{a}\bar{b} \qquad\qquad f_{14}: \quad ab, \bar{a}\bar{b}$$
$$z_3: \quad \bar{b}c, ac, ab \qquad f_{34}: \quad \bar{a}b, ab, b\bar{c}, \bar{a}\bar{c}$$
$$z_4: \quad \bar{c}, \bar{a}, b \qquad\quad f_{134}: \quad \bar{a}b, ab.$$
$$f_{13}: \quad ab, \bar{a}\bar{b}$$

$a\,b\,c$	z_1	z_3	z_4	f_{13}	f_{14}	f_{34}	f_{134}
0 0 0	1	–	–	1	1	–	1
0 0 1	–	1	1	1	1	1	1
0 1 1	0	0	–	0	0	0	0
0 1 0	0	–	1	0	0	1	0
1 1 0	1	–	–	1	1	–	1
1 1 1	1	1	1	1	1	1	1
1 0 1	0	1	0	0	0	0	0
1 0 0	0	0	1	0	0	0	0

FIG. 3.49.

The minimal circuit table is shown in Figure 3.50. Terms ab and $\bar{a}\bar{b}$ are essential to z_1. Consequently ab and bc, or $\bar{a}\bar{b}$ and ac are used to represent z_3. $\bar{c}$ is essential to z_4. To represent 1, $\bar{a}\bar{b}$ or $\bar{a}$ can be used; b or ab can be used to represent 7.

There are therefore eight possible solutions. We take the solutions:

$$z_1 = ab + \bar{a}\bar{b}$$
$$z_3 = ab + \bar{b}c$$
$$z_4 = \bar{c} + b + \bar{a}\bar{b}.$$

Thirteen diodes are necessary for this circuit.

		z_1			z_2			z_3				Cost
		0	6	7	1	5	7	1	2	4	7	
z_3	$\bar{b}\,c$				×	×						3
	$a\,c$					×	×					3
z_4	$\bar{c}$								×	×		1
	$\bar{a}$							×	×			1
	b								×		×	1
f_{34}	$b\,\bar{c}$								×			3 or 4
	$\bar{a}\,\bar{c}$								×			3 or 4
f_{134}	$a\,b$		×	×			×					3,4 or 5
	$\bar{a}\,\bar{b}$	×			×			×				3,4 or 5

FIG. 3.50.

If the z_1, z_3, z_4 functions had been separately studied, the minimal solution would have been:

$$z_1 = ab + \bar{a}\bar{b}$$
$$z_3 = \bar{b}c + ac$$
$$z_4 = \bar{a} + b + \bar{c},$$

calling for 15 diodes or 11 relay contacts.

Note that if we had sought the minimal relay solution, ab and $\bar{a}\bar{b}$ would be essential to z_1 giving a 0 cost. z_3 could be represented only by $\bar{c}$ (essential), ab and $\bar{a}\bar{b}$. We take the solution:

$$z_1 = ab + \bar{a}\bar{b}$$
$$z_3 = \bar{a}\bar{b} + ac$$
$$z_4 = \bar{c} + ab + \bar{a}\bar{b}$$

which needs 7 relay contacts.

3.5.2.1.9. *Conclusion.* McCluskey's extended and approximation methods are not only easily applicable to diode circuits, but also to transistor circuits. There are, however, restrictions in their application to relay circuits.

In fact, consider the following two solutions

$$f_1 = abc + d$$
$$f_2 = abc + e.$$

Eight contacts are needed as in Figure 3.51 to separately represent these two functions.

The extended Quine-McCluskey method reduces the cost of the preceding circuit to 5 contacts, but this circuit can no longer be represented by Figure 3.52 because the contacts have bilateral conduction with respect to the current. Rectifiers, therefore, become necessary as in Figure 3.53. Figure 3.52 leads to the equation:

$$z_1 = z_2 = abc + d + e.$$

The extended method, because it necessitates rectifiers in the contact realization, thus seems less appropriate for relay circuits. For this

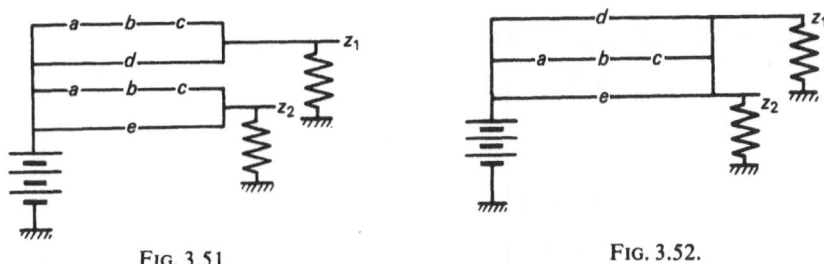

FIG. 3.51.   FIG. 3.52.

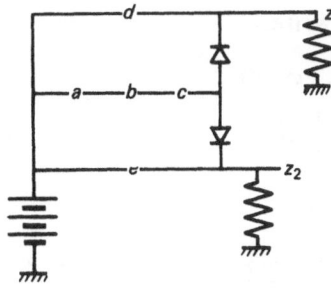

FIG. 3.53.

reason, we use a method called 'matrix analysis' when working in this and only this technology.

3.5.2.2. *Utilization of Boolean matrices in multipole design*

The method using Boolean matrices to be employed in this section, closely follows the one used in the case of dipoles. Given diverse functions $f_1, ..., f_k$, we can see if they have common subfunctions by considering the possibilities of choice in the different matrices (column permutation, etc.). We could, also, given diverse subfunctions, $f_1, ..., f_k$, see if they are decomposable in terms of n subfunctions of a set of p functions $(\varphi_1, ..., \varphi_p)$. In this case the method is exactly the same as for dipoles, but successively applied to the k functions to be considered. We shall give an example of the first fashion to proceed.

Reconsider the three functions studied, (a is the least weight variable)

$$f_1(a, b, c) = R(1, 3, 6, 7)$$
$$f_2(a, b, c) = R(0, 2, 3, 7)$$
$$f_3(a, b, c) = R(0, 1, 3, 6)$$
$$\div f_1 = 0\ 1\ 0\ 1\quad 0\ 0\ 1\ 1$$
$$\div f_2 = 1\ 0\ 1\ 1\quad 0\ 0\ 0\ 1$$
$$\div f_3 = 1\ 1\ 0\ 1\quad 0\ 0\ 1\ 0.$$

We seek $E^1_{c;ab}$, $E^2_{c;ab}$, $E^3_{c;ab}$ which are:

$$E^1 = \begin{bmatrix} 0 & 1 & 0 & 1 \\ 0 & 0 & 1 & 1 \end{bmatrix}$$

$$E^2 = \begin{bmatrix} 1 & 0 & 1 & 1 \\ 0 & 0 & 0 & 1 \end{bmatrix}$$

$$E^3 = \begin{bmatrix} 1 & 1 & 0 & 1 \\ 0 & 0 & 1 & 0 \end{bmatrix}.$$

We see that we may write:

$$f_1 = F_1(\varphi_1, \varphi_2, c)$$
$$f_2 = F_2(\varphi_3, \varphi_4, c)$$
$$f_3 = F_3(\varphi_5, c)$$

where

$$\varphi_i = \varphi_i(a, b).$$

If we had taken $E^1_{a;bc}$, $E^2_{a;bc}$, $E_{a;bc}$ we would have had the three following matrices:

$$E^1_{a;bc} = \begin{bmatrix} 0 & 0 & 0 & 1 \\ 1 & 1 & 0 & 1 \end{bmatrix}$$

$$E^2_{a;bc} = \begin{bmatrix} 1 & 1 & 0 & 0 \\ 0 & 1 & 0 & 1 \end{bmatrix}$$

$$E^3_{a;bc} = \begin{bmatrix} 1 & 0 & 0 & 1 \\ 1 & 1 & 0 & 0 \end{bmatrix}$$

which would have led to the three G_k functions:

$$f_1 = G_1(\psi_1, \psi_2, a)$$
$$f_2 = G_2(\psi_3, \psi_4, a)$$
$$f_3 = G_3(\psi_5, \psi_6, a).$$

If we had taken $E^1_{b;ac}$, $E^2_{b;ac}$, $E^3_{b;ac}$

$$E^1_{b;ac} = \begin{bmatrix} 0 & 1 & 0 & 0 \\ 0 & 1 & 1 & 1 \end{bmatrix}$$

$$E^2_{b;ac} = \begin{bmatrix} 1 & 0 & 0 & 0 \\ 1 & 1 & 0 & 1 \end{bmatrix}$$

$$E^2_{b;ac} = \begin{bmatrix} 1 & 1 & 0 & 0 \\ 0 & 1 & 1 & 0 \end{bmatrix}$$

we would have had

$$f_1 = H_1(\chi_1, \chi_2, b)$$
$$f_2 = H_2(\chi_3, \chi_4, b)$$
$$f_3 = H_3(\chi_5, \chi_6, b).$$

No technological restraint imposes the choice of a partition. We take the one which is the most convenient for us; note that $(ac; b)$ give a larger choice since E^1 and E^2 have three distinct columns which consequently gives the possibility of taking the T_{JI} matrices which best suit our interests.

The matrix T^1 associated with E^1 will have a row in which a 1 is in a 0 position and another row with a 1 in a 1 position, but the two following rows may be taken either 0011 and 0000, or 0010 and 0001. It is the same for T^2. There are 4 rows imposed for E^3; they have respectively a 1 in each of the 4 possible positions. This leads to a T

matrix common to the three functions which can be, for example:

$$T = \begin{bmatrix} 1 & 0 & 0 & 0 \\ 0 & 1 & 0 & 0 \\ 0 & 0 & 1 & 0 \\ 0 & 0 & 0 & 1 \end{bmatrix}.$$

But the functions X which thus appear are no other than a and c which are of little use. Note, however, that if we take

$$T^1 = \begin{bmatrix} 1 & 0 & 0 & 0 \\ 0 & 1 & 0 & 0 \\ 0 & 0 & 0 & 0 \\ 0 & 0 & 1 & 1 \end{bmatrix}$$

$$T^2 = \begin{bmatrix} 1 & 0 & 0 & 0 \\ 0 & 1 & 0 & 1 \\ 0 & 0 & 0 & 0 \\ 0 & 0 & 1 & 0 \end{bmatrix}.$$

We have:

$$\chi_1 = a + c$$
$$\chi_2 = c$$
$$\chi_3 = a + c = \chi_1$$
$$\chi_4 = \bar{a}c.$$

T^3 corresponds to $\chi_5 = a$. Hence, $\chi_6 = \chi_2 = c$. Therefore,

$$f_1 = H_1(\chi_1, \chi_2, b)$$
$$f_2 = H_2(\chi_1, \chi_4, b)$$
$$f_3 = H_3(\chi_5, \chi_2, b).$$

Leading to the same computation as the usual case:

$$f_1 = \chi_1(\bar{\chi}_2 + b)$$
$$f_2 = \bar{\chi}_4(\bar{\chi}_1 + b)$$
$$f_3 = b\bar{\chi}_2 + \chi_5\bar{\chi}_2 + b\chi_2\bar{\chi}_5 = \chi_2(\bar{b} + \chi_5) + b\chi_2\bar{\chi}_5.$$

3.6. MATRIX ANALYSIS OF COMBINATIONAL RELAY SYSTEMS

3.6.1. *Introduction to the method*

Reconsider the system of two Boolean output functions in Section 3.5.2.1.9.

$$z_1 = abc + d \qquad z_2 = abc + e.$$

Application of the extended Quine-McCluskey method produces the circuit in Figure 3.54.

We could have written:

$$z_1 = abc\bar{d} + d$$
$$z_2 = abc\bar{e} + e.$$

These equations which are not minimal according to the Quine-McCluskey method, give the circuit shown in Figure 3.55 which has 7 contacts, while a z_1, z_2 realization in terms of independent circuits needs 8 contacts. The Figure 3.55 circuit, more economic with respect to contacts than the Figure 3.51 circuit, is less economic than the Figure 3.54 circuit, but has the advantage of needing no diodes. The Figure 3.55 circuit is easily determined by matrix analysis of the combinational relay systems.

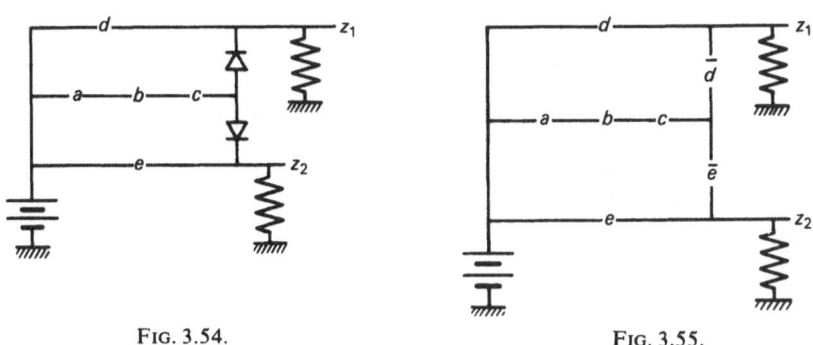

FIG. 3.54.　　　　　　　　FIG. 3.55.

3.6.2. Connection matrix

In Chapter 1 we gave a general definition of Boolean matrices. We shall now extend the notion of determinant to the set $(0, 1)$ and study a particular Boolean matrix related to the physical structure of the circuit; it is called the connection matrix.

3.6.2.1.

DEFINITION. The determinant, noted Δ, of an $(n \times n)$ Boolean matrix is the Boolean sum of the n terms obtained by multiplying one and only one element in each row and each column.

The minor of this determinant, δ_{ij}, is the determinant derived from the original by suppressing row i and column j.

The reader can verify that the determinant can be equally developed by following a row or a column and Sarrus' rule can be generalized for determinants of order 3.

Consider the following matrix A:

$$A = \begin{bmatrix} 1 & 0 & a & 1 \\ 1 & 0 & b & b \\ c & 1 & 0 & 1 \\ 0 & d & 0 & 1 \end{bmatrix}$$

$$\Delta = \begin{vmatrix} 1 & 0 & a & 1 \\ 1 & 0 & 0 & b \\ 0 & 1 & 0 & 1 \\ 0 & d & 0 & 1 \end{vmatrix} = \begin{vmatrix} 0 & 0 & b \\ 1 & 0 & 1 \\ d & 0 & 1 \end{vmatrix} + \begin{vmatrix} 0 & a & 1 \\ 1 & 0 & 1 \\ d & 0 & 1 \end{vmatrix} + c\begin{vmatrix} 0 & a & 1 \\ 0 & 0 & b \\ d & 0 & 1 \end{vmatrix}$$

$$\Delta = 0 + a + ad + abcd = a$$

$$\delta_{34} = \begin{vmatrix} 1 & 0 & a \\ 1 & 0 & 0 \\ 0 & d & 0 \end{vmatrix} = ad,$$

Consider Figure 3.56. The conductibility between i and j is written:

(a) $c_{ij} = c_{ji} = 1$
(b) $c_{ij} = c_{ji} = 0$
(c) $c_{ij} = 1$ $c_{ji} = 0$
(d) $c_{ij} = 0$ $c_{ji} = 1$
(e) $c_{ij} = a$ $c_{ji} = a$

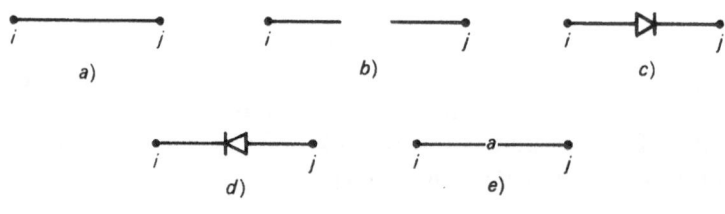

FIG. 3.56.

(notice for (c) and (d) that in one sense the rectifier is a conductor and in the other sense an open circuit; in (e) a is a Boolean variable corresponding to the contact at button A).

Note that the connection matrix of a relay network without rectifiers is symmetric while it is asymmetric in the opposite case.

Example. Consider the circuits in Figures 3.57a and b. Their connection matrices are:

$$M = \begin{bmatrix} 1 & a & 0 & c \\ a & 1 & d & b \\ 0 & d & 1 & e \\ c & b & e & 1 \end{bmatrix} \qquad N = \begin{bmatrix} 1 & a & 0 & c \\ a & 1 & d & 0 \\ 0 & d & 1 & e \\ 0 & b & 0 & 1 \end{bmatrix}$$

M is symmetric but N is not.

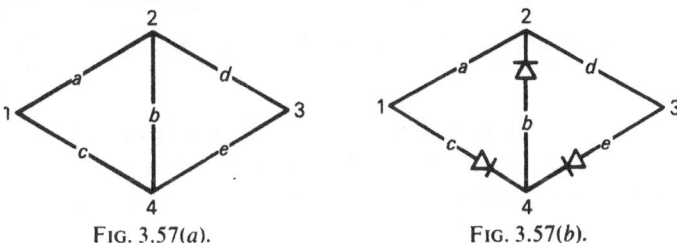

FIG. 3.57(a).   FIG. 3.57(b).

3.6.2.2. *Properties of the connection matrix*

(a) *Conductibility between two nodes of a network.* Let $A = (a_{ij})$ be the connection matrix of a combinational contact system.

$$A = i \begin{bmatrix} 1 & & \vdots & & \\ & & \vdots & & \\ \cdots & \cdots & \cdots & a_{ij} & \\ & & & & 1 \end{bmatrix}.$$

Consider the minor δ_{ij} of A's determinant Δ. It is obtained by suppressing the i row and j column.

$$\delta_{ij} = \begin{bmatrix} 1 & a_{1,2} & \cdots & a_{1,j-1} a_{1,j+1} & \cdots & a_{1n} \\ a_{j-1,1} & & \cdots\cdots\cdots\cdots\cdots\cdots & & a_{j-1,n} \\ a_{i+1,1} & & \cdots\cdots\cdots\cdots\cdots\cdots & & a_{i+1,n} \\ a_{n,1} & & \cdots\cdots\cdots\cdots\cdots & & 1 \end{bmatrix}.$$

a_{ik} and a_{kj} ($1 \leqslant k \leqslant n$) do not exist in δ_{ij}. The terms in the development of δ_{ij} can be put in the form:

$$a_{j,\alpha_1} a_{\alpha_1,\alpha_2} a_{\alpha_{n-3},\alpha_{n-2}} a_{\alpha_{n-2},i}$$

and can be separated into three classes.

(1) Certain elements $a_{\alpha_i,\alpha_{i+1}}$ are on the main diagonal: $\alpha_i = \alpha_{i+1}$ and $a_{\alpha_i,\alpha_{i+1}} = 1$.

(2) Part of the term under consideration is of the form

$$a_{\alpha_k, \alpha_{k+1}} \cdot a_{\alpha_{k+1}, \alpha_{k+2}} \cdots \cdots a_{\alpha_{k+p}, \alpha_k}.$$

This set therefore constitutes a loop.

(3) After excluding the first two cases, there remain terms in the general form such that $\alpha_1 \neq \alpha_2 \neq \cdots \neq \alpha_{n-2} \neq 1$ and no loop is included in these terms.

The expression for the conductibility between j and i is written:

$$C_{ji} = a_{ji} + \sum_{\alpha_k \neq i,j} a_{j,\alpha_1} a_{\alpha_1,i} + \cdots + \sum_{\alpha_k \neq i,j} a_{j,\alpha_1} a_{\alpha_1,\alpha_2} \cdots a_{\alpha_{n-2},i},$$

which expresses the fact that it equals the Boolean sum of the conductibilities of the paths which directly join j and i, passing another point, two other points, ..., or the $n-2$ other points (nodes) of the network.

We observe that in the development of δ_{ij} the first type terms correspond to the different terms of the conductibility C_{ji} except for

$$b = \sum_{\alpha_k \neq i,j} a_{j,\alpha_1} a_{\alpha_1,\alpha_2} \cdots a_{\alpha_{n-2},j} \quad (1 \leqslant k \leqslant n-2)$$

and the length of the paths corresponding to the different terms is $(n-1)$ minus the number of elements of the form: $a_{\alpha_i,\alpha_i} = 1$ (two points i and j of a circuit are connected by a path of length $q+1$ if the path passes q other points).

The second type terms correspond to the same conductibilities multiplied by a factor which corresponds to the conductibilities of the loops they contain. They are therefore redundant.

The third type terms correspond to b; we may hence write:

$$C_{ji} = \delta_{ij} \tag{3.3}$$

Example. Consider the circuit in Figure 3.58. The connection matrix is:

$$A = \begin{bmatrix} 1 & a & 0 & d \\ a & 1 & b & 0 \\ 0 & b & 1 & 0 \\ d & c & e & 1 \end{bmatrix}$$

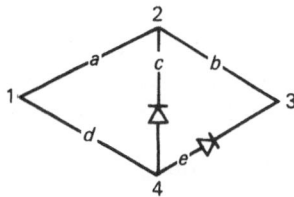

FIG. 3.58.

The conductibility from node 1 to node 3 is;

$$C_{13} = \delta_{31} = \begin{vmatrix} a & 0 & d \\ 1 & b & 0 \\ c & e & 1 \end{vmatrix} = ab + de + bcd.$$

The conductibility from node 3 to node 1 is:

$$C_{31} = \delta_{13} = \begin{vmatrix} a & 1 & 0 \\ 0 & b & 0 \\ d & c & 1 \end{vmatrix} = ab.$$

(b) *Successive powers of the connection matrix.* Every element of A^2 ($A \otimes A$) is in the form:

$$a_{ij}^2 = \sum_{k=1}^{n} a_{ik} a_{kj}.$$

This expression can be written:

$$a_{ij}^2 = \sum_{k \neq i,j} a_{ik} a_{kj} + a_{ij}$$
$$a_{ii}^2 = 1.$$

a_{ij}^2 is the set of paths of maximum length 2 which join i and j.

Since for all i and j, a_{ij} is contained in a_{ij}^2 ($a_{ij} \leqslant a_{ij}^2$), A is contained in A^2 ($A \leqslant A^2$).

In the general case, suppose A^{p-1} (A to the $p-1$ power) corresponds to the set of paths of maximum length $p-1$ which join the pairs of the circuit nodes.

We may write: $A^p = A^{p-1}A$

a_{ij}^p the element defining A^p is expressed:

$$a_{ij}^p = \sum_k a_{ik}^{p-1} a_{kj} = a_{ij} + \sum_{k \neq i,j} a_{ik}^{p-1} a_{kj} + a_{ij}^{p-1}.$$

a_{ij}^p is the set of paths of maximum length p; therefore A^{p-1} is contained in A^p.

If n is the order of A, the longest paths joining two of the circuit's nodes are of order $n-1$ (there are at most $n-1$ intervals between the two points). Every path of order greater than $n-1$ equals a path of which the length is between 1 and $n-1$; therefore

$$a_{ij}^n = a_{ij}^{n-1} \quad \text{for any } i \text{ and } j,$$

that is, $A^n = A^{n-1}$ and $A^q = A^{n-1}$ if $q \geqslant n$.
   Finally, $A \leqslant A^2 \leqslant A_3 \leqslant \cdots \leqslant A^{n-1} = A^n = A^{n+1}$.

THEOREM.   Given a connection matrix of order n, there exists a positive integer p less than or equal to n such that:

$$A \leqslant A^2 \leqslant \cdots \leqslant A^p = A^{p+1} = \cdots = A^n = \cdots$$

(the matrix A^p corresponds to the set of all paths joining the pairs of nodes in the circuit).

Example. Consider the connection matrix of the circuit in Figure 3.58.

$$A = \begin{bmatrix} 1 & a & 0 & d \\ a & 1 & b & 0 \\ 0 & b & 1 & 0 \\ d & c & e & 1 \end{bmatrix}$$

$$A^2 = \begin{bmatrix} 1 & a+cd & ab+de & d \\ a & 1 & b & ad \\ ab & b & 1 & 0 \\ d+ac & c+ad+be & e+bc & 1 \end{bmatrix}$$

$$A^3 = A^2A = \begin{bmatrix} 1 & a+cd+bde & ab+de+bcd & d \\ a & 1 & b+ade & ad \\ ab & b & 1 & abd \\ d+ac+abe & c+ad+be & e+bc+abd & 1 \end{bmatrix}$$

We can verify that $A^3 = A^4$ and we observe that the elements of A^2 and A^3 are paths of respective maximum lengths 2 and 3 joining the pairs of nodes.

3.6.3. *Application of connection matrices to combinational multipoles*

3.6.3.1. *Node removal or addition in a network*
Consider the circuit in Figure 3.59. If we take the nodes in the in-

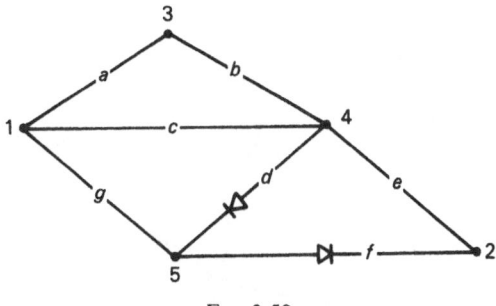

FIG. 3.59.

creasing order of the numbers which characterize them, the connection matrix is:

$$A = \begin{bmatrix} 1 & 0 & a & c & g \\ 0 & 1 & 0 & e & 0 \\ a & 0 & 1 & b & 0 \\ c & e & b & 1 & d \\ g & f & 0 & 0 & 1 \end{bmatrix}.$$

If a_{ij} is the general term of the connection matrix A to a p node circuit in which we eliminate node k without modifying the conductibilities between pairs of nodes different from k, we must add to every a_{ij} term representing the conductibility from node i directly to node j, the conductibility of the path joining i and j which passes k but only if it passes k ($i, j = 1, 2, ..., p$).

A' the new connection matrix is hence defined by

$$\boxed{a'_{ij} = a_{ij} + a_{ik}a_{kj}.} \tag{3.4}$$

In the preceeding example the new connection matrix A' resulting from the suppression of node 4 is:

$$A' = \begin{bmatrix} 1 & ce & a+bc & g+cd \\ ce & 1 & be & ed \\ a+bc & be & 1 & bd \\ g & f & 0 & 1 \end{bmatrix}$$

The corresponding network is shown in Figure 3.60. We observe that the conductibility between nodes 1, 2, 3, 5 is the same in both networks.

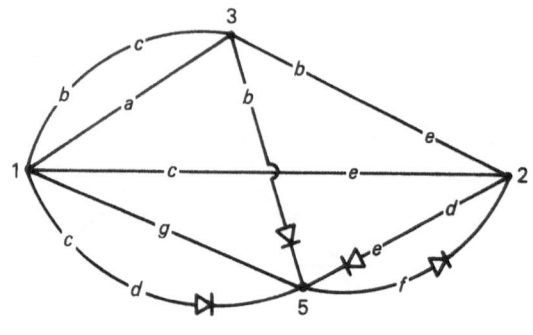

FIG. 3.60.

We compute, for example, C_{12}, for the circuit in Figure 3.59

$$C_{12} = \begin{vmatrix} 0 & a & c & g \\ 0 & 1 & b & 0 \\ e & b & 1 & d \\ f & 0 & 0 & 1 \end{vmatrix} = e \begin{vmatrix} a & c & g \\ 1 & b & 0 \\ 0 & 0 & 1 \end{vmatrix} + f \begin{vmatrix} a & c & g \\ 1 & b & 0 \\ b & 1 & d \end{vmatrix}$$

$$C_{12} = abe + abdf + gf + ce + cdf,$$

for the circuit in Figure 3.60

$$C_{12} = \begin{vmatrix} ce & a+bc & g+cd \\ be & 1 & bd \\ f & 0 & 1 \end{vmatrix} = \begin{aligned} & ce + bfd(a+bc) \\ & \quad + f(g+cd) + be(a+bc) \end{aligned}$$

$$C_{12} = ce + abdf + abe + gf + cdf.$$

Generally, we consider a p-node circuit which has for its connection coefficients (or elements of the connection matrix) the a_{ij}.

THEOREM. The connection matrix A' of the circuit derived from the initial circuit by eliminating a node k, is defined by:

$$a'_{ji} = a_{ij} + a_{ik} a_{kj}.$$

To prove this theorem we shall show that the conductibility between two nodes, i and j, is conserved, since the passage from A to A' has already been established by relation (3.4).

For the initial circuit, we may write:

$$C_{ij} = \delta_{ij} = \sum a_{i,l_1} a_{l_1,l_2} \cdots a_{l_{p-2},j}$$

$l_1, \ldots, l_{p-2}$ can take all values between 1 and p including i and j.

From relation (3.4)

$$C'_{ij} = \delta'_{ij} = \sum_{l_1,\ldots,l_{p-3}\neq k} a'_{i,l_1} \cdots a'_{l_{p-3},j}$$

$$C'_{ij} = \sum_{l_1,\ldots,l_{p-3}\neq k} (a_{i,l_1} + a_{ik}a_{kl_1}) \cdots (a_{l_{p-3},j} + a_{l_{p-3},k}a_{k,j}).$$

$$\tag{3.5}$$

The term

$$\sum_{l_1,\ldots,l_{p-3}\neq k} a_{i,l_1}a_{l_1,l_2} \cdots a_{l_{p-3}\,j}$$

corresponds to the set of paths which join i to j without passing k.

In the development of (3.5) the term

$$\sum_{l_1,\ldots,l_{p-3}\neq k} a_{i,l_1} \cdots a_{l_{m-2},l_{m-1}}(a_{l_{m-1},k}a_{k,l_m})a_{l_m,l_{m+1}} \cdots a_{l_{p-3}\,j}$$

corresponds to only one factor analogous to (3.4) and hence represents the set of paths passing the point k. Every term in the development of (3.5) having several factors analogous to (3.4) is a path joining i to j and passing k; it therefore belongs to the preceding category. In fact, this type term is written:

$$\sum_{l_1,\ldots,l_{p-3}\neq k} a_{il_1} \cdots a_{\alpha_1 k}a_{k\alpha_2} \cdots a_{\beta_1 k}a_{k\beta_2} \cdots a_{\delta_1 k}a_{k\delta_2} \cdots a_{l_{p-3}\,j}$$

or

$$\sum_{l_1,\ldots,l_{p-3}\neq k} (a_{il_1} \cdots a_{\alpha_1 k}a_{k\delta_2} \cdots a_{l_{p-3}\,j})a_{k\alpha_2} \cdots a_{\delta_1 k}. \tag{3.6}$$

The term $a_{k\alpha_2}\cdots a_{\delta_1 k}$ corresponds to a loop passing the node k and the product $(a_{i,l_1} \cdots a_{\alpha_1,k}a_{k,\delta_2} \cdots a_{l_{p-3}\,j})$ is a path passing k and joining i and j already obtained. The term (3.6) is therefore redundant and:

$$C'_{ij} = C_{ij}. \tag{3.7}$$

Comment. In the elimination of a node k, the relation (3.4) shows that for a given row of the connection matrix, a_{ik} is the same for all a'_{ij} (for any $j \neq k$). In the same way, for a given column j, the a'_{ij} have the same a_{kj}.

3.6.3.2. *Addition of supplementary nodes to a circuit*

By virtue of the preceding comment, it will be possible to add supplementary nodes to a network if the elements of row i are in the form:

$$a'_{ij} = a_{ij} + ba_{kj} \tag{3.8}$$

or if the elements of column j are in the form:

$$a'_{ij} = a_{ij} + a_{ik}c. \tag{3.9}$$

In (3.8) b is the a_{ik} term at the intersection of row i and the new column; a_{kj} is at the intersection of the new row and the j column. Relation (3.9) has an analogous interpretation.

Interpretation from the connection matrix. Figure 3.61a represents the i and k rows followed by the j and k columns of the connection matrix under consideration $a_{kk} = 1$.

In Figure 3.61b where node k has been removed, the coefficient a'_{ij} is defined by relation (3.4). Working with the connection matrix it is sufficient to find the term in column k situated in row i and the term in row k situated in column j, then take the Boolean product of these terms.

	j		k	
i	a_{ij}		a_{ik}	
k	a_{kj}		1	

FIG. 3.61(a).

	j	
i	a'_{ij}	

FIG. 3.61(b).

Example. Consider the connection matrix A (Figure 3.62a) and the corresponding circuit (Figure 3.62b). Let 1, 2, 3, 4 be the four nodes of the initial circuit corresponding to A.

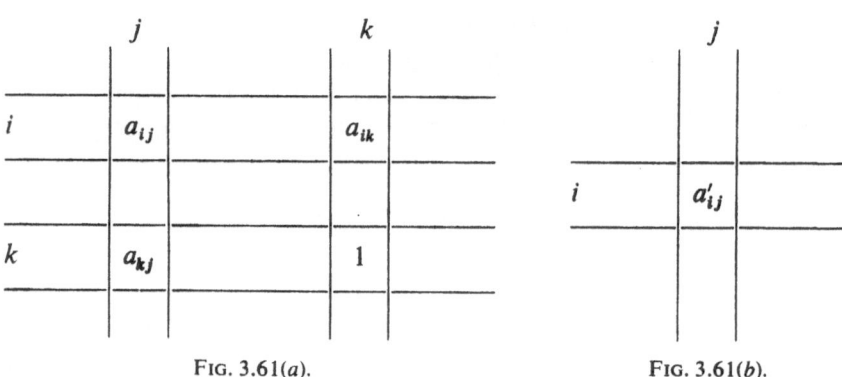

$$A = \begin{bmatrix} 1 & ce & a+bc & g+cd \\ 0 & 1 & bc & ed \\ a & bc & 1 & bd \\ g & f & 0 & 1 \end{bmatrix}$$

FIG. 3.62(a).

FIG. 3.62(b).

Note that in the first row of A, c is a factor in the terms ce, bc, cd. If we add a 5th node, we have A, in Figure 3.63a and the circuit in Figure 3.63b.

Observe that since $a_{11} = 1$, we can put any term in the place of a_{51}. We take c so that we will have one rectifier less thus economizing two contacts.

$$
A' = \begin{bmatrix}
1 & 0 & a & g & c \\
0 & 1 & bc & ed & 0 \\
a & bc & 1 & bd & 0 \\
g & f & 0 & 1 & 0 \\
c & e & b & d & 1
\end{bmatrix}
$$

FIG. 3.63(*a*).   FIG. 3.63(*b*).

Note that in the case of a symmetrical connection matrix (circuit without rectifiers) supplementary nodes can be created either by introduction of rectifiers as before (the new circuit's connection matrix is unsymmetrical) which has little interest, or without using rectifiers (the new circuit's connection matrix is symmetrical). However, if we operate on a row (or column) of the initial connection matrix (use of rectifiers) to create a supplementary node, we generally obtain a connection matrix which doesn't give the matrix of the circuit without rectifiers by symmetry. This means that we cannot operate on only one row (or column) of the initial connection matrix and complete by symmetry to create supplementary nodes without introducing rectifiers. This is shown in the following example.

Consider the connection matrix A (Figure 3.64a).

A 5th node due to the common factor c is created (use of rectifiers). The connection matrix in Figure 3.65(a) is obtained.

We now create a 5th node without using rectifiers (note that this operation cannot be performed in the absence of the term 'b' of a_{23} and a_{32} in matrix A). The matrix in Figure 3.65(b) and the circuit in Figure 3.65(c) are obtained. We see that this matrix is different from the one previously obtained by symmetry.

$$A = \begin{bmatrix} 1 & ce & a+bc & g+cd \\ ce & 1 & bc+be & ed \\ a+bc & bc+be & 1 & bd \\ g+cd & ed & bd & 1 \end{bmatrix}$$

FIG. 3.64(a).

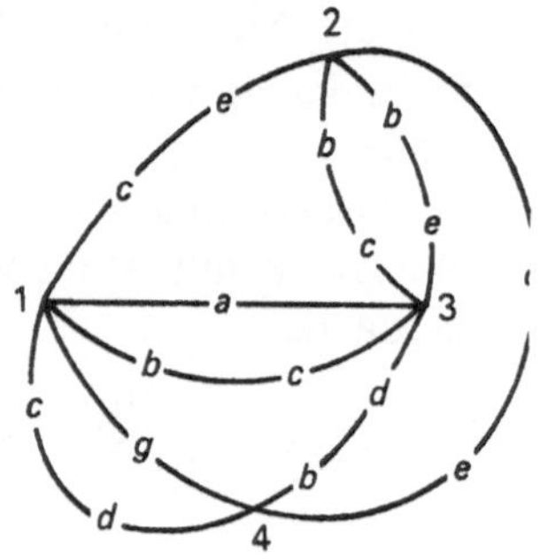

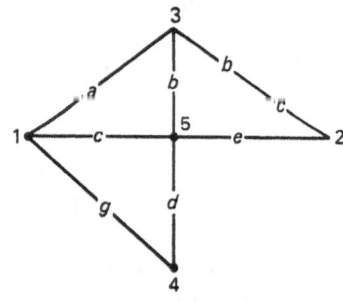

FIG. 3.64(b).

$$\begin{bmatrix} 1 & 0 & a & g & c \\ ce & 1 & bc+be & ed & 0 \\ a+bc & bc+be & 1 & bd & 0 \\ g+cd & ed & bd & 1 & 0 \\ 0 & e & b & d & 1 \end{bmatrix}$$

FIG. 3.65(a).

$$\begin{bmatrix} 1 & 0 & a & g & c \\ 0 & 1 & bc & 0 & e \\ a & bc & 1 & 0 & b \\ g & 0 & 0 & 1 & d \\ c & e & b & d & 1 \end{bmatrix}$$

FIG. 3.65(b).

FIG. 3.65(c).

Another procedure consists in working with the half of the connection matrix above the principal diagonal (Ref. [7]). In fact, the relation:

$$a'_{ij} = a_{ij} + a_{ik}a_{kj}$$

can be written:

$$a'_{ij} = a_{ij} + a_{ik}a_{jk} = a'_{ji}.$$

Consider row i or j depending on whether i is the larger or smaller of the two. For the preceding example the top half matrix A is:

$$
\begin{matrix}
1 & ce & a+bc & g+cd \\
  & 1 & bc+be & ed \\
  &   & 1 & bd \\
  &   &   & 1
\end{matrix}
$$

Addition of a 5th node gives the half matrix:

$$
\begin{matrix}
1 & 0 & a & g & c \\
  & 1 & bc & 0 & e \\
  &   & 1 & 0 & b \\
  &   &   & 1 & d \\
  &   &   &   & 1
\end{matrix}
$$

which permits the construction of A'.

Comment. Addition of supplementary nodes in the case of symmetric matrices simplifies the initial circuit. This is due to the fact that the factorization considered eliminates some of the contacts. In the case of rectifiers (Figures 3.62 and 3.63) there is simplification if we operate either on a subnetwork having rectifiers in each branch or on a subnetwork without rectifiers. One term is always factorized in either case. This does not involve the addition of rectifiers and decrease the number of contacts.

If we operate on a mixed subnetwork (some branches have rectifiers and others don't) addition of supplementary nodes complicates the circuit and should definitely not be done in this case. As a matter of fact, the rectifiers lead to two branches instead of one without rectifiers and the economy due to the factorization does not compensate the cost of the operation.

A common factor in all the terms of one row or one column (c) corresponds to a contact which is identical in every branch from or to a 1 node.

Consider Figure 3.66a. Three nodes, j, k, l, part from i and the conductibility directly between i and j, k, l is as in Figure 3.66a. By factorizing c and adding a supplementary node, m, the circuit in Figure 3.66b is realized. Its effect is to complicate instead of simplify the circuit.

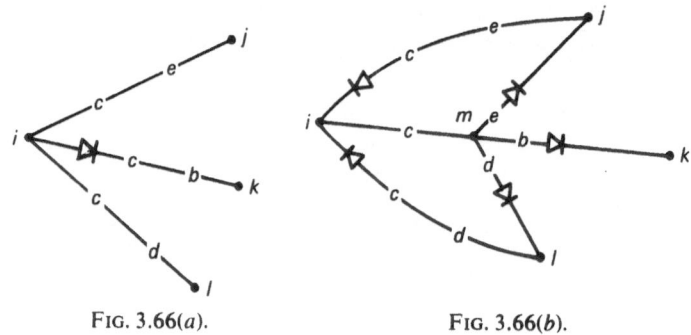

FIG. 3.66(a).   FIG. 3.66(b).

3.6.4. *Elimination of redundant terms*

(a) *Systems having nothing but rectifiers in all branches.* Consider a circuit which has a number of nodes at least two greater than k and part of which has k nodes as in Figure 3.67(a).

3.6.4.1. *Type one*

The type 1 redundant elements are the terms which disappear when a supplementary node is added to the network.

In the preceding example, addition of a 5th node removed the terms ce, bc and cd from the first row of the connection matrix A. They are therefore type 1 redundant elements.

3.6.4.2. *Type two of series redundant terms*

We propose to answer the following question: Can the connection matrix be used to determine the network's redundant elements?

We classify three types of redundancy.

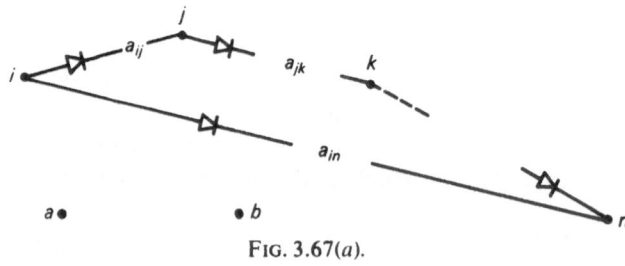

FIG. 3.67(a).

Let a and b be any two nodes of the network different from i, j, ..., n. To evaluate the conductibility C_{ab} between a and b, we separate the different paths going from a to b into 3 categories.

(a) Those which use neither the branch (i, n), nor the set of branches $(i, j), (j, k), \ldots, (m, n)$.
Let $C_{\neq ij \ldots n}$ be their conductibility.

(b) Those which use the branches (i, j), $(j, k), \ldots, (m, n)$. Let $C_{ij \ldots n}$ be their conductibility.

(c) Those which use the branch (i, n). Let C_{in} be their conductibility.

Note that there exist indirect paths going from i to j, from j to k, from m to n. Let C be the conductibility of the set of paths going from a to i and from n to b.

C_{ab} can be written:

$$C_{ab} = C_{\neq i,j \ldots n} + C_{ij \ldots n} + C_{in}.$$

Furthermore, C_{in} and $C_{ij \ldots n}$ can be expressed in terms of C:

$$C_{in} = C \cdot a_{in}$$

$$C_{ij \ldots n} = C \cdot (a_{ij} \cdot \cdots \cdot a_{mn})$$

from which we deduce the relation:

$$C_{ab} = C_{\neq ij \ldots n} + C(a_{in} + a_{ij} \cdot \cdots \cdot a_{mn}) \qquad (3.10)$$

If a_{in} is included in the product $a_{ij} \ldots a_{mn}$, C_{ab} is not modified. This holds even if the (i, n) branch is removed and either a or b or both are among the points $i, j, \ldots, n$ (Figure 3.67b).

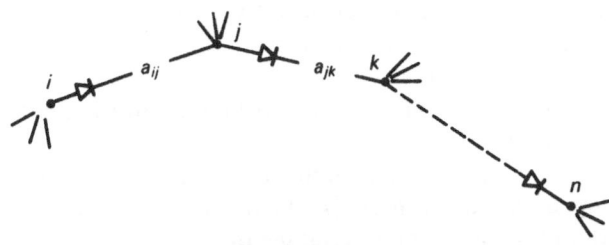

FIG. 3.67(b).

THEOREM. The circuits in Figures 3.67a and b are equivalent. This statement means that the conductibilities between corresponding points are equal if the condition $a_{ij} a_{jk} \cdots a_{mn} \geqslant a_{in}$ realized.

(b) *Relay systems without rectifiers.* A branch ij (Figure 3.68(a)) can be represented as in Figure 3.68(b) since the conductibilities are equal in both directions.

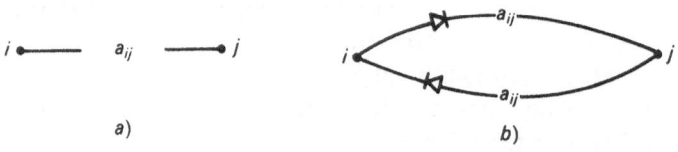

FIG. 3.68.

Figure 3.67(a) in the case of systems without rectifiers can, due to Figure 3.68(b), be represented as indicated by Figure 3.69.

We may proceed by superposing as in Figure 3.67(a). If we have the relation $a_{in} \leqslant a_{ij}a_{jk} \cdots a_{mn}$ the (i, n) branch can be removed and the conductibility of the paths between any two points of the circuit is not modified due to the presence of branches (i, j), (j, k), ..., (m, n).

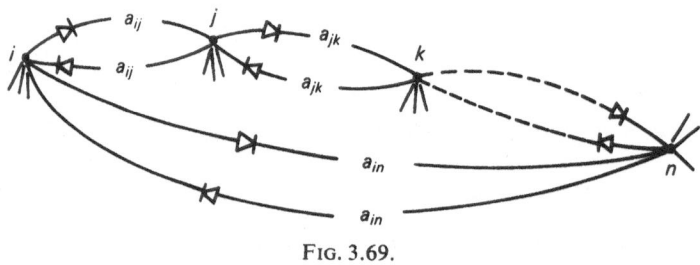

FIG. 3.69.

In the same way, removal of the (n, i) branch does not modify the conductibility of paths between any two points of the circuit since branches (n, m), ..., (j, i) are present.

Therefore, in this case, branches (i, n) and (n, i) can be eliminated without causing modification of the conductibility between any two points of the network.

(c) *Mixed systems.* Here certain loops (k, l, k) in Figure 3.69 are replaced by a simple branch, (k, l) or (l, k), if there is a rectifier between the two corresponding nodes of the circuit.

If we have the configuration $(i, j, ..., m, n)$ or $(n, m, ..., j, i)$ of Figure 3.69, (n, i) or (i, n) can be removed if one of the following conditions hold:

$$a_{in} \leqslant a_{ij}a_{jk} \cdots a_{mn}$$
$$a_{ni} \leqslant a_{nm} \cdots a_{ji}.$$

No reduction can be made under other conditions .

(d) *Interpretation on a connection matrix.*

(d.1) *Geometrical configuration relative to terms in series.* Let a be the conductibility between two points i and j: $a_{ij} = a$.

We wish to represent the conductibilities b, c, d of points k, l, m on a connection matrix. We suppose that these quantities are as indicated in Figure 3.70(a). We assume the conductibility from i to m to be the product of the conductibilities (i, j) (j, k) (k, l) (l, m), i.e. we suppose all rectifiers to be oriented in the same direction.

Looking at the connection matrix in Figure 3.70(b), we see that each row corresponds to a branch origin and each column to a branch extremity (a in the case ij corresponds to a branch with origin i and extremity j). Starting from j (extremity of ij), we descend the j column to the square marked '1' which is on the j row corresponding to the fact that j is the origin of the jk branch (next step in the product). We then cross the j row to the k column (extremity of the jk branch). This intersection is marked b. In the same way, we descend the k column to

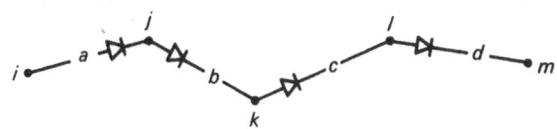

FIG. 3.70(a).

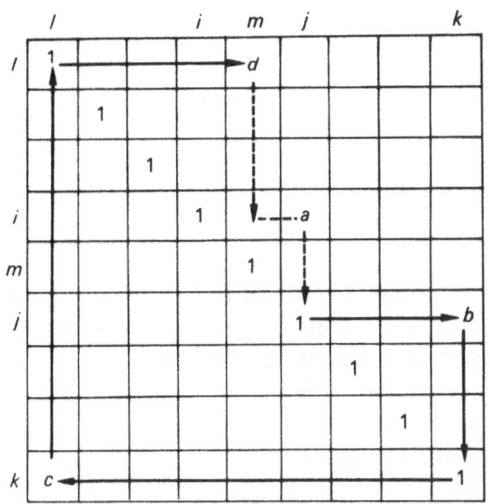

FIG. 3.70(b).

the square marked '1' which is in the k row corresponding to the fact that k is the origin of the kl branch then cross the k row to c which is in the l column corresponding to the fact that it is the extremity of the kl branch. We continue in this way moving up the l column to '1' in the l row (origin of the lm branch) and across the l row to d in the m column.

We have thus drawn a broken line of arrows $a1b1c1d$. a_{im} is at the intersection of row i and column m since the origin of the branch is i and its extremity m.

(d.2) *Geometrical configuration relative to type 2 redundant terms.* The preceding shows that if $a_{im} = abcd$, it is redundant. To see if a term $abcd$, for example, is redundant, we examine the connection matrix to see if a term containing it is in its row (for example, a in Figure 3.66). We then search a polygonal line starting from this point and ending in the $abcd$ term column.

Example. Consider the connection matrix A in Figure 3.71(a). We shall show that the term $\bar{a}cde$ is a type 2 redundant term.

FIG. 3.71(a).

In the second column $\bar{a}$ is in the same row as $\bar{a}cde$. In the 3rd row e is in the same column as $\bar{a}cde$. We search a polygonal line from $\bar{a}$ to e.

We move along the column which contains $\bar{a}$ until we reach '1', then across the row containing this '1' to c, etc. The result is the polygonal contour indicated on the matrix A showing $\bar{a}cde$ to be a redundant term. The network's nodes being $1, 2, 3, 4, 5$ respectively, the polygonal path $\bar{a}cde$ corresponds to the route 1 2 4 3 5.

Terms be in a_{25} and a_{52} are redundant. We have b in the same row as a_{25} and e in the same column as a_{25}; these two terms correspond to a polygonal contour (rectangle).

In the same way, $a_{42} = de$, $a_{41} = bed + \bar{b}\bar{c}$, $a_{13} = b$, be of a_{31}, $a_{34} = \bar{c}e$ are redundant terms. The matrix A is shown in Figure 3.71b. (We keep the term bc in a_{14} which is redundant in order to use it in the next section.

(e) *Utilization of redundant terms for simplification of the connection matrix*. Part of the connection matrix under consideration is shown in Figure 3.72(a), where no redundant terms appear. We observe that addition of the redundant term ab to $\bar{a}b$ would simply give b and, therefore, the submatrix in Figure 3.72(b) which is a simplification of the initial connection matrix.

$$A = \begin{bmatrix} 1 & \bar{a}+b & 0 & b\bar{e}+bc & 0 \\ b & 1 & b & c & 0 \\ \bar{c} & e & 1 & 0 & e \\ 0 & 0 & d & 1 & \bar{c} \\ \bar{b} & 0 & e & \bar{c} & 1 \end{bmatrix}$$

FIG. 3.71(b).

1	$\bar{a}b$		a	
	1			
		1		
	b		1	
				1

FIG. 3.72(a).

1	b		a	
	1			
		1		
	b		1	
				1

FIG. 3.72(b).

Example. Reconsider the preceding example, (Figure 3.73a). The redundant term $be\bar{c}$ can be added to $a_{14} = b\bar{e} + bc$ giving:

$$a_{14} = b\bar{e} + bc + be\bar{c} = b\bar{e} + bc + b\bar{c} = b$$

and we thus obtain the simplified matrix A' (Figure 3.73b). The corresponding circuit is shown in Figure 3.73(c).

$$A = \begin{bmatrix} 1 & \bar{a}+b & 0 & b\bar{e}+bc & 0 \\ b & 1 & \bar{b} & c & 0 \\ \bar{c} & e & 1 & 0 & e \\ 0 & 0 & d & 1 & \bar{c} \\ \bar{b} & 0 & e & \bar{c} & 1 \end{bmatrix}$$

FIG. 3.73(a).

$$A' = \begin{bmatrix} 1 & \bar{a}+b & 0 & b & 0 \\ b & 1 & b & c & 0 \\ \bar{c} & e & 1 & 0 & e \\ 0 & 0 & d & 1 & \bar{c} \\ \bar{b} & 0 & e & \bar{c} & 1 \end{bmatrix}$$

FIG. 3.73(b).

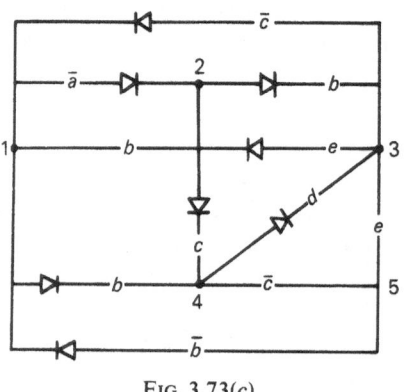

FIG. 3.73(c).

(f) *Symmetrical connection matrices.* In this case it is sufficient to search the redundant terms in the top half matrix and complete the simplified matrix by symmetry.

Consider the matrix in Figure 3.74(a). We observe that it is symmetric and the redundant terms in the top half matrix are:

$$a_{12} = a\bar{b} + \bar{a}bc$$
$$bc \text{ in } a_{14}$$
$$a_{15} = a\bar{b}c$$
$$a_{45} = acd.$$

If we add the redundant term ac to $a_{23} = \bar{a}c$, this term becomes c giving the matrix in Figure 3.74(b).

It is possible to work strictly with the top half matrix which actually would only have the advantage of gaining the time it would take to write the lower half.

$$\begin{bmatrix} 1 & a\bar{b}+\bar{a}bc & b & a+bc & a\bar{b}c \\ a\bar{b}+\bar{a}bc & 1 & \bar{a}c & \bar{b} & c \\ b & \bar{a}c & 1 & c & a \\ a+bc & \bar{b} & c & 1 & acd \\ a\bar{b}c & c & a & acd & 1 \end{bmatrix}$$

FIG. 3.74(a).

$$\begin{bmatrix} 1 & 0 & b & a & 0 \\ 0 & 1 & c & \bar{b} & c \\ b & c & 1 & c & a \\ a & \bar{b} & c & 1 & 0 \\ 0 & c & a & 0 & 1 \end{bmatrix}$$

FIG. 3.74(b).

3.6.4.3. *Type 3 redundant terms*

(a) DEFINITION. These redundant terms are an application of Theorem 5 in Section 1.3.2.

If we have $f = ax + \bar{a}y + xy$, simplification gives $f = ax + \bar{a}y$; xy is a redundant term. It can exist in a term a_{ij} of the connection matrix; but terms like ax and $\bar{a}y$ which make xy a type 3 redundant term do not explicitly figure in the matrix because they would be type 2 redundant terms. They can in fact be created from other terms a_{kl}.

(b) *Method of research for type 3 redundant terms.* If we have $a_{ij} = xy$, we must see if there are two polygonal contours joining a_{ij} to two terms of the form ax and $\bar{a}y$. ax and $\bar{a}y$ are type 2 redundant terms which cause $a_{ij} = xy$ to be a type 3 redundancy.

Figure 3.75 represents this type configuration. We note, considering the cell containing xyz, that ax and $\bar{a}y$ can be added to it causing no modification of conductibilities between pairs of points in the initial circuit. Their consensus xy, makes xyz a type 3 redundant term.

(c) *Example.* Consider Figures 3.76a and b. The variables a and e figure uniquely in their normal or complemented form.

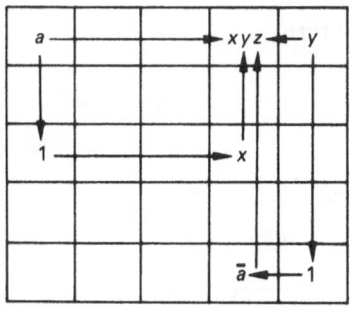

FIG. 3.75.

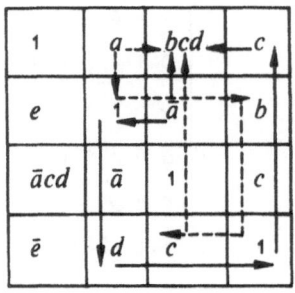

1	a bcd c		
e	1 ā		b
ācd	ā	1	c
ē	d	c	1

FIG. 3.76(a).

1	a	b c d	c
e	1	ā	b
ācd	ā	1	c
ē	d	c	1

FIG. 3.76(b).

1	a	0	c
e	1	ā	b
0	ā	1	c
ē	d	c	1

FIG. 3.76(c).

Variable a. The two polygonal contours $a1b1c$ and $\bar{a}1d1c$ (Figure 3.76a) give the consensus bcd which makes $a_{13} = bcd$ a type 3 redundant term in the initial matrix.

Variable 3. The two polygonal lines $e1\bar{a}$ and $\bar{e}1c$ (Figure 3.76b) give the consensus $\bar{a}c$. The term $a_{31} = \bar{a}cd$ becomes a type 3 redundant term. The reduced connection matrix is represented in Figure 3.76(c).

Comment. Whenever the connection matrix is symmetric, it is sufficient, as in the search for type 2 redundant terms, to simplify the top half matrix and complete it by symmetry.

3.6.5. *Example of a multipole synthesis*

Consider the connection matrix of a multipole as in Figure 3.77(a). It is symmetric. We study the top half matrix. The reader can verify that

$$acde \quad \text{in} \quad a_{13}$$
$$a_{15} = \bar{a}\bar{d} + ad$$
$$a_{24} = b\bar{d}e$$
$$be \quad \text{in} \quad a_{25}$$

are type 2 redundant terms.

$$
\begin{bmatrix}
1 & a & bc\bar{d}e+acde & \bar{a} & \bar{a}\bar{d}+ad \\
a & 1 & b & b\bar{d}e & d+be \\
bc\bar{d}e+acde & b & 1 & c & e+bc \\
\bar{a} & b\bar{d}e & c & 1 & \bar{d}+\bar{e}c \\
\bar{a}\bar{d}+ad & d+be & e+bc & \bar{d}+\bar{e}c & 1
\end{bmatrix}
$$

FIG. 3.77(a).

Addition of ec, a type 2 redundancy, to the term a_{45} results in a simplification.

$bc\bar{d}e$ in a_{13} and bc in a_{35} are type 3 redundant terms. Figure 3.77(b) shows the simplified matrix and Figure 3.77(c) the corresponding circuit.

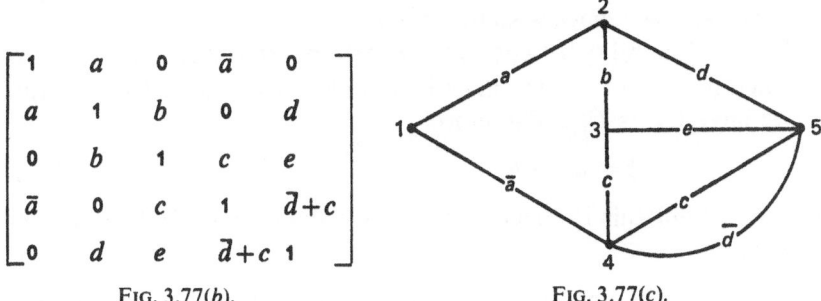

$$\begin{bmatrix} 1 & a & 0 & \bar{a} & 0 \\ a & 1 & b & 0 & d \\ 0 & b & 1 & c & e \\ \bar{a} & 0 & c & 1 & \bar{d}+c \\ 0 & d & e & \bar{d}+c & 1 \end{bmatrix}$$

FIG. 3.77(b).   FIG. 3.77(c).

3.6.6. Partial equivalence of combinational multipoles

3.6.6.1. Definition

The methods described in Sections 3.4.3, 3.4.4, 3.4.5 conserve the conductibility between all pairs of nodes in the circuit. After using these methods, the original and final networks are therefore, completely equivalent. But this total equivalence goes too far when we are interested in only certain pairs of nodes; a correspondence of partial equivalence between two networks would be all that is necessary. In this case it would be sufficient to perform transformations which simplify the circuit and conserve the conductibilities between the pairs of nodes which interest us independently of the others. After such modification the initial and final circuits are only *partially equivalent*.

3.6.6.2. Application to combinational dipoles

If we look at the combinational dipole from a topological point of view, it is really a multipole. As we are interested in only 2 nodes, we call one input and the other output. On the other hand, the multipole is really a dipole from the point of view of performance.

We shall show that an n terminal multipole which has its connection matrix A defined by a_{ij} in the i row and j column, can be reduced in the case in which the conservation of conductibility between only two nodes is envisaged (let h and k be the two nodes). The method which we shall extend to the case of circuits with rectifiers is due to Seman.

Consider an element $a_{ij} = l$ of the connection matrix. How can it be modified without changing the conductibility C_{hk} between h and k?

Developing the minor δ_{kh} of the determinant Δ corresponding to A, we may write this conductibility: $C_{hk} = al + b$, where a and b are Boolean expressions depending on other coefficients $a_{ij} \neq l$. Let m be the term with which we wish to replace l.

The conductibility between h and k in the new circuit is $C'_{hk} = am + b$.

Since these two circuits must be equivalent for input h and output k, we have $C_{hk} = C'_{hk}$. Therefore,

$$al + b = am + b. \tag{3.11}$$

Before solving this Boolean equation, we shall establish the following lemma.

LEMMA. The necessary and sufficient condition that two Boolean expressions, A and B, be equal is:

$$A\bar{B} + \bar{A}B = 0. \tag{3.12}$$

The sufficiency is evident since $A = B$ implies (3.12). Reciprocally (3.12) implies (3.13) and (3.14):

$$A\bar{B} = 0 \tag{3.13}$$
$$\bar{A}B = 0. \tag{3.14}$$

(3.13) is written $AB + A\bar{B} = AB$. Therefore, $A = AB$ $(B + \bar{B} = 1)$ which means that A is equal to or belongs to B.

(3.14) indicates that B is equal to or belongs to A. Consequently $A = B$.

In virtue of (3.12), (3.11) implies (3.15) and reciprocally

$$\overline{(al + b)}(am + b) + (al + b)\overline{(am + b)} = 0. \tag{3.15}$$

Let

$$(\bar{a} + \bar{l})\bar{b}(am + b) + (al + b)\bar{b}(\bar{a} + \bar{m}) = 0$$

that is

$$\bar{l}bam + al b\bar{m} = 0, \tag{3.16}$$

which means

$$\bar{l}bam = 0 \tag{3.17}$$
$$alb\bar{m} = 0. \tag{3.18}$$

(3.17) is written $m \leqslant \overline{a\overline{l}b}$ or $m \leqslant \bar{a}+l+b$.

(3.18) is written $a\bar{l}b \leqslant m$.

The preceding inequalities are summarized by

$$a\bar{l}b \leqslant m \leqslant \bar{a}+l+b \ . \tag{3.19}$$

3.6.6.3 . *Application to combinational multipoles*

If we wish to conserve the conductibility between several pairs of nodes, instead of just two, a certain number of simultaneous inequalities must be solved:

$$a_{i_1}l\overline{b_{i_1}} \leqslant m \leqslant \overline{a_{i_1}}+l+b_{i_1}$$
$$\cdots\cdots\cdots\cdots\cdots\cdots\cdots\cdots\cdots \tag{3.20}$$
$$a_{i_p}l\overline{b_{i_p}} \leqslant m \leqslant \overline{a_{i_p}}+l+b_{i_p}.$$

In fact, consider the term l in the connection matrix, which we wish to replace by m. Let $(i_1, j_1) \cdots (i_p, j_p)$ be the pairs of nodes between which conductibility must be conserved. These conductibilities are:

$$C_{i_1 j_1} = a_{i_1}l + b_{i_1}$$
$$\cdots\cdots\cdots\cdots\cdots\cdots$$
$$C_{i_p j_p} = a_{i_p}l + b_{i_p}.$$

Application of (3.19) leads to system (3.20) which may be summarized by

$$\sum_{k=1}^{p} a_{i_k}l\overline{b_{i_k}} \leqslant m \leqslant \prod \overline{a_{i_k}}+l+b_{i_k} \tag{3.21}$$

3.6.6.4. *Example*

(a) *Dipole*. Consider the two-terminal dipole (one input one output) such that its connection matrix is as in Figure 3.78(a).

We seek a term m which can replace the term $a_{23} = xz\bar{t}$ without modifying C_{13} the conductibility between 1 and 3.

$$A = \begin{bmatrix} 1 & \bar{x} & \bar{y} & z \\ x & 1 & xz\bar{t} & \bar{x} \\ z & 0 & 1 & b \\ 0 & \bar{t} & t & 1 \end{bmatrix}$$

FIG. 3.78(*a*).

$$A = \begin{bmatrix} 1 & \bar{x} & \bar{y} & z \\ 0 & 1 & x & \bar{x} \\ 0 & 0 & 1 & 0 \\ 0 & \bar{t} & t & 1 \end{bmatrix}$$

FIG. 3.78(*b*).

We substitute m for a_{23} and compute C_{13}

$$C_{13} = \begin{vmatrix} \bar{x} & \bar{y} & z \\ 1 & m & \bar{x} \\ \bar{t} & t & 1 \end{vmatrix} = m(\bar{x}+\bar{t}z)+\bar{y}+t(\bar{x}+z).$$

If we use the notation employed in Section 3.6.6.2 we may write:

$$a = \bar{x}+\bar{t}z \qquad \bar{a} = x(t+\bar{z})$$
$$b = \bar{y}+t(\bar{x}+z) \qquad \bar{b} = y(\bar{t}+x\bar{z})$$
$$l = xz\bar{t}.$$

Therefore

$$\bar{a}\bar{b}l = (\bar{x}+\bar{t}z)(\bar{t}+x\bar{z})yxz\bar{t} = xyz\bar{t}$$
$$\bar{a}+\bar{b}+l = x(t+\bar{z})+\bar{y}+t(\bar{x}+z)+xz\bar{t}$$
$$= t+\bar{y}+x\bar{z}+xz$$
$$= x+\bar{y}+t.$$

(3.22) is written

$$xyz\bar{t} \leqslant m \leqslant x+\bar{y}+t.$$

The simplest relation is to take $m = x$ which corresponds to the matrix in Figure 3.78(b). In the same way it can be shown that we may let $a_{21} = a_{31} = a_{41} = a_{34} = 0$. The corresponding circuit is represented on Figure 3.78(c).

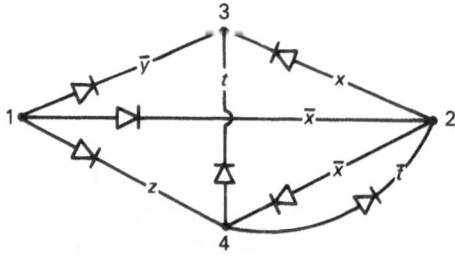

FIG. 3.78(c).

(b) *Multipole.* Consider the 4-terminal multipole 1, 2, 3, 4 which has 1 input (1) and 2 outputs (2, 3). The connection matrix is shown in Figure 3.79(a). We wish to conserve conductibilities C_{12} and C_{13}.

We study the term $a_{14} = b$. Let $a_{14} = m$ (notation of Section 3.6.6.3)

$$C_{12} = \begin{vmatrix} a+b & 0 & m \\ c+d & 1 & ad \\ \bar{c} & 0 & 1 \end{vmatrix} = \bar{c}m+(a+b)$$

$$\begin{bmatrix} 1 & a+b & 0 & b \\ a+b & 1 & c+d & 0 \\ 0 & c+d & 1 & ad \\ b & \bar{c} & 0 & 1 \end{bmatrix}$$

FIG. 3.79(a).

$$\begin{bmatrix} 1 & a+b & 0 & 0 \\ a+b & 1 & c+d & 0 \\ 0 & (c+d) & 1 & 0 \\ 0 & 0 & 0 & 1 \end{bmatrix}$$

FIG. 3.79(b).

$$C_{13} = \begin{vmatrix} a+b & 0 & m \\ 1 & c+d & 0 \\ \bar{c} & 0 & 1 \end{vmatrix} = \bar{c}dm + (a+b)(c+d).$$

Since $l = b$, (3.21) is written

$$\bar{c}a\bar{b}b + \bar{c}d(\bar{a}\bar{b} + \bar{c}\bar{d})b \leqslant (a+b+c)[c+\bar{d}+b+(a+b)(c+d)]$$

that is

$$0 \leqslant m \leqslant a+b+c.$$

We take $m = 0$. We study the term $a_{42} = \bar{c}$. Let $a_{42} = m$, note that actually $a_{14} = 0$

$$C_{12} = \begin{vmatrix} a+b & 0 & 0 \\ c+d & 1 & ad \\ m & 0 & 1 \end{vmatrix} = a+b$$

$$C_{13} = \begin{vmatrix} a+b & 0 & 0 \\ 1 & c+d & 0 \\ m & 0 & 1 \end{vmatrix} = (a+b)(c+d).$$

Since $l = \bar{c}$ (3.21) is written

$$0 \leqslant m \leqslant 1$$

We take $m = 0$. The reader can verify that the following solution can be adopted

$$a_{14} = 0 \qquad a_{34} = 0.$$

This leads to the connection matrix in Figure 3.79(b) and the circuit in Figure 3.79(c) which corresponds to the removal of node 4. It is

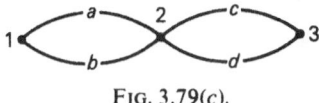

FIG. 3.79(c).

unnecessary to consider solutions $a_{21} = 0$ and $a_{32} = 0$ which have no effect on the output solutions because supplementary rectifiers would have to be introduced.

3.6.6.5. *Comments*

If A is symmetric, the conductibilities C_{ij} and C_{ji} are equal for all pairs of nodes i, j. If a term a_{hk} is replaced by a term l without modification of the conductibilities $C_{i_1 j_1}, \ldots, C_{i_p j_p}$, then the conductibilities $C_{j_1 i_1}, \ldots, C_{j_p i_p}$ will not be modified as long as a_{k_h} is not modified.

If we wish to avoid the introduction of rectifiers and still have a symmetrical connection matrix, we use a_{hk} and a_{kh} at the same time, substituting m for them in order to apply the method in Section 3.6.6.3.

Consider, for example, the symmetrical connection matrix (Figure 3.80(a)) of the circuit in Figure 3.80(b). If we wish to conserve C_{12} and C_{13}, there are two solutions possible. The choice depends on whether or not we accept the introduction of rectifiers.

$$\begin{bmatrix} 1 & a+b & 0 & b \\ a+b & 1 & c+d & \bar{c} \\ 0 & c+d & 1 & ad \\ b & \bar{c} & ad & 1 \end{bmatrix}$$

Fig. 3.80(a).

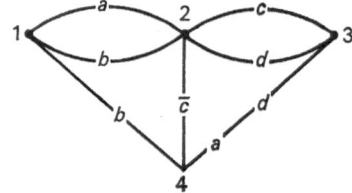

Fig. 3.80(b).

(1) *Case with rectifiers.* The reader can verify that the following solution is possible

$$a_{14} = a_{41} = 0 \qquad a_{21} = 0 \qquad a_{24} = a_{42} = 0 \qquad a_{32} = 0$$
$$a_{34} = a_{43} = 0.$$

The connection matrix in Figure 3.81(a) is obtained and the corresponding circuit is represented in Figure 3.81(b).

$$\begin{bmatrix} 1 & a+b & 0 & 0 \\ 0 & 1 & c+d & 0 \\ 0 & 0 & 1 & 0 \\ 0 & 0 & 0 & 1 \end{bmatrix}$$

Fig. 3.81(a).

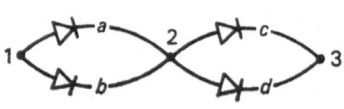

Fig. 3.81(b).

(2) *Case without rectifiers.* We study the term

$$C_{12} = \begin{vmatrix} a+b & 0 & b \\ m & 1 & ad \\ \bar{c} & ad & 1 \end{vmatrix} = a+b$$

$$C_{13} = \begin{vmatrix} a+b & 0 & b \\ 1 & m & \bar{c} \\ \bar{c} & ad & 1 \end{vmatrix} = m(a+b) + ad(b+\bar{c}).$$

Since $c + d = l$, application of (3.21) gives:

$$(c+d)(a+b)(\bar{a}+\bar{d}+\bar{b}c) \leqslant m \leqslant \bar{a}\bar{b}+c+d$$
$$(c+d)(a\bar{d}+a\bar{b}c+\bar{a}b+b\bar{d}) \leqslant m \leqslant \bar{a}\bar{b}+c+d.$$

We must therefore take $m = c + d$.

In the same way we show that we must take $a_{12} = a_{21} = a+b$ and we may take

$$a_{24} = a_{42} = a_{14} = a_{41} = a_{34} = a_{43} = 0.$$

We obtain the connection matrix in Figure 3.82(a) and the circuit in Figure 3.82(b).

$$\begin{bmatrix} 1 & a+b & 0 & 0 \\ a+b & 1 & c+d & 0 \\ 0 & c+d & 1 & 0 \\ 0 & 0 & 0 & 1 \end{bmatrix}$$

Fig. 3.82(a).   Fig. 3.82(b).

3.6.7. *Graph of a circuit-matrix associated with the graph*

A graph can be associated with a relay circuit whether or not it has rectifiers. If the branch under consideration has a rectifier, the corresponding branch on the graph will be oriented. (Figures 3.83a and b.) If the branch does not have a rectifier (Figure 3.84a), it can be

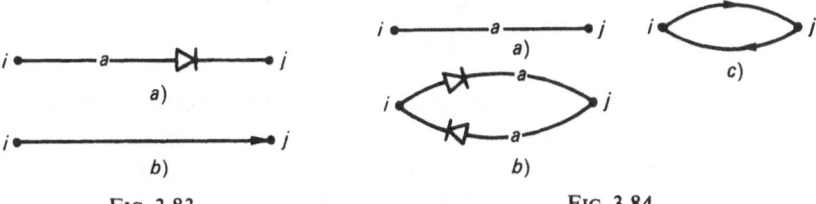

Fig. 3.83.   Fig. 3.84.

separated into two branches having rectifiers as shown in Figure 3.84(*b*) and its graphic representation will be two oriented branches (Figure 3.84*c*).

A Boolean variable l_{ij} is associated with every ij branch of the graph. This variable can be the direct conductibility from i to j.

We can associate a Boolean matrix $B = (b_{ij})$ with the graph. It is defined in the following way:

$b_{ij} = 0$, if there are no branches from i to j,

$b_{ij} = l_{ij}$, if there is one branch from i to j and l_{ij} is the variable associated with this branch.

$$b_{ii} = 0$$

Consider the circuit in Figure 3.85(*a*). Its graph is shown in Figure 3.85(*b*).

We associate a Boolean variable with each branch of the oriented graph of the circuit, as in Figure 3.85(*b*) for example.

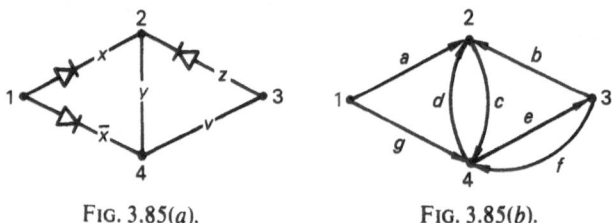

FIG. 3.85(*a*).   FIG. 3.85(*b*).

The connection matrix B associated with this graph is shown in Figure 3.85(*c*).

$$B = \begin{bmatrix} 0 & a & 0 & g \\ 0 & 0 & 0 & c \\ 0 & b & 0 & f \\ 0 & d & e & 0 \end{bmatrix}$$

FIG. 3.85(*c*).

Note that each branch of the graph of a circuit can correspond to the direct conductibility between the two corresponding nodes of the circuit. We could let 1 be the value of all branches of the graph and search the hamiltonian circuits (see Kaufmann[8], pp. 275–80).

In the following, we shall associate different variables with every branch of the graph. The corresponding matrix will be called the circuit's *topological matrix*.

3.6.8. *Properties of a circuit's topological matrix*

We shall define a certain number of properties of the topological matrix in the same way as we did for the connection matrix.

3.6.8.1. *Determination of the number of loops in a circuit*

A. Let the Boolean variable b_{ij} be the element at the intersection of row i and column j in the topological matrix B of order n (Figure 3.86).

$$B = \begin{bmatrix} 0 & b_{12} \cdots b_{1j} & \cdots & b_{1n} \\ b_{i1} & 0 \cdots b_{ij} & \cdots & b_{in} \\ b_{n1} & \cdots\cdots\cdots\cdots\cdots & & 0 \end{bmatrix}$$

Fig. 3.86.

The corresponding circuit can be with or without rectifiers.

We develop the determinant Δ_n of B.

$$\Delta_n = \sum_i b_{i,\alpha_1} b_{\alpha_1,\alpha_2} \cdots b_{\alpha_{n-1},i}$$

(Σ represents a Boolean sum).

The terms $b_{\alpha_k,\alpha_{k+1}}$ can be of three different types:

(1) On the principal diagonal $(b_{\alpha_k,\alpha_{k+1}} = 0)$, the corresponding terms in the Δ development are zero.

(2) Certain terms are such that

$$i \neq \alpha_1, ..., i \neq \alpha_{n-1} \qquad \alpha_1 \neq \alpha_2, ..., \alpha_{n-2} \neq \alpha_{n-1}$$

they correspond to the set of loops passing n of the circuit's nodes.

(3) Certain terms are a product of groups in the following form:

$$b_{\beta_1,\beta_2} b_{\beta_2,\beta_3} \cdots b_{\beta_p,\beta_n} \quad (p < n).$$

Each corresponds to a set of loops passing at most $(n-2)$ points.

Note that if we consider a submatrix of order $n-k$ $(0 < k < n)$, denoted B_{n-k} and obtained by the suppression of k rows and the k corresponding columns of B, it corresponds to the network of the $(n-k)$ remaining points (k nodes were removed from the original network; they correspond to the rows and columns taken out of B).

The development of Δ_{n-k}, determinant of B_{n-k}, has 3 types of terms the same as Δ_n:

(1) Zero terms corresponding to the b_{ij} on the principal diagonal.

(2) Terms corresponding to the loops which pass the $(n-k)$ points of the subnetwork.

(3) Terms corresponding to the loops of order less than $(n-k)$, i.e. passing at most $n-k-1$ nodes in the subnetwork.

THEOREM.   To obtain all the network's loops, we form the Boolean sum of all developments of the determinants of the topological matrix and all submatrices formed around the principal diagonal.

B. *Example.* Consider the circuit in Figure 3.87(*a*). Its graph is represented in Figure 3.87(*b*). The circuit's topological matrix is written as in Figure 3.87(*c*). We search the different loops of the circuit.

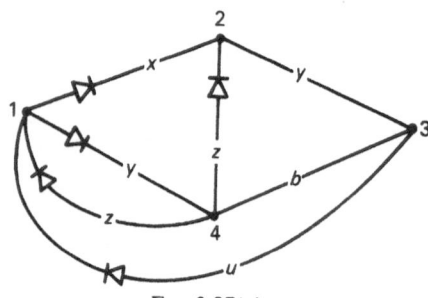

FIG. 3.87(*a*).   FIG. 3.87(*b*).

$$B = \begin{bmatrix} 0 & a & 0 & b \\ 0 & 0 & e & 0 \\ i & f & 0 & h \\ c & d & g & 0 \end{bmatrix},$$

FIG. 3.87(*c*).

(a) *Loops of order 2*

$$\text{node 1:} \quad \begin{vmatrix} 0 & a \\ 0 & 0 \end{vmatrix} = 0 \quad \begin{vmatrix} 0 & 0 \\ i & 0 \end{vmatrix} = 0 \quad \begin{vmatrix} 0 & b \\ c & 0 \end{vmatrix} = bc \quad (\text{loop } 14)$$

$$\text{node 2:} \quad \begin{vmatrix} 0 & e \\ f & 0 \end{vmatrix} = ef \quad (\text{loop } 23) \quad \begin{vmatrix} 0 & 0 \\ d & 0 \end{vmatrix} = 0$$

$$\text{node 3:} \quad \begin{vmatrix} 0 & h \\ g & 0 \end{vmatrix} = gh \quad (\text{loop } 34).$$

There are therefore 3 loops of order 2: (14, 23, 34).

(b) *Loops of order 3*

$$\text{nodes } 123: \begin{vmatrix} 0 & a & 0 \\ 0 & 0 & e \\ i & f & 0 \end{vmatrix} = aci \, (\text{loop } 123)$$

$$\text{nodes } 124: \begin{vmatrix} 0 & a & b \\ 0 & 0 & 0 \\ c & d & 0 \end{vmatrix} = 0$$

$$\textit{nodes } 134 \begin{vmatrix} 0 & 0 & b \\ i & 0 & h \\ c & g & 0 \end{vmatrix} = bgi \, (\text{loop } 143)$$

$$\text{nodes } 234: \begin{vmatrix} 0 & e & 0 \\ f & 0 & h \\ d & g & 0 \end{vmatrix} = dch \, (\text{loop } 234).$$

(c) *Loops of order 4 (nodes 1, 2, 3, 4).* Let Δ be the determinant of the matrix B;

$$\Delta = \begin{vmatrix} 0 & a & 0 & b \\ 0 & 0 & e & 0 \\ i & f & 0 & h \\ c & d & g & 0 \end{vmatrix} = e \begin{vmatrix} 0 & a & b \\ i & f & h \\ c & d & 0 \end{vmatrix} = e \left[i \begin{vmatrix} a & b \\ d & 0 \end{vmatrix} + c \begin{vmatrix} a & b \\ f & h \end{vmatrix} \right]$$

$$\Delta = eibd + ecah + ecbf.$$

ecbf corresponds to two loops of order 2: (14) and (23). There are therefore 2 true loops of order 4: (2314) and (1234). The system has a total of 8 loops.

Comment. The search for the loops on a circuit's graph can be done independently of the technology used. It can, for example, be extended to transistor circuits, i.e. NOR and NAND circuits.

3.6.8.2. *Determination of paths of a given length*

DEFINITIONS. The matrix product (Section 1.8.1) of p matrices all equal to a circuit's graph matrix B, is called B to the power p and written B^p:

$$B^p = \underbrace{B \otimes B \otimes \cdots \otimes B.}_{p \text{ times}}$$

A. *Study of* $(B^t)^2$. Consider the topological matrix B^t of the circuit under study. Its general term is b_{ij} ($1 \leqslant i, j \leqslant n$). The circuit has n nodes. The general term of $(B^t)^2$ is:

$$b_{ij}^2 = \sum_{k=1}^{n} b_{ik}b_{kj}$$

which can also be written

$$b_{ij}^2 = \sum_{k \neq i,j} b_{ik}b_{kj} \quad (b_{ii} = b_{jj} = 0).$$

$\sum_{k \neq i,j} b_{ik}b_{kj}$ is the set of paths from i to j of length 2.

In the same way,

$$\sum_{k \neq i} b_{ik}b_{ki} = b_{ii}^2$$

is the set of loops of length 2 which pass i.

B. *Study of* $(B^t)^p$ ($p < n$). We use the recurrence procedure. Assume b_{ij}^{p-1}, the general term of $(B^t)^{p-1}$, to be the set of length $(p-1)$ paths from i to j and b_{ii}^{p-1} the set of length $(p-1)$ loops which pass the point i. b^p general term of $(B^t)^p$ is written

$$b_{i,j}^p = \sum_{k=1}^{n} b_{ik}^{p-1}b_{kj} = \sum_{k \neq i,j} bb_{ik}^{p-1}b_{k,j} + b_{i,j}b_{i,i}^{p-1}$$

$b_{ii}^{p-1}b_{ij}$ is trivial (it belongs to the set of length 1 paths)

$$b_{ii}^p = \sum_{k \neq 1} b_{ik}^{p-1}b_{ki}.$$

b_{ij}^p and b_{ii}^p are therefore sets of paths and loops of length p. The paths go from i to j and the loops pass the point i.

THEOREM. If B^t is the topological matrix of an n node circuit, there exists a positive integer p, less than or equal to n, such that the Boolean sum

$$\sum_p = B + B^2 + \cdots + B^p$$

is constant.

First of all, we see that all branches going from a point i to a point j have a maximum length of $n-1$. If this were not true, a longer branch would use, a certain number of times, branches which were already considered and hence disappear from the sum.

Secondly, no loop longer than n exists. If, in fact, a loop had a length greater than n, it would pass the same branch several times and not figure in the Boolean sum of all the coefficients $\sum_{p \geqslant 1} b_{ii}^p$.

Consequently:

$$\sum_{n+1} = B^t + \cdots + (B^t)^{n+1} = \sum_{n} = B^t + \cdots + (B^t)^n$$

$$\sum_{q} B^t + \cdots + (B^t)^q \quad (q \geqslant n) \quad \text{is constant.}$$

Therefore, there exists a number p less than or equal to n such that the relation

$$\sum_{p} = \sum_{k>p}$$

is true.

C. *Physical interpretation.* The sum precedingly defined, is an $n \times n$ matrix. Its terms b_{ij} have the following property:

(a) if $i = j$, the Boolean sum

$$\sum_{i=1}^{n} \sum_{k=1}^{p} b_{ii}^k$$

represents the set of all the graph's loops.

(b) if $i \neq j$, the Boolean sum

$$\sum_{k=1}^{p} b_{ij}^k$$

is the set of all paths which go from i to j.

If each term b_{mn} of B^t is replaced by the conductibility of the circuit's corresponding branch, we obtain the circuit's conductibility function between points i and j.

D. *Example.* Reconsider Figure 3.87(a).

$$B = \begin{bmatrix} 0 & a & 0 & b \\ 0 & 0 & e & 0 \\ i & f & 0 & h \\ c & d & g & 0 \end{bmatrix}$$

$$B^2 = \begin{bmatrix} bc & bd & ae+bg & 0 \\ ei & ef & 0 & eh \\ ch & ai+dh & ef+gh & bi \\ gi & ac+fg & de & bi+gh \end{bmatrix}$$

$$B^3 = \begin{bmatrix} (ae+bg)i & abc+f(ae+bg) \\ ehc & aei+deh \\ (ef+gh)i+bic & ach+f(e+gh)+bid \\ dei+c(b+gh) & agi+def+d(bc+gh) \end{bmatrix}$$

$$\begin{bmatrix} ebd & bc+h(ae+bg) \\ ef+egh & bei \\ e(ai+dh)+big & bch+h(g+ef) \\ e(ac+fg)+g(bc+h) & bgi+deh \end{bmatrix}.$$

It is unnecessary to compute the b_{ij}^4 terms $(i \neq j)$ of B^4 because the longest path from a point i to a point j is of length 3.

$$b_{11}^4 = ebdi + bc + chae$$
$$b_{22}^4 = aehc + ef + bdei$$
$$b_{33}^4 = aech + ef + bdei + hg$$
$$b_{44}^4 = bdei + bc + gh + ehac.$$

(e) *Application.* (1) Determination of C_{32}, the conductibility between nodes 3 and 2:

$$(b_{32} + b_{32}^2 + b_{32}^3) = f + ai + dh + ach + bid.$$

We replace a, b, c, d, f, h, i, by the conductibilities of the circuit's corresponding branches.

$$a = x \qquad b = f = y \qquad c = d = z \qquad h = t \qquad i = u$$
$$C_{32} = y + xu + zt.$$

(2) Determination of the circuit's loops. We compute the Boolean sum of the terms on the principal diagonal of the matrix.

The system therefore has 8 loops: (14), (23), (34), (123), (143), (234), (2314), (1234). We find the result of Section 3.6.8.1.

Comment. The results of Section 3.6.8.2 relative to the determination of the number of loops in a relay circuit can be extended to the general case in which any of the technologies is used. To draw a circuit's graph, we assume each of the circuit's operators to correspond to a node on the graph. It is thus sufficient to determine the circuit's topological matrix from its graph.

Conductibility between 2 nodes no longer has any signification. In fact, on the one hand, if the system has loops, as will be shown in the next chapter, it is no longer purely combinational. On the other hand, since the input terminal (supply in relays) is no longer unique, even if the direct conductibility between 2 nodes of a relay system is replaced by the output operator under consideration, the conductibility between 2 nodes no longer corresponds to the definition of a system's output functions.

Consider the transistor circuit in Figure 3.88(a), where each transistor corresponds to a NOR operator. Figure 3.88(b) represents the

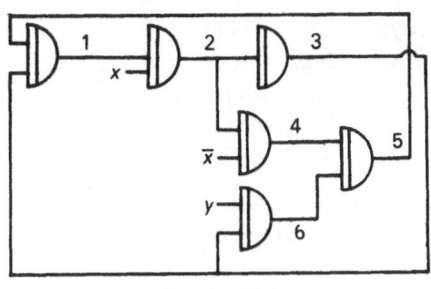

FIG. 3.88(a). FIG. 3.88(b).

circuit's graph. The circuit's topological matrix, taking into account Figure 3.88(b), is written

$$B = \begin{bmatrix} 0 & a & 0 & 0 & 0 & 0 \\ 0 & 0 & b & e & 0 & 0 \\ c & 0 & 0 & 0 & 0 & d \\ 0 & 0 & 0 & 0 & f & 0 \\ h & 0 & 0 & 0 & 0 & 0 \\ 0 & 0 & 0 & 0 & g & 0 \end{bmatrix}$$

from which we derive:

$$B^2 = \begin{bmatrix} 0 & 0 & ab & ae & 0 & 0 \\ bc & 0 & 0 & 0 & ef & bd \\ 0 & ac & 0 & 0 & dg & 0 \\ fh & 0 & 0 & 0 & 0 & 0 \\ 0 & ah & 0 & 0 & 0 & 0 \\ gh & 0 & 0 & 0 & 0 & 0 \end{bmatrix}$$

$$B^3 = \begin{bmatrix} abc & 0 & 0 & 0 & aef & abd \\ efh & abc & 0 & 0 & bdg & 0 \\ dgh & 0 & abc & aec & 0 & 0 \\ 0 & afh & 0 & 0 & 0 & 0 \\ 0 & 0 & abh & aeh & 0 & 0 \\ 0 & agh & 0 & 0 & 0 & 0 \end{bmatrix}$$

$$B^4 = \begin{bmatrix} aefh & abc & 0 & 0 & abdg & 0 \\ bdgh & aefh & abc & abce & 0 & 0 \\ abc & adgh & 0 & 0 & acef & abcd \\ 0 & 0 & abfh & aefh & 0 & 0 \\ abch & 0 & 0 & 0 & aefh & abdh \\ 0 & 0 & abgh & aegh & 0 & 0 \end{bmatrix}$$

$$B^5 = \begin{bmatrix} abdgh & aefh & abc & abce & 0 & 0 \\ abc & abdgh & abefh & aefh & abcef & 0 \\ acefh & abc & abdgh & adegh & abcdg & 0 \\ abcfh & 0 & 0 & 0 & aefh & abdfh \\ aefh & abch & 0 & 0 & abdgh & 0 \\ abcgh & 0 & 0 & 0 & aefgh & abdgh \end{bmatrix}.$$

Since the longest possible elementary path between 2 distinct points is length 5, we compute only the terms on the principal diagonal of B^6.

$$b^6_{11} = abc$$
$$b^6_{22} = abc$$
$$b^6_{33} = abc$$
$$b^6_{44} = 0$$
$$b^6_{55} = 0$$
$$b^6_{66} = 0$$

from which we derive:

$$\sum_{p=1}^{6} \sum_{i=1}^{6} b^p_{ii} = abc + aefh + abdgh.$$

The different loops of the system are: (123), (1245), (12365).

3.7. COMPARISON BETWEEN THE GENERAL SIMPLIFICATION METHOD OF BOOLEAN FUNCTIONS AND THE MATRIX ANALYSIS METHOD IN RELAY SYSTEMS

The general methods, Karnaugh, McCluskey, and Boolean function decomposition seek common terms or common groups of terms in the set, or part of the set, of the Boolean functions under consideration. In general, this requires rectifiers in the case of relay realizations.

Reconsider the example in Section 3.4.4. If 1 is the input terminal and 2 and 3 are the output terminals, the Boolean equations are written

$$C_{12} = abc + d \qquad C_{13} = abc + e.$$

The circuit obtained by factorizing the common term *abc* is represented in Figure 3.89.

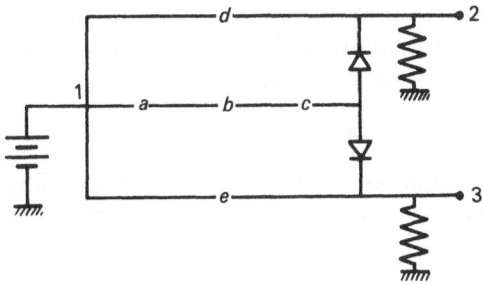

FIG. 3.89.

Generally, the problem is defined in the following way: Given the conductibilities $C_{12}, ..., C_{1p}$ between the input terminal 1 and the output terminals $2, ..., p$, find the simplest circuit representing all these functions.

Observe that the conductibilities between each pair of output terminals $(2, 3, ..., p)$ are not defined. We let them equal 0. The problem to be solved is one of partial equivalence; find a circuit partially equivalent to the one in Figure 3.90(a) where the functions $C_{12}, ..., C_{1p}$ have been separately minimized. The circuit we seek will have the same conductibilities between the 1 terminal and any one of the $2, ..., p$ terminals as the initial circuit.

Applying the extended McCluskey method, we consider a term A to be a common factor in the $C_{1\alpha_1}, ..., C_{1\alpha_k}$ functions for the minimal solu-

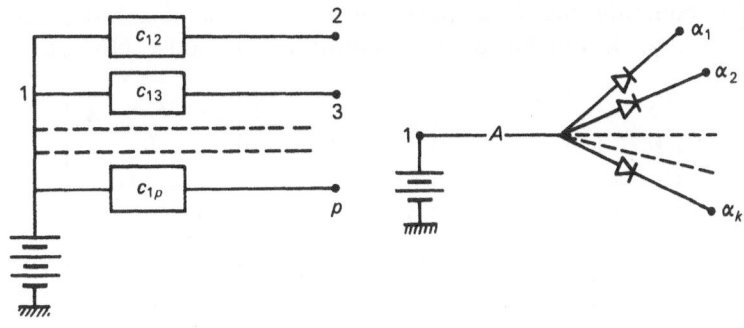

FIG. 3.90(a).   FIG. 3.90(b).

tion found. This means that the common factor A in all the branches going from 1 to one of the $\alpha_1, ..., \alpha_k$ terminals, must be in series with a rectifier as in Figure 3.90(b). In the example in Figure 3.89 the term abc is a common factor of the 12 and 13 branches.

We now apply the matrix analysis method. The conductibilities of branches $1\alpha_1, ..., 1\alpha_k$ are written

$$C_{1\alpha i} = C'_{1\alpha i} + A,$$

because A is a common factor in the corresponding conductibility functions. Figure 3.91 is the connection matrix.

$$\begin{bmatrix} 1 & C_{12} & C_{13} & ... & (C'_{1\alpha_1}+A) & ... & (C'_{1\alpha k}+A) & ... & C_{1p} \\ \emptyset & 1 & 0 & ... & 0 & ... & 0 & ... & 0 \\ \emptyset & & & & & & & & \\ \vdots & & & & & & & & \\ & & & & & & & & \\ \emptyset & 0 & 0 & ... & 0 & ... & 0 & ... & 1 \end{bmatrix}$$

FIG. 3.91.

The symbol $\emptyset$ corresponds to a non-specification. In fact, as we are considering only the conductibilities from terminal 1, every term in the first column can be whatever we wish. All terms which are neither on the principal diagonal nor in the first column are zeros. Since A is a common factor of p terms in the first row, we create a $(p+1)$ node.

The reader can verify that this operation results in the matrix in Figure 3.92 and the subnetwork in Figure 3.90(b) if the $(p+1)$ node is the A output.

Consequently, matrix analysis results in the same solutions as the McCluskey, Karnaugh or decomposition methods. Note that by

$$\begin{bmatrix} 1 & C_{12} & C_{13} & ... & C'_{1\alpha_1} & C'_{1\alpha_2} & ... & C'_{1\alpha k} & ... & C_{1p} & A \\ \emptyset & 1 & 0 & ... & 0 & 0 & ... & 0 & ... & 0 & 0 \\ & & & & & & & & & & \\ & & & & & & & & & & \\ & & & & & & & & & & \\ & 0 & 0 & ... & 0 & 0 & ... & 0 & ... & 1 & 0 \\ A & 0 & 0 & ... & 1 & 1 & ... & 1 & ... & 0 & 1 \end{bmatrix}$$

FIG. 3.92.

introducing redundant terms, we obtain other solutions without having to use rectifiers.

If we consider the preceeding example; C_{12} and C_{13} can be written:

$$C_{12} = abc\bar{d} + d$$
$$C_{13} = abc\bar{e} + e.$$

The connection matrix is written (using the symmetrical form) as in Figure 3.93(a).

Addition of a supplementary node leads to the connection matrix in Figure 3.93(b) and the circuit in Figure 3.93(c) because we are not concerned with the conductibility between nodes 2 and 3 (we introduce the redundant terms, in the Seman sense $a_{23} = a_{32} = \bar{d}\bar{e}$ in the matrix of Figure 3.93a).

$$\begin{bmatrix} 1 & abc\bar{d}+d & abc\bar{e}+e \\ abc\bar{d}+d & 1 & 0 \\ abc\bar{e}+e & 0 & 1 \end{bmatrix}$$

FIG. 3.93(a).

$$\begin{bmatrix} 1 & d & e & abc \\ d & 1 & 0 & \bar{d} \\ e & 0 & 1 & \bar{e} \\ abc & \bar{d} & \bar{e} & 1 \end{bmatrix}$$

FIG. 3.93(b).

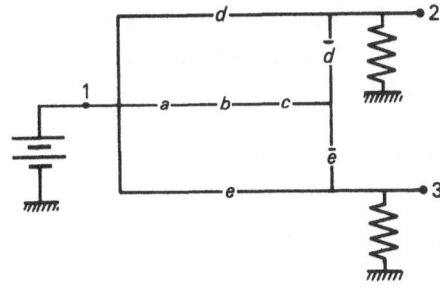

FIG. 3.93(c).

Matrix analysis is therefore the method most adaptable to combinational relay circuits. It goes further than classical simplification methods, but it is more intuitive and less systematic.

APPENDIX

We have not yet envisaged a certain number of questions relative to combinational circuits and particularly with respect to relay technology. Subjects such as circuit realizations which have symmetric conductibility functions or iterative circuits have not been treated. There also exists another important type of combinational circuit which was not discussed, the selector, specifically designed for computers and realized with relays, diodes or ferrites.

We shall only define these different elements, and indicate to the interested reader, the principal works to which he may refer for more detailed information.

3.A.1. SYMMETRIC FUNCTIONS

DEFINITION. A Boolean function of n variables is symmetric if any permutation of its variables leaves its expression unchanged.

Thus, the function

$$f(a, b, c) = a\bar{b}\bar{c} + \bar{a}b\bar{c} + \bar{a}\bar{b}c$$

is symmetric, but

$$g(a, b, c) = \bar{a}bc + a\bar{b}c$$

is not.

Note that if the canonical form of the symmetric function contains a term in which $n-k$ variables are complemented and k non-complemented, C_k^n terms should have $n-k$ complemented variables and the last k non-complemented.

Hence, a symmetric Boolean function of n variables of order k, takes the value 1 only if k variables have a 1 value.

Symbolically, it is noted S_k^n and we notice the analogy between this definition and that of the majority function ($k \geqslant n/2$).

3.A.2. ELEMENTARY SYMMETRIC FUNCTIONS

The elementary symmetric functions of a Boolean function of n variables are written:

$$S_0^n = \bar{a}_1 \bar{a}_2 \cdots \bar{a}_n$$

$$S_1^n = \sum_{i=1}^{n} \bar{a}_1 \cdots \bar{a}_{i-1} a_i \bar{a}_{i+1} \cdots \bar{a}_n$$

$$S_n^p = \sum_{i=1}^{n} \bar{a}_1 \cdots \bar{a}_{i-1} a_i \cdots a_{\ i+p-1} \bar{a}_{i+p} \cdots \bar{a}_n$$

$$\dots\dots\dots\dots\dots\dots\dots\dots\dots\dots\dots\dots\dots\dots\dots\dots$$

$$S_n^n = a_1 a_2 \cdots a_n.$$

There are $n+1$ elementary symmetric functions, therefore 2^{n+1} symmetric functions of n variables. The reader can verify that the product of any two elementary symmetric functions is zero:

$$S_p^n S_q^n = 0 \quad \text{if} \quad p \neq q.$$

3.A.3. PROPERTIES OF THE SYMMETRIC FUNCTIONS

(a) *Expression of a symmetric Boolean function*
Every symmetric Boolean function can be expressed as the disjunction of elementary symmetric functions. This form is unique. In fact, suppose that the function under consideration is $S_{p,q,r}^n$. It takes the value 1 if p or q or r of the variables are 1. We may write:

$$S_{p,q,r}^n = S_p^n + S_q^n + S_r^n.$$

Since the elementary functions are unique, the decomposition is also unique.

(b) *Disjunction of 2 symmetric functions*

$$S_{p,q}^n + S_{r,s}^n = S_{p,q,r,s}^n.$$

In fact, by (a):

$$S_{p,q}^n = S_p^n + S_q^n$$
$$S_{r,s}^n = S_r^n + S_s^n$$
$$S_{p,q}^n + S_{r,s}^n = S_p^n + S_q^n + S_r^n + S_s^n = S_{p,q,r,s}^n.$$

The function takes the value 1 if p, q, r, or s variables are 1.

(c) *Conjunction of two symmetric functions*

In fact, by (a):

$$S_{p,q,r}^n \cdot S_{p',q',r}^n = S_r^n$$
$$S_{p,q,r}^n = S_p^n + S_q^n + S_r^n$$
$$S_{p',q',r}^n = S_{p'}^n + S_{q'}^n + S_r^n$$
$$S_{p,q,r}^n \cdot S_{p',q',r}^n = (S_p^n + S_q^n + S_r^n)(S_{p'}^n + S_{q'}^n + S_r^n) = S_r^n.$$

(d) *Complement of a symmetric function*

The definition of the elementary symmetric functions gives:

$$S_0^n + S_1^n + \cdots + S_n^n = 1,$$

that is, simply

$$\overline{(S_{a_1}^n + \cdots + S_{a_k}^n)} = \overline{S_{a_1,\dots,a_k}^n} = S_{a_{k+1}}^n + \cdots + S_{a_n}^n = S_{a_{k+1},\dots,a_n}^n$$

for example:

$$S_{2,3}^5 = S_{1,4,5}^5.$$

3.A.4. REALIZATION OF THE SYMMETRIC FUNCTIONS

Graphically, the set of the elementary symmetric functions of 5 variables is easily represented (Figure 3.94).

If we wish to represent some five variable symmetric function, it is sufficient to consider part of this circuit. The reader may refer to the bibliography [3, 6, 8, 12].

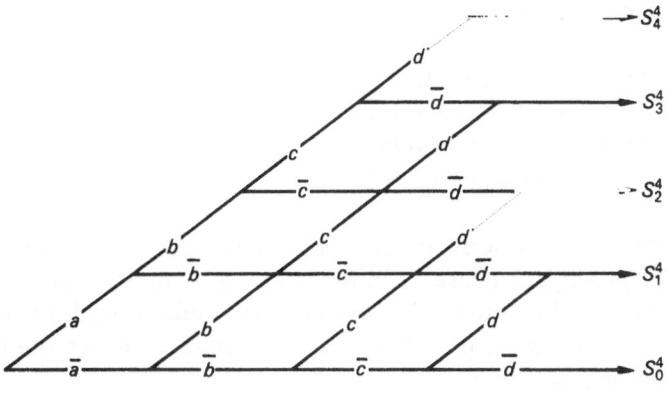

FIG. 3.94.

3.A.5. ITERATIVE CIRCUITS

An iterative system is a repeated structure consisting of a chain of identical cells. Each cell has a certain number of relays; the number of input and output terminals is the same. These cells are part of a complete circuit submitted to certain conditions. Taking into account the imposed specifications, the realization of each cell is based on inductive reasoning by studying the behavior of any one of the cells.

As an example we treat the following problems: An iterative circuit must satisfy the following condition: each cell has 2 relays. The output is 1 if any 2 cells, and only 2, have an even total number of closed relays in them. The circuit's output is 1, therefore, if 2 cells have their relays, X and Y, in the positions indicated in Figure 3.95.

First cell	01	01	10	10	11
Second cell	10	01	01	10	11

FIG. 3.95.

Given any cell, the following must be envisaged:

(1) no cell has closed relays,
(2) one cell has 1 closed relay,
(3) one cell has 2 closed relays,
(4) the output condition is realized.

Figure 3.96 is a performance table. If we have case 1, commands X, Y are possible. In case 3, on the contrary, X and Y cannot operate alone because the number of closed relays would be odd. In case 4, it is the same; we must not operate relays because the required condition is already satisfied.

xy	00	01	11	10
1	1	2	3	2
2	2	4		4
3	3		4	
4	4			

FIG. 3.96.

Given the state at the input of the cell under consideration (n), the table indicates, in function of the state of this cell (X and Y), what the situation at the input of the next cell is.

We may write that there are 4 outputs S_1, S_2, S_3, S_4 and only the last corresponds to the real output of the system. Let e_1, e_2, e_3, e_4 be the 4 inputs corresponding to the 4 possible situations of the cell: we may draw the corresponding circuit (Figure 3.97).

The reader wishing to obtain supplementary precisions can refer to the bibliography [1, 3, 8, 10].

Selectors

The selector is very useful in digital computers; it separates the 2^n signals susceptible to appear together at the input, giving a 1 input 2^n

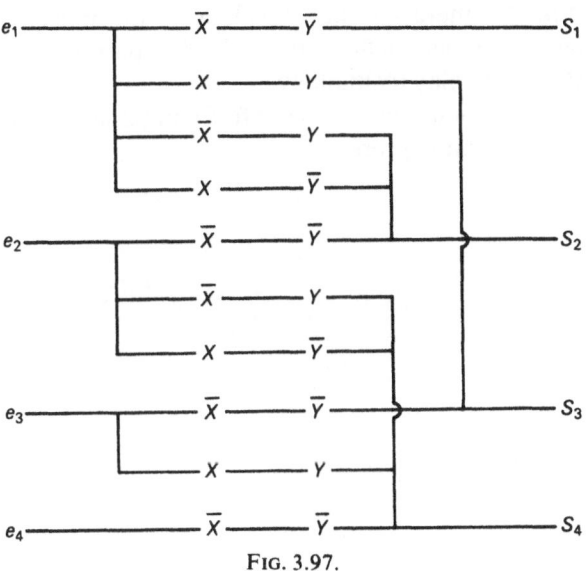

FIG. 3.97.

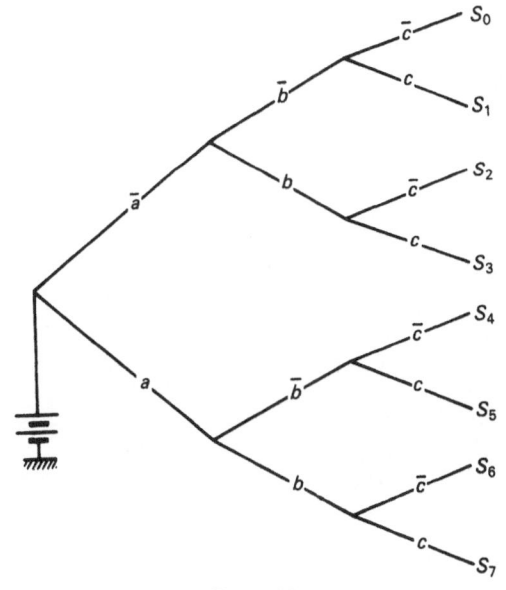

FIG. 3.98.

output multipole: there can be 2^n values of the input; each output characterizes an input value. Figure 3.98 represents the complete 2^3 input selector in relay technology.

These circuits can be realized with few components. The interested reader can refer to bibliography.

BIBLIOGRAPHY

[1] WATTS, S. and HUMPHREY, Jr., W. S., *Switching Circuits with Computer Applications*, McGraw-Hill, New York, 1958.

[2] BARTEE, T. C., LEBOW, I. L., and REED, I. S., *Theory and Design of Digital Machines*, McGraw-Hill, New York, 1962.

[3] FLORINE, J., *La synthèse des machines logiques et son automatisation*, Presses Académiques Européennes, Bruxelles, 1964.

[4] MALEY, G. and EARLE, J., *The Logic Design of Transistor Digital Computers*, Prentice Hall, Englewood Cliff, N.J., 1963, U.S.A., pp. 114–59.

[5] MILLER, R. E., *Switching Theory*, Vol. 1, *Combinational Circuits*, Wiley, New York, 1965.

[6] MOISIL, GR. C., *Circuite cu Tranzistori*, Vols. 1 and 2, Editure Académiei Republicii Populare Romîne, 1961.

[7] NASLIN, P., *Circuits logiques et automatismes à séquences*, Dunod, Paris, 1965.

[8] DENIS PAPIN, M., KAUFMANN, A. and FAURE, R., *Cours de calcul booléen*, Albin Michel, Paris, 1963.

[9] CALDWELL, S. H., *Switching Circuits and Logical Design*, Wiley, New York, 1958.

[10] MOISIL, GR. C., 'Axiomatisation of the Theory of Simplification of Combinational Automata', in *Proceedings of the International Congress of I.F.A.C.*, 1963.

[11] CONSTANTINESCU, P., 'Synthesis of the Multi-terminal Networks with Relay-Contacts and Rectifiers', *Bull. Math. Soc. Sci. Math. Phys. R.P.R.* 2 (1958) 50.

[12] FLORINE, J., 'Fonctions de sortie d'un système logique', *Rev. Automatisme* 1 (1965).

[13] McCLUSKEY, E. J., Jr and SCHORR, M., 'Essential Multiple-output Prime Implicants', in *Proc. Symp. Math. Theory of Automata*, New York, 1962.

[14] PELEGRIN, M., *Machines à calculer électroniques*, Dunod, Paris, 1964.

[15] MARCUS, M. P., *Switching Circuits for Engineers*, Prentice-Hall, Englewood Cliff, N.J., U.S.A., 1962.

[16] HARRISON, M. A., *Introduction to Switching and Automata Theory*, McGraw-Hill, New York, 1965.

[17] DENOUETIE, M., avec la collaboration de J. P. Perrin et E. Daclin, 'Détermination des boucles d'un graphe orienté, *Compt.-rend. Acad. Sci. Paris* 262 (1966) 1274–76.

EXERCISES

3.1. Realize the minimal 2 level diode or relay circuits (operators AND, OR, NOT conjunctive and disjunctive forms) then the same with transistors (NAND then NOR operators) where the conductibility function is:

(a) $f = R(0, 2, 3, 6, 10, 11, 15) + R_\phi(7, 8, 14)$
(b) $f = R(3, 4, 5, 6, 9, 11, 13) + R_\phi(1, 7, 12, 15)$
(c) $f = R(0, 4, 8, 10, 13, 15, 16, 20, 21, 23, 24, 26) + R_\phi(2, 5, 7, 18, 29, 31)$
(d) $f = R(0, 4, 5, 13, 14, 28, 32, 37, 39, 52, 62) + R_\phi(12, 15, 16, 29, 36, 38, 48, 54, 60)$.

3.2. Decompose the function:

$$f = R(2, 3, 9, 12, 13, 14, 15, 17, 18, 19, 20, 23, 29, 30)$$

into sub-functions.

3.3. Realize the minimal diode, relay, then transistor circuits corresponding to the following system of equations:

$$f_1 = R(0, 2, 3, 4, 5, 11, 12, 13, 14, 15)$$
$$f_2 = R(0, 4, 5, 7, 11, 13, 15)$$
$$f_3 = R(0, 4, 5, 9, 11, 13, 15).$$

3.4. Same question for the system:

$$f_1 = R(0, 4, 5, 6, 7, 8, 9, 15)$$
$$f_2 = R(0, 4, 5, 9, 11, 15)$$
$$f_3 = R(0, 1, 2, 3, 4, 5, 8, 9, 10, 11, 12, 13, 14).$$

3.5. Same question for the system:

$$f_1 = R(0, 7, 9, 11, 14, 15)$$
$$f_2 = R(1, 3, 4, 6, 10, 15)$$
$$f_3 = R(1, 2, 6, 8, 9, 11)$$
$$f_4 = R(1, 3, 4, 5, 6, 7, 9, 11, 13, 14)$$
$$f_5 = R(0, 5, 6, 7, 8, 11, 13, 14).$$

3.6. Simplify the following connection matrix knowing that the conductibilities are conserved with respect to all the terminals.

$$\begin{bmatrix} 1 & a+c+d & \bar{a}+cd & a+\bar{c}d \\ a+c+d & 1 & c & \bar{a}c+d \\ \bar{a}+cd & c & 1 & \bar{a}\bar{c} \\ a+\bar{c}d & \bar{a}c+d & \bar{a}\bar{c} & 1 \end{bmatrix}.$$

3.7. Represent simply the dipole which has the following conductibility:

$$Z = a(b + c\bar{d}) + d(bc + \bar{b}\bar{c}) + \bar{a}(\bar{b} + \bar{c}\bar{d})$$

by creating three supplementary nodes.

3.8. Represent the simplest circuit having the conductibility function:

$$C_{12}(a, b, c, d) = R(3, 5, 6, 9, 10, 12).$$

Use the connection matrix.

3.9. Same question for the conductibility function:

$$C_{12}(a, b, c, d) = R(7, 11, 13, 14, 15).$$

3.10. Simplify the circuit having the following connection matrix:

$$\begin{bmatrix} 1 & \bar{a}b & \bar{d} & \bar{b} + \bar{a}\bar{c} & 0 \\ a\bar{b} & 1 & b & 0 & \bar{c} \\ \bar{d} & b & 1 & c & \bar{a} \\ \bar{b} + \bar{a}\bar{c} & 0 & c & 1 & a \\ 0 & \bar{c} & \bar{a} & a & 1 \end{bmatrix}$$

knowing that only the C_{12} conductibility should be conserved.

3.11. Determine algebraically the loops of the graphs in Figures 3.99a and b.

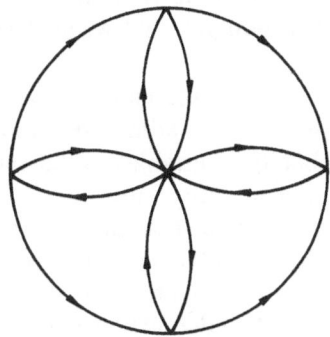

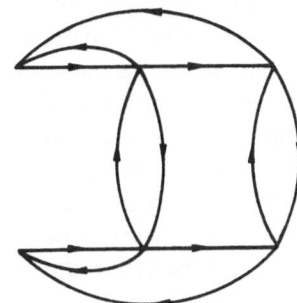

FIG. 3.99(a).   FIG. 3.99(b).

CHAPTER 4

INTRODUCTION TO SEQUENTIAL SYSTEMS

We have studied the first class of logical systems which we have called combinational systems. In these systems, the output function does not depend on time. The study of the second class, sequential systems, remains to be undertaken.

In this chapter we shall see that the intervention of a time factor induces two types of consequences. First, the introduction of one or more feedback loops. This will be shown by comparison of combinational and sequential systems. The second type is that time must become the same kind of variable as the logical variables we have been using. This is less apparent than the first consequence, but we shall see that it is absolutely necessary.

From what we have already seen, the characteristic of logical variables is 'quantification'. In other words, we admitted, in our discussion of combinational systems, that the variables could take only a finite number of values; this was a quantity supposition. In order to take into account the passage of time in a sequential system, it will be necessary to consider time on a quantitative basis; that is, we shall be interested in the state of the parameters which define the system at given instants. As a result of this, we shall define new variables which, in a way, realize the time variable. They are the internal or secondary variables which translate the systems' state at a given moment in a logical fashion.

4.1. REVIEW OF THE GENERAL PROPERTIES OF TRANSIENT PHENOMENA IN COMBINATIONAL SYSTEMS

4.1.1. *Equation and graph of combinational systems*
The essential property of combinational systems is that the state of the inputs determines the state of the outputs at any given moment independently of what input conditions were before the moment in

question. This results in the fact that two identical configurations of all inputs give two identical configurations of all outputs in a combinational system.

The form of this type of system's equation is:

$$z_i = f_i(x_1, \ldots, x_p) \tag{4.1}$$

$x_1, \ldots, x_p$ are the different binary input variables $z_1, \ldots, z_m$ are the different binary output variables.

We shall see, by an example, that this property exerts a direct influence on the structure of the logical diagram associated with a Boolean function.

Consider

$$z = [(a+b)c + d(b+c)](e+f).$$

Using the NOR operator it becomes:

$$z = [((a \downarrow b) \downarrow \bar{c}) \downarrow ((b \downarrow c) \downarrow \bar{d})] \downarrow (e \downarrow f)$$

or, using the NAND operator:

$$\bar{z} = [((\bar{a} / \bar{b}) / c) / ((\bar{b} / \bar{c}) / d)] / (\bar{e} / \bar{f}).$$

The different logical diagrams representing z are shown in Figures 4.1, 4.2, and 4.3.

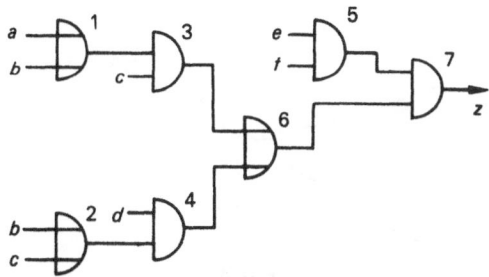

FIG. 4.1.

In the following, we shall consider only the systems realized either in terms of AND, OR, NOT or NOR and NAND.

Figure 4.4 is representative of all logical diagrams in that they have no loops. The nodes of this graph represent logical operators, (AND, OR, NOT, NOR or NAND) and the branches represent these operators' connection wires. For the general case, we may announce the following theorem:

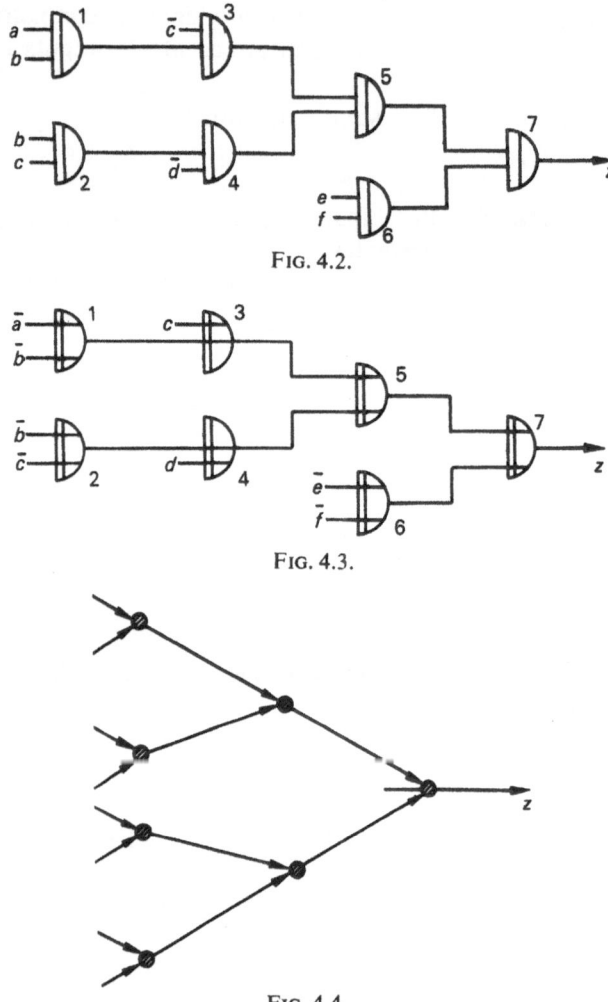

Fig. 4.2.

Fig. 4.3.

Fig. 4.4.

THEOREM. The combinational circuit corresponding to a given Boolean function (expressed in terms of NOR, AND, NOT, or NOR or NAND) can always be represented by an oriented graph with no loops.

In fact, an oriented graph gives the output expressed as a function of only the inputs:

$$z_i = f_i(x_1, \ldots, x_p).$$

Reciprocally, given a Boolean function of $(x_1, ..., x_p)$ where the operators are AND, OR, NOT or NOR or NAND, the preceding representation leads step by step to a graph in the form of a tree and therefore without loops.

4.1.2. *Transients in combinational systems*

In the study of transistorized combinational systems in Chapter 3, we neglected the time it took for a signal to cross the transistors and run through a conducting wire. That is, we supposed that the signal was propagated at an infinite velocity. In reality, it is propagated at a finite velocity (300 000 km/sec) from one part of the circuit to the other. Therefore, two types of delays must be considered; those due to the operators' response time and those due to the length of the path which must be covered.

A 12-m wire implies at least a 4/100 microsecond delay. Therefore the length of connection wires should be taken into consideration only if the operators' response time reaches the nanosecond (10^{-9} sec) range. Since transistor response time is in the order of some hundreths of a microsecond in computer circuits (or microsecond in digital training devices), only these will have a real influence from this point of view.

To study the transient state of an electronic combinational system and thus complete the Chapter 3 study of the steady state, we shall suppose all operators to have the same delay, Δ. We shall consider the connections between operators to be instantaneous because there is a very small time constant between connections as compared to semiconductor elements.

With these hypotheses in mind we study the transient state of the circuit in Figure 4.5. Its equation is:

$$z = (a \downarrow b) \downarrow [((c \downarrow d) \downarrow e) \downarrow (a \downarrow d)]$$

or, in terms of AND, OR, NOT:

$$z = (a+b)[\bar{a}\bar{d} + \bar{e}(c+d)].$$

We impose the inputs:

$$a = b = c = d = e = 0.$$

The output is: $z = 0$.

We examine a possible transition.

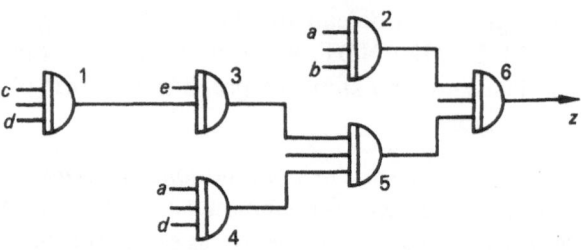

FIG. 4.5.

We can group the NOR circuits, which make up the logical diagram, according to their distances from the inputs. Thus, circuits 1, 2, and 4 have only input specifications; their outputs will change state after a delay proportional to the change of state of the input variables. Circuit 3 will also change state with a delay of $\Delta + \Delta = 2\Delta$ with respect to the variation in a or b, etc. Hence, we see that the different operator outputs only change value after a delay of Δ. Consequently, we may study the circuit by considering only instances $0, \Delta, 2\Delta, ..., N\Delta$, which comes down to sampling the time variable, causing it to intervene uniquely in the form of discrete instants.

Initial state: $a = b = c = d = e = 0$
      1: operator 2 output
      0: operator 5 output
      1: operator 4 output
      0: system's output (operator 6).

We apply the command: $a = 1$, $b = c = d = e = 0$. Instantaneously, nothing happens and operators 2, 5, 4 keep their output values.

Instant Δ:
      0: operator 2 output
      0: operator 5 output
      0: operator 4 output
      0: system's output.

The variable a simultaneously passed the outputs of operators 2 and 4 from 1 to 0.

Instant 2Δ:
      0: operator 2 output

1: operator 5 output
0: operator 4 output
1: system's output.

Since c, d, and e are unchanged and the operator 3 output 0, the operator 4 output also remains 0. Therefore, the operator 5 output is 1 and the system's output 1.

Instant 3Δ:

0: operator 2 output
1: operator 5 output
0: operator 4 output
0: system's output.

The change during instant 2Δ in the operator 5 output modified the system's output. The system has thus reached a steady state after 3Δ length time intervals. During the transient state, the output received a positive pulse for a time Δ, while in steady state that output was zero for the two commands: $a\, b\, c\, d\, e = 0\ 0\ 0\ 0\ 0$ and $a\, b\, c\, d\, e = 1\ 0\ 0\ 0\ 0$.

The transient state in combinational circuits lasts such a short time that it cannot be measured by ordinary instruments. Its energy is too weak to visibly modify certain steady states in neighbouring circuits. Only an oscilloscope detects it with precision.

Two possible cases occur during application of old and new commands to the steady state. The corresponding outputs are equal (case a) or different (case b). If the output does not vary during the transient state, case a, or if it doesn't change value several times, case b (Figure 4.6). Chapter 3's analysis method is correct, since the transient state has no effect. If the system's output changes during the transition, the analysis method does not account for all phenomena and therefore is no longer sufficient. We say that the system presents a *hazard*. We shall return to this question in more detail in Chapter 6.

4.2. SEQUENTIAL SYSTEMS–ANALYSIS

4.2.1. *Single loop systems*

4.2.1.1. *Method of study*

Consider the circuit of the logical diagram in Figure 4.7(*a*). It is impossible to express z solely in terms of a, b, c at the given instant. We must introduce a supplementary variable corresponding to the

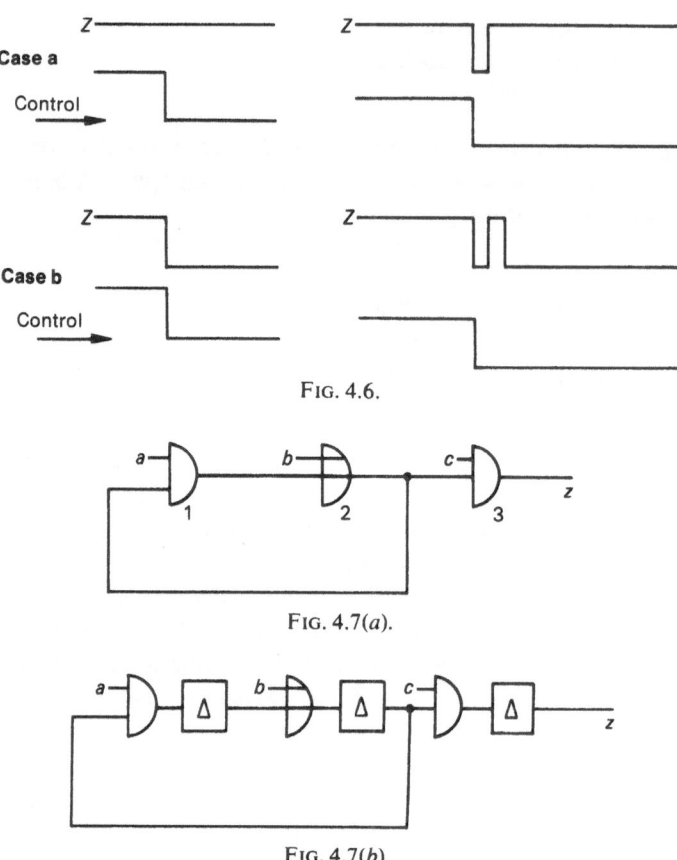

Case a

Control

Case b

Control

FIG. 4.6.

FIG. 4.7(a).

FIG. 4.7(b).

operator 2 output. Figure 4.7(b) represents the system and shows the different delays.

Intuitively, we see that the feedback loop transmits the new output from operator 2 to operator 1, which results in output modification. For the moment, we don't take into account the feedback branch delay. We attribute a fictional delay, Δ, to operator 2 in order to represent the time necessary for y to change value and be reinjected at the feedback loop input. y will be the Boolean value of the output signal from the delay Δ (Figure 4.8). The circuit of Figure 4.8 is an approximation of the circuit in Figure 4.7b. We are thus led to sample time in intervals of length Δ, which we take as the time unity. We study the output and y values for each time interval.

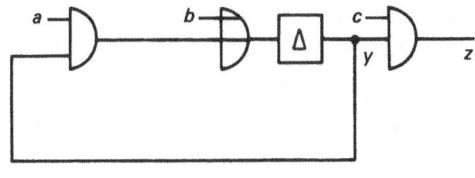

FIG. 4.8.

We shall now examine how the circuit in Figure 4.7(a) operates. The output circuit is purely combinational. We suppose that at the instant under consideration, which we take as the initial instant (instant 0), y has the value y_0 and the inputs are respectively a_0, b_0, c_0.

In Figures 4.9(a) and (b) we have represented the Figure 4.8 diagram with the output and feedback loop separated.

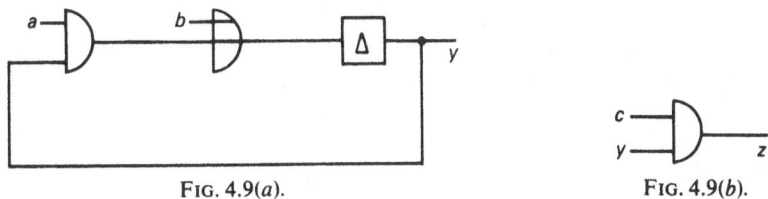

FIG. 4.9(a).   FIG. 4.9(b).

The circuit's equations are written:

$$z = cy \qquad\qquad (4.2)$$
$$y = b + ay. \qquad\qquad (4.3)$$

The first equation presents no difficulty, but the second is delicate because the variable y appears in both members. The influence of the Δ delay must be taken into account in order to interpret this equation. In the second member all commands and the value of y are taken at instant $N\Delta$: the first member indicates what value y will have when introduced in operator 1 at time $(N+1)\Delta$. The output equation corresponds to a combinational circuit and the c and z signals are considered at time $N\Delta$.

If y' is the Boolean variable associated with the signal coming from operator 2 (Figure 4.8) before the Δ delay, we may write:

$$y'_{N\Delta} = y_{(N+1)\Delta}.$$

This means that the value of y' at the instant under consideration will be the value of y at the next sample instant. In order not to have a too complicated notation, we take Δ as the unit of time. (The values of the variables at this instant are a_N, b_N, c_N, y_N.) We may therefore write:

$$y'_N = y_{N+1} = b_N + a_N y_N \qquad (4.4)$$

$$z_N = c_N y_N. \qquad (4.5)$$

Starting from an initial state, $N = 0$ (a_0, b_0, c_0), with the preceding conventions, we can in this way analyze step by step how the circuit of Figure 4.6 operates. We shall study the values of y and z for every time interval.

Furthermore, we shall suppose that the command does not vary, i.e., we have the relations:

$$a_0 = a_1 = \cdots = a_N$$
$$b_0 = b_1 = \cdots = b_N$$
$$c_0 = c_1 = \cdots = c_N.$$

Instant 0: The value of y is y_0. The (z) inputs are y_0 and c_0, from which we deduce the output value

$$z_0 = c_0 y_0. \qquad (4.6)$$

y' will take the value y_0 defined by the relation

$$y'_0 = y_1 = b_0 + a_0 y_0. \qquad (4.7)$$

Instant 1: y will be modified: y' will take the value y'_1 defined by relation (4.8):

$$y'_1 = y_2 = b_0 + a_0 y_1. \qquad (4.8)$$

During this time interval, the other functional block (z) input has not varied. From this we deduce the new output expression:

$$z_1 = c_0 y_1. \qquad (4.9)$$

Instant 2: (4.3) gives the new y' value:

$$y'_2 = y_3 = b_0 + a_0 y_2 \qquad (4.10)$$

and the output value is:

$$z_2 = y_2 c_0. \qquad (4.11)$$

Relation (4.5) defines the new output value corresponding to each new y value.

At any given time p, two cases are possible:

(a) either, the system has reached its final stable state, that is, y_p and z_p no longer change value;

(b) or the system continues to be transient.

In both cases, we assume that at any given instant p, we apply inputs a_p, b_p, c_p. To determine the system's future, it is sufficient to apply the previous process; in fact, the new initial y value at time p will be the y_p value determined during the past evolution when the inputs were a_0, b_0, c_0.

Therefore, equations (4.4) and (4.5) with the new initial conditions, determine step by step the system's new states.

4.2.1.2. *Validity of the method*

In order to study the validity of the proposed method, the different delays in the system under consideration must be foreseen. Another very important factor to be considered, is the feedback branch. In practice, the technology used will lead us to separate sequential systems into two types: relay systems (type 1) and transistor (or other) systems (type 2). In the latter type systems, the feedback loop is visible and has a delay which can be neglected or in the order of the other operators' delays. Let Δ' be the delay due to the feedback branch, and let Δ_1, Δ_2, ..., be the delays due to the operators.

(a) *Relay systems* (type 1). In relay systems, contacts furnish the coil and relay their supply or prevent their supply. Every modification in the state of the current induces a modification in the state of the contact of this relay after a delay of Δ', (if Δ' is the commutation time of the relay). The response time of the Boolean operators composed of series or parallel contacts, is negligible compared to relay response time, (in the order of a millisecond). The feedback branch is not visible; it is the electromagnetic field.

Relay performance (see Chapter 2) may be described in the following way: let i be the Boolean variable associated with the coil current and let y be the Boolean variable associated with the contact;

$i = 0$ no current in the coil,
$i = 1$ current circulates in the coil,
$y = 0$ the contact is open (the relay opens the circuit),
$y = 1$ the contact is closed (the relay closes the circuit).

Relay performance is studied by taking samples of the time, given Δ' the commutation time. The relay's Boolean equation is written (Figure 4.10):

$$i_N = y_{N+\Delta'}.$$

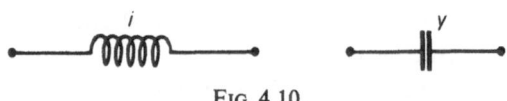

FIG. 4.10.

In fact, if at a given instant N, current circulates in the coil, y is closed, but if at time N, i is zero, the contact y is open at time $N+\Delta'$.

The Figure 4.7(a) circuit is represented by the relay design in Figure 4.11.

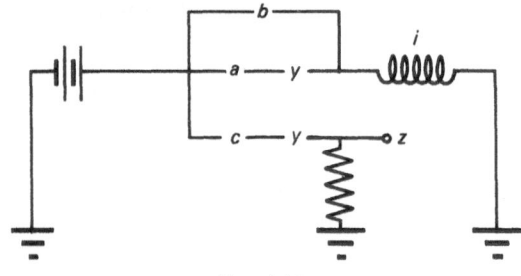

FIG. 4.11.

We take the time interval Δ' as the unit of time. To study the system's performance, it is sufficient to see what happens at every time interval. Assume that at time N the commands are a_N, b_N, c_N and $y = y_N$. The circuit's Boolean equations (Chapter 3) are written:

$$l_N = y_{N+1} = b_N + a_N y_N$$
$$z_N = c_N y_N.$$

These equations are analogous to (4.4) and (4.5).

The symbolic representation in Figure 4.8 is in accordance with real relay circuit performance because the output at time N depends on the value of y at time N.

(b) *Electronic systems* (type 2). Consider the circuit in Figure 4.12, obtained by separating the technological functional element and the delay associated with it for each circuit. The complete study of the system will be very complicated if we take into account the quantities of the different delays, Δ_i, Δ', especially since these delays are difficult to evaluate. A first approximation consists in considering the different delays, Δ_i, to be equal quantities. We then study two possible cases: Δ' is zero or equal to Δ. Let $y_1, y_2, ...,$ be the Δ output delays corresponding to operators $1, 2, ...$ We always envisage the case where the command slowly varies with respect to the time Δ.

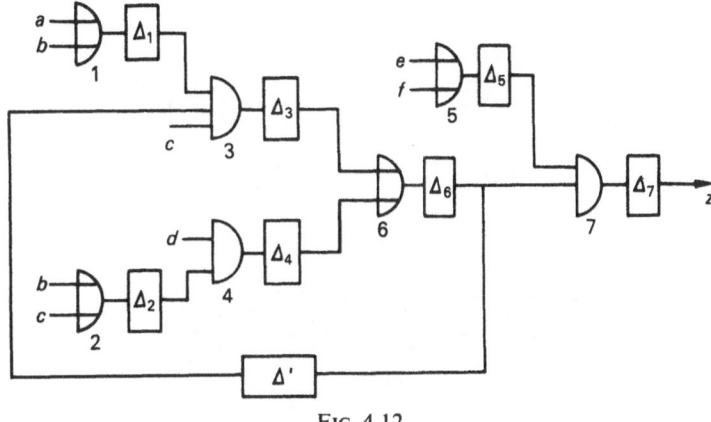

FIG. 4.12.

First case $\Delta' = 0$. It is possible to write the recurrence equations of this type of system. We shall study the value of the different signals at each of the instants Δ.

$$y_{1,N+1} = a_N + b_N$$
$$y_{2,N+1} = b_N + c_N$$
$$y_{3,N+1} = c_N y_{1,N} y_{6,N}$$
$$y_{4,N+1} = d_N y_{2,N}$$
$$y_{5,N+1} = e_N + f_N$$
$$y_{6,N+1} = y_{3,N} + y_{4,N}$$
$$z_{N+1} = y_{5,N} y_{6,N}.$$

By assuming that from a certain instant N on, the state of the commands is unstable, these equations can be condensed:

$$y_{6,N+3} = y_{3,N+2} + y_{4,N+2} = c_N(a_N + b_N)y_{6,N+1} + d_N(b_N + c_N)$$
$$z_{N+2} = y_{6,N+1}(e_N + f_N).$$

These recurrence equations are not the same as the ones we would have obtained by the proposed method for this type of system.

If the initial conditions are $y_{1,N}, \ldots, y_{6,N}$ a transient state, due to the input signals' propagation time, is produced. At the end of this time delay, the operators' inputs corresponding to the commands of the system $a_N, \ldots, f_N$ are no longer subject to change; only y_6 will be modified: the delays $\Delta_1, \Delta_2, \Delta_4, \Delta_5$ no longer have any effect on the system and the symbolic diagram is that of Figure 4.13. It can also be represented by Figure 4.14.

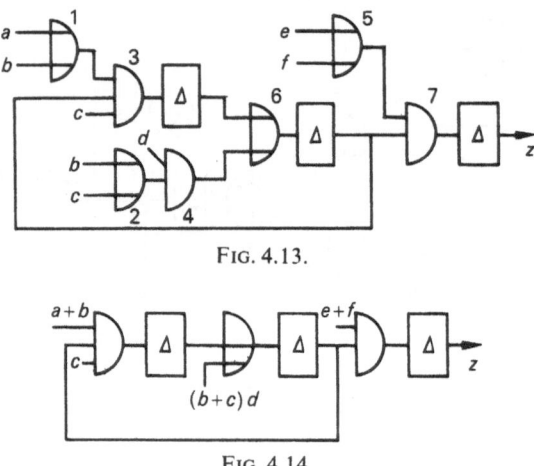

FIG. 4.13.

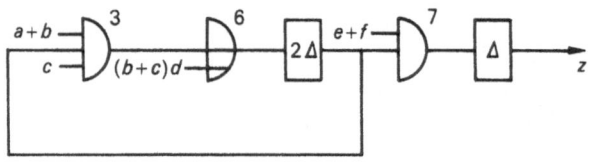

FIG. 4.14.

The two Δ delays can be replaced by a single delay, 2Δ, placed at the operator 6 output as in Figure 4.15.

FIG. 4.15.

We thus see that the system will evolve at every 2Δ interval. The proposed approximation method of study of the systems having a feedback loop therefore neglects the transition corresponding to the command variation transmission. Only the steady state is studied assuming that the command variation instantaneously reaches operators which intervene in the feedback loop or are connected to it.

Second case: $\Delta' = \Delta$. Everything done in the case $\Delta' = 0$ (neglecting the transition corresponding to the input variation transmission) remains valid. After a certain length of time, when the inputs of the operators corresponding to the system's commands are no longer modified, the delays, Δ_1, Δ_2, Δ_4, Δ_5 have no influence on the system. The symbolic diagram of the system can be that of Figure 4.16(a). Only the equation defining the y_N variable is changed:

$$y_{6,N+3} = c_N(a_N + b_N)y_{6,N} + d_N(b_N + c_N).$$

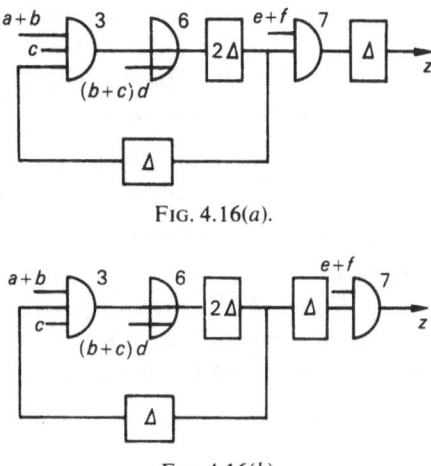

FIG. 4.16(a).

FIG. 4.16(b).

From the point of view of output, the Figure 4.16a circuit's performance is analogous to the circuit in Figure 4.16(b) in which the Δ delay is placed in front of the operator 7. From the point of view of performance, the Figure 4.16(b) circuit is analogous to the Figure 4.17 circuit, which, in turn is analogous to the Figure 4.15 circuit. In fact, it only differs by the 3Δ delay. The conclusions relative to the validity of the method are therefore the same in the case $\Delta' = 0$ and the case $\Delta' = \Delta$.

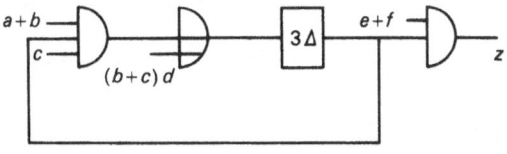

FIG. 4.17.

Comment. The case $\Delta' \gg \Delta$ has already been studied in Section 4.2.1.2a.

4.2.1.3. *First series of conclusions*

What should be retained from this first section? In the first place, the fact that transient phenomena appear in combinational systems as well as in sequential systems. In the second place, the fact that in circuits having one loop, the state of the system's variables depend on both present and past states by means of a variable associated with the loop. In the following we shall extend this last result to systems having several loops; but, we shall however, show that it is not necessary to associate a variable with each of the circuit's loops. We shall call these variables associated with the loops *internal or secondary variables*.

4.2.2. *Systems having several loops*

We shall, as in Section 4.2.1, separately study the type 1 circuits (relays) and the type 2 circuits (electronic).

4.2.2.1. *Relays systems*

Consider the circuit in Figure 4.18. If we suppose that the switching time of the 4 relays are the same and we take this interval as the time unit, then the circuit's equations are written as in Section 4.2.1.2:

$$i_{1,N} = y_{1,N+1} = a_N y_{2,N}(d_N + y_{1,N} + y_{6,N})$$
$$i_{2,N} = y_{2,N+1} = b_N + y_{1,N}$$
$$i_{3,N} = y_{3,N+1} = y_{2,N} y_{6,N}$$
$$i_{6,N} = y_{6,N+1} = y_{3,N}(d_N + y_{1,N} + y_{6,N})$$
$$z_{1,N} = c_N + y_{3,N}$$
$$z_{2,N} = a_N + y_{6,N}.$$

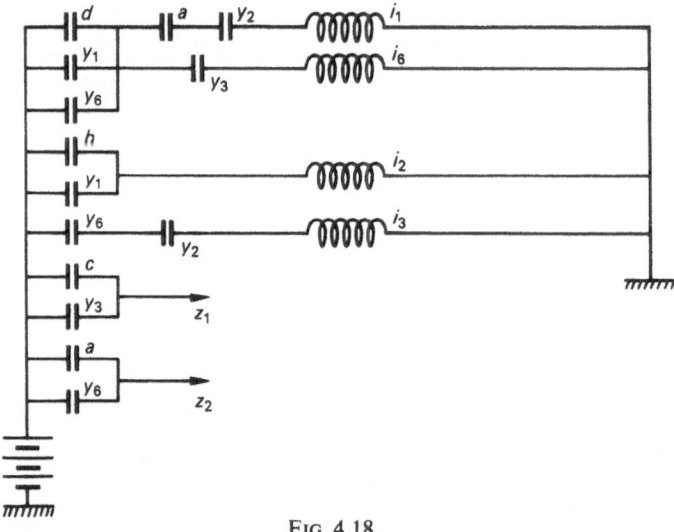

FIG. 4.18.

It can be noticed that the different internal variables of a sequential relay system are imposed: a secondary variable corresponds to each relay. The only restriction to the method used is to admit the equality of the different relays switching times. Except in the case of timed relays, this approximation is justified by the fact that it leads to very simple and accurate computation. In Chapter 6 we shall see how to avoid problems whenever this hypothesis is not entirely satisfied.

4.2.2.2. *Type 2 systems*

In this type of system, the feedback loops are real and the internal variables do not explicitly appear. Consider the circuit in Figure 4.19.

We proceed as in Section 4.2. Since it was impossible to express the output solely as a function of the inputs, we introduce a parameter (secondary variable) which gives a Boolean output expression.

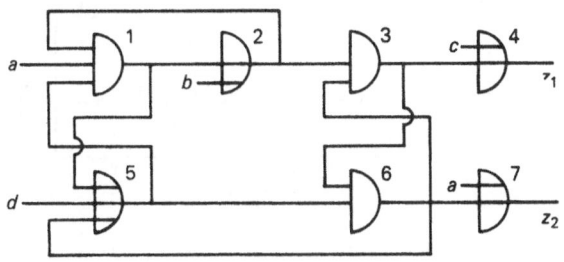

FIG. 4.19.

As in Section 4.2, all delays due to operators are replaced by as many delays as there are secondary variables necessary to be defined. Each of them is attributed to the operator having one of the secondary variables in its output.

In the present example, the system has five loops; 12, 15, 36, 56 and 12365. If we are given the output variables, y_1, y_2, y_3, y_6 of the operators 1, 2, 3, 6, we can show that the system is perfectly defined.

We make a second fundamental hypothesis for the sake of simplicity and in order to be able to perform sampling as in Section 4.1. We suppose that all fictional delays introduced into the system are equal to a delay Δ that we take as the unit of time.

The operation of the circuit in Figure 4.19 is represented as that in Figure 4.20. Figure 4.21 and 4.22 represent the output circuits and definition of the internal variables.

From Section 4.1, we have the equations

$$y_{1,N+1} = a_N y_{2,N}(d_N + y_{1,N} + y_{6,N})$$
$$y_{2,N+1} = b_N + y_{1,N}$$

$$y_{3,N+1} = y_{2,N}y_{6,N}$$
$$y_{6,N+1} = y_{3,N}(d_N + y_{1,N} + y_{6,N})$$
$$z_{1,N} = c_N + y_{3,N}$$
$$z_{2,N} = a_N + y_{6,N}$$

Notice that these equations correspond to the circuit in Figure 4.18.

Figure 4.20 is therefore the symbolic representation of the Figure 4.18 circuit.

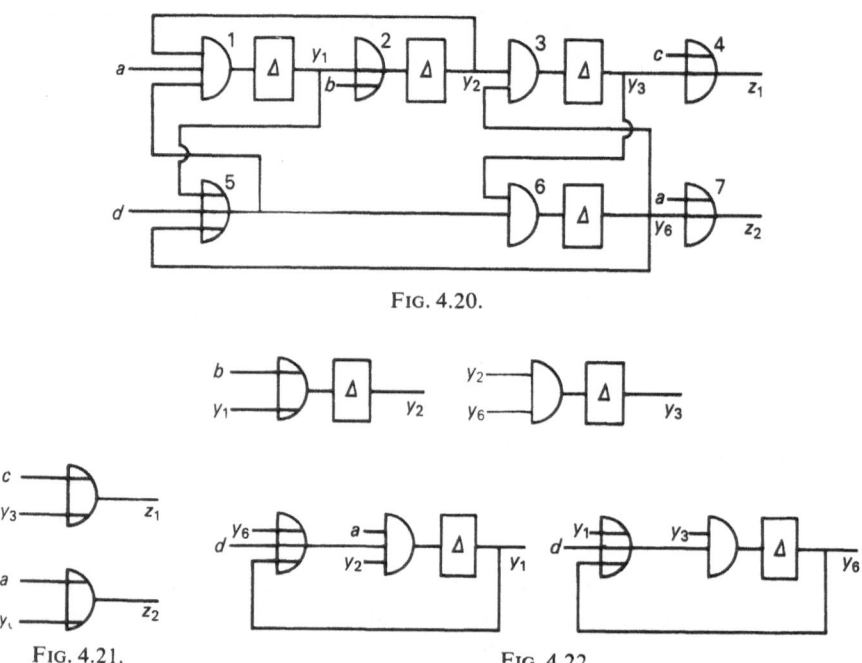

FIG. 4.20.

FIG. 4.21.

FIG. 4.22.

4.2.3. *Equations and representation of a sequential system*

We were led to take time samples in intervals of amplitude Δ (fictional delay). Generally if we consider a p input $x_1, \ldots, x_p$ system with loops and m outputs, $z_1, \ldots, z_m$, it is necessary to introduce a certain number of variables $y_1, \ldots, y_n$, in order to define all the outputs in a combinational way. This comes down to the introduction of n fictional Δ delays, then studying the circuit's performance at every Δ instant. The symbolic diagram of this kind of circuit appears in Figure 4.23. We take the interval of length Δ as the time unit for the study of the sys-

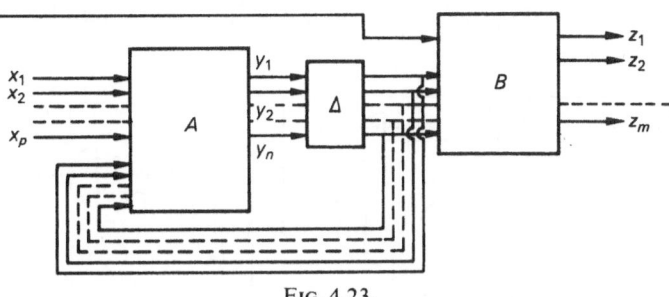

FIG. 4.23.

tem's performance. We seek the value of the y_i variables and the outputs z_i for each time interval. Let $x_{k,N}$ and $y_{i,N}$ be the values of the x_k inputs and the y_i variables at instant N. From this we derive the expressions for the y_i variables at instant $N+1$, and the z_j outputs at instant N.

$$y_{i,N+1} = g_i(x_{1,N}, \ldots, x_{p,N}, y_{1,N}, \ldots, y_{n,N}$$
$$z_{j,N} = f_i(x_{1,N}, \ldots, x_{p,N}, y_{1,N}, \ldots, y_{n,N}). \tag{4.12}$$

By definition, any system which has the equations describing its performance analogous to (4.12) is a *sequential system*.

The function y, previously defined, is called the sequential system's *internal or secondary variable*.

The inputs are sometimes called *primary variables*.

Note. The essential difference between a combinational and sequential system is in the forced introduction of internal variables which in certain cases, prevent the system from reaching a definitive stable state.

THEOREM. A sequential system of which the basic functions are AND, OR, NOT, or NOR, or NAND, is represented by an oriented graph with loops.

The proof of the theorem is based on the *reductio ad absurdum* and Theorem 1 (Section 4.1.1). In fact, if the graph had not any loops, it would correspond to a combinational system.

Comment. Certain graphs can have loops without corresponding to a sequential system. As a matter of fact, the definitive state of the circuit can depend only on the inputs in spite of the fact that the system has certain transitions before reaching its definitive state.

Consider, for example, the circuit which has its logical diagram in

Figure 4.24 and its graph as in Figure 4.25. The system has 3 loops, (1245), (1238), (387512).

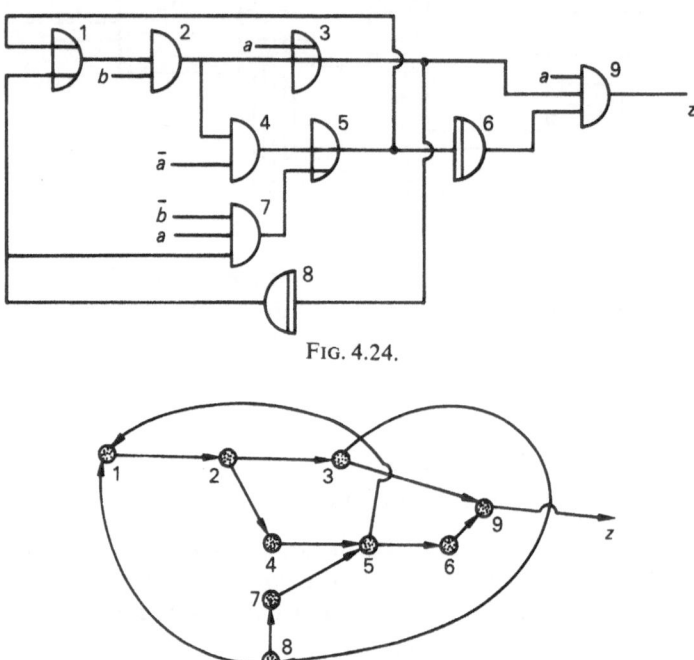

FIG. 4.24.

FIG. 4.25.

Operators 3 and 5's output variables, y_3 and y_5, are sufficient for the definition of the system. By applying the study process in the preceding section, the circuit's decomposition diagrams permits the writing of the Boolean equations. The representation appears in Figure 4.26.

As before, we suppose that the system's transition begins at an instant N when the state of the commands is a_N, b_N. We envisage an autonomous system, that is $a_N = a_{N+p}$ and $b_N = b_{N+p}$ at any instant p:

$$y_{3,N+1} = a_N + b_N(\overline{y_{3,N}} + y_{5,N}) \tag{4.13}$$
$$y_{5,N+1} = a_N \bar{b}_N \bar{y}_{3,N} + \bar{a}_N b_N(\overline{y_{3,N}} + y_{5,N}) \tag{4.14}$$
$$z_N = a_N y_{3,N} \overline{y_{5,N}}. \tag{4.15}$$

The recurrence Equations (4.13) and (4.14), together with Equation (4.15), lead to an explicit expression of z_{N+2}:

$$z_{N+2} = a_N y_{3,N+2} \bar{y}_{5,N+2}.$$

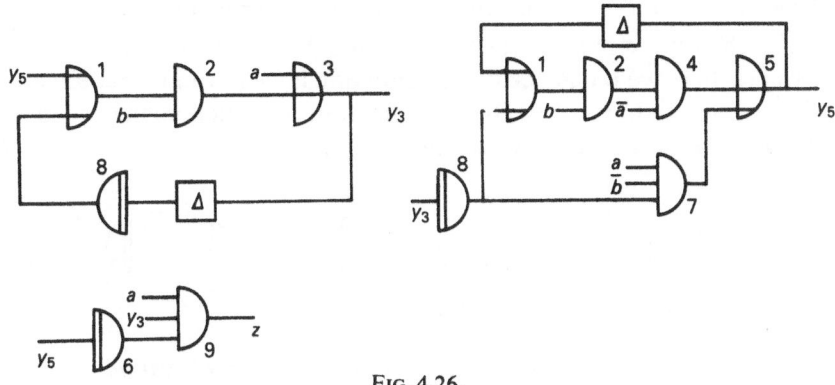

FIG. 4.26.

But from (4.13):

$$a_N y_{3,N+2} = a_N$$
$$\bar{y}_{5,N+2} = (\bar{a}_N + b_N + y_{3,N+1})(a_N + \bar{b}_N + y_{3,N+1}\bar{y}_{5,N+1})$$
$$a_N \bar{y}_{5,N+2} = a_N(b_N + y_{3,N+1})$$

We derive:

$$z_{N+2} = a_N.$$

At time $N + 2$ the output depends only on the input at time N, that is a_N. We say that the system is pseudo-sequential.

DEFINITION. We call system pseudo-sequential if all the equations can be put in the form of Equations (4.16)

$$y_{i,N+1} = g_i(x_{1,N}, \ldots, x_{p,N}, y_{1,N}, \ldots, y_{n,N}$$
$$z_{j,N+q_j} = f_j(x_{1,N}, \ldots, x_{p,N}). \tag{4.16}$$

When studying the autonomous transition of the system, that is, the commands are the same at times N and $N + q$ for any q.

THEOREM. Any system which has its autonomous performance equations in the form:

$$y_{j,N+q_j} = g_i(x_{1,N}, \ldots, x_{p,N}) \tag{4.17}$$
$$z_{i,N} = f_i(x_{1,N}, \ldots, x_{p,N}, y_{1,N}, \ldots, y_{n,N}) \tag{4.18}$$

is a pseudo-sequential system. The converse is false.

In fact, if we study the output value at instant $N + q_r$ (q_r is the largest of the q_j), Equation (4.18) gives:

$$z_{i,N+q_r} = f_i(x_{1,N}, \ldots, x_{p,N}, y_{1,N+q_r}, \ldots, y_{n,N+q_r}).$$

If we replace the $y_{j,N+q_r}$ by their expressions derived from Equation (4.17), the output is no longer a function only of the inputs at time N.

In practice, we come across this situation if we introduce redundant wires in a circuit. They create annoying transient phenomena and give response delays in the system (Figure 4.27).

$a+y_N$ or ay_N ⟩ $a+y_N$ ⟩ ay_N ⟩ $a+y_N$ or ay_N ⟩

a ⟩ y_{N+1} a ⟩ y_{N+1} a ⟩ y_{N+1} a ⟩ y_{N+1}

FIG. 4.27.

4.2.4. *Internal variables of a type 2 sequential system*

4.2.4.1. *Search for internal variables*

Reconsider the example in Section 4.2.2.2. In order to study the corresponding circuit, we defined four secondary variables. Two, however, would have been sufficient. In fact, it is simply a question not only of being able to express the outputs in terms of the secondary variables and inputs, but also of defining each of them by recurrence in terms of the inputs and all the secondary variables.

We consider the outputs of operators 1 and 6 as secondary variables.

From the point of view of performance, the circuit in Figure 4.19 can be represented by Figure 4.28. Figures 4.29 and 4.30 represent the circuits defining the outputs and secondary variables. From these, we deduce the Boolean equations of the circuit:

$$y_{1,N+1} = a_N(b_N + y_{1,N})(d_N + y_{1,N} + y_{6,N})$$
$$y_{6,N+1} = y_{6,N}(b_N + y_{1,N})(d_N + y_{1,N} + y_{6,N})$$
$$z_{1,N} = c_N + y_{6,N}(b_N + y_{1,N})$$
$$z_{2,N} = a_N + y_{6,N}.$$

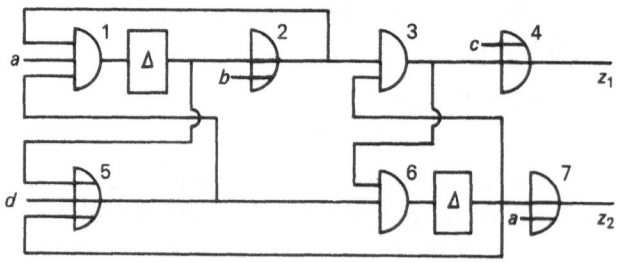

FIG. 4.28.

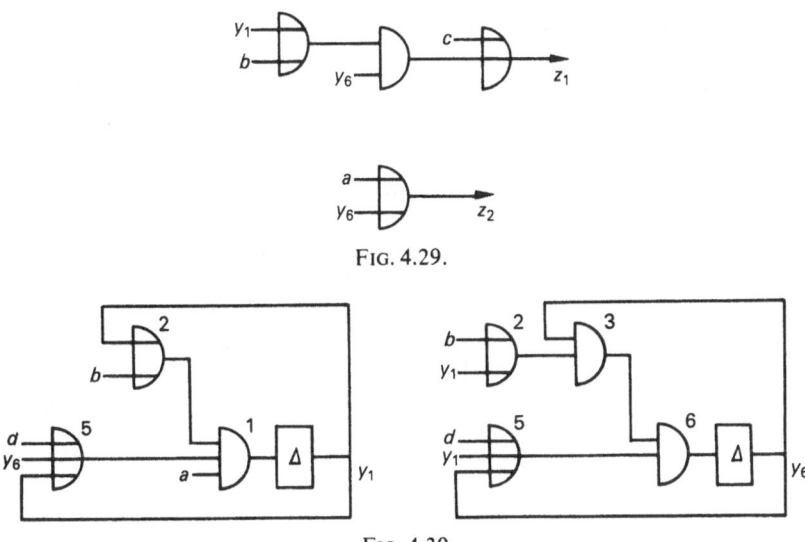

FIG. 4.29.

FIG. 4.30.

We thus see that the choice of internal variables in type 2 circuits is not unique. This is the main difference in the two types of circuits (1 and 2).

In the present section we shall try to give a method of study which permits, in the case of type 2 circuits:

–to find the sufficient number of secondary variables,

–to find, among all the possible choices, the one having the minimal number of secondary variables. (From Section 4.2.1.2 we know that this is unnecessary in the case of type 1 circuits.)

4.2.4.2. *Determination of the sufficient number of internal variables*
We saw in Section 4.2 that the determination of the internal variables made the output circuit combinational. It is then quite simple to define the signal running through each branch. When we define an internal variable, we in fact define an operator output. We therefore know the value of the signal running through a certain number of branches. We can therefore remove all branches and see if the remaining circuit still has loops. In this case, we define a new internal variable which implies the opening of a certain number of branches in the residual graph. We continue in this way, until we have a graph which has no loops. A fictional delay is associated with each internal variable as in Section 4.2.2. We can decompose the original circuit into several circuits

defining the internal variables and several output circuits if the system has different outputs.

Consider the circuit in Figure 4.31. Its graph is in Figure 4.32.

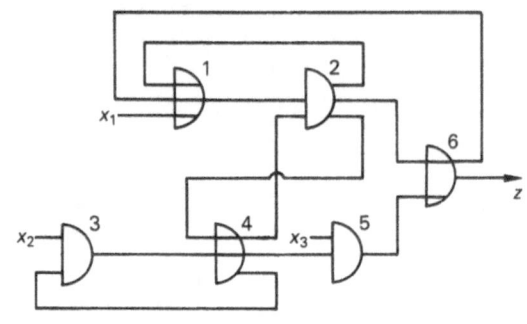

FIG. 4.31.

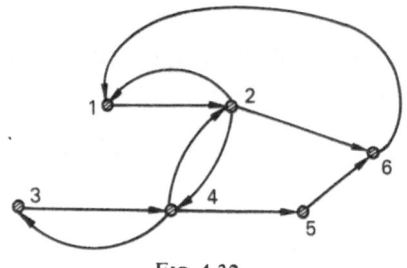

FIG. 4.32.

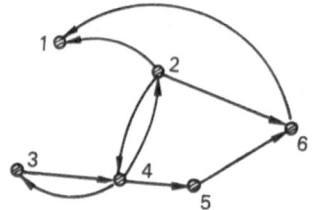

FIG. 4.33.

There are several choices of internal variables possible. First, we eliminate loop 12 and take the operator 1 output, (y_1) as first internal variable. The circuit's graph becomes that of Figure 4.33 if we open all the branches coming from operator 1.

We now open loop 34 taking the operator 3 output as second internal variable. Figure 4.34 is the new graph obtained by opening all the branches coming from operator 3 (y_3). In order to remove the last loop from the graph, we open the branches coming from operator 4 (the last internal variable is y_4; the operator 4 output) and obtain Figure 4.35. The system no longer has loops. The Figure 4.31 diagram can therefore be represented by Figure 4.36. Figure 4.37 represents the different circuits defining the secondary variables and the output circuit, from which we deduce the following equations:

$$y_{1,N+1} = y_{1,N}y_{4,N}(1+x_{3,N}y_{4,N})+x_{1,N} = x_{1,N}+y_{1,N}y_{4,N}$$
$$y_{3,N+1} = x_{2,N}y_{4,N}$$
$$y_{4,N+1} = y_{3,N}+y_{1,N}y_{4,N}$$
$$z_N = y_{4,N}(x_{3,N}+y_{1,N}).$$

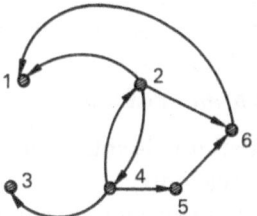

FIG. 4.34.

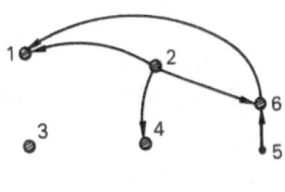

FIG. 4.35.

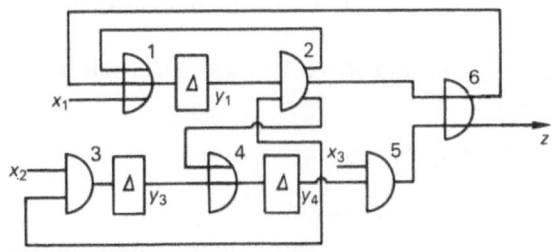

FIG. 4.36.

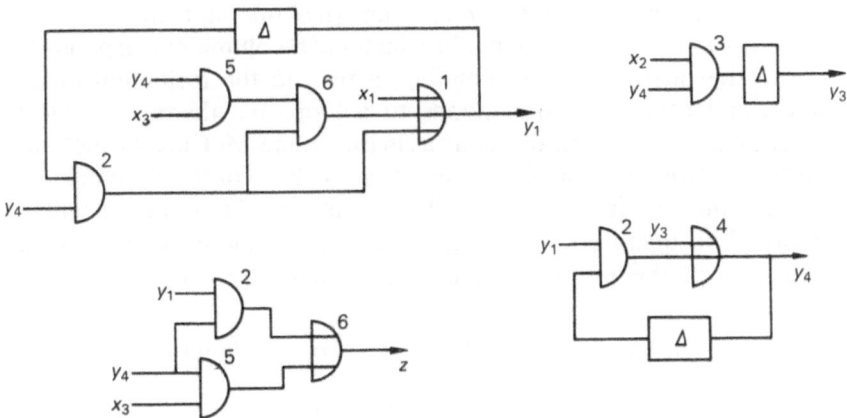

FIG. 4.37.

4.2.4.3. *Determination of the minimal number of internal variables*
We know how to determine the internal variables step by step. We wish to find the minimal number of these variables in order to write the Boolean performance equations. For this, we must determine the minimal number of operators for which we open the output branches. To start with, we must find all the circuit's loops and therefore the operators intervening in these loops. We can proceed using the Boolean connection matrices described in Chapter 3.

We shall consider particular loops called *primitive loops*.

DEFINITION.   If no subset of a loop's operators is sufficient in itself to form a loop, then we call the loop a primitive loop.

For example, if we consider loops 123, 12345, assuming that no pair of operators form a loop, then 123 is a primitive loop, but 12345 is not.

The opening of primitive loops leads to the opening of the non-primitive loops. There is therefore no reason to keep the primitive loops.

Consider the circuit in Figure 4.31 and its graph (Figure 4.32). The circuit has 5 loops:

$$12, 24, 34, 126, 12456.$$

Only loops 12, 24, 34 are primitive.

We seek, among all the primitive loops, the minimum number of operators intervening in the composition of all these loops.

For this, we suppose that the first loop is composed of operators $a_1, \ldots$, the second of operators $b_1, \ldots$, the nth of operators $n_1, \ldots,$.

We draw a rectangular table in which each column corresponds to one of the operators corresponding in turn to the formation of the loops, and each row corresponds to a loop. We therefore solve a covering problem much the same as in the Quine-McCluskey method. There is a cross in a cell if the operator at the head of the column intervenes in the loop indicated at the left of the row; if not, the cell will be empty. The operators which intervene in minimum number in the formation of the primitive loops are obtained by solving Equation (4.19):

$$(a_1 + a_2 + \cdots)(b_1 + b_2 + \cdots) \cdots (n_1 + n_2 + \cdots) = 1. \quad (4.19)$$

The shortest term is the solution to the problem.

In the example under discussion the table in Figure 4.38 is the table

	1	2	3	4	5	6
12	×	×				
24		×		×		
34			×	×		

FIG. 4.38.

described in the preceding paragraph. The Boolean equation determining the minimum number of internal variables is written:

$$(1+2)(2+4)(3+4) = 1$$
$$(2+14)(4+23) = 1.$$

The solutions are:

$$14 \qquad 23 \qquad 24.$$

There are therefore 3 possible assignments.

We intend to discuss at the end of the chapter the physical interpretation of these different assignments.

The method just proposed therefore allows the determination of the internal variables and at the same time this determination completely defines the sequential system by giving the recurrence equations for the definition of the internal variables and the Boolean output expression (Equations (4.12)), starting from the graph of a type 2 sequential system.

$$y_{j,N+1} = g_j(x_{1,N}, \ldots, x_{p,N}, y_{1,N}, \ldots, y_{n,N}) \tag{4.20}$$
$$z_{i,N} = f_i(x_{1,N}, \ldots, x_{p,N}, y_{i,N}, \ldots, y_{n,N}). \tag{4.21}$$

These equations are valid for the two types of sequential systems.

By definition, every part of the system satisfying a relation analogous to (4.20) will be called a *memory*. This term signifies that the state, at a given instant, of the output of this subsystem is a function of the system's past state (the output depends on the past state of subsystems therefore we see that it is a question of the subsystem's memory).

DEFINITION.   The *internal state* of a sequential system is a given state of the internal variables, i.e., a given state of all the sequential system's memories.

DEFINITION.   The *total state* of a sequential system is a given state of the inputs and internal variables.

The relations (4.20) and (4.21) can be represented in the form of tables called excitation matrix and output matrix.

The outputs being themselves in binary code, the matrix term is well adapted to express them because we effectively deal with Boolean matrices (see Chapter 1).

In these two matrices, each column corresponds to a given state of inputs and each row corresponds to an internal state of the system (state of the internal variables). Each cell at the intersection of a row and a column indicates the following internal state in the excitation matrix (in binary code) and the output at the instant under consideration in the output matrix. We give an example of the construction and utilization of these matrices.

4.2.5. *Performance of a sequential system*

Consider the sequential system in Figure 4.39. Its graph is shown in Figure 4.40. The graph has three loops: 125, 468, 1365. Those three loops are primitive. The implicant chart for the determination of the minimal number of secondary variables is represented in Figure 4.41. The Boolean equation of the determination of the minimal number sought is:

$$(1+3+6+5)(1+2+5)(4+6+8) = 1.$$

The different possible choices are:

14, 16, 18, 26, 45, 56, 58.

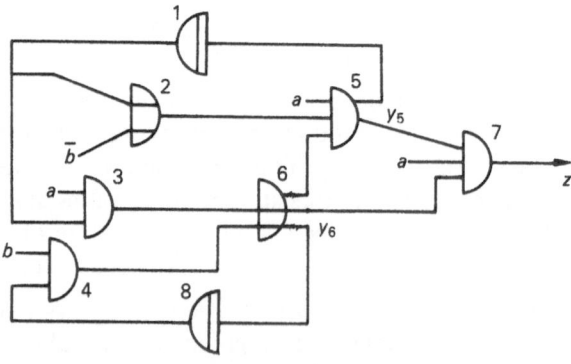

FIG. 4.39.

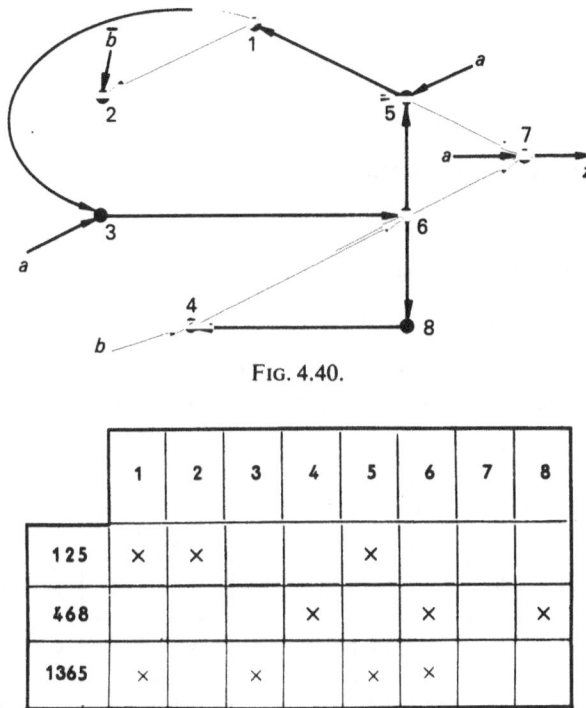

FIG. 4.40.

	1	2	3	4	5	6	7	8
125	×	×			×			
468				×		×		×
1365	×		×		×	×		

FIG. 4.41.

Two secondary variables are sufficient to define the system. We shall consider the operators 5 and 6 output variables: y_5 and y_6.

Figure 4.42 represents the circuits defining the secondary variables and the output.

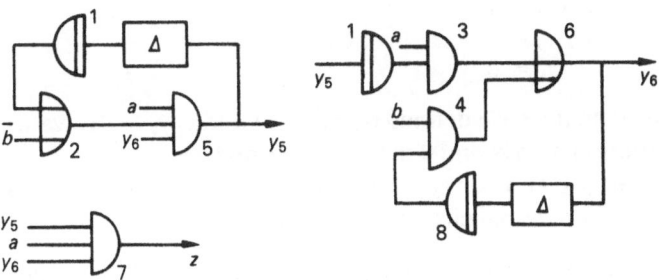

FIG. 4.42.

The system's Boolean equations of performance are written:

$$y_{5,N+1} = (\overline{b_N} + \overline{y_{5,N}})a_N y_{6,N} \qquad (4.22)$$
$$y_{6,N+1} = a_N \overline{y_{1,N}} + b_N \overline{y_{6,N}} \qquad (4.23)$$
$$z_N = a_N y_{5,N} y_{6,N}. \qquad (4.24)$$

The system's different internal states are:

$$y_5 y_6 = 00, 01, 11, 10$$

and the different inputs are:

$$ab = 00, 01, 11, 10.$$

The excitation and output matrices are represented by the maps in Figures 4.43 and 4.44. They represent Equations (4.20), (4.21), (4.22).

ab / $y_5 y_6$	00	01	11	10
00	00	01	01	01
01	00	00	11	11
11	00	00	00	10
10	00	01	01	00

FIG. 4.43.

ab / $y_5 y_6$	00	01	11	10
00	0	0	0	0
01	0	0	0	0
11	0	0	1	1
10	0	0	0	0

FIG. 4.44.

In fact, suppose that we apply the input $ab = 11$ to the system in the initial state $y_1 y_2 = 01$. From Equations (4.20), (4.21), (4.22) we have:

$$y_{1,N+1} = 1$$
$$y_{2,N+1} = 1$$
$$z_N = 0.$$

Therefore, in the case defined by $ab = 11$ and $y_1 y_2 = 01$, we write 11 in the excitation matrix and 0 in the output matrix.

We shall use another type of table called the transition map in order to realize a sequential circuit with τ flip-flops.

DEFINITION. Given the values $y_{i,N}$ and $y_{i,N+1}$ of a sequential system's internal variable at two consecutive instants N and $N + 1$, we call transition variable, noted $\underset{N\to N+1}{\tau_i}$, a variable which equals 0 if the quantity y_i does not vary during the interval of time under consideration, and 1 in the opposite case; this leads to the relation:

$$\underset{N\to N+1}{\tau_i} = y_{i,N} \oplus y_{i,N+1}.$$

The transition map will be derived from the excitation matrix by substituting $\underset{N\to N+1}{\tau_i}$ for $y_{i,N+1}$.

Figure 4.45 represents the transition map of the sequential system under study.

y_1y_2 \ ab	00	01	11	10
00	00	01	01	01
01	01	01	10	10
11	11	11	11	01
10	10	11	11	10

FIG. 4.45.

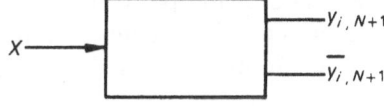

FIG. 4.46.

For example, in the case, $ab = 11$, $y_1 y_2 = 01$, we mark 10 since:

$$\underset{N\to N+1}{\tau_1} = y_{1,N} \oplus y_{1,N+1} = 0 \oplus 1 = 1$$
$$\underset{N\to N+1}{\tau_2} = y_{2,N} \oplus y_{2,N+1} = 1 \oplus 1 = 0.$$

In conclusion the internal state is an important concept, intervening as a consequence of the presence of internal variables in the problem of the analysis of a sequential system.

Comment. The transition variable τ_i will be useful when we wish to use τ flip-flops to create values of the y_i variables at the instant $N+1$ from the values at the instant N.

Consider the τ flip-flop in Figure 4.46. From the discussion in Chapter 2 we know that if $y_{i,N}$ is the y_i value at instant N, and $y_{i,N+1}$ its value at instant $N+1$, then corresponding to the application of X, we have the relations:

$$X = 0 \quad \text{implies} \quad y_{i,N} = y_{i,N+1}$$
$$X = 1 \quad \text{implies} \quad y_{i,N} = y_{i,N+1}.$$

We deduce the relation:

$$X = y_{i,N} \oplus y_{i,N+1} = \underset{N \to N+1}{\tau_i}.$$

If we attack symmetric flip-flops with the transition $\underset{N \to N+1}{\tau_i}$ between instants N and $N+1$, the τ flip-flop output will be the y_i value taken at instant $N+1$.

4.3. SYNTHESIS PROBLEMS–DEFINITION OF THE INTERNAL STATE

In analysis of the performance of a sequential system, we know the state of the different inputs (input vector) the state of the different internal variables (internal state) and we deduce the state of the different outputs (output vector) (Equations (4.20) and (4.21)).

We have already shown that, by knowing the vector $x_N = (x_{1,n}, \ldots, x_{p,N})$ and the internal state $Q_N = (y_{1,N}, \ldots, y_{n,N})$, the output circuit becomes a combinational system.

The circuits which define the secondary variables y_i are the memories, that is, they take into account the system's past transitions.

$(x_1, \ldots, x_p)$ is the input vector X,
$(z_1, \ldots, z_r)$ is the output vector Z.

If we introduce the internal state and the input and output vectors, Equations (4.20) and (4.21) are written:

$$Q_{N+1} = G(X_N, Q_N) \tag{4.25}$$
$$Z_N = F(X_N, Q_N). \tag{4.26}$$

Equations (4.25) and (4.26) appear in both analysis and synthesis problems.

Knowing the initial state Q_0 and the different input vectors, the different internal states attained and the different output vectors can be deduced in an analysis problem of a sequential system.

We note an important property of the F and G functions:

$$\left. \begin{array}{l} F(X_N, Q_N) \div F(X_N, Q'_N) \\ G(X_N, Q_N) = G(X_N, Q'_N) \end{array} \right\} \text{ imply } Q_N = Q'_N.$$

DEFINITION. We call input sequence of a sequential system, a sequence of q possible input vectors. If $X_1, \ldots, X_q$ are the q input vectors, the sequence $X_1, \ldots, X_q$ is an input sequence, that is, we successively apply the q input vectors, $X_1, X_2, \ldots$, then X_q to the sequential system.

We call output sequence of a sequential system, the sequence of q output vectors corresponding to an input sequence. For example, the output sequence $Z_1 Z_2, \ldots, Z_q$ corresponds to the input sequence $X_1 X_2, \ldots, X_q$.

In a sequential system synthesis problem, we are given groups of input-output sequences, from which the internal states Q as well as the functions F and G must be determined.

A combinational system synthesis was presented in the form of a truth table. A sequential system synthesis problem is a notebook of changes defining a correspondence between input and output sequences. By two examples, we shall show how the internal states of a given system are defined.

Example 1. Consider a two push button device in which A and B command two motors M_1 and M_2. We wish to have a system so designed that if the two motors are off and we push A, motor M_1 will not only start, but keep running when we release A. Next, pushing B a first time, M_2 should start and continue running when we let B go off. The M_1 motor stops when A is pushed a second time and stays off when we release A. M_2 stops with the second push of B and stays off when we release B. We eliminate the case of A and B both being pushed at the same time, and any other manipulation of A and B in a different order than that described above has no effect on the motors.

Let a and b be the Boolean variables associated with the push buttons A and B. Let m_1 and m_2 be those associated with the motors M_1 and M_2.

$$a \text{ (or } b) = 1 \quad \text{if we press } A \text{ (or } B),$$
$$a \text{ (or } b) = 0 \quad \text{if we release } A \text{ (or } B),$$
$$m_1 \text{ (or } m_2) = 1 \quad \text{if the motor } M_1 \text{ (or } M_2) \text{ is running,}$$
$$m_1 \text{ (or } m_2) = 0 \quad \text{if } M_1 \text{ (or } M_2) \text{ is off.}$$

Taking into account the specifications imposed in the text of the problem, we can construct the truth table (Figure 4.47).

In fact, at the command $a\,b = 0\,0$, the motors do not change. If we push B, M_1 cannot run alone because M_2 is immediately turned on. If we push A, both motors cannot remain off or on as they were.

The system is not combinational because there are many possible output values (m_1, m_2) corresponding to a given value of ab. It is

ab	00	01	11	10
$m_1\, m_2$	00, 01, 11, 10	00, 11	—	01, 10

FIG. 4.47.

necessary to define four internal states:

state 1: both motors are off,
state 2: M_1 is on,
state 3: both motors are running,
state 4: only M_2 is running.

We can therefore define a Karnaugh output map (Figure 4.48).

ab	00				01				11				10			
Internal state	1	2	3	4	1	2	3	4	1	2	3	4	1	2	3	4
$m_1\, m_2$	00	10	11	01	00	11	11	00	—	—	—	—	10	10	01	01

FIG. 4.48.

The system is combinational with respect to the different command values and the different internal states. Notice that in this problem an internal state is attributed to each output value. This is not a general rule because in most cases the number of internal states is not the same as the number of outputs. We justify this statement by an example.

Example 2. We wish to determine a 3 push button (A, B, C) system which has a motor M designed so that if we push and release A, a manipulation of B starts the motor M which continues running when B is released. A manipulation of C stops the motor. In the same manner, if C is pushed after a manipulation of A, B has no effect on the motor and C is a reset to 0. Any simultaneous action of two buttons is excluded. Several successive manipulations of A, B, or C do not change the system's state attained by a first manipulation of these buttons.

The Boolean variables a, b, c have the same signification as in example 1. From the specifications imposed; we determine the system's truth table (Figure 4.49).

abc	000	001	011	010	110	111	101	100
m	0,1	0	—	0,1	—	—	—	0,1

FIG. 4.49.

This system is sequential because the motor can run as well as be stopped by states 000, 010, and 100 of the command. Notice that the output values are not specified for the command values 011, 110, 101, 111.

If the command value is 000, the past state of the motor, on or off, must be known in order to deduce its actual state. This leads to the consideration of two internal states:

state 1: the motor runs,
state 2: the motor is off.

We define a new truth table (Figure 4.50). Notice that we cannot specify what the motor M will do if it was off and we push B. What it

abc	000		001		011		010		110		111		101		100	
Internal state	1	2	1	2	1	2	1	2	1	2	1	2	1	2	1	2
m	1	0	0	0	—	—	—	1,0	—	—	—	—	—	—	1	0

FIG. 4.50.

will do depends on whether A or C was previously manipulated. We shall therefore consider a total of three internal states:

state 1: the motor runs,
state 2: the motor is off and A is not pushed,
state 3: the motor is off and A has just been pushed.

The system's truth table is written (Figure 4.51). The system has become combinational by definition of the three internal states. Notice that in this example the two internal states 2 and 3 correspond to the same output value, $m = 0$.

abc	000	001	011	010	110	111	101	100
Internal state	1 2 3	1 2 3	1 2 3	1 2 3	1 2 3	1 2 3	1 2 3	1 2 3
m	1 0 0	0 0 0	– – –	1 0 1	– – –	– – –	– – –	1 0 0

FIG. 4.51.

4.4. INTERNAL STATE–TECHNOLOGICAL STATE

Consider the sequential system in Figure 4.52. Its realization is accomplished by the sole use of NOR circuits. The system is defined with the help of two secondary variables y_1 and y_2 which will be the operators 4 and 6 outputs. The system's Boolean equations are written:

$$y_{1,N+1} = (\overline{a_N} + y_{1,N})(a_N + b_N)$$
$$y_{2,N+1} = \overline{y_{1,N}}(b_N + y_{2,N})$$
$$z_N = \overline{y_{2,N}}(a_N + y_{1,N}).$$

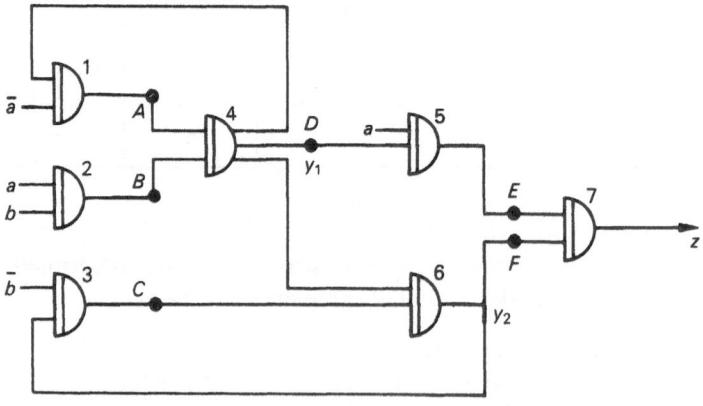

FIG. 4.52.

Figures 4.53 and 4.54 represent the excitation and output matrices of this system.

We have mentioned (Section 4.2.4) that the internal state of a sequential system was the state of the internal variables. Consequently, this system has four internal states: 00, 01, 11, 10.

y_1y_2 \ ab	00	01	11	10
00	01	10	00	01
01	01	11	01	01
11	00	10	10	10
10	00	10	10	10

FIG. 4.53.

y_1y_2 \ ab	00	01	11	10
00	0	0	1	1
01	0	0	0	0
11	0	0	0	0
10	1	1	1	1

FIG. 4.54.

Another method for defining present states of a system in order to foresee its future states exists. It is sufficient to consider each operator block output and the input vector at the instant under consideration. We shall call a given state of inputs and output signal of all operators of the circuit the 'technological state' of the sequential system.

THEOREM. To every technological state there corresponds a single total state and vice-versa. A total state is defined by the pair of 'internal state-input vector'.

Since the internal variables define the system, the signal at all points of the system is defined by the internal state and input vector. Conversely, if we know the signal's value at all points of the circuit and the inputs, we can deduce the value of the internal variables, therefore the total state.

Example. In the circuit of Figure 4.52 consider the total state:

$$(aby_1y_2) = 0\ 1\ 1\ 0.$$

The value of the signal i at the circuit's different points is the following:

$$A:i=0 \qquad D:i=1$$
$$B:i=0 \qquad E:i=0$$
$$C:i=1 \qquad F:i=0.$$

THEOREM. To every technological state there corresponds a single internal state, but several technological states can correspond to each internal state.

This is a result of the preceding theorem. In fact, the correspondence between the total state and the technological state is one-to-one. Since the total state is defined both by the internal state and the input vector to be given, the technological state is the same thing as to be given the total state. Therefore to be given the pair, 'input vector-internal state', that is, to say one internal state. Conversely, given the internal state, there are as many technological states as there are possible input vectors which are associated with this internal state.

In the preceding example, if X_A, X_B, ..., X_F, X_G, are the Boolean variables attributed to the signals at points A, B, C, D, E, F, G, there are four total states corresponding to the internal state 10,

$$(aby_1y_2) = 0\ 0\ 1\ 0, 0\ 1\ 1\ 0, 1\ 1\ 1\ 0, 1\ 0\ 1\ 0$$

and therefore four technological states. To determine these states, we refer to Figure 4.55, in which the Figure 4.52 circuit is decomposed.

The initial conditions are $y_1y_2 = 10$. We have decomposed the given circuits starting at instant 0, by giving the new y_1y_2 and output values under the hypotheses of simplification in Section 4.2.4. The four technological states we are looking for are represented on Figure 4.56.

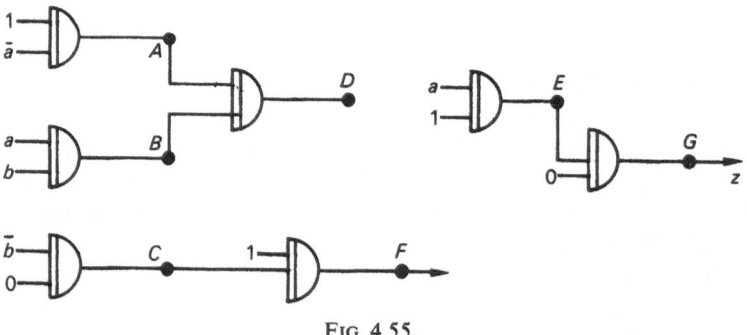

FIG. 4.55.

Comment. If the circuit has p functional elements and q distinct inputs (independent Boolean variables) the system would not have 2^{p+q} technological states. For example, it is impossible in a NOR circuit or OR gate, that one of the inputs and one of the outputs be 1 in

a	b	x_A	x_B	x_C	x_D	x_E	x_F	x_G
0	0	0	1	0	0	0	0	1
0	1	0	0	1	1	0	0	1
1	1	0	0	1	1	0	0	1
1	0	0	0	0	1	0	0	1

FIG. 4.56.

the first case and 0 in the second. In the same way, it is impossible in an NAND circuit or AND gate, to have one of the inputs 0 and the first operator output 0 and the second 1.

4.5. CONCLUSION

The essential concept of the chapter is the notion of a sequential system's internal variable, which is nothing but a supplementary variable introduced to make the output circuit combinational. The number of internal variables is connected to the machine structure in two ways: first, the presence of loops in the logical diagram of the realized circuit; second the fact that the output function can be different for several identical input combinations. There are therefore two consequences of the introduction of these variables: first, because of the loops, if the technological circuit is not monitored, it can engage itself in cycles (we shall study this subject in detail in the following chapters). Then, according to the state of the internal variables (which define the system's internal state) the sequential machine can store a certain memory of its past transitions.

APPENDIX

PHYSICAL INTERPRETATION OF THE CHOICE OF INTERNAL VARIABLES

The problem which we wish to solve is to give a physical interpretation of the different choices possible of internal variables for type 2 circuits. Consider the circuit in Figure 4.57.

The system has three primitive loops:

$$(6, 7, 8) \qquad (3, 2, 1) \qquad (8, 9, 10, 11).$$

The table in Figure 4.58 represents the implicant chart for the determination of the minimal number of internal variables. The equation of

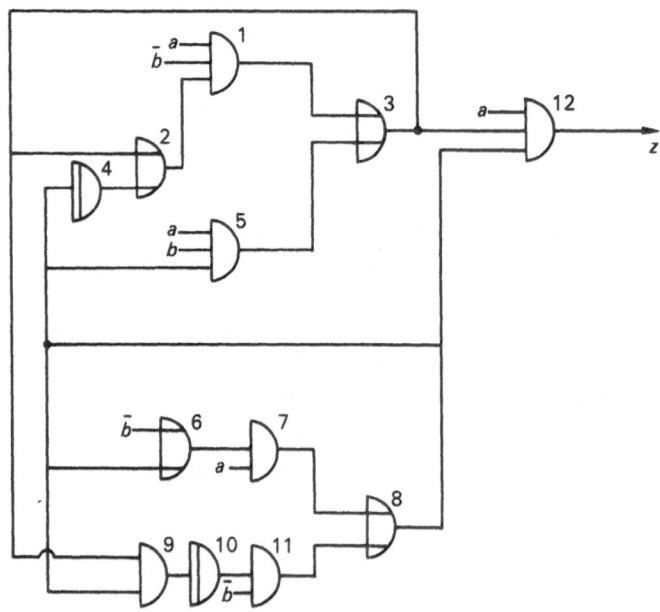

FIG. 4.57.

this determination is written:

$$(6+7+8)(1+2+3)(8+9+10+11) = 1$$
$$[8+(6+7)(9+10+11)](1+2+3) = 1.$$

	1	2	3	4	5	6	7	8	9	10	11
678						×	×	×			
321	×	×	×								
8, 9, 10, 11								×	×	×	×

FIG. 4.58.

The different minimal solutions are:

18   28   38.

Let us seek the different Boolean equations, excitation and output matrices corresponding to the different choices of secondary variables. We establish in detail the determination of the equations in the case of the minimal solution 18. We shall give the results in the two other cases leaving the computation as an exercise for the reader.

Variables y_1 and y_8 output of operators 1 and 8
From Figure 4.57 we can write the following equations since the fictional delays are placed at the output of operators 1 and 8.

$$y_{1,N+1} = (\overline{y_{8,N}} + y_{3,N})a_N\overline{b_N}$$
$$y_{3,N} = y_{1,N} + a_Nb_Ny_{8,N}$$
$$y_{8,N+1} = a_N(\overline{b_N} + y_{8,N}) + \overline{b_N}(\overline{y_{8,N}} + \overline{y_{3,N}})$$
$$\overline{y_{3,N}} = \overline{y_{1,N}}(\overline{a_N} + \overline{b_N} + \overline{y_{8,N}})$$
$$a_N\overline{b_N} + a_Ny_{8,N} + \overline{b_N}\overline{y_{8,N}} = a_Ny_{8,N} + \overline{b_N}\overline{y_{8,N}}$$
$$z_N = a_Ny_{8,N}y_{3,N},$$

from which we derive the final equations:

$$y_{1,N+1} = a_N\overline{b_N}(y_{1,N} + \overline{y_{8,N}})$$
$$y_{8,N+1} = a_Ny_{8,N} + \overline{b_N}(\overline{y_{1,N}} + \overline{y_{8,N}})$$
$$z_N = a_Ny_{8,N}(y_{1,N} + b_N).$$

Figures 4.59 and 4.60 are the excitation and output matrices.

ab / y_1y_8	00	01	11	10
00	01	00	00	11
01	01	00	01	01
11	00	00	01	11
10	01	00	00	11

FIG. 4.59.

ab / y_1y_8	00	01	11	10
00	0	0	0	0
01	0	0	1	0
11	0	0	1	1
10	0	0	0	0

FIG. 4.60.

Variables y_2 and y_8
The system's equations are written:

$$y_{2,N+1} = \overline{y_{8,N}} + a_N(b_N + y_{2,N})$$
$$y_{8,N+1} = \overline{b_N} + a_N y_{8,N}$$
$$z_N = a_N y_{8,N}(b_N + y_{2,N}).$$

Figures 4.61 and 4.62 are the excitation and output matrices.

ab / y_2y_8	00	01	11	10
00	11	10	10	11
01	01	00	11	01
11	01	00	11	11
10	11	10	10	11

FIG. 4.61.

ab / y_2y_8	00	01	11	10
00	0	0	0	0
01	0	0	1	0
11	0	0	1	1
10	0	0	0	0

FIG. 4.62.

Variables y_3 and y_8
The system's equations are written:

$$y_{3,N+1} = a_N[b_N y_{8,N} + \overline{b_N}(y_{3,N} + \overline{y_{8,N}})]$$
$$y_{8,N+1} = a_N y_{8,N} + \overline{b_N}(\overline{y_{3,N}} + \overline{y_{8,N}})$$
$$z_N = a_N y_{3,N} y_{8,N}.$$

Figure 4.63 and 4.64 are the excitation and output matrices.

If we consider the choices 18, 28, 38 (tables in Figures 4.59 and 4.64) we notice that if the system is in the total state $y_1y_2y_3y_8ab = 111110$ and inputs 11 and 10 are successively applied, the output sequence is 111 for 28 and 38 and it is 110 for 18.

y_3y_8 \ ab	00	01	11	10
00	01	00	00	11
01	01	00	11	01
11	00	00	11	11
10	01	00	00	11

FIG. 4.63.

y_3y_8 \ ab	00	01	11	10
00	0	0	0	0
01	0	0	0	0
11	0	0	1	1
10	0	0	0	0

FIG. 4.64.

This is easily explained when we consider that the choices of the internal variables correspond to different operations in the system in type 2 circuits (transistor). The performance of the system corresponds to one or several well defined assignments. A priori, it is difficult to choose the correct assignment. If we adopt a given choice of variables, either the system will operate according to the excitation and output matrices which indicates that the method is useful, or it will not function in this way and we say that there is a *hazard* in the system. In the latter circumstance we see that it will be possible to avoid hazards either by modification of the choice of internal variables, which is rather delicate, or by introduction of delays at certain points of the circuit, which comes down to modifying the circuit in such a way that the choice of internal variables is justified. We can simulate this kind of study on a 'LOGIMORS' device (digital training device having NOR and OR circuits).

Logical simulation

The diagram used is that of Figure 4.65. We study the values of the variables $y_2' = \bar{y}_2, y_1, y_3, y_8$ and the output z on the digital training device.

The operator 2's output is in fact $y_2' = \bar{y}_2$ (y_2 has the same significication as in the preceding example).

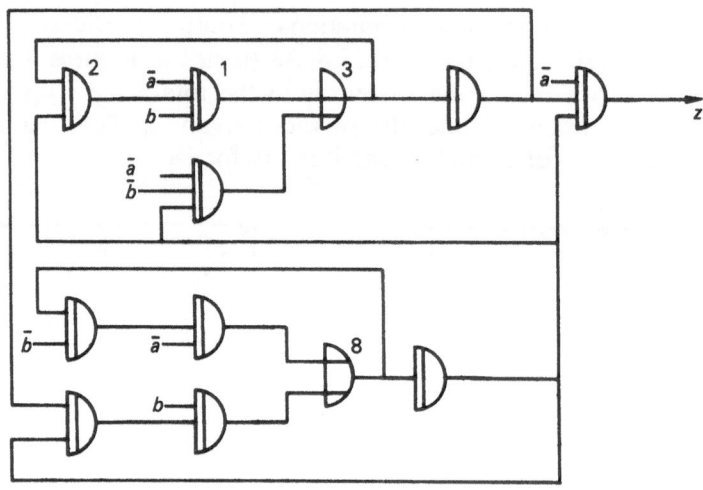

FIG. 4.65.

The circuit's Boolean equations are written:

$$y'_{2,N+1} = y_{8,N}[\bar{a}_n + \bar{b}_N y'_{2,N}]$$
$$y_{8,N+1} = \bar{b}_N + a_N y_{8,N}$$
$$z_N = a_N y_{8,N}[b_N + \bar{y}'_{2,N}].$$

Figure 4.66 represents the excitation and output matrices, with y'_2 and y_0 chosen as internal variables.

$\begin{array}{c}ab\\\hline y_2 y_8\end{array}$	00	01	11	10
00	01/0	00/0	00/0	01/0
01	11/0	10/0	01/1	01/1
11	11/0	10/0	01/1	11/0
10	01/0	00/0	00/0	01/0

FIG. 4.66.

We notice that when simulated the choices of y'_2 and y_8 or y_3 and y_8 represent the real performance of the system while the choice of y_1 and y_8 do not.

BIBLIOGRAPHY

[1] PERRET, G. and DEGUERRY, M., 'Analyse de circuits séquentiels à l'aide de graphes', exposé fait au Colloque d'algèbre de Boole, Grenoble, 1965.

[2] DENOUETTE, M., PERRIN, J. P. and DACLIN, E., 'Analyse des systèmes séquentiels', *Bull. Acad. Polonaise Sci.*, Série des sciences techniques (présenté par S. WEGRZYN) 13 (1965) No. 9.

EXERCISES

4.1. Study the transient flow of the combinational circuit in Figure 4.67 when $b = d = 0$, $c = 1$, and a goes from 1 to 0 (the switching delay of the three 'NORs' is assumed to be Δ).

FIG. 4.67.

4.2. Determine the equations of the system in Figure 4.68 when all transistors have the same switching delay.

Compare the equations obtained with those derived by the analysis method proposed in Section 4.2.1.

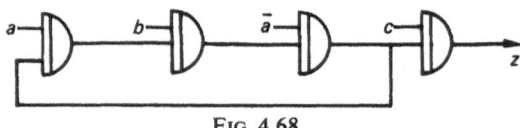

FIG. 4.68.

4.3. Consider the same question for the circuit in Figure 4.69. Compare this transistor circuit with the relay circuit in Figure 4.70.

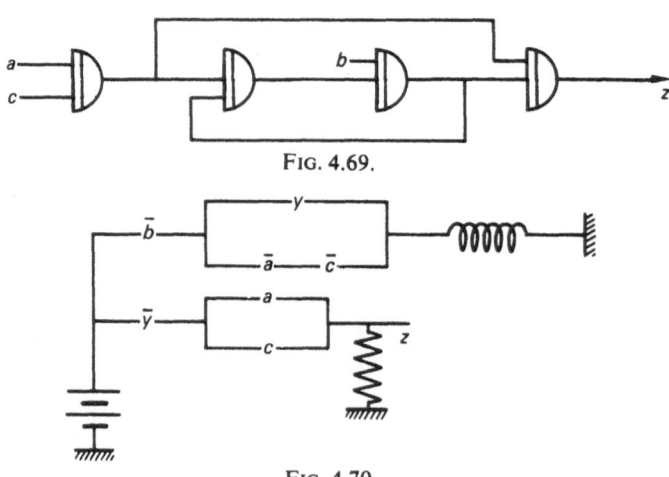

FIG. 4.69.

FIG. 4.70.

4.4. Assuming that all the transistors have the same delay Δ, write the equations of the sequential system in Figure 4.71.

Compare the results with those of the method proposed in Section 4.2.2.

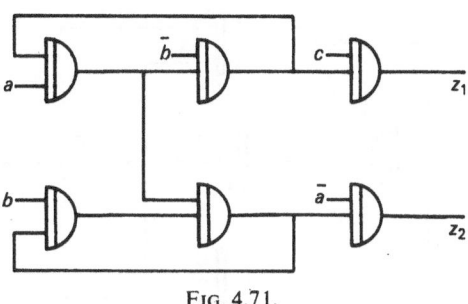

FIG. 4.71.

4.5. Same questions for the circuit in Figure 4.72.

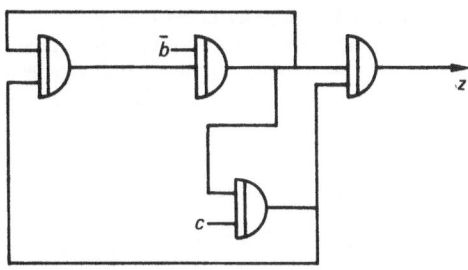

FIG. 4.72.

4.6. Determine the different choices of internal variables for the circuit in Exercise 2.3.

4.7. Same question for the circuit in Exercise 2.4.

4.8. Same question for the circuit in Exercise 2.5.

4.9. Represent the circuit described by the equations below in terms of 'NOR' operators.

$$Y_1 = y_1y_2 + z\bar{b}y_1 + ay_2 + \bar{b}y_2$$
$$Y_2 = a\bar{y}_1 + aby_2 + b\bar{y}_1 + \bar{y}_1y_2$$
$$Z_1 = ay_1y_2$$
$$Z_2 = ay_1 + \bar{b}y_2.$$

4.10. Show that the circuit in Figure 4.73 is pseudo-sequential. A single secondary variable can be used for its study. Consider that all the 'NOR' operators imply a unity delay.

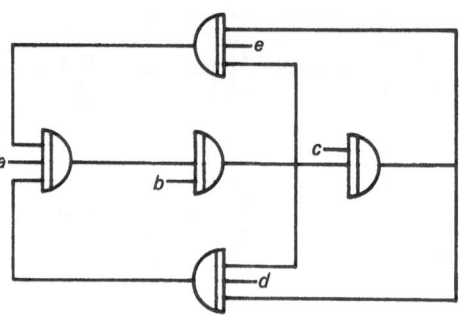

FIG. 4.73.

4.11. Write the equations of the relay circuit in Figure 4.74.

Write the equations of the electronic circuit of Figure 4.75 taking the operators 3 and 5 then 3 and 6 outputs as internal variables. Compare the systems of equations obtained with those of the preceding relay system. What conclusions can be drawn?

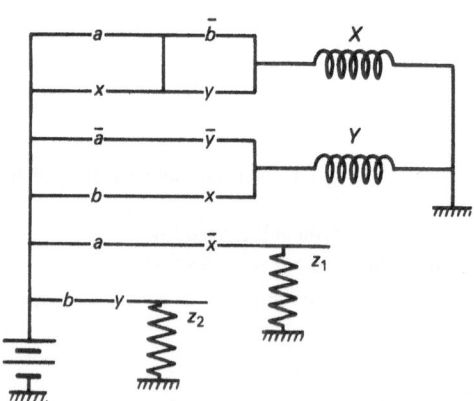

FIG. 4.74.

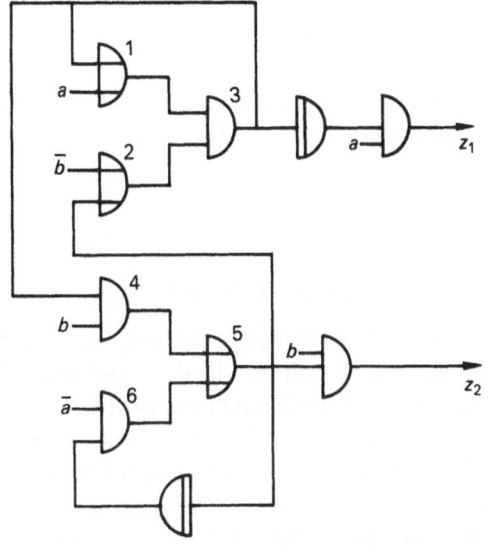

FIG. 4.75.

CHAPTER 5

REPRESENTATION AND CLASSIFICATION OF
SEQUENTIAL SYSTEMS

5.1. INTRODUCTION

In the preceding chapter a first analysis showed that the main property characterizing sequential systems is the existence of *memory functions* which we specified in the form of *internal states*.

These internal states are determined by referring to a certain number of internal variables and in reality our development was principally based on these variables. We assume that the property of storing its past transitions is admitted and understood for sequential systems. In this chapter, we want to put some order into the collection of notions and problems implied by the definitions which were given. We shall equally try to give the principles of sequential system representation independently of the technology used.

In order that the study be as systematic as possible, it is necessary, that a system's representation be independent of the technology used to realize them. Consequently, without going too far from the reality of the problems, the present chapter will be relatively abstract. We shall try to order the questions relative to the nature and representation of a machine without bothering too much about what technology realized it (this aspect will be developed in Chapters 8 and 9).

Since there is a definite connection between problems of classification and representation for sequential systems, the plan we shall follow may seem somewhat confused. We shall begin with a few words about tabulated representation in order to have a tool at hand which will be used in all the following chapters. Next, we shall separate sequential machines into two large classes depending on the nature of their inputs. Thus, we shall come to the notion of synchronous and asynchronous machines. Once this has been discussed, we shall see what influence the classification of systems can have on the way in which they are represented and what new separation can be made among the machines (Moore machine and Mealy machine). Finally, we shall give some brief notions of one or two synthesis properties of sequential systems and a few examples of other types of representations.

5.2. FLOW TABLE OF A SEQUENTIAL SYSTEM

5.2.1. *Necessity of the flow table*

Reconsider Examples 1 and 2 of Section 4.2.6. In both cases, we defined the output matrix in terms of different commands and a certain number of internal states. We showed that the output is expressed in a combinational way in terms of different inputs and internal states: a single output value corresponds to each pair–'internal state, input value'. However, the output matrix, established in this way, is not sufficient for a complete definition of the system. In fact, if the system is in a given state, the table can give the output value for every input value. But if the system is in a given state, the output matrix alone cannot give the output sequence corresponding to an input sequence. There is therefore need of a table analogous to the excitation matrix defined in Sections 4.2.4.3 and 4.2.5 defining the future state of the system if it undergoes a given input for a certain present internal state.

5.2.2. *Construction of the flow table*

We shall consider example 2 of Section 4.3. From the specifications of the problem it is possible to construct the desired table representing the equation:

$$Q_{j,N+1} = G_j(X_N, Q_N),$$

where X_N and Q_N are the input vector and internal state of the system at the instant N. This table is shown in Figure 5.1.

Q_N \ abc	000	001	011	010	110	111	101	100
1	1	2	–	1	–	–	–	1
2	2	2	–	2	–	–	–	3
3	3	2	–	1	–	–	–	3

FIG. 5.1.

Thus, a, b, c being zero, let us push B. We observe that if the system is in its initial state 1 (the motor M is running), it remains in state 1 (the motor continues to run). If it is initially in state 2 (the motor is off and A is not pushed) it remains in state 2. If it is originally in state 3 (the motor is off but A has previously been pushed) it changes to state 1 (the motor starts running).

In order to completely define the system, the output table must be added to this new table. These two tables can be condensed into a single table as in Figure 5.2, which is called the flow table of the sequential system. It is a tabulated representation of the sequential system's equations.

$$Q_{j,N+1} = G_j(X_N, Q_N)$$
$$Z_{i,N} = F_i(X_N, Q_N)$$

abc / Q_N	000	001	011	010	110	111	101	100
1	1/1	2/0	–/–	1/1	–/–	–/–	–/–	1/1
2	2/0	2/0	–/–	2/0	–/–	–/–	–/–	3/0
3	3/0	2/0	–/–	1/1	–/–	–/–	–/–	3/0

FIG. 5.2.

5.2.3. *Utilization of the flow table*

Suppose that the system was initially in state 2 and the following input sequence is applied:

000, 100, 000, 010, 000, 001, 000.

We seek the corresponding output sequence. We successively search the different input vectors in the order of the input sequence, then seek the transition of the internal state and the different values of the output from the flow table (Figure 5.3). The output sequence is 0001100 and the system is in the internal state 2 after the input sequence is applied.

5.2.4. *Flow table – excitation and output matrices*

It can be observed that the main difference between the flow table and

abc	Q_N	Q_{N+1}	m
000	2	2	0
100	2	3	0
000	3	3	0
010	3	1	1
000	1	1	1
001	1	2	0
000	2	2	0

FIG. 5.3.

the excitation and output matrices is in the representation of the internal state. In fact, in the flow tables, the internal state is represented by a decimal number, while in the excitation and output matrices, a coded word is associated with each internal state. This observation shows that the flow table of a system can be determined from its excitation and output matrices.

Consider the excitation matrices in Figures 5.4a and b (see example in Section 4.2.5). We derive the flow table in Figure 5.4.c. We shall return to the question of the different properties of these tables later. For the moment, we shall make a first classification of sequential machines.

ab / y_5y_6	00	01	11	10
00	00	01	01	01
01	00	00	11	11
11	00	00	00	10
10	00	01	01	00

FIG. 5.4(a).

ab / y_5y_6	00	01	11	10
00	0	0	0	0
01	0	0	0	0
11	0	0	1	1
10	0	0	0	0

FIG. 5.4(b).

ab Q_N	00	01	11	10
1	1/0	2/0	2/0	2/0
2	1/0	1/0	3/0	3/0
3	1/0	1/0	1/1	4/1
4	1/0	2/0	2/0	1/0

FIG. 5.4(c).

5.3. ASYNCHRONOUS AND SYNCHRONOUS MACHINES

5.3.1. *Introduction*

As a first approximation, we might say that the main difference between the two types of sequential machines which we are going to examine is in the nature of their inputs and the way in which we can make these inputs play on the machine's control facilities. Schematically, we may say that an asynchronous machine is a sequential machine having an internal transition which cannot be controlled from the exterior while a synchronous machine has a transition which can be controlled from the exterior. We begin with asynchronous machines.

5.3.2. *Example of an asynchronous machine*

Consider the table in Figure 5.5. It has four input vectors (which are the four possible combinations of the two commands X_1 and X_2) and four internal states (numbered from 1 to 4). Suppose that the machine

$X_1 X_2$	00	01	11	10
1	2,0	1,0	2,0	2,0
2	3,1	1,0	2,0	3,0
3	4,1	2.1	3,0	4,0
4	1,1	4,1	3,1	4,1

FIG. 5.5.

is in state 1 and inputs $X_1 = 1, X_2 = 1$ are applied (X_1 and X_2 are step inputs). The system's reaction time is very small as compared to the duration of the input. Consequently, the system goes from state 1 to state 2. Since X_1 and X_2 have not changed, once in state 2, the system goes through no further transition. We say that 2 is stable for input 11: as long as $X_1 X_2$ is 11, the system will remain in state 2. We now change the inputs to $X_1 = 1$, $X_2 = 0$. We pass the neighbouring column. At this moment, we see that the machine will go to state 3 since $3 = G$ $(X_1 X_2 = 10, Q = 2)$, but it will not stop there. As a matter of fact, $X_1 X_2 = 10$ but $G(X_1 X_2 = 10, Q = 3) = 4$ in state 3. The machine therefore changes, to state 4 where it will remain as long as $X_1 X_2 = 10$. The machine therefore follows the path $2 \rightarrow 3 \rightarrow 4$ by itself and we can do nothing to change it. But this is the least troublesome thing which happens. Our machine has a stable state at 4 for input 10. Suppose that we bring X_1 back to 0. The new input is therefore 00 and we go from the 4th column to the first. Following an analogous treatment, we see that the machine will indefinitely go through the cycle $\rightarrow 1 \rightarrow 2 \rightarrow 3 \rightarrow 4 \rightarrow$ as long as X_1 and X_2 remain 0 and we have no means of stopping someplace in this column nor of controlling the system in any way. This is not necessarily a handicap in the realization of a sequential system: we can seek to produce cycles, for example, to obtain periodic oscillations at the output.

Comment. By hypothesis the machines under consideration have a finite number of states. Consequently, during an autonomous transition, the system will go through a cycle if it periodically repasses the same states or will stop at a stable state. It cannot indefinitely undergo transition without passing the same state which would contradict the previous hypothesis.

5.3.3. *Definition of synchronous machines*

We have just seen that for certain inputs, an asynchronous machine has no stable state. The system goes through a cycle which can be annoying since it is impossible to know at what point of the cycle the system is at a given instant. If a new command is applied for which the system has several stable states, it is impossible to determine the future transition of the system.

In order to avoid this inconvenience, we shall try to control the system from the exterior: for a given state of the command, the system will evolve only if given the order to do so.

There are two possible solutions: we can first observe that in an asynchronous system the transition during a cycle is directly connected to the presence of the command; generally, the system leaves the cycle as soon as the command disappears. It thus seems that the system could be controlled from the inputs. All that would be necessary would be that the length of the input signal be less than the system's response time. This means that in an electronic system, the inputs are pulses; they could or could not be synchronized to a clock; these systems are called *pulsed systems*. Since the system evolves only in the presence of a command, it would remain in the state it was during the time interval separating two consecutive inputs.

Another solution is the following: during asynchronous performance, given a certain initial state of the internal variables and a certain command, the system instantaneously supplies an output and determines the initial values of the internal variables at the following sample instant.

In order to control the system, it would therefore be sufficient that the new initial values of the internal variables be injected after a certain time delay connected to a clock. This kind of delay would be placed on each feedback branch connected to a secondary variable; for example, it would be a shift register commanded by a clock. These systems are called *synchronized asynchronous systems*. Here again, the system would be blocked between two clock or control signals.

Observe that in these systems, the inputs have the same nature as in the asynchronous systems (that is, the levels); the internal variables also have the same nature as the two kinds of systems.

In pulsed systems, the internal variables will be levels; if not, there would be a very delicate problem of synchronization with input pulses to solve. To realize a system in which the inputs are pulses and the outputs levels, it is necessary to use flip-flops.

5.3.4. *Comparison between the different realizations*
Consider an asynchronous sequential system which has a flow table as in Figure 5.6a (in reality the output function is of no interest to us).

In asynchronous performance, for a given value of the command, all the states are not generally stable; if the input is $\bar{a}\bar{b}$ only states 1 and 3 are stable; if the input is $\bar{a}b$, there are no stable states: the system goes through a cycle. We shall see how a synchronous performance can be represented.

	$\bar{a}\bar{b}$	$\bar{a}b$	$a\bar{b}$
1	1	2	2
2	3	3	2
3	3	4	4
4	1	1	4

FIG. 5.6(a).

	$\bar{H}$	$H\bar{a}\bar{b}$	$H\bar{a}b$	$Ha\bar{b}$
1	1	1	2	2
2	2	3	3	2
3	3	3	4	4
4	4	1	1	4

FIG. 5.6(b).

Synchronized asynchronous systems

The table in Figure 5.6(a) represents the performance of the system. The inputs and the internal states are the same as in asynchronous functioning. For a given state of the input ($\bar{a}b$, for example) the system will only change, as shown in the flow table, if given the order to do so from the outside: if the system is initially in state 1, for the command $\bar{a}b$, it changes to state 2 at the first clock pulse, to state 3 at the second, and so on. The cyclic transition is controlled by the clock.

Pulsed systems

The table in Figure 5.6(b) shows the representation of how the system operates. The inputs are pulses and hence respectively, $H\bar{a}\bar{b}$, $H\bar{a}b$, $Ha\bar{b}$. Another state of the inputs depending on the control of the system must be foreseen, namely, the interval between two clock-pulses ($\bar{H}$). All internal states are stable for this input state because only the pulses of the clock permit the system's transition. Suppose that the system is in the 1 state between two pulses and the command $\bar{a}b$ is permanently applied. At the first pulse of the clock the system, in column $H\bar{a}b$, reaches the 3 state and remains there when H disappears ($\bar{H}$); at the next pulse of the clock, the system goes to the next state, and so on.

5.3.5. *Realization of the synchronous system*

(a) *Synchronized asynchronous systems*

These are the synchronous systems which are modified by the introduction of delays controlled by a clock in some branches. As an exercise, we consider the Figure 5.6(a), the flow table of an asynchronous system.

Suppose that we have given assignments to the internal states in the following way:

$$1 \rightarrow 10 \qquad 2 \rightarrow 00 \qquad 3 \rightarrow 11 \qquad 4 \rightarrow 01.$$

The excitation matrix is represented in Figure 5.7. The recurrence equations of the internal variables are written:

$$Y_1 = \bar{a}\bar{b} + \bar{a}\bar{y}_1$$
$$Y_2 = y_2(a + y_1) + \bar{a}\bar{y}_1\bar{y}_2.$$

	$\bar{a}\bar{b}$	$\bar{a}b$	ab	$a\bar{b}$
10	10	00	- -	00
00	11	11	- -	00
11	11	01	- -	01
01	10	10	- -	01

FIG. 5.7.

Assume that we have found the output expressed in the form:

$$z = ay_1 + by_2.$$

Figures 5.8(a) and (b) represent the realizations of asynchronous systems and synchronized asynchronous systems in terms of the Boolean functions AND, OR, NOT.

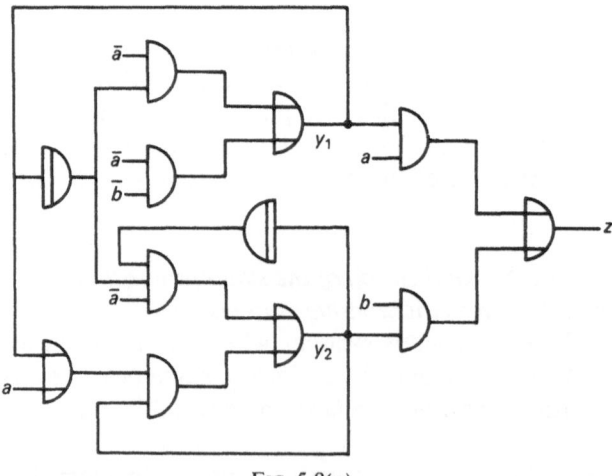

FIG. 5.8(a).

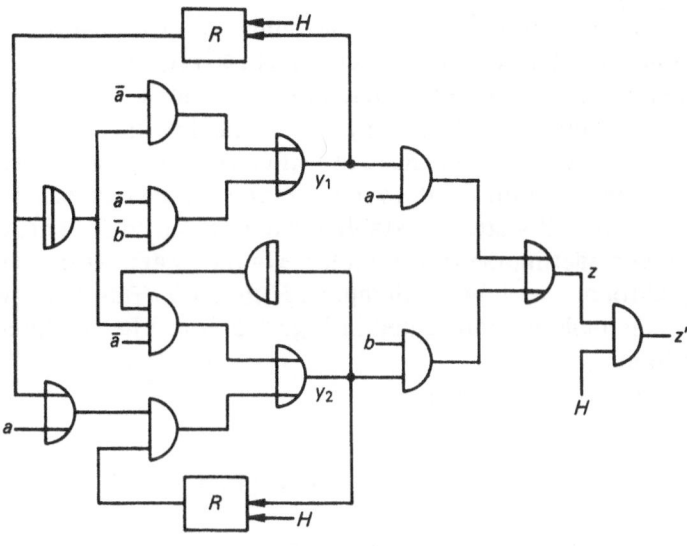

FIG. 5.8(b).

COMMENT.   The output can be a synchronized pulse (z') on H, or a level (z) depending on which we prefer.

(b) *Pulsed systems*

We shall successively study systems with symmetric flip-flops and then *SR* flip-flops.

Symmetric flip-flops. The excitation matrix of the pulsed system (cf. Figure 5.6b) is represented in Figure 5.9(a) (the internal state assignments are the same as used at the beginning of this section). The expressions Y_1 and Y_2 are written:

$$Y_1 = \bar{H}y_1 + H(\bar{a}\bar{b} + \bar{a}\bar{y}_1)$$
$$Y_2 = \bar{H}y_2 + H(ay_2 + y_1y_2 + \bar{a}\bar{y}_1\bar{y}_2).$$

	$\bar{H}$	$H\bar{a}\bar{b}$	$H\bar{a}b$	Hab	$Ha\bar{b}$
00	00	11	11	- -	00
01	01	10	10	- -	01
11	11	11	01	- -	01
10	10	10	00	- -	00

FIG. 5.9(a).

	$H\bar{a}\bar{b}$	$H\bar{a}b$	Hab	$Ha\bar{b}$
00	11	11	- -	00
01	11	11	- -	00
11	00	10	- -	10
10	00	10	- -	10

FIG. 5.9(b).

These expressions differ from those found for the asynchronous and synchronized asynchronous systems respectively by $\bar{H}y_1$ and $\bar{H}y_2$: they signify that the system is held in the absence of a control pulse. To obtain the quantities Y_1 and Y_2, two symmetric flip-flops are used. They are acted on by the τ_1 and τ_2 transitions of the y_1 and y_2 variables. It can be remarked that $\bar{H}$ does not intervene in the expressions of τ_1 and τ_2 because all states are stable for the command $\bar{H}$. This comes down to considering the transition table of the system as operating in an asynchronous way, but with inputs, $H\bar{a}\bar{b}$, $H\bar{a}b$, Hab, $Ha\bar{b}$, respectively. This table is represented in Figure 5.9(b). The τ_1 expressions are written:

$$\tau_1 = H(b + \bar{a}\bar{y}_1 + ay_1)$$
$$\tau_2 = H\bar{a}\bar{y}_1.$$

The corresponding circuit is represented in Figure 5.10.

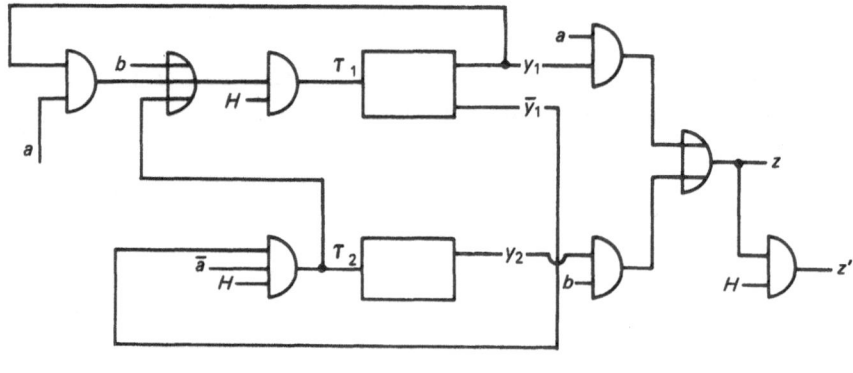

FIG. 5.10.

Here again the output can be a level (z) or a pulse (z'). We could have made each signal a pulse ($a, \bar{a}, b, \bar{b}$) which would have given the same result.

SR flip-flops. We recall that a SR flip-flop has two Boolean inputs S and R with the following property (cf. Section 2.7.4):

if $R = 1$ and $S = 0$ the system's output takes or holds the value 0,

if $R = 0$ and $S = 1$ the system's output takes or holds the value 1,

if $R = 0$ and $S = 0$ the system's output does not change (recall that R and S cannot simultaneously be 1).

To realize a sequential system with SR flip-flops, as many flip-flops as there are secondary variables must be used: suppose that the R_iS_i flip-flop produces the variable y_i. The present value of the variable is y_i and at the next pulse of the clock it is Y_i. We compute the value of R_iS_i so that if the flip-flops output is y_i, whenever RS applied, it will be Y_i at the next pulse of the clock.

The quantities R_i, S_i, y_i, Y_i are related as shown in Figures 5.11(a) and (b).

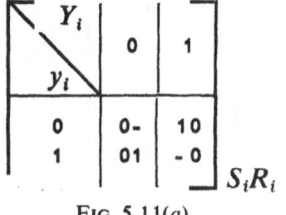

FIG. 5.11(a).   FIG. 5.11(b).

In practise the system's excitation matrix will be considered as asynchronous, but the different inputs will be, respectively, $H\bar{a}\bar{b}$, $H\bar{a}b$, $Ha\bar{b}$: in fact, the column corresponding to $\bar{H}$ has only zeros in its simplest form. We construct the (R_iS_i) table for each input and each internal state (Figure 5.12).

y_1y_2	R_1S_1	R_2S_2	R_1S_1	R_2S_2	R_1S_1	R_2S_2	R_1S_1	R_2S_2
00	01	01	01	01	- -	- -	−0	−0
01	01	10	01	10	- -	- -	−0	0−
11	0−	0−	10	0−	- -	- -	10	0−
10	0−	−0	10	−0	- -	- -	10	−0

FIG. 5.12.

For example, consider the total state $(H, \bar{a}, b, 0, 1)$; from Figure 5.9(a), $Y_1Y_2 = 10$. We derive from this the values of the pairs R_1S_1, R_2S_2;

$$R_1S_1 = 01 \qquad R_2S_2 = 10,$$

and we may then derive the expression of R_1, S_1, R_2, S_2:

$$R_1 = H(a+b)y_1 \qquad S_1 = H\bar{a}\bar{y}_1$$
$$R_2 = H\bar{a}\bar{y}_1 y_2 \qquad S_2 = H\bar{a}y_1\bar{y}_2.$$

Figure 5.13 represents the corresponding circuit. The output can be a level (z) or a pulse (z').

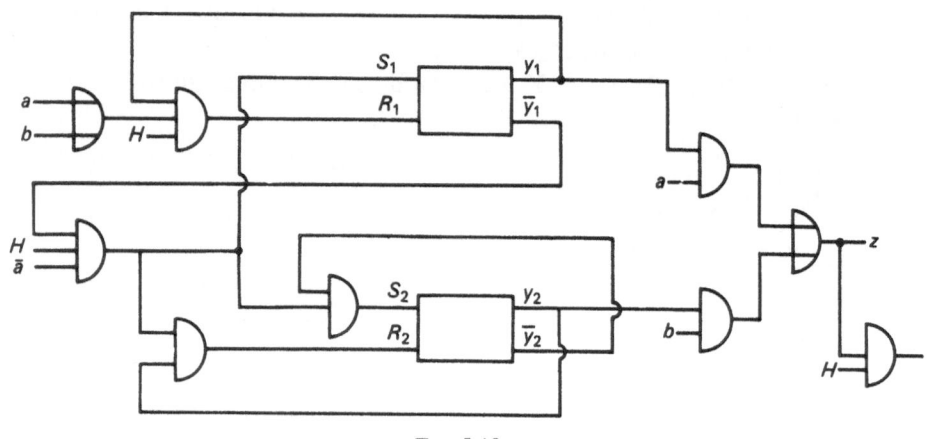

FIG. 5.13.

Comment. This method can be used for the realization of *JK* or *PQ* pulsed flip-flop systems.

The principle is the same as in the *RS* flip-flop system. We could proceed in the following way: from the excitation matrix (Figure 5.9*a*) the next internal state corresponding to a given input and a given internal state is known. In particular the value of an internal variable at the next instant and that at the present instant y_i. We may write the relations:

$$Y_i = g_i(Q_i, X_i)$$
$$Z_i = f_i(Q_i, X_i),$$

where Q_i is the system's internal state at the present instant and X_i the input vector. We wish, in the proposed realization, that the *JK* (or *PQ*) flip-flop relative to y_i which has a present output value of y_i, will have the value Y_i at the next pulse of the clock. We may, therefore, compute the values of the pairs $J_iK_i(P_iQ_i)$ acting on the *JK* (*PQ*) flip-flops at the next pulse of the clock. The values of these pairs can be determined for each total state.

We recall that the *JK* and *PQ* flip-flop operate as shown in Figures 2.37(*c*) and (*d*). From these figures we derive the values of *JK* (*PQ*) in function of the values Y_i and y_i (Figure 5.14).

y	Y	J	K	P	Q
0	0	0	–	0 / –	– / 1
0	1	1	–	1	0
1	1	–	0	– / 1	0 / –
1	0	–	1	0	1

FIG. 5.14.

We observe that in all cases of the column $\bar{H}$ where we have the relation $y_i = Y_i$, the value 00 can be attributed to the pairs JK (PQ). That is, $\bar{H}$ does not appear in the final expression of J, K, P, Q. We may, therefore, as in the case of symmetric flip-flops or RS realizations, operate from the asynchronous system's excitation matrix in which the inputs will respectively be replaced by $H\bar{a}\bar{b}$, $H\bar{a}b$, Hab, $Ha\bar{b}$. The output will again be a pulse or level depending on whether or not it was synchronized with an external clock.

5.4. MOORE, MEALY, AND HUFFMAN MACHINES

5.4.1. *Mealy and Moore machines*

In the preceding section flow tables were used with two symbols marked in every cell: the first indicated the next state and the second the output. These flow tables therefore take into account the two relations which define a sequential system:

$$Z_t = F(X_t, Q_t)$$
$$Q_{t+1} = G(X_t, Q_t).$$

A machine which has this type of flow table is called a Mealy machine. But other types of machines derived from this one exist. As a matter of fact, it is always possible to write $Q_{t+1} = G(Q_t, X_t)$ but not $Z_t = F(X_t, Q_t)$. It is possible that X_t or Q_t do not intervene in the Z_t. Consequently, there are two cases possible:

(1) $Z_t = F(X_t)$ and we thus deal with a combinational or pseudosequential system.

(2) $Z_t = F(Q_t)$ which signifies that the outputs are associated with the machine's internal states, that is, considering the flow table representation, they correspond to the table's rows. This means that there will be one output per row in the table. An example of this type machine is given in Section 5.2.1 (operation of two motors). We actually gave the output value at this moment as definition of the states. This means that the sequential machine in Figure 5.3 can have its table written in complete form as given here (Figure 5.15). By reference to the definitions of the states in Chapter 4 concerning this example, it can be seen that the outputs associated with each state are really the same. The outputs were placed opposite the states and not in the cells of the flow table in order that we could immediately recognize that we were dealing with this type of machine (called Moore machine) and not a Mealy machine.

	00	01	10	m_1	m_2
1	1	1	2	0	0
2	2	3	2	1	0
3	3	3	4	1	1
4	4	1	4	0	1

FIG. 5.15.

Now we come to the problem of knowing what relation can exist between the two principal types of sequential machines which we have just defined. Is there a particular kind of work for which each one is especially adapted? What do they have in common? In Appendix A.5.1 we shall show that a Mealy machine corresponds to each Moore machine and conversely a Moore machine can be associated with each Mealy machine. These results are extremely important; for they mean that all the demonstrations to be undertaken for one type of machine will be valid for the other.

5.4.2. Asynchronous machines – representation by Huffman flow table*

We have seen that while synchronous machines are stable for each of their internal states no matter in which of the table's columns the row corresponding to this state was reached, it was not at all the same in the case of asynchronous machines which evolved by themselves until reaching (or not) a stable state situated in this column. Since all the states have the same function, it is unnecessary to specify in detail one or another. On the contrary, if we wish to have a representation which tells us more, in the sense of an asynchronous system, it can be very interesting to note the stable and unstable states in a different way. We shall begin by circling the stable states situated in the different columns of the flow table in Figure 5.16(a).

ab \	00	01	10
1	①	①	3
2	②	3	②
3	③	③	4
4	④	1	④

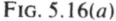

FIG. 5.16(a).

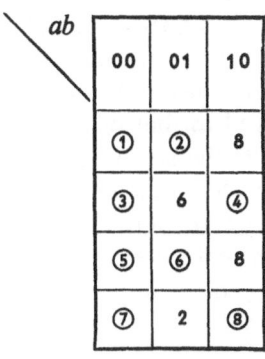

ab \	00	01	10
	①	②	8
	③	6	④
	⑤	⑥	8
	⑦	2	⑧

FIG. 5.16(b).

It is insufficient as a representation because this type of notation can lead to error, since it might appear that the internal states are the ones which are stable. Therefore, we prefer to individually number each total stable state and give the same number to the unstable states which lead to it in the same column. In this way Figure 5.16(a) becomes what is called the Huffman flow table in Figure 5.16(b).

This notation has great advantage in asynchronous systems synthesis. It allows the synthesis of a system without the advance preoccupation of the number of internal states which will be needed to finally realize the machine. In sum, we can operate in the following way for the synthesis of the table of an asynchronous system:

* Which we shall also call 'phase table

We begin with the construction of the Huffman flow table (said to be primitive) which contains a single total stable state per row. Then, by different processes of reduction, we try to decrease the number of states in this table. Consequently, in a certain measure, the number of internal variables to be used is also decreased.

Two things must be noted with respect to the Huffman flow table. First, this table in itself does not give all the information concerning the system. For example, the output values are not noted in the table. Consequently, the Huffman flow table of the asynchronous system under study must be coupled with the output matrix if a description of the entire sequential system is to be obtained.

The second remark is related to the first. It concerns the determination of the output matrix. In the case most commonly met with, the value of the input devices changes and the system's transitions through a certain number of unstable states during a very short time as compared to the command step strictly speaking. The Huffman flow table translates this by the fact that the duration of a stable state is very long compared to that of an unstable state. Generally, we therefore consider just the steady state (corresponding to the stable states) and do not, hence, indicate the outputs associated with unstable states (a 'don't care' in the output matrix replaces those which correspond to the transient state).

Thus, for example, the output matrix in Figure 5.17(b) can correspond to the Huffman flow table in Figure 5.17(a).

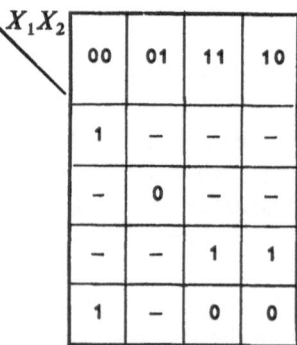

FIG. 5.17(a).   FIG. 5.17(b).

5.4.3. *Correspondence between the Huffman flow table and the flow table*

In the preceding section we have seen how to go from a flow table to a Huffman flow table. We are now concerned with the inverse process. For this, we first give some definitions with respect to the subject.

5.4.3.1. *Mealy transform of a Huffman flow table*

Consider, for example, the system defined by the two tables (Huffman and output) in Figures 5.18(*a*) and (*b*).

00	01	11	10
①	3	6	⑧
②	4	5	⑦
2	③	⑤	8
1	④	⑥	7

00	01	11	10
00	—	—	10
00	—	—	01
—	10	11	—
—	01	11	—

Fig. 5.18(*a*).   Fig. 5.18(*b*).

To obtain the Mealy transform of these two tables, we proceed in the following way;
  – each row is numbered,
  – each stable state of row i is given the same number i,
  – each unstable state of row i is given the number j of the corresponding stable state,
  – the Huffman flow table is superposed onto the output matrix.

For our example these steps are schematized below (Figures 5.19*a*, *b*, *c*, *d*).

5.4.3.2. *Mealy tables associated with Huffman flow tables*

In an output matrix (we remind the reader that here only the outputs corresponding to the stable states are defined) we attribute the values associated with the stable states of the same number to the outputs corresponding to the unstable states. We obtain a machine in which the outputs take their permanent state before arriving at a stable state: these are the rapid outputs. Thus, the output matrix in Figure 5.18(*b*) becomes that of Figure 5.20. On the contrary, if an input modification

First step

	00	01	11	10
1				
2				
3				
4				

FIG. 5.19(a).

Second step

	00	01	11	10
1	1			1
2	2			2
3		3	3	
4		4	4	

FIG. 5.19(b).

Third step

	00	01	11	10
1	1	3	4	1
2	2	4	3	2
3	2	3	3	1
4	1	4	4	2

FIG. 5.19(c).

Fourth step

	00	01	11	10
1	1,00	3,—	4,—	1,10
2	2,00	4,—	3,—	2,01
3	2,—	3,10	3,11	1,—
4	1,—	4,01	4,11	2,—

FIG. 5.19(d).

00	01	11	10
00	10	11	10
00	01	11	01
00	10	11	10
00	01	11	01

FIG. 5.20.

does not immediately provoke an output charge, the result is a system with slow outputs.

Note, however, that, by construction, there exists only one rapid output system while many slop output systems can be designed. Actually, to obtain a slow output, suppose that the unstable state of a row j has the same output as a stable state in the same row (which is the starting state of the system). If several stable states exist in one row, they are not generally associated with identical outputs. Therefore, to be precise, we must speak of slow outputs with respect to a given transition.

Thus, the table in Figure 5.18(b) has been transformed into the table in Figure 5.21(a) which is a slow output matrix with respect to the transitions: $1 \rightarrow 3, 2 \rightarrow 4, 8 \rightarrow 6, 7 \rightarrow 5, 3 \rightarrow 2, 4 \rightarrow 1, 5 \rightarrow 8, 6 \rightarrow 7$. In Figure 5.21($b$) it has been transformed into a slow output matrix with respect to the transitions: $8 \rightarrow 3, 7 \rightarrow 4, 1 \rightarrow 6, 2 \rightarrow 5, 3 \rightarrow 8$,

00	01	11	10
00	00	10	10
00	00	01	01
10	10	11	11
01	01	11	11

FIG. 5.21(a).

00	01	11	10
00	10	00	10
00	01	00	01
11	10	11	10
11	01	11	01

FIG. 5.21(b).

	00	01	11	10
1	1,00	3,00	4,10	1,10
2	2,00	4,00	3,01	2,01
3	2,10	3,10	3,11	1,11
4	1,01	4,01	4,11	2,11

FIG. 5.22.

$4 \rightarrow 7$, $5 \rightarrow 2$, $6 \rightarrow 1$. It is evidently possible to associate the Huffman flow table representation with an output matrix – hence, a Mealy table is outlined – by a process analogous to that of Section 5.4.3.1. Figure 5.22 represents the Mealy machine associated with the Huffman flow table and output matrix in Figures 5.18(a) and 5.21(a).

Comment. There exist several flow tables associated with one Huffman table. They differ by the nature of the transients. Only one Huffman table however, corresponds to a flow table. We can, nevertheless, associate the Huffman flow table and the Mealy transform in a one-to-one correspondence. It is unique. This particular flow table will be used in Chapter 8.

5.5. COMPLEMENTARY NOTIONS

The essential part of the present chapter has already been discussed. We should now like to give some complementary notions which can be useful in certain problems and more strongly tie sequential systems to the rest of automata theory. First, we shall give some brief ideas on the flow diagrams of sequential machines. Here we will be dealing with a concept which is very useful because it is pictorial. Furthermore, it seems that a junction between the general theory of flow graphs and that of the flow diagrams of sequential machines is currently under study (cf. Brozozowski and McCluskey). This will lead to a documentary discussion of sequential systems' transition matrices. In conclusion, and as a preface to Chapters 7 and 8, we shall explain what we mean by identical internal states in a sequential machine.

5.5.1. Flow diagram

As in Section 5.4.1 we shall discuss the Mealy and Moore diagrams. We begin with the Mealy diagram.

5.5.1.1. Flow diagram of a Mealy machine

Consider the flow table in Figure 5.23. It represents a two input, X_1, X_2, synchronous machine (for the reasons given in Section 5.3, we have not represented the stable column $\bar{X}_1\bar{X}_2$). We associate a small circle in the plan with each state of this flow table. In order to have a reference system, we mark the number of the corresponding state inside the circle. This is what was done in Figure 5.24(a). Circles a and b are connected by an oriented branch from a to b if $b = G(X_i, a)$. I.e., if we go from state a to state b by action of the command X_i. The input variable X_i which provokes the passage from one state to the

	X_1	X_2
1	2,0	3,1
2	5,–	6,1
3	1,1	5,–
4	2,0	4,–
5	3,1	6,0
6	1,–	4,0

FIG. 5.23.

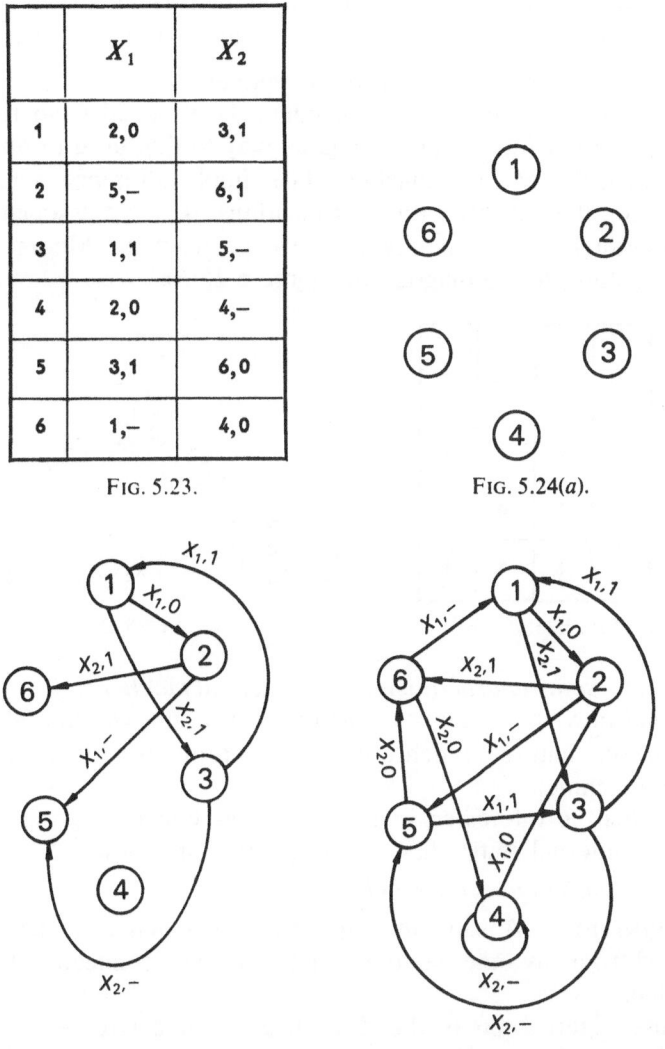

FIG. 5.24(a).

FIG. 5.24(b).

FIG. 5.24(c).

other, then the output associated with the passage in question, are indicated on the oriented branch from *a* to *b*.

In Figure 5.24(*b*), we have represented the partial flow diagram for the transitions coming from states 1, 2 and 3. There is no problem for state 4, and input X_1. On the contrary, we see that 4 is stable with respect to input X_2. Hence an arrow is looped around the circle representing 4. We finish the diagram in this way, arriving at Figure 5.24c.

5.5.1.2. *Flow diagram of Moore machines*

The flow diagram of Moore's machine is obtained from the table defining the machine in an analogous way to that used to obtain the flow diagram of Mealy's machine. The simple difference is instead of associating the outputs with the transitions, they are associated with the diagram's states. In this way, we go from the Moore table in Figure 5.25(a) to the diagram in Figure 5.25(b).

	X_1	X_2	X_3	Z
1	1	2	2	0
2	2	3	3	1
3	1	3	1	0

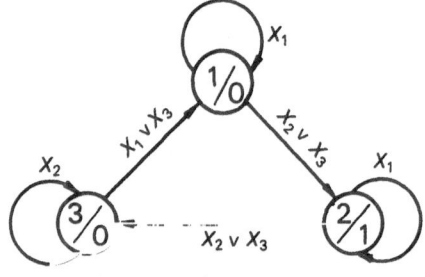

FIG. 5.25(a).   FIG. 5.25(b).

5.5.1.3. *Some characteristics of sequential machines*

We shall now speak about a machine's structure without taking into account its nature (synchronous, asynchronous, Moore machine, Mealy machine).

We shall be interested in the properties concerning the relations between internal states, first in groups, then in pairs.

(a) *Strongly connected machines.*

DEFINITION. A sequential machine such that any state can be attained from any other state is called a strongly connected sequential machine.

Thus, Figure 5.26 is the flow diagram of a strongly connected machine. Beginning with state 1, for example, we can attain state 2 through the input sequence X_1; state 3 through X_1X_2, 4 through $X_1X_2X_2$, 5 through $X_1X_2X_2X_1$, and 1 itself through X_2 or $X_1X_2X_2X_1X_2$ or $X_1X_2X_2X_1X_1$. The same as we go from 2 to 3 through X_2, from 2 to 4 through X_2X_2, from 2 to 5 through $X_2X_2X_1$, from 2 to 1 through $X_2X_2X_1X_2$ or $X_2X_2X_1X_1$, from 2 to 2 by X_2X_1 (via state 3), by $X_2X_2X_2$ (via 3 then 4) by $X_2X_2X_1X_2X_1$ (via 3, 4, 5, 1), by $X_2X_2X_1X_1X_1$ (via the

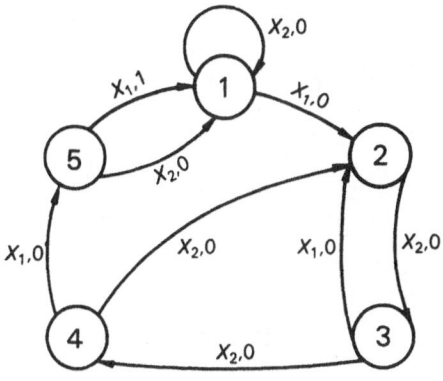

Fig. 5.26.

same path) or by $X_2 X_2 X_1 X_2 \dots X_2$ or by $X_2 X_2 X_1 X_1 X_2 \dots X_2$; $X_2 \dots X_2$ means that the command X_2, for which 1 is stable, can be sent as many times as we wish.

The same properties can be verified for all the states.

We give an example of the opposite case; that is, sequential machines which are not strongly connected.

Consider the machine represented by the flow diagram in Figure 5.27. It is impossible to reach state 1 from 2 or 3. In this case, we say 1 is a *source* or *initial state*.

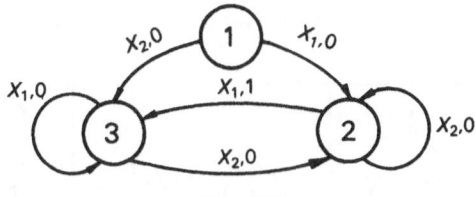

Fig. 5.27.

DEFINITION.   We say that an internal state of a sequential machine is a source or initial state if it is impossible to reach it from other states of the machine to which it belongs.

The Figure 5.28 machine is not the same case; starting from state 5 it is impossible to go to another state. Here state 4 is an initial state and state 5 is called a *final* or *sink state*.

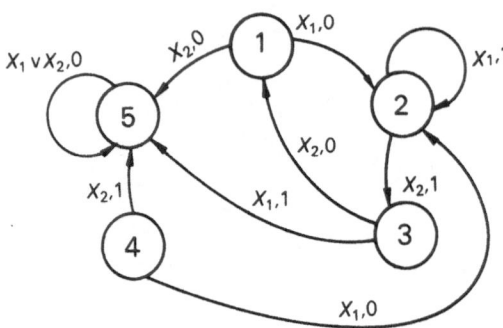

Fig. 5.28.

DEFINITION.   We say that an internal state of a sequential machine is a final state if it is impossible to go to other states in the same machine starting from the state in question. Notice that determining the structure of a machine is very simple if we start from its flow diagram. We call convergent branches towards state i, all branches which go from j to i; we call divergent branches from the state i all branches going from i to another state j. Hence, an initial state is connected only to divergent branches and a final state only to convergent branches.

If we consider groups of states arranged in sequential submachines instead of single states, we can extend the preceding definitions to the diagram in Figure 5.29, for example, where 3 submachines have been isolated: M_1 composed of states 1, 2, 3, M_2, composed of 4, 5, 6, and M_3, composed of 7, 8. M_1 is an initial submachine and M_3 a final sub-

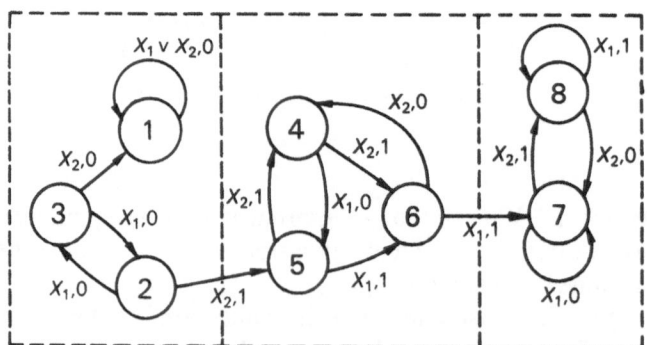

FIG. 5.29.

machine. Consequantly, as soon as we leave M_1, we cannot return and as soon as we enter M_3, we cannot leave it.

We often come across this type of case in practice. An example is the realization of machines which must recognize a certain input sequence. Generally, there is an initial and a final state; in order that we can put the machine back in the state in which the input sequence can be recognized, special reset commands are generally necessary; these are not inputs already existing in the machine but can always be represented on a table.

(b) *Identical states.* We shall now discuss a concept which will be very useful in the chapters dealing with the reduction of the number of states of a sequential machine. Consider the flow diagram in Figure 5.30. The Figure 5.31 flow table corresponds to it. States 1 and 4 both have the same next state and the outputs associated with their transitions are the same:

$$\begin{cases} G(1, X_1) = 2 = G(4, X_1) \\ F(1, X_1) = 0 = F(4, X_1) \end{cases}$$
$$\begin{cases} G(1, X_2) = 1 = G(4, X_2) \\ F(1, X_2) = 0 = F(4, X_2). \end{cases}$$

We say that states 1 and 4 are identical.

DEFINITION. We say that two states of a sequential machine, Q_i, Q_j, are identical if we have:

$$G(Q_i, X_k) = G(Q_j, X_k) \qquad F(Q_i, X_k) = F(Q_j, X_k)$$

for any input X_k.

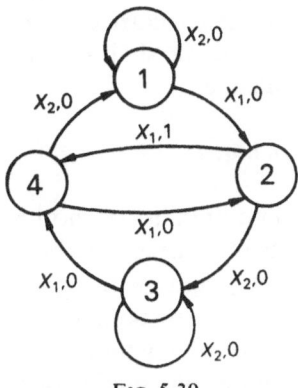

	X_1	X_2
1	2,0	1,0
2	4,1	3,0
3	4,0	3,0
4	2,0	1,0

FIG. 5.30.   FIG. 5.31.

In the flow table (or on the flow diagram) every time state *j* appears, it can be replaced by state *i* without changing the behaviour of the machine.

For our example Figure 5.32 shows the flow table and diagram where 4 has been replaced by 1 every time it appeared. Verification that the new machine M' obtained in this way, is the same, in as much as performance is concerned, as our original machine M, can be done by a sequence. The first machine was supposed in state 1 or 4 and the

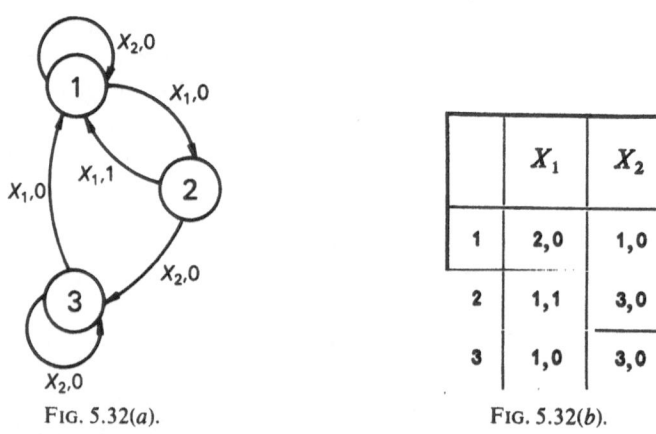

	X_1	X_2
1	2,0	1,0
2	1,1	3,0
3	1,0	3,0

FIG. 5.32(*a*).   FIG. 5.32(*b*).

input sequence $X_1 X_2 X_2 X_1 X_2$ gave a 2, 3, 3, 4, 1 sequence of states and 00000 output sequence (which in reality is the only thing of interest). The sequence of states in machine M' becomes 2, 3, 3, 1, 1 and the output sequence 0, 0, 0, 0, 0, that is, exactly the same as the first machine. Consequently as far as the user is concerned, it operates in exactly the same way as M. In Chapter 8 we shall return in more detail, to the subject of machine equivalence.

5.5.2. *Transition matrix*

5.5.2.1.

In ending this brief chapter, we are going to indicate another way of representing sequential systems in terms of matrices. In the same way as in classical algebra we associate flow graphs with flow matrices. In order to do this, we study the machine corresponding to the flow diagram in Figure 5.33. We draw a 6 row 6 column table (row = state, column = next state). We mark $(X_2, 1)$ at the intersection of row 1 and

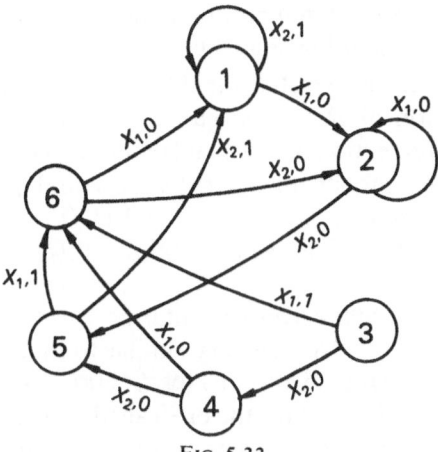

FIG. 5.33.

column 1. This signifies that we can go from state 1 to state 1 by application of input X_2 and that the output at the moment of this transition
is $Z = 1$. $(X_1, 0)$ is marked at the intersection of row 1 and column 2
since we go from state 1 to state 2 by applying input X_1 and the output
at that moment is $Z = 0$. The remaining cells of row one are zeros
because it is impossible to go from 1 to 3, 4, 5, or 6 by a single input.
We continue the table in this way which results in the matrix in Figure
5.34.

	1	2	3	4	5	6
1	$(X_2, 1)$	$(X_1, 0)$	0	0	0	0
2	0	$(X_1, 0)$	0	0	$(X_2, 0)$	0
3	0	0	0	$(X_2, 0)$	0	$(X_1, 1)$
4	0	0	0	0	$(X_2, 0)$	$(X_1, 0)$
5	$(X_2, 1)$	0	0	0	0	$(X_1, 1)$
6	$(X_1, 0)$	$(X_2, 0)$	0	0	0	0

FIG. 5.34.

In the general case we can therefore define a transition matrix from the flow diagram in the following way:

(a) If the machine has n states, the transition matrix will be $(n \times n)$.

(b) The transition allowing the passage from state i to state j is indicated at the intersection of row i and column j, i.e.,

(c) If a diagram branch exists between i and j, the indications figuring above this branch are noted in cell (i, j)

(d) If there is no branch between i and j, cell (i, j) is noted 0 in the matrix.

5.2.2.2. *Properties of the transition matrix*

The properties of this matrix are very similar to those of the topological matrix for combinational systems (cf. Section 3.4.7). We compute, for example, $M^2 = (M \otimes M)$ for the envisaged matrix (for the moment without bothering about the outputs associated with the transitions). The result is given in Figure 5.35.

	1	2	3	4	5	6
1	$X_2 X_2$	$X_1 X_1 \vee X_2 X_1$	0	0	$X_1 X_2$	0
2	$X_2 X_2$	$X_1 X_1$	0	0	$X_1 X_2$	$X_2 X_1$
3	$X_1 X_1$	$X_1 X_2$	0	0	$X_2 X_2$	$X_2 X_1$
4	$X_2 X_2 \vee X_1 X_1$	$X_1 X_2$	0	0	0	$X_2 X_1$
5	$X_2 X_2 \vee X_1 X_1$	$X_2 X_1 \vee X_1 X_2$	0	0	0	0
6	$X_1 X_2$	$X_1 X_1 \vee X_2 X_1$	0	0	$X_2 X_2$	0

FIG. 5.35.

We see that this matrix gives all the input sequences of length 2, which permit the passage from state i to state j. The length 2 cycles appear on the principal diagonal. In an analogous way, the length 2 loops appear between the different nodes of a combinational system on the squared topological matrix. The same occurs in M^3, where all order 3 transitions between states i and j appear.

APPENDIX

5.A.1. REPRESENTATION OF THE ASYNCHRONOUS MACHINES BY SEQUENCE CHARTS

In the flow table representation of an asynchronous system, we remarked that if, for example, the system had p inputs, the flow table had 2^p columns. This can be difficult to handle in certain industrial automata where the number of commands can be a very important consideration. In this case, it can be interesting to use a graph method, which represents, in an exact way, the phases of the system. We shall give a glimpse of this method in the following. The reader can find in the bibliography, two or three references (we cite those of Brunin and Naslin).

Principle of the method

We begin by recognizing which variables are which in the system (inputs, internal, outputs). A row, to be thickened if the value of the variable under consideration is 1, is associated with each of the variables. The passage of time of the input operations will thus be represented.

Example of usage

Consider the following system: a motor M is commanded by four relays; A, B, C, and D. A starts the motor, B stops it. C is on when a default appears (of very short duration) which also stops the motor. The motor starts again when D is on. (D corresponds to the termination of the default.) The duration of 'the end' of the default is also very short.

The sequence chart is shown in Figure 5.36, where we see four rows representing the commands and one row for the output M (motor running $M = 1$, motor off $M = 0$) and one row for the secondary variable S.

Analysis of this chart shows that the sequence is represented in the order A, C, D, B (note that C is always followed by D and B by A). At the start (phase 0) the system is at rest. Pushing A (phase 1) M starts.

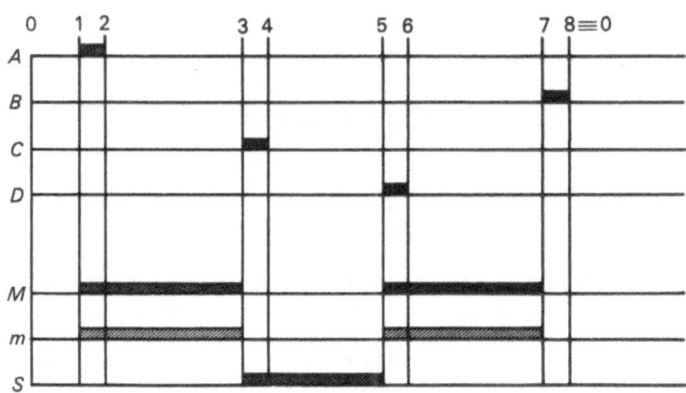

FIG. 5.36.

When A is released (at rest) (phase 2), M continues running. A default appears (phase 3) and M stops since C appears. M remains off even when C disappears (phase 4). Here, consequently, a secondary variable must be introduced, S, which stores the fact that M has stopped and to make it start again D must appear and not A. This secondary variable disappears as soon as D signals the end of the default (phase 5) thus provoking the motor M to start again. It will not be stopped by the end of D, (phase 6), but when B is pushed (phase 7) and will remain off (phase 8) when we let go of B.

How can this chart give the system's logical equations? Two of them interest us: the equation of M and the equation of S. We have $M = 1$, if $A = 1$ and $B = C = D = 0$ and $S = 0$, $A = 0$ and M already equal to 1 or if $A = 0 = B = C$ and $D = 0$ or 1 and $S = 0$.

Thus, we have decomposed M in two terms:

(1) term of establishment corresponding to A being pushed and S at rest.

(2) memory term: A is released, all the other quantities are zero (except perhaps D) and the exciation relay of M, which we note m, already has the logical value 1 (it is the row represented between M and S).

We therefore have: $M = \bar{s}(a - m\bar{b})$ (supposing that two commands cannot both be 1 at the same time). By analogous reasoning (S goes from 0 to 1 under a C action and remains equal to 1 as long as D does not appear) we find $S = c + s\bar{d}$.

Comment

We have simplified the sequence chart in this presentation in order that the principle of this representation be completely understood. Without going any further (we shall continue the study in Chapter 9) note that, in order to be complete, a sequence chart should (as in Huffman's table) include the study of all possible sequences (logical and physical) in the system. This would have forced us to complicate the one given as an example by examination of other input sequences $(A, B; A, C; A, D; A, C, B; D;$ etc.).

Note also that the sequence chart, while very useful in sequential systems' analysis, is more complicated to use in the case of synthesis because the introduction of secondary variables is not done automatically as in the case of the Huffman flow table (we shall see this in a later chapter).

5.A.2. MOORE'S MACHINE AND MEALY'S MACHINE

5.A.2.1. *Introduction: passage from a Moore machine to an equivalent Mealy machine*

(a) One of the problems which can be posed with respect to sequential machines and finite automata is that of the equivalence between the two proposed models, Moore's and Mealy's. There exist different proofs of the equivalence of these two types of machines; we note particularly those of Gill, Gloushkov and Aizerman (see references). We shall review these different proofs and seek the relations which exist among them by giving examples of their applications. We shall be particularly concerned with the passage from a Mealy machine to a Moore machine. As a matter of fact the passage in the inverse sense is quite simple: it is sufficient to associate each next state in the Moore flow table with its corresponding output. To make this explicit, we consider an example. Examine the flow table in Figure 5.37 which is a Moore table.

The equivalent Mealy machine is obtained by associating each state which has the next state 3 with the output Z_3, and each state having its next state 1 with the output Z_1. The table in Figure 5.38 is obtained. Note that the machine A_2 produced the same output sequence as the

	X_1	X_2	Z
1	3	2	Z_1
2	1	3	Z_2
3	2	1	Z_3

FIG. 5.37.   Machine A_1.

	X_1	X_2
1	3, Z_3	2, Z_2
2	1, Z_1	3, Z_3
3	2, Z_2	1, Z_1

FIG. 5.38.   Machine A_2.

machine A_1 if the same input sequence is imposed upon it. However, A_2 will in a way be ahead of A_1.

For example, assuming that A_1 and A_2 are in state 1, we apply a sequence to them. Suppose that this sequence starts with X_1. Both machines will change to state 3, but A_1 will go with output Z_1 (associated with state 1) and A_2 will go immediately with output Z_3. If the next input is X_1, A_1 goes to 2 with output Z_3, and A_2 with output Z_2, etc. The A_1 output sequence will therefore really be an instant behind the A_2 output sequence.

(b) We can put this in a general explicit way by the following theorem.

THEOREM.   To every Moore machine there corresponds a Mealy machine having the following properties: to every initial state of the Moore machine there corresponds an initial state of the Mealy machine such that the same output sequence is obtained from both machines (the Mealy machine being quicker than the Moore machine), from the two corresponding states for any input sequence applied to both machines.

Proof. Consider a Moore machine defined by:

$$\begin{cases} Q_{k+1} = G(Q_k, X_k) \\ Z_k = F(Q_k) \end{cases}$$

and a Mealy machine defined by

$$\begin{cases} Q'_{k+1} = G(Q'_k, X_k) \\ Z'_k = F[G(Q'_k, X_k)] = F^*(Q'_k, X_k) \end{cases}$$
$$\begin{cases} X'_k = X_k \\ Q'_0 = Q_0. \end{cases}$$

For $k = 0$ the Mealy machine's equations are:

$$\begin{cases} Q_1' = G(Q_0', X_0) = Q_1 \\ Z_0' = F[G(Q_0', X_0)] = F^*(Q_1') = F(Q_1) = Z_1 \end{cases}$$

for $k = 1$ we have:

$$\begin{cases} Q_2' = Q_2 \\ Z_1' = Z_2, \end{cases}$$

for $k > 1$:

$$\begin{cases} Q_{k-1}' = Q_{k-1} \\ Z_{k-1}' = Z_k, \end{cases}$$

and finally:

$$\begin{cases} Q_k' = Q_k \\ Z_k' = Z_{k+1}. \end{cases}$$

The theorem is thus proven.

5.A.2.2. *First proof of the existence of a Moore machine equivalent to a given Mealy machine*

(a) In this section we shall give different proofs of the following theorem:

THEOREM 2. To every Mealy machine corresponds a Moore machine having the following characteristics: to every initial state of the Mealy machine there corresponds an initial state of the Moore machine such that starting from these states in both machines the same output sequence is obtained for all input sequences applied to both machines, the Moore machine having a time unit delay.

We shall successively expose the Aizerman, Gloushkov and Gill methods.

(b) The Aizerman method is reminicient of the method used to prove Theorem 1. Since the Moore machine equivalent to the Mealy machine has a time unit delay compared with the latter, we shall associate a type (1) given Mealy machine with a machine given by the following recurrence equations:

$$Q'_{k+1} = G^*(Q'_k, X'_k)$$
$$Z'_k = F^*(Q'_k, X'_k).$$

Q'_k, Z'_k, X'_k are taken in the same alphabet as Q_k, Z_k, X_k, but we define $X'_{k+1} = X_k$ in order to make the time difference intervene. We are going to choose the pair (Q', X') as being the internal state in the new machine. From the relation giving Z' we see that we deal with a Moore machine. But M' is not completely defined since at instant 0 (when we apply the first input), X'_0 is not defined. The specification of X'_0 must therefore be introduced in the following way:

$$G^*(Q', X'_0) = Q \tag{a}$$
$$F^*(Q', X'_0) \quad \text{unspecified} \tag{b}$$

The second relation introduced expresses the fact that at instant 0, M has the Z_0 output, but M' will have a different output. In order that both machines have the same output sequence we let:

$$\begin{cases} G^* = G \\ F^* = F. \end{cases}$$

We verify that both machines have the same output sequence whenever the same input sequence is applied. As in Theorem 1 we reason by induction.

$k = 0$. M is therefore in state Q_0. We apply X_0.

$$\begin{cases} Q_1 = G(Q_0, X_0) \\ Z_0 = F(Q_0, X_0). \end{cases}$$

M' is in state (Q'_0, X'_0) which we take equal to (Q_0, X_0). The characteristic equations of M' are:

$$\begin{cases} Q'_1 = G^*(Q'_0, X'_0) = Q_0 & \text{following (a)} \\ Z'_0 \quad \text{unspecified} & \text{following (b).} \end{cases}$$

$k = 1$. M is in state Q_1. Under the influence of X_1 its characteristic equations become:

$$\begin{cases} Q_2 = G(Q_1, X_1) \\ Z_1 = F(Q_1, X_1). \end{cases}$$

M' is in state $Q_1' = Q_0$. At this instant we apply input $X_1' = X_0$ (elaborated at instant 0) and we have:

$$\begin{cases} Q_2' = G^*(Q_1', X_1') = G(Q_1', X_1') = G(Q_0, X_0) = Q_1 \\ Z_1' = F^*(Q_1', X_1') = F(Q_1', X_1') = F(Q_0, X_0) = Z_0. \end{cases}$$

We elaborate the next input $X_2' = X_1$.

$k > 1$. Suppose that

$$\begin{cases} Z_k' = Z_{k-1} \\ Q_k' = Q_{k-1} \end{cases}$$
(remember $X_k' = X_{k-1}$).

From the characteristic equations, we easily see that:

$$\begin{cases} Z_{k+1}' = Z_k' \\ Q_{k+1}' = Q_k'. \end{cases}$$

M' is equivalent to M (the same input sequences give the same output sequences) but with a unit time delay.

(c) *In practice.* Consider a Mealy machine M in an initial state Q_0. To obtain the equivalent Moore machine, we proceed in the following manner:

(a) We define the initial state $Q_0' = Q_0$.

(b) We associate a state Q_{k+1}' with each pair (Q_k, X_k).

(c) We associate an output $Z_{k+1}' = Z_k$ with each internal state Q_{k+1}' (Z_0' is unspecified).

(d) Whenever the Moore machine is in state Q_{k+1}', input $X_{k+1}' = X_k$ is applied.

Example of application

The application is the construction of a Moore machine equivalent to a Mealy machine given by Figure 5.39, assuming the initial state to be 1 and applying the input sequence $X_1 X_2 X_2 X_1$. In order to avoid confusion the time indices relative to machine M' will be noted as powers. We may therefore draw the table defining M' for the imposed sequence as in Figure 5.39.

Note that the time unit difference is intuitively guessed. In fact, a finite automaton produces the output associated with its present state (the state from which we begin). For a Mealy machine, the output at instant k is associated with the initial state. For a Moore machine, this output is associated with the state after the initial state (state which is attained after the input is applied). Since both machines

	X_1	X_2
1	$2, Z_1$	$4, Z_2$
2	$3, Z_2$	$1, Z_1$
3	$4, Z_2$	$2, Z_1$
4	$1, Z_1$	$3, Z_2$

Q'	Z'	X'
$Q'^0 = Q^0 = 1$	$Z'^0 —$	$X'^0 —$
$Q'^1 = (1, X_1)$	$Z'^1 = Z_1$	$X'^1 = X_1$
$Q'^2 = (2, X_2)$	$Z'^2 = Z_1$	$X'^2 = X_2$
$Q'^3 = (1, X_2)$	$Z'^3 = Z_2$	$X'^3 = X_2$
$Q'^4 = (4, X_1)$	$Z'^4 = Z_1$	$X'^4 = X_1$

Moore machine

Q	Z	X
$Q^0 = 1$	$Z^0 = Z_1$	$X^0 = X_1$
$Q^1 = 2$	$Z^1 = Z_1$	$X^1 = X_2$
$Q^3 = 1$	$Z^2 = Z_2$	$X^2 = X_2$
$Q^4 = 4$	$Z^3 = Z_1$	$X^3 = X_1$

Mealy machine

FIG. 5.39.

attain their next state only after the end of the input pulse and are blocked between two commands or orders k and $k+1$, we see that the Moore machine output will only reveal the output corresponding to X_k at the next instant when it will leave this state under the influence of a new command.

(d) With respect to the number of states in a Moore machine equivalent to a Mealy machine, it can be noted that if the Mealy machine has m inputs and n states, $nm+1$ states in the equivalent Moore machine can correspond to each initial state of the Mealy machine. Since the Mealy machine has n internal states, the equivalent Moore machine will have $(m+1)n$ states for any sequence and any initial state. Nevertheless, it must be observed that this is the maximum number of possible states because the table representing the Moore machine, obtained in this way, can be simplified.

5.A.2.3. *Second Proof*

(a) We now give the Gloushkov proof. The basic idea is the same as in the Aizerman proof (that is, we associate a new state in the Moore machine with each pair (Q, X) of the Mealy machine). Generally, the application is slightly different. We no longer consider the quantities X and Z intervening at an instant k, but taken as letters of the alphabet of inputs $(x_1 \ldots x_m)$ or output $(z_1 \ldots z_r)$. As in the Aizerman method, we shall consider that the Mealy machine is in the initial state q_1 when we begin: q_1 is part of the alphabet $(q_1 \ldots q_n)$. The indices do not indicate a succession in time.

(b) Therefore, to the automaton of Mealy, M, defined by $F_k G_k$ and the quantities Q, X, and Z defined by the alphabets previously discussed, we correspond an automaton of Moore M' with the following characteristics: its inputs and outputs are defined by the same letters as the inputs and outputs of M; its states are defined by:

The state when we begin is

$$q_1' = q_1.$$

The internal states

$$q_{ij}' = (q_i, x_j) \quad [i = 1 \text{ to } n, j = 1 \text{ to } m].$$

The next state

$$q_{jk}' = (q_1, x_k)$$

$$q_{ij}' x_k = (q_i, x_j) x_k = (q_i, x_j, x_k).$$

The output function

$$F^*(q_1') \quad \text{undefined}$$

$$F^*(q_i', x_j) = F(q_i, x_j) \quad \text{every time } F(q_i, x_j) \text{ exists.}$$

We must now prove the equivalence between M and M'. To do this, we consider any input sequence $x_{i_1}, x_{i_2} \ldots x_{i_t}$. Under the influence of these inputs, M describes the sequence of states $q_1, q_{j_1}, \ldots, q_{j_{t-1}}$ starting from the initial state q_1. The machine M' describes the sequence of internal states $q_1, (q_1, x_{i_1}), (q_{j_1}, x_{i_2}), \ldots, (q_{j_{t-1}}, x_{i_t})$. From the definitions of the next states and outputs of M' in function of the corresponding quantities of M, it is clear that M and M' will produce the same outputs but with a unit time difference.

(c) *In practice.* To construct a Moore automaton equivalent to a

Mealy automaton, we are thus led to associate $(mn+1)$ states, which are q_i and mn states in the form (q_j, x_k), with each state q_i.

Example of application

We seek the Moore machine equivalent to the Mealy machine given by the table in Figure 5.40. State 1 is associated with

$$\begin{cases} A = 1 \\ B = (1, X_1) \\ C = (1, X_2), \end{cases}$$

state 2 with

$$\begin{cases} D = 2 \\ E = (2, X_1) \\ F = (2, X_2), \end{cases}$$

and state 3 with

$$\begin{cases} G = 3 \\ H = (3, X_1) \\ I = (3, X_2). \end{cases}$$

	X_1	X_2
1	2, 0	2, 1
2	2, 1	3, 0
3	3, 1	2, 0

FIG. 5.40.

	X_1	X_2	Z
A	B	C	–
B	E	F	0
C	E	F	1
D	E	F	–
E	E	F	1
F	H	I	0
G	H	I	–
H	H	I	1
I	E	F	0

FIG. 5.41.

The flow table of the Moore machine equivalent to the Mealy machine 4 is given in Figure 5.41. We examine its construction by the example of states A, B, and C. 1 is taken as the initial state. Hence,

(1) The output of state A is not specified.

(2) Under the influence of input X_1, we go from A to $B = (1, X_1)$ of which the output is 0.

(3) Under the influence of X_2, we go from A to $C = (1, X_2)$ of which the output is 1.

Action of X_1 leads from B to E, X_2 from B to F (these two states are not initial states, which correspond to state 2 in the Mealy table).

The table thus obtained is not minimal, but can be minimized (which necessitates evidently additional work). The table in Figure 5.42 is therefore obtained: with:

$$Q_0 = (A)$$
$$Q_1 = (B, D, I)$$
$$Q_2 = (G, H)$$
$$Q_3 = (F)$$
$$Q_4 = (C, E).$$

	X_1	X_2	Z
Q_0	Q_1	Q_4	–
Q_1	Q_4	Q_3	0
Q_2	Q_2	Q_1	1
Q_3	Q_2	Q_1	0
Q_4	Q_4	Q_3	1

FIG. 5.42.

(d) The method comes down to separating each state in two, considered as the state in which we arrive, by associating an output with each of the pairs thus created.

5.A.2.4. *Utilization of the transition matrix*

(a) This method (due to Gill) of seeking the Moore machine equivalent to a given Mealy machine is not, strictly speaking, a proof of the theoretical equivalence of the two types of machines, but rather a process which permits to go rapidly from one to the other.

In Section 5.5.2 the Moore and Mealy machines were characterized by their transition matrices. Figures 5.43 and 5.44 recall the matrices associated with the two machines.

$$\begin{bmatrix} (X_{11}, Z_{11}) \dots (X_{1j}, Z_{1j}) \dots (X_{1n}, Z_{1n}) \\ (X_{i1}, Z_{i1}) \dots (X_{ij}, Z_{ij}) \dots (X_{.i}, Z_{.n}) \\ (X_{n1}, Z_{n1}) \dots (X_{nj}, Z_{nj}) \dots (X_{nn}, Z_{nn}) \end{bmatrix}$$

Fig. 5.43.   Transition matrix of a Mealy machine.

$$\begin{bmatrix} (X_{11}, Z_1) \dots (X_{1j}, Z_j) \dots (X_{1n}, Z_n) \\ (X_{i1}, Z_1) \dots (X_{ij}, Z_j) \dots (X_{in}, Z_n) \\ (X_{n,1}, Z_1) \dots (X_{nj}, Z_j) \dots (X_{nn}, Z_n) \end{bmatrix}$$

Fig. 5.44.   Transition matrix of a Moore machine.

(b) It is therefore a question of going from a Mealy type transition matrix (one output per cell) to a Moore type transition matrix (one output per column). We proceed differently than in the two previous methods. Instead of considering pairs (Q, X), we shall consider the pairs (Q, Z) or more precisely $(Q_{arrival}, Z)$. We shall perform about the same method as that to which we are in practice led to by application of the Gloushkov method. For that, new quantities are called for; we call $(X_{ij}, Z_{ij})_{\bar{z}_k}$ a term of the transition matrix which *contains* the output z_k and $(X_{ij}, Z_{ij})_{z_k}$ a term which does not contain z_k. We shall systematically create new arrival states each associated with r possible Mealy automaton outputs. Therefore, each column of the transition matrix will be split in two columns $(X_{ij}, Z_{ij})_{z_k}$ and $(X_{ij}, Z_{ij})_{\bar{z}_k}$ as a beginning. The same transitions toward the next states are kept for these new states. In order to do this the j row will be repeated (since the j column has just been divided into two). This row corresponds to the j state considered as an initial state instead of a final state. The operation is repeated for the $(s-1)$ remaining outputs associated with the Q_j state $(s \leqslant r)$ and for the $(n-1)$ remaining states of the machine. The transition matrix thus obtained will have a maximum of nr columns and nr rows; therefore, a Moore machine will have at most nr states.

(c) *Example of application.* Figure 5.45 represents a transition matrix. We see that state 1 is purely initial (since column 1 is empty). On the contrary, state 2 is not purely initial; we therefore apply the method. We create (Figure 5.46) a fourth column where only the first line contains the term associated with the output $Z = 1$. State 2, considered as a final state, has been split in two. In order that state 4, just created, also be an initial state, with the same transitions as 2, we create a fourth row by copying the second row of the transition matrix. We operate in the same way for state 3 and obtain the transition matrix

	1	2	3
1		$X_1, 0$ $X_2, 1$	
2		$X_1, 0$	$X_2, 0$
3		$X_2, 0$	$X_1, 1$

FIG. 5.45.

	1	2	3	4
1		$X_1, 0$		$X_2, 1$
2		$X_1, 0$	$X_2, 0$	
3		$X_2, 0$	$X_1, 1$	
4		$X_1, 0$	$X_2, 0$	

FIG. 5.46.

	1	2	3	4	5
1		$X_1, 0$		$X_2, 1$	
2		$X_1, 0$	$X_2, 0$		
3		$X_2, 0$			$X_1, 1$
4		$X_1, 0$	$X_2, 0$		
5		$X_2, 0$			$X_1, 1$

FIG. 5.47.

in Figure 5.47 and the flow table in Figure 5.48. We see that the Figure 5.48 table will be identical to the table obtained in the preceeding section if we group (I, B), (C, D, E) and (G, H) instead of (B, D, I), (C, E) and (G, H) in the Figure 5.41 table.

	X_1	X_2	Z
1	2	4	–
2	2	3	0
3	5	2	0
4	2	3	1
5	5	2	1

Fig. 5.48.

5.A.2.5. *Comparison of the methods*

The three methods exposed above have diverse interests. The Aizerman method seems of little interest in practice since it requires the separate consideration of each of the possible sequences from an initial state.

The Gloushkov and Gill methods are easier to handle in practice. The Gloushkov methods generally leads to a non-minimal table while the Gill method immediately gives the reduced form. This comes from the fact that a purely initial state with empty output is not created as in the Gloushkov method, for each state in the Mealy machine under consideration.

The other advantage of the Gill method is that simple inspection of the transition matrix the number of states in the Moore machine that we wish to obtain is a priori determined. As a matter of fact, we see that, to a column in which there is only one output, there will correspond a single column in the modified transition matrix; therefore, a single state in the Moore machine. If a column has two outputs, two columns of the modified transition matrix will correspond to it, therefore two states.

Thus we see that the number of states in the Moore table will be $n_1 + \cdots + n_a = \Sigma n_i$ where n_i is the number of outputs associated with each column of the transition matrix of the Mealy machine. If the Mealy machine has p outputs and n states, we obtain an n state Moore machine with

$$n_p \geqslant n' \geqslant n + p - 1.$$

Note that this happens if we really have a Mealy machine to start with. This means that we have outputs by pairs (X, Q), i.e., a machine such that its transition matrix has more than one output per column.

BIBLIOGRAPHY

To the preceeding books we must add:

[1] MOORE, E. F., 'Gedanken Experiments on Sequential machines', *Automata Studies*, Princeton University Press, 1956.

[2] MEALY, G. M., 'A Method for Synthetizing Sequential Circuits', *Bell System Technical J.* **34** (1955) 1045–79.

[3] CADDEN, W. J., 'Equivalent Sequential Circuits', *IRE Trans. Circuits Theory* **C.T. 6** (1959) 30–34.

[4] GILL, A., 'Comparison of Finite State Models', *IRE Trans. Circuits Theory* **C.T. 7** (1960) 178–72.

[5] AIZERMAN, M. A., GOUCER, L. A., SMIRNOVA, I. M., TAL, A. A., and ROZONOER, L. I., *Logique, automates, algorithmes*, Phys. Math., Éditions d'état, Moscou, 1963.

[6] GLOUSHKOV, V. M., 'Théorie abstraite des automates', *Ann. roumaines-soviétiques*, *Math. Phys.* **2** (1962).

[7] GILL, A., *Introduction to the Theory of Finite-state machines*, McGraw-Hill, New York, 1962.

[8] FLORINE, J., *La synthèse des machines logiques*, Presses Académiques Européennes, Bruxelles, Dunod, Paris, 1964.

[9] BRUNIN, J., *Logique binaire et communications*, Dunod, Paris, 1966.

EXERCISES

5.1. Determine the internal states and the flow table of a push-button system which gives a 1 output only when the button is consecutively pushed twice.

5.2. A motor M can rotate in two directions (left and right). Closing a contact d provokes its turning to the right, and closing a contact g provokes its turning to the left. The notebook of changes is the following:

If we push only button A when the motor is at rest, it starts turning to the right and continues if A is released and eventually A is manipulated in other ways. B plays the same role for the motor turning to the left as A does for the motor turning to the right.

A and B cannot be pushed at the same time. The rest position must be passed in order to go from the right turning to the left turning.

The motor is stopped by a third button C (which has priority over A and B); it is a reset. Determine the internal states and the flow table of the motor's command system.

5.3. Represent the phase tables of the systems studied in Section 4.2.6.

$y_1\,y_2\,y_3$ \ a	0	1	Z
000	100	001	0
001	100	001	1
011	000	000	0
010	001	000	0
110	001	010	0
111	000	010	1
101	100	111	1
100	100	111	0

FIG. 5.49.

5.4. Consider a sequential machine's excitation and output matrices shown in Figure 5.49 (Moore machine). Perform a realization of:
(a) an asynchronous system with relays then with transistors;
(b) a synchronized asynchronous system;
(c) with symmetrical flip-flops;
(d) with RS flip-flops;
(e) with JK flip-flops;
(f) with PQ flip-flops;

5.5. Same questions for the system which has its excitation and output matrices represented in Figure 5.50 (Moore machine).

$y_1\ y_2\ y_3$ / a	0	1	Z
000	011	000	0
001	010	001	0
011	000	011	1
010	001	010	0
110	100	010	1
111	101	011	1
101	111	001	0
100	110	000	0

FIG. 5.50.

5.6. Same questions for the system which has its excitation and output matrices represented in Figures 5.51 and 5.52 (Mealy machine).

5.7. For each of the three preceeding exercises, determine the transition matrix of the system and the set of length 2 and length 3 sequences.

5.8. Determine the conditions in which the functions τ, $(RS)(JK)$, (PQ) defining the variable Y are expressed independently of y. Write Y in the form:

$$Y = Ay + B\bar{y},$$

where A and B are Boolean functions of variables other than y and $\bar{y}$.

a	0	1
$y_1\ y_2\ y_3$		
000	011	101
001	010	100
011	000	110
010	001	111
110	001	011
111	000	010
101	010	000
100	011	001

FIG. 5.51.

a	0	1
$y_1\ y_2\ y_3$		
000	0	1
001	1	0
011	1	0
010	0	1
110	0	1
111	1	0
101	0	0
100	0	0

FIG. 5.52.

CHAPTER 6

ANALYSIS OF SEQUENTIAL SYSTEMS
HAZARDS IN SEQUENTIAL AND
COMBINATIONAL SYSTEMS

Chapters 4 and 5 showed what a sequential system is, how it can be defined, and gave its equations. The complexity of these equations led to tabulated representations of these machines in the form of a flow table, excitation matrix, and output matrix. The two large categories of sequential systems were mentioned: asynchronous and synchronous.

6.1. ANALYSIS OF ASYNCHRONOUS SEQUENTIAL SYSTEMS

An asynchronous sequential system evolves in an autonomous way (without outside intervention). The duration of the input (or command) T is much longer that the system's response time T'. Hence, if a certain input X_i is applied to this system, its internal state is modified after a time T', while X continues to be applied. The system is then susceptible to undergo a new transition. The most characteristic example of asynchronous systems is the relay system.

6.1.1. *Asynchronous relay systems*

Consider the relay system in Figure 6.1. Let i_1, i_2, i_3 be the Boolean variables associated with the currents running through coils 1, 2, and 3. Taking into account what was discussed in Chapter 4, the Boolean equation which defines the state of the current in coil 1 at instant N (state of this relay's contacts at instant $N+1$) is written:

$$i_{1,N} = y_{1,N+1} = (\bar{a}_N y_{3,N} + \bar{b}_N \bar{y}_{3,N}) y_{1,N} \bar{y}_{2,N} + \bar{a}_N y_{2,N} \bar{y}_{3,N} + a_N b_N y_{1,N}.$$

In the same way, we have the Boolean equation which defines the z output:

$$z_{1,N} = a_N \bar{y}_{1,N} + b_N \bar{y}_{2,N}.$$

In order to simplify the writing we leave out the time indices; in order

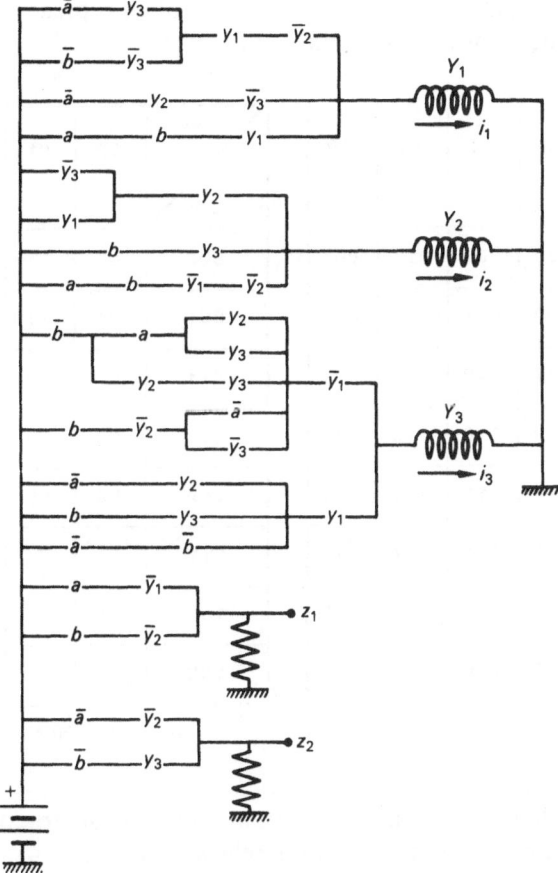

FIG. 6.1.

to show that the state of the secondary variable y in the first term of $i_{1,N}$ is taken at $N+1$, we let $y_{1,N+1} = Y_1$. There is no ambiguity in the equation of z because both terms are taken relative to instant N. The set of Boolean equations for the Figure 6.1 circuit is:

$$Y_1 = (\bar{a}y_3 + \bar{b}\bar{y}_3)y_1\bar{y}_2 + \bar{a}y_2\bar{y}_3 + aby_1$$
$$Y_2 = y_2(y_1 + \bar{y}_3) + by_3 + ab\bar{y}_1\bar{y}_2$$
$$Y_3 = \bar{y}_1[a\bar{b}(y_2 + y_3) + \bar{b}y_2y_3 + b\bar{y}_2(\bar{a} + \bar{y}_3)]$$
$$+ y_1[\bar{a}(\bar{b} + y_2) + by_3]$$
$$z_1 = a\bar{y}_1 + b\bar{y}_2 \qquad z_2 = \bar{a}\bar{y}_2 + \bar{b}y_3.$$

These equations describe how the system operates. To give a more concrete representation of its transition we shall represent its excitation and output matrices in Figures 6.2 and 6.3.

ab / $y_1\,y_2\,y_3$	00	01	11	10
000	000	001	011	000
001	000	011	010	001
011	001	010	010	001
010	110	110	010	011
110	111	111	110	010
111	011	011	111	010
101	101	111	111	000
100	101	000	100	100

FIG. 6.2.   Excitation matrix.

ab / $y_1\,y_2\,y_3$	00	01	11	10
000	01	11	10	10
001	01	11	10	11
011	01	00	10	11
010	00	00	10	10
110	00	00	00	00
111	01	00	00	01
101	01	11	10	01
100	01	11	10	00

FIG. 6.3.   Output matrix.

6.1.1.1. *Construction of the flow table*
The flow table of the sequential system under consideration is determined from the excitation and output matrices (Figure 6.4).

6.1.1.2. *Construction of the Huffman flow table*
The Huffman table is derived from the flow table. It gives only the system's stable states, indicating the connections between these states, but without any particular specifications as to how the connections are made. It gives no description of the transient.

If certain sequences do not lead to stable states, the corresponding terms in the excitation matrix or flow table are replaced by 'don't cares'. Thus, the second column of the Huffman table has only 'don't cares'. This Huffman table appears in Figure 6.5.

6.1.1.3. *Construction of the flow diagram*
We easily go from Figure 6.4 to the diagram in Figure 6.6 (cf. Section 5.5.).

	00	01	11	10
1	1/01	2/11	3/10	1/10
2	1/01	3/11	4/10	2/11
3	2/01	4/00	4/10	2/11
4	5/00	5/00	4/10	3/10
5	6/00	6/00	5/00	4/00
6	3/01	3/00	6/00	4/01
7	7/01	6/11	6/10	1/01
8	7/01	1/11	8/10	8/00

FIG. 6.4. Flow table.

	00	01	11	10
1	①	—	4	②
2	1	—	4	③
3	1	—	4	3
4	1	—	④	3
5	1	—	⑤	3
6	1	—	⑥	3
7	⑦	—	6	2
8	7	—	⑧	⑨

FIG. 6.5. Huffman flow table.

6.1.1.4. *Graph of performance of an asynchronous system*

We are going to construct a table in the following way: it will be derived from the excitation matrix by placing an empty circle in each cell which corresponds to a stable state and a dot in each cell corresponding to a secondary state. Arrows will connect the stable and secondary states as indicated in the excitation matrix.

Thus, in the Figure 6.7 table which represents the performance of the Figure 6.1 circuit, the unstable state 111 in column $ab = 01$, is connected to the unstable state 011 as in the Figure 6.2 excitation matrix. This representation makes it easy to visualize how the proposed sequential system (Figure 6.7) operates.

6.1.1.5. *Construction of the transition table*

As in Section 4.2.5, it is possible to represent the Figure 6.1 relay system's transition table which is shown in Figure 6.8.

The fact that an internal state in one of the excitation matrix's columns is stable, tells us that there is no change of secondary variables. The transition (τ_1, τ_2, τ_3) corresponding to the three secondary variables y_1, y_2, y_3, is 000. In Figure 6.8 a rectangle has been put around all the stable states.

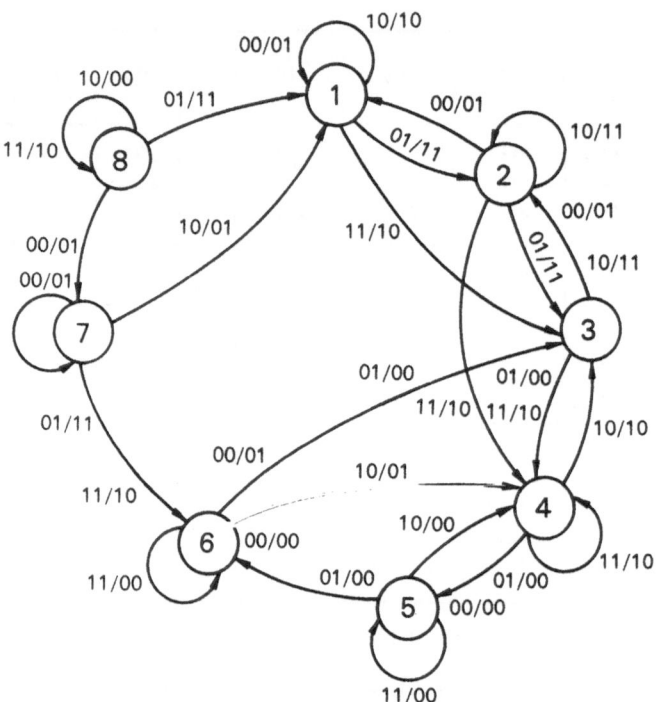

FIG. 6.6.   Flow diagram.

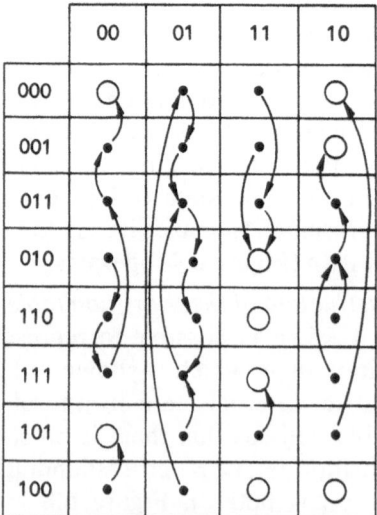

FIG. 6.7.   Performance diagram.

	00	01	11	10
000	000	001	011*	000
001	001	010	011*	000
011	010	001	001	010
010	100	100	000	001
110	001	001	000	100
111	100	100	000	101*
101	000	010	010	101*
100	001	100	000	000

FIG. 6.8.   Transition table.

The weight (arithmetic sum of the numbers which make up the term) of the term $(\tau_1\tau_2\tau_3)$ gives the number of secondary variables which change value in that transition.

6.1.1.6. *Construction of the transition matrix*
Let the different inputs be noted as follows:

$$X_1 = 00 \qquad X_3 = 11$$
$$X_2 = 01 \qquad X_4 = 10$$

The transition matrix is constructed according to the indications given in Section 5.5.2. The reader can verify that the transition matrix of the Figure 6.1 example is that shown in Figure 6.9.

6.1.2. *Characteristic properties of asynchronous sequential systems*
The asynchronous sequential systems are generally characterized by a stable state's autonomous transition, for a given input, to another stable state corresponding to a new input. This passage can be made directly or by passing unstable secondary states. Two phenomena of asynchronous systems should be pointed out: races and cycles.

6.1.2.1. *Cycles*
A sequential system can, under a given input, constantly evolve, periodically going through the same succession of states, instead of evolv-

	1	2	3	4	5	6	7	8
1	X_1+X_4	X_2	X_3	0	0	0	0	0
2	X_1	X_4	X_2	X_3	0	0	0	0
3	0	X_1+X_4	0	X_2+X_3	0	0	0	0
4	0	0	X_4	X_3	X_1+X_2	0	0	0
5	0	0	0	X_4	X_3	X_1+X_2	0	0
6	0	0	X_1+X_2	X_4	0	X_3	0	0
7	X_4	0	0	0	0	X_2+X_3	X_1	0
8	X_2	0	0	0	0	0	X_1	X_3+X_4

FIG. 6.9.   Transition matrix.

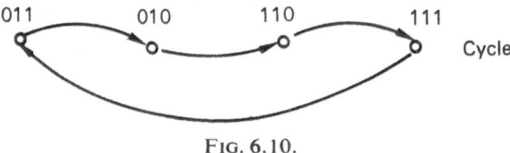

FIG. 6.10.

ing to a stable state. We say that it goes through a cycle. Thus, if we consider two stable states in column 00 (Figure 6.7) and apply a 01 input, the system will go through the cycle (011-010-110-111) (Figure 6.10) after a certain period of time. If input 11 is then applied, it is impossible to foresee toward which stable state 010, 110 or 111 the system will evolve.

This uncertainty of future transition causes the existence of cycles to generally be dangerous in an asynchronous sequential system and we therefore try to avoid them.

6.1.2.2. *Races*

Reference to the Figure 6.8 transition table, shows that certain transitions have the following property: the weight of $(\tau_1\tau_2\tau_3)$ is greater than 1, which means that it corresponds to a simultaneous value change of several secondary variables. Physically this translates the simultaneous commutation of several contacts in the relay systems. But, the relay systems are not ideal switching devices. That is, perfect coincidence in the opening or closing of two relays' contacts cannot be assured. Technologically, it is difficult to foresee the order in which this operation will happen. This is why we study the different possibilities. This succession of switchings which replace a single commutation is called a "race". If its result is that determined by the flow table we say that it is *not a critical race*; if, on the contrary, this succession of operations due to the relay itself, leads to a solution which differs from the one in the flow table, we say that it is a *critical race*.

6.1.2.3. *Example of a critical race*

Consider Figure 6.11 which corresponds to column 10 in Figure 6.7. We study the transition from state 101 to state 000 which corresponds to the simultaneous change of y_1 and y_3 from 1 to 0. Physically, this cannot be realized. The switching can therefore be made starting either with y_1 or y_3.

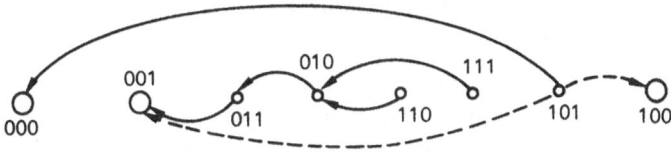

FIG. 6.11. Critical race.

Starting with y_1, the system goes from 101 to 001; starting with y_3, the intermediate state is 100. These transitions are indicated in Figure 6.11. States 001 and 100 are stable. The system therefore cannot continue to 000 after reaching one of these intermediate states.

This is a *critical race*.

6.1.2.4. *Example of a non-critical race*

Consider Figure 6.12. It corresponds to column 11 in Figure 6.7. We study the transition from 000 to 001. Starting from 000, the system

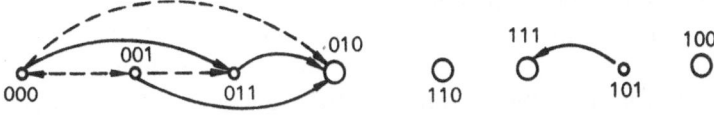

FIG. 6.12. Non-critical race.

can reach 010 or 001 depending on whether y_2 or y_3 changes first. 010 is stable. The system's final state will be 010 even if it passes 001. The race is not critical.

As an exercise the reader can verify that the races between 001 and 010 in Figures 6.12, and 111 and 010 in Figure 6.11 are not critical.

Comment. We have just studied races of the sequential system's secondary variables. In a like manner we could study races on inputs corresponding to the simultaneous change of the state of several input variables.

6.1.2.5. *Example of a critical race on primary variables*
Consider Figure 6.7. Suppose that the system is in the stable state corresponding to input 11 and the internal state 100.

For the preceding technological reasons, if input 00 is applied, we must assume that the inputs will attain one of the intermediate states 01 or 10.

In the first case, the system will be in cyclic transition. Input 00 will stabilize it in state 000.

In the second case, the system will remain in the same internal state and input 00 will bring it to state 101.

The race is critical.

6.1.2.6. *Example of non-critical races of primary variables*
Suppose (Figure 6.7) the sequential system is in the stable state 111 corresponding to input 11 and input 00 is applied.

As before, the intermediate states 01 and 10 of primary variables are possible.

A 01 input leads to a cycle; then a 00 input leads to the stable state 000.

A 10 input leads to 001, a 00 input leads to the stable state 000.

The race is not critical.

6.1.2.7. *Adjacency condition in an asynchronous sequential system*
In the preceding section we saw the danger that critical races present to a system. Since we cannot know, when realizing an asynchronous sequential system, if the possible races will be critical, we eliminate the risk by removing the causes of races.

In order to do this, we must have the following condition: every input change will be made by modifying the value of only one primary variable at a time; every transition from one internal state to another will be made by modifying only one secondary variable at a time.

In the case of primary variables, mechanical configuration in which the buttons are placed at a distance will prevent two buttons being pushed at the same time.

For the secondary variables, the internal states' assignment in the flow table will impose the adjacency condition. Two internal states which are connected during a transition can differ only (by assignment) by the state of a *single* secondary variable.

6.1.3. *Electronic asynchronous systems*

Consider the transistor circuit in Figure 6.13. (The logical function NOR is realized by the transistors.)

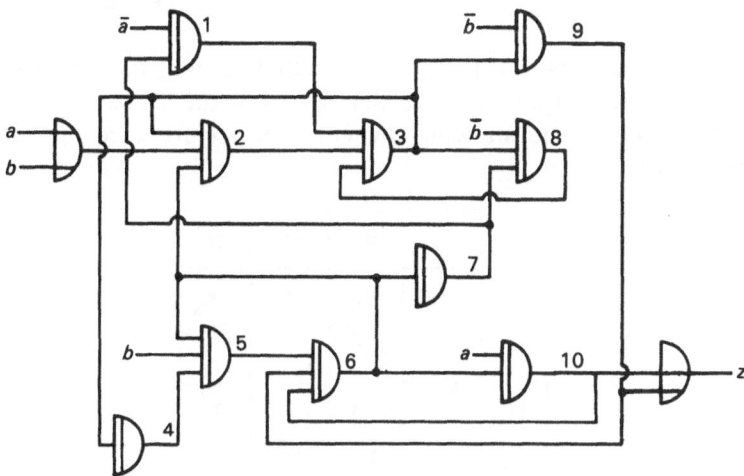

Fig. 6.13.

As in Section 4.2.4.2 we take the operators 3 and 6 outputs as internal variables.

The Boolean equations describing how the system operates are written:

$$Y_3 = y_3(\bar{a} + \bar{y}_6) + \bar{b}\bar{a}y_6 + (a+b)\bar{y}_6$$
$$Y_6 = (\bar{b} + y_3)y_6 + a(by_3 + \bar{b}\bar{y}_3)$$
$$Z = b\bar{y}_3 + \bar{a}\bar{y}_6.$$

Figures 6.14 and 6.15 are the excitation and output matrices of this sequential system.

The simulation by digital training device of this electronic circuit

ab / $y_3\,y_6$	00	01	11	10
00	00	10	10	11
01	11	00	00	01
11	11	11	01	01
10	10	10	11	10

FIG. 6.14.

ab / $y_3\,y_6$	00	01	11	10
00	1	1	1	0
01	0	1	1	0
11	0	0	0	0
10	1	1	0	0

FIG. 6.15.

shows that the Figure 6.13 circuit actually functions according to the excitation and output matrices derived from the choice of internal variables. The table showing the circuit's performance appears in Figure 6.16.

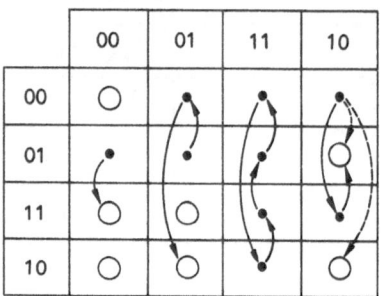

	00	01	11	10
00				
01				
11				
10				

FIG. 6.16.

The presence of a cycle for input 11 can be noticed. In the column corresponding to input 10 the passage from the internal state 00 to internal state 11 cannot be instantaneous. Due to the differences in the paths of the electric circuits generating Y_3 and Y_6, the signals corresponding to the new values of Y_3 and Y_6 are not simultaneously transmitted. As in the case of relays, the intermediate states 01 or 10, depending on whether Y_3 or Y_6 is transmitted first, must be envisaged. Both 01 and 10 are stable. The system has a critical race. The self-operating electronic system in Figure 6.13, where the inputs are steps, evolves like the relay circuit in Figure 6.1.

6.2. ANALYSIS OF SYNCHRONOUS SEQUENTIAL SYSTEMS

6.2.1. *Synchronized asynchronous systems*

Consider the circuit in Figure 6.17. It differs from the Figure 6.13 circuit by two delays Δ controlled by an external clock. If the variables y_3 and y_6 reach a certain value at instant N, these values can be reinjected into the circuit only at the next pulse of the clock. In this way, the system will always be under control.

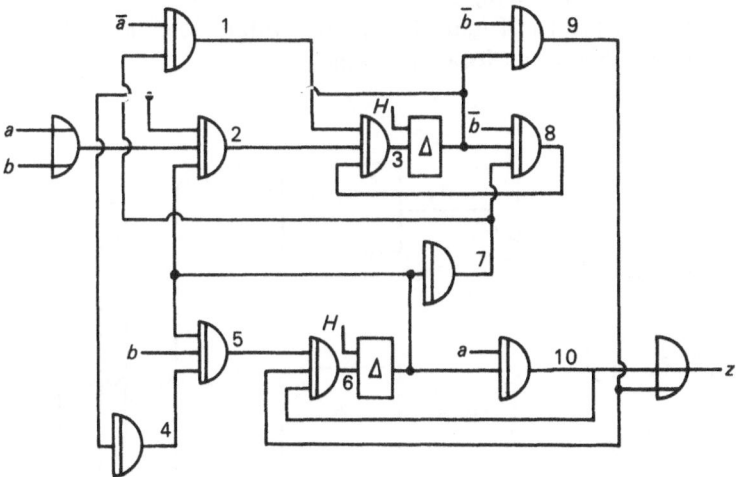

FIG. 6.17.

The duration of the clock's pulse is less than the system's response time. The system's inputs are always levels. The same tables (flow table) and matrices (excitation, output) as for the Figure 6.13 system will be used to study how this system operates. The only thing to be pointed out is that the transition is no longer autonomous, but controlled by a clock.

In these circumstances the cycles are not annoying. In fact, the system advances one step of the cycle with each pulse of a clock, if input 11 continues to be applied.

There is no fear of races. In fact, assuming the system to be in state 00 and input 10 applied (Figure 6.16), Figure 6.17 shows that y_3 takes the value 1, but this value does not cross the Δ element because of the clock. It is the same for y_6. The system is therefore blocked in state 11 until the next clock pulse.

In general, if a level-controlled circuit is considered, we cannot really speak of an asynchronous or synchronous system. What we really consider is the system *operating asynchronously or synchronously*.

6.2.2. *Pulsed systems*

We shall study two kinds of pulsed systems: those which use symmetric flip-flops and those which use SR flip-flops.

6.2.2.1. *Symmetrical flip-flop circuits*

Consider the circuit in Figure 6.18. The output does not depend just on the input; we have a Moore machine.

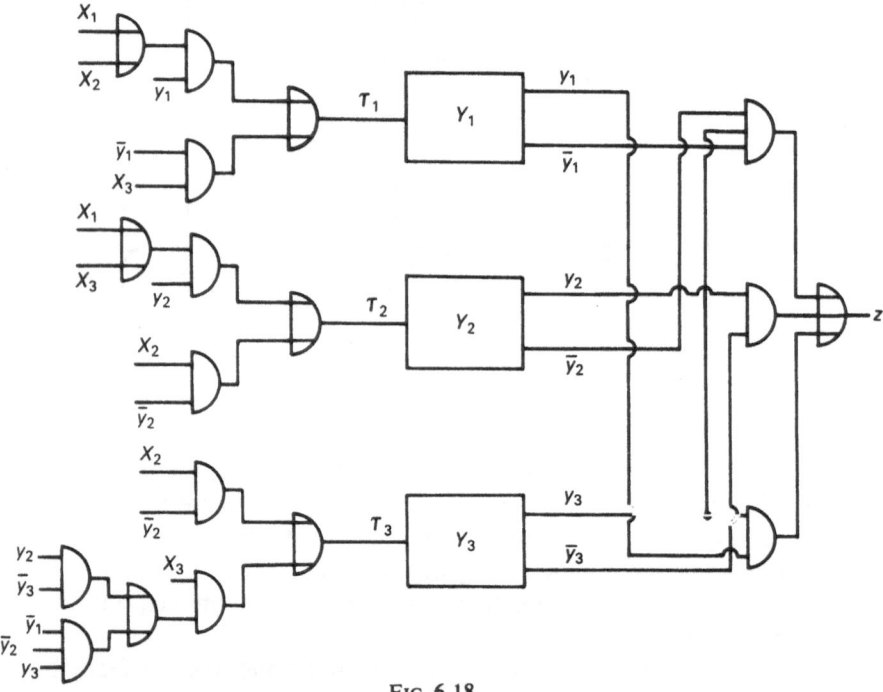

FIG. 6.18.

The Boolean equation is:

$$Z = \bar{y}_1 \bar{y}_2 y_3 + y_2 \bar{y}_3 + y_1 y_3.$$

The output matrix is shown in Figure 6.19. In Section 4.2.5 it was shown that, if the quantity $\tau_i = (y_{i,N} \oplus y_{i,N+1})$ acts on the flip-flop in a symmetrical flip-flop circuit, the output of the flip-flop is $y_{i,N+1} = Y_i$.

$y_1\,y_2\,y_3$	X_1	X_2	X_3
000	0	0	0
001	1	1	1
011	0	0	0
010	1	1	1
110	1	1	1
111	1	1	1
101	1	1	1
100	0	0	0

FIG. 6.19. Output matrix.

$y_1\,y_2\,y_3$	X_1	X_2	X_3
000	000	011	100
001	000	011	101
011	010	000	110
010	010	000	111
110	110	100	011
111	110	100	010
101	100	111	000
100	100	111	000

FIG. 6.20. Transition table.

We derive the Boolean expressions of the τ_i from Figure 6.18

$$\tau_1 = (X_1 + X_2)y_1 + X_3\bar{y}_1$$
$$\tau_2 = (X_1 + X_3)y_2 + X_2\bar{y}_2$$
$$\tau_3 = X_2\bar{y}_2 + X_3(y_2\bar{y}_3 + \bar{y}_1\bar{y}_2y_3).$$

Figure 6.20 shows the corresponding transition table. The relation defining the τ_i allows us to write $Y_i = y_i \oplus \tau_i$, that is,

$$Y_1 = y_1 \oplus \tau_1 = X_3\bar{y}_1 + y_1\overline{(X_1 + X_2)} = X_3$$
$$Y_2 = y_2 \oplus \tau_2 = X_2\bar{y}_2 + y_2\overline{(X_1 + X_3)} = X_2$$
$$Y_3 = y_3 \oplus \tau_3 = X_1y_3 + X_2\bar{y}_2\bar{y}_3 + X_3(y_2 + y_1y_3) + y_2y_3.$$

Notice that the relation $X_1 + X_2 + X_3 = 1$ signifies that the command takes one of the three states X_1, X_2, or X_3, the command $\bar{H}$ introduced in Section 5.3.4 is one of the X_i.

Figure 6.21 shows the corresponding excitation matrix which permits the determination of the system's flow table shown in Figure 6.22.

Figure 6.21 (or 6.22) and 6.19 give a representation of how the Figure 6.18 circuit operates.

$y_1\,y_2\,y_3$	X_1	X_2	X_3
000	000	011	100
001	001	010	100
011	001	011	101
010	000	010	101
110	000	010	101
111	001	011	101
101	001	010	101
100	000	011	100

FIG. 6.21.   Excitation matrix.

	X_1	X_2	X_3
1	1/0	3/0	8/0
2	2/1	4/1	8/1
3	2/0	3/0	7/0
4	1/1	4/1	7/1
5	1/1	4/1	7/1
6	2/1	3/1	7/1
7	2/1	4/1	7/1
8	1/0	3/0	8/0

FIG. 6.22.   Flow table.

6.2.2.2. SR flip-flop circuits

Consider the circuit in Figure 6.23. The output expression can immediately be derived:

$$z = \bar{y}_1\bar{y}_2 y_3 + y_2\bar{y}_3 + y_1 y_3.$$

It corresponds to the Figure 6.19 matrix. Again we are dealing with a Moore machine.

Figure 6.23 permits us to determine the Boolean expressions for the quantities $R_1, S_1, R_2, S_2, R_3, S$.

$$R_1 = X_1 + X_2 \qquad\qquad S_1 = X_3$$
$$R_2 = X_1 + X_3 \qquad\qquad S_2 = X_2$$
$$R_3 = \bar{y}_2(X_2 y_3 + X_3 \bar{y}_1) \qquad S_3 = X_3 y_2 + X_2 \bar{y}_2 \bar{y}_3.$$

Figure 6.25 shows the table defining the R_i and S_i. The reader can verify that Figure 6.21 is the corresponding excitation matrix and Figure 6.22 the flow table.

As an example, consider the internal state 010 and input X_2 in Figure 6.25. From the figure we have the relations

$$S_1 R_1 = 01 \qquad S_2 R_2 = 10 \qquad S_3 R_3 = 00.$$

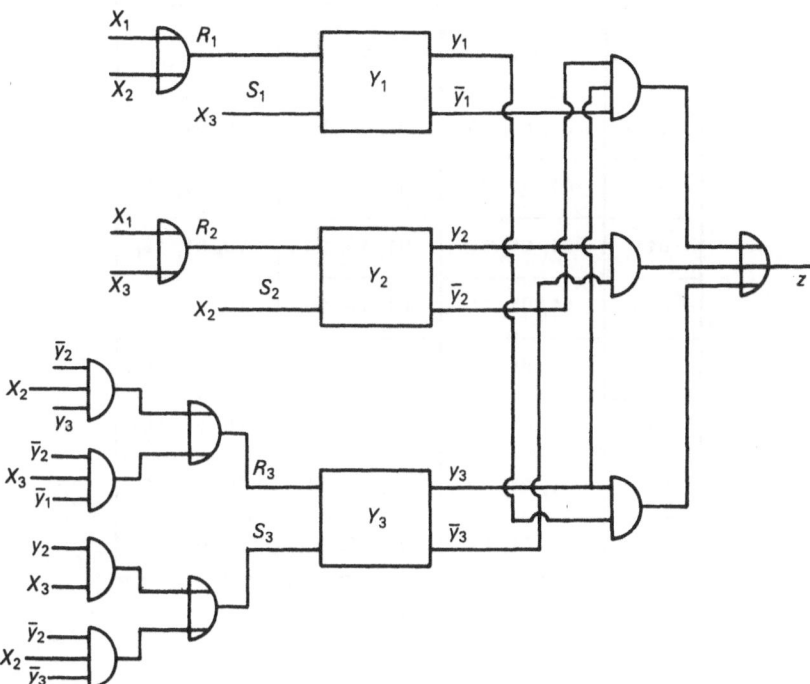

FIG. 6.23.

SR. $\diagdown$ y	00	01	10
0	0	0	1
1	1	0	1

Y

FIG. 6.24.

But, $y_1 y_2 y_3 = 010$. From the Figure 6.24 table, we find: $Y_1 = 0$, $Y_2 = 1$, $Y_3 = 0$.

The next state in the excitation matrix is therefore 010.

Comment. We have examined Moore machines in pulsed systems because machines which have a level output were considered. Since the input was a pulse, the output could not therefore depend on the input $[z_i = f_i(y_1, \ldots, y_q)]$.

$y_1\,y_2\,y_3$	X_1	X_2	X_3
000	01, 01, 00	01, 10, 10	10, 01, 01
001	01, 01, 00	01, 10, 01	10, 01, 01
011	01, 01, 00	01, 10, 00	10, 01, 10,
010	01, 01, 00	01, 10, 00	10, 01, 10
110	01, 01, 00	01, 10, 00	10, 01, 10
111	01, 01, 00	01, 10, 00	10, 01, 10
101	01, 01, 00	01, 10, 01	10, 01, 00
100	01, 01, 00	01, 10, 10	10, 01, 00

FIG. 6.25.　S_1R_1, S_2R_2, S_3R_3.

It is possible to imagine pulsed Mealy machines. The input pulses control both the flip-flops (symmetrical or SR) and the combinational systems defining the outputs.

Since flip-flop response time is not negligible, delays on the connections from input pulses to output circuits must be introduced as in Figure 6.26.

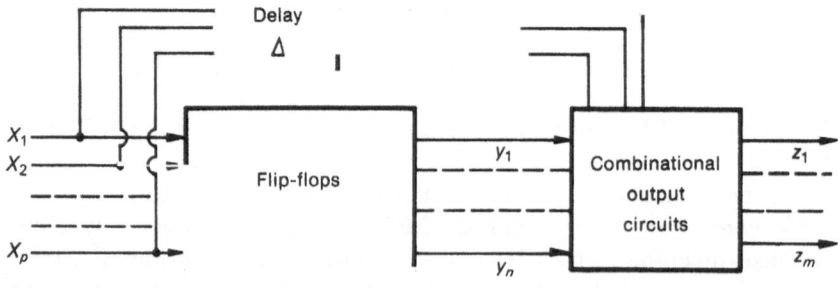

FIG. 6.26.

6.3. HAZARDS IN COMBINATIONAL AND SEQUENTIAL SYSTEMS

6.3.1. *Nature of the problem*

We studied combinational systems in Chapter 3, then introduced sequential systems. Both are combinations of switching devices which function either naturally (relays) or artificially (electronic) on two levels 0, 1. The system is sequential or combinational depending on whether the circuit contains loops.

Our analysis of such circuits was based on a fundamental hypothesis: the algebra of relay, diode, and transistor circuits is the algebra of Boole. This was shown in Chapter 3. We supposed in our discussion that the technological devices were perfect.

In all cases the only solutions envisaged were

$$(x, \bar{x}) = (0, 1) \quad \text{or} \quad (1, 0).$$

We only considered the two following cases: make-contacts closed and break-contacts open, make-contacts open and break-contacts closed. We never considered the case in which they were both closed or open; we only considered the steady state and omitted the transient phenomena.

We implicitly assumed the *relay acting time to be zero*. In the same way, we assumed the influence of the length of connection wires in diode or transistor circuits to be negligible. But, these different wires imply delays, which are of course very short when taken individually, but not negligible if considered in their entirety.

Furthermore, the signals are assumed to be perfect square waves; but they often have a certain slope, parasitic pulses, or even energy such that certain switching devices can be sensible to it and overshoot.

We have not considered the transition during the change of state of a switching device and these changes influence the transition of signals in the systems under consideration.

Under these conditions, should we seek a more complicated algebra which would take into account the reality or can binary logic be modified in a simple way to cope with the situation?

Have these transient phenomena an influence on combinational and sequential systems?

These are the questions which we shall ask ourselves in this chapter. Let us be modest and temporarily eliminate one of these questions:

a more complicated algebra can be used to take into account the transient, but we shall discuss it only in an appendix where we deal with many-valued logics (Chapter 13). In this chapter we shall successively study hazards of combinational systems then of sequential systems.

Combinational systems are characterized uniquely by the output signal value. Performance hazards will be classed in diverse categories according to the transient of this output. We shall distinguish three types of hazards:

(1) static hazards,
(2) dynamic hazards,
(3) multiple input-change hazards (race hazards).

Note that during the discussions of static and dynamic hazards, we shall study only the control modifications which cause one input variable at a time to intervene. When discussing the race hazards, we shall make modifications concerning several input variables simultaneously.

6.3.2. *Static hazards*

6.3.2.1. *Definition*

We say that a combinational system has a static hazard if for two adjacent inputs, the system's output must be constant (0 or 1) but takes a different value (1 or 0) during the transient which exists.

Suppose that the Boolean input variable a distinguishes the two adjacent inputs. The output function can be written

$$z = f(a, X).$$

X is a vector which has its components the Boolean input variables different from a.

We may also write:

$$z = af(1, X) + \bar{a}f(0, X) \tag{6.1}$$
$$z = [a + f(0, X)][\bar{a} + f(1, X)] \tag{6.2}$$

We shall study z in the (6.1) form.

Suppose that for a certain value of X, X_0

$$f(1, X_0) = 1 \qquad f(0, X_0) = 1$$

The output value, for input X_0, is written:

$$z = a + \bar{a}.$$

The necessary and sufficient condition that the output equal 0 during the transient corresponding to the change of value of a, is

$$a + \bar{a} = 0 \qquad (6.3)$$

In the same way, if $f(1, X_0) = f(0, X_0) = 0$, consideration of (6.2) gives he necessary and sufficient condition that $z = 1$ during the ti ansient:

$$a\bar{a} = 1 \qquad (6.4)$$

Relations (6.3) and (6.4) are the causes of static hazards.

6.3.2.2. *Static hazards and technology*
We shall consider three different technologies: relays or contacts, diodes, and transistors. There will really be only two classes of circuits: relay or contact circuits and electronic circuits.

Relay circuits. Consider a switch A with one make-contact a and one break-contact $\bar{a}$ (Figure 6.27). If the switch is off, the break-contact is closed and the make-contact open (position 2 is also called rest position). If the switch is on the make- and break-contacts are in reverse positions (position 1 is also called work position).

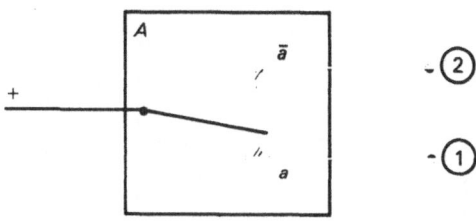

FIG. 6.27.

The action time is not zero and during a short instant there will be a transient state depending upon the armature: if the armature opens one contact before closing the other, these contacts are called break-before-make-contacts (cf. Figure 6.27) and during the transient a and $\bar{a}$ satisfy the relation:

$$a = \bar{a} = 0 \quad \text{let} \quad a + \bar{a} = 0.$$

We also say that the relay has ordinary contacts.

If the armature closes one contact before opening the other, these contacts are called make-before-break (or special) contacts (Figure 6.28) and during the transient a and $\bar{a}$ satisfy the relation:

$$a = \bar{a} = 1 \quad \text{let} \quad a\bar{a} = 1.$$

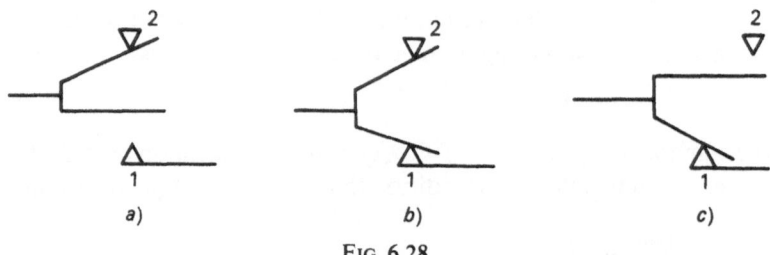

FIG. 6.28.

Notice that in the first case the relation $a\bar{a} = 0$ is true, whereas in the second it is the relation $a + \bar{a} = 1$ which is true.

Boolean algebra is therefore insufficient for a perfect description of how a relay system functions.

Electronic circuits. Transmission in diode or transistor circuits is done by signals in steps or square waves. The delays due to the fact that the propagation velocity is not infinite and the acting time of electronic circuits is much smaller than that of relays, make the waves of the two complementary signals rarely coincide; there is a time difference τ as shown in Figure 6.29.

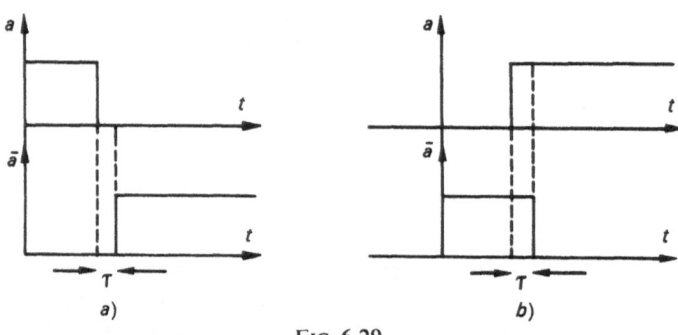

FIG. 6.29.

Suppose that the complementary signal $\bar{a}$ is derived from a (a is $\bar{a}$). In case (a) during the time τ, we have $a + \bar{a} = 0$; in case (b), we have $a\bar{a} = 1$.

Note the following property: while in relay circuits we may have either relation (6.3) or (6.4) during the transient, both cases can occur in electronic systems (whether the signal a passes from 1 to 0 or from 0 to 1). Extreme care must therefore be exercised in the realization of circuits which are static hazard free.

6.3.2.3. *Notions of cut-sets and tie-sets*

Consider the relay circuit in Figure 6.30. The output equation is written

$$z = \bar{a}c + acd + bd + a\bar{a}b.$$

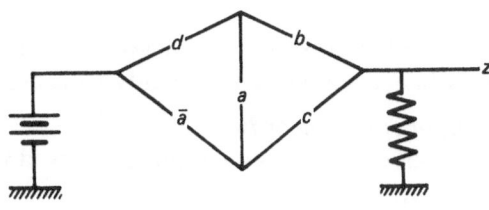

FIG. 6.30.

In a less evident way it can also be written:

$$z = (a+c+d)(\bar{a}+d)(b+c)(a+\bar{a}+b).$$

DEFINITION. We call *tie-set* a set of contacts which, if closed, make the output value 1 (*bd* for example is a tie-set); a tie-set is called unstable if it has a same variable y appearing in two forms (complemented and uncomplemented) and stable in the opposite case: *bd* is a stable tie-set and *aāb* an unstable tie-set.

DEFINITION. We call *cut-set* a set of contacts, which, if opened, make the output value 0. A cut-set is called unstable if it contains the same variable in two forms (complemented and uncomplemented), and stable in the opposite case. The second form given for z is the intersection of the functions associated with such branches; $(b+c)$ is a stable cut-set and $(a+\bar{a}+b)$ an unstable cut-set.

Other definitions can be given for these groups. In fact, if we consider the output function's disjunctive and corresponding conjunctive forms, the different terms of the disjunctive form correspond to the tie-sets and the different terms of the conjunctive form correspond to the cut-sets.

From a circuit's topological structure, we may write:

$$z = A_C B_C \cdots L_C \tag{6.5}$$
$$z = A_D + B_D + \cdots + M_D. \tag{6.6}$$

We suppose that no simplification of the form $x\bar{x} = 0$ or $x + \bar{x} = 1$ has been performed.

Let K_D be one of the terms in (6.6). If $K_D = 1$, then $z = 1$. K_D corresponds to a path which, if closed, makes the output 1. K_D is a tie-set.

Let H_C be one of the terms in (6.5). If $H_C = 0$ then $z = 0$. H_C is a set of contacts which, if opened (conductibility 0) make the output 0; it is a cut-set.

Comment. A tie-set corresponds to a grouping of the '1's' in a Karnaugh map, while a cut-set corresponds to a grouping of '0's'.

6.3.2.4. *Search for static hazards*

Every Boolean output equation of a circuit, expressed with respect to a variable a, can be written:

$$z = Aa + B\bar{a} + C + Da\bar{a} \tag{6.7}$$

or

$$z = (H + a)(K + a)L(M + a + \bar{a}) \tag{6.8}$$

We shall distinguish two types of hazards:

(1) Hazards in tie-sets correspond to relation (6.3). The output which is 1 takes the value 0 during the transient.

(2) Hazards in cut-sets correspond to relation (6.4). The output which is 0 takes the value 1 during the transient.

In both cases an output expression in the form of (6.7) or (6.8) must be envisaged.

Hazards in tie-sets. In order to have an equation in the form $z = a + \bar{a}$, we must solve either

$$A = B = 1 \qquad C = D = 0 \tag{6.9}$$

or

$$H = K = L = 1 \qquad M = 0 \tag{6.10}$$

Which system must be solved depends on whether z is expressed by (6.7) or (6.8). If (6.9) or (6.10) can be solved, the system will have hazards in the tie-sets. In the case of the Figure 6.30 circuit, we have:

$$A = cd \qquad B = c \qquad C = bd \qquad D = b.$$

System (6.9) is written:

$$cd = 1 \qquad c = 1 \qquad bd = 0 \qquad b = 0.$$

We have the solution:

$$c = d = 1 \qquad b = 0.$$

Hazards in cut-sets. In order to have an equation in the form $z = a\bar{a}$, one of the following systems, depending on whether z is of type (6.7) or (6.8), must be solved:

$$A = B = C = 0 \qquad D = 1 \tag{6.11}$$

or

$$H = K = 0 \qquad L = M = 1. \tag{6.12}$$

The system will have hazards in the cut-sets if (6.11) or (6.12) can be solved.

For the Figure 6.30 system (6.11) is written

$$cd = 0 \qquad c = 0 \qquad bd = 0 \qquad b = 1,$$

from which the solution is derived:

$$b = 1 \qquad d = 0 \qquad c = 0.$$

6.3.2.5. *Elimination of static hazards*

In contrast with the preceding problem (where a circuit risks having a static hazard), we try to see what conditions a combinational system's Boolean equations must satisfy in order that the corresponding circuit be static hazard free.

By reference to Equations (6.7) and (6.8) in the preceding section, and writing the circuit's Boolean equations in the form

$$z = Aa + B\bar{a} + C \tag{6.13a}$$
$$z = (H + a)(K + \bar{a})L, \tag{6.13b}$$

we eliminate the hazards in the cut-sets with the help of (6.13a) and in the tie-sets with the help of (6.13b).

Note that since AB in (6.13a) and $(H + K)$ in (6.13b) are the consensus (cf. Appendix 1.A.3) of aA and $\bar{a}B$ on one hand and $(H + a)$ and $(K + \bar{a})$ on the other hand, the equations

$$z = Aa + B\bar{a} + AB \tag{6.14a}$$
$$z = (H + a)(K + \bar{a})(H + K) \tag{6.14b}$$

are static hazard free.

There are no longer hazards in the tie-sets in (6.14a). In fact, if $A = 1$ and $B = 1$, the output remains 1 during the transient.

The cut-sets in (6.14b) are also hazard-free. In fact, if $H = K = 0$, the output remains 0 during the transient $(a = \bar{a} = 1)$.

The Boolean equation with respect to every Boolean variable of a static hazard free circuit is in the (6.13a) or (6.13b) form with the conditions

$$AB \leqslant C$$
$$H + K \leqslant L. \tag{6.15}$$

Two cases can occur in practice:

(1) $C \leqslant AB$ or $L \leqslant H + K$.

The equation of the static hazard free circuit is written:

$$Z = Aa + B\bar{a} + AB$$

or

$$Z = (H + a)(H + \bar{z})(H + K).$$

(2) $C > AB$ or $L > H + K$.

The equation of the static hazard free circuit is written:

$$Z = Aa + B\bar{a} + C$$
$$Z = (H + a)(K + \bar{a})L. \tag{cf. (6.13)}$$

Comment. (a) The preceding results are valid for diode, transistor and relay circuits, note that the given conditions are too restrictive for relays. In fact, if the *contacts are special*, there cannot be hazards in the tie-sets and we may write:

$$Z = Aa + B\bar{a}.$$

If ordinary contacts are used, there cannot be hazards in the cut-sets and we may write:

$$Z = (H + a)(K + \bar{a}).$$

(b) The terms Aa, $B\bar{a}$, $(H + a)$, $(K + \bar{a})$, as well as C and L, can be prime implicants of the function in order to use fewer technological components.

Example 1. Case of completely specified functions. Consider the circuit defined by the Karnaugh map in Figure 6.31 (Figure 6.32 shows the complementary function).

The prime implicants of z are:

$$\bar{a}c, \bar{a}b, b\bar{c}.$$

The minimal disjunctive form is written:

$$z = \bar{a}b + \bar{a}c + b\bar{c}.$$

ab \ cd	00	01	11	10
00	0	1	1	0
01	0	1	1	0
11	1	1	0	0
10	1	1	0	0

FIG. 6.31.

ab \ cd	00	01	11	10
00	1	0	0	1
01	1	0	0	1
11	0	0	1	1
10	0	0	1	1

FIG. 6.32.

The prime implicants of $\bar{z}$ are:

$$a\bar{b}, \bar{b}\bar{c}, ac.$$

The minimal disjunctive form of $\bar{z}$ is written:

$$\bar{z} = a\bar{b} + \bar{b}\bar{c} + ac$$

from which we have the minimal conjunctive form of z:

$$z = (\bar{a}+b)(b+c)(\bar{a}+\bar{c}).$$

Both forms of z are static hazard free because the consensus which can be formed are 0.

Example 2. Case of not entirely specified functions (functions with 'don't cares'). Consider the Boolean functions defined by the Karnaugh maps in Figure 6.33. The verification that

$$\bar{a}\bar{b}\bar{e}, \bar{a}\bar{d}\bar{e}, \bar{a}\bar{b}e, bcd, \bar{b}\bar{d}, \bar{a}bd, bde, ade$$

are the prime implicants of f is left to the reader. One of the minimal solutions is

$$z = \bar{b}\bar{d} + bcd + \bar{a}\bar{b}\bar{e} + bde + a\bar{b}e.$$

This form presents static hazard. The consensus which can be formed are ade and $\bar{a}cd\bar{e}$, where ade is a prime implicant and $\bar{a}cd\bar{e}$ is contained in the prime implicant $\bar{a}d\bar{e}$.

A reduced form, free from static hazards, is written:

$$z = \bar{b}\bar{d} + bcd + \bar{a}\bar{b}\bar{e} + bde + a\bar{b}e + ade + \bar{a}d\bar{e}.$$

ab \\ cd	00	01	11	10
00	–	0	0	1
01	1	–	0	0
11	1	1	1	0
10	1	0	0	–

$e = 0$

ab \\ cd	00	01	11	10
00	–	0	0	1
01	0	1	–	1
11	0	–	–	1
10	–	0	0	1

$e = 1$

FIG. 6.33.

At present, we seek a reduced conjunctive form which is static hazard free.

The complementary function of the given function is represented in Figure 6.34 (the theorem proven in Appendix 4 of Chapter 1 is applied). We leave the verification that

$$a\bar{b}d\bar{e}, a\bar{c}d\bar{e}, a\bar{b}c\bar{e}, acd\bar{e}, \bar{a}\bar{c}\bar{d}, \bar{a}be,$$
$$b\bar{c}\bar{e}, \bar{a}ce, b\bar{d}e, ab\bar{c}, bce, abe, \bar{a}d\bar{e}, b\bar{d}$$

are prime implicants of $\bar{z}$, to the reader.

One possible minimal form is:

$$\bar{z} = b\bar{d} + \bar{a}\bar{b}e + a\bar{c}d\bar{e} + a\bar{b}d\bar{e}.$$

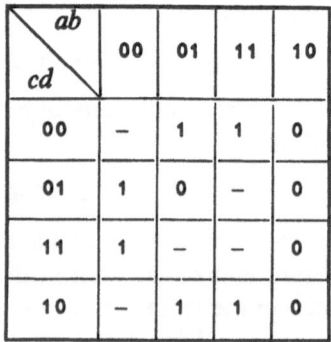

ab \\ cd	00	01	11	10
00	–	1	1	0
01	0	–	1	1
11	0	0	0	1
10	0	1	1	–

$e = 0$

ab \\ cd	00	01	11	10
00	–	1	1	0
01	1	0	–	0
11	1	–	–	0
10	–	1	1	0

$e = 1$

FIG. 6.34.

This form contains static hazards. The consensus which can be formed are $\bar{a}\bar{d}e$ and $abc\bar{e}$. But, $\bar{a}e\bar{d}$ is a prime implicant of $\bar{z}$ and $abc\bar{e}$ belongs to the prime implicant $b\bar{c}\bar{e}$. A reduced form free from static hazards is written

$$\bar{z} = b\bar{d} + \bar{a}\bar{b}e + a\bar{c}d\bar{e} + a\bar{b}d\bar{e} + \bar{a}e\bar{d} + b\bar{c}\bar{e}$$

or

$$z = (\bar{b}+d)(a+b+\bar{e})(\bar{a}+c+\bar{d}+e)(\bar{a}+b+\bar{d}+e)$$
$$(a+\bar{e}+d)(\bar{b}+c+e).$$

6.3.3. *Dynamic hazard*

6.3.3.1. *Definition.*

During our discussion of a circuit's static hazards, the case in which a relay or contact has several make-contacts and several break-contacts, was not mentioned. In fact, during switching all contacts cannot be simultaneously opened or closed. There is a slight time difference in their respective transitions. We wish to know what effect this phenomenon has on the value of the circuit's different outputs.

For this, consider the circuit in Figure 6.35. In order to characterize the different contacts of a switch, we have attributed a different index to each of them.

The circuit's Boolean output function is:

$$z = a_1 c_1 + a_1 \bar{c}_2 d + b_1 \bar{c}_2 c_1 + b_1 d + \bar{a}_2 b_2 \bar{c}_3. \tag{6.15}$$

We may immediately write the Boolean output equation for steady state. The steady state Karnaugh map is represented in Figure 6.36.

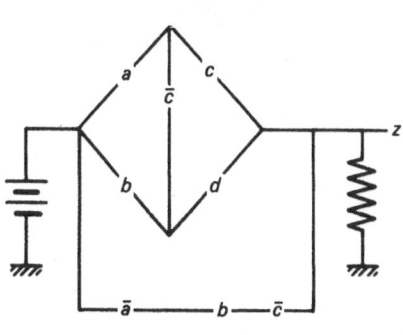

	ab			
cd	00	01	11	10
00	0	1	0	0
01	0	1	1	1
11	0	1	1	1
10	0	0	1	1

FIG. 6.35.   FIG. 6.36.

Consider the following two values of the input: $(abcd) = 0\ 1\ 1\ 0$ and $(abcd) = 0\ 1\ 0\ 0$.

We shall study the output's transient phenomena, when these two inputs are applied one after the other. We assume that the contacts $c_1 c_2 c_3$ switch in the order c_2, c_1, c_3.

We have the output equation:

$$z = c_1 c_2 + \bar{c}_3.$$

The system's transient is the following:

time 0: $\quad c_1 = 1 \quad \bar{c}_2 = 0 \quad \bar{c}_3 = 0 \quad z = 0$
time 1: $\quad c_1 = 1 \quad \bar{c}_2 = 1 \quad \bar{c}_3 = 0 \quad z = 1$
time 2: $\quad c_1 = 0 \quad \bar{c}_2 = 1 \quad \bar{c}_3 = 0 \quad z = 0$
time 3: (steady state) $\quad c_1 = 0 \quad \bar{c}_2 = 1 \quad \bar{c}_3 = 1 \quad z = 1.$

Instead of going directly from 0 to 1, the output gives the sequence 0 1 0 1. We say that the system has a *dynamic hazard*.

DEFINITION. We say that a dynamic hazard is present in a combinational system if for two adjacent inputs (the system should go from 0 to 1 or 1 to 0) there exists a very brief transient during which the output gives the sequence 0 1 0 1 or 1 0 1 0.

6.3.3.2. *Search for dynamic hazards*
We are going to consider the case in which the switch A has two contacts of the same type a_1^* and a_2^*, and a third of a different type a_3^*. In general, the output equation is written:

$$z = Aa_1^* a_2^* \bar{a}_3^* + Ba_1^* a_2^* + Ca_1^* \bar{a}_3^* + Da_2^* \bar{a}_3^* + Ea_1^* + Fa_2^* + G\bar{a}_3^* + H. \qquad (6.16)$$

The terms $A, B, ..., H$ are Boolean equations of variables other than a.

We seek the dynamic hazards, if any. By definition one of the following conditions

(1) $\qquad a = 0 \qquad z = 0$
$\qquad\qquad a = 1 \qquad z = 1$
(2) $\qquad a = 1 \qquad z = 0$
$\qquad\qquad a = 0 \qquad z = 1$

must be satisfied in steady state.
  Case 1.

$$0 = B + E + F + H \qquad G = 1.$$

The output equation is written:

$$z = Aa_1^* a_2^* \bar{a}_3^* + Ca_1^* \bar{a}_3^* + Da_2^* \bar{a}_3^* + \bar{a}_3^* = \bar{a}_3^*.$$

There is no dynamic hazard during the command transient.

Case 2. The conditions to be satisfied are:

$$0 = G = H \qquad 1 = B + E + F.$$

We study the different cases:

(a) $E = 1, B = F = 0$.

$$z = Aa_1^* a_2^* \bar{a}_3^* + Ca_1^* \bar{a}_3^* + Da_2^* \bar{a}_3^* + a_1^* = a_1^* + Da_2^* \bar{a}_3^*.$$

The interesting case is that in which $D = 1$

$$z = a_1^* + a_2^* \bar{a}_3^*.$$

If the contact a^* switches from 0 to 1 in the index order of 2.3.1 or from 1 to 0 in the index order of 1.3.2, the system presents a dynamic hazard.

(b) $F = 1, B = E = 0$.

$$z = Aa_1^* a_2^* \bar{a}_3^* + Ca_1^* \bar{a}_3^* + Da_2^* \bar{a}_3^* + a_2^* = a_2^* + Ca_1^* \bar{a}_3^*.$$

The interesting case is where $C = 1$.

If the contact a^* switches from 0 to 1 in the index order 1.3.2 or from 1 to 0 in the index order 2.3.1, the system presents a dynamic hazard.

(c) $B = 1, E = F = 0$.

$$z = Aa_1^* a_2^* \bar{a}_3^* + a_1^* a_2^* + Ca_1^* \bar{a}_3^* + Da_2^* \bar{a}_3^* =$$
$$= a_1^* a_2^* + Ca_1^* \bar{a}_3^* + Da_2^* \bar{a}_3^*.$$

(1) $C = 0, D = 0$. There is no dynamic hazard.

(2) $C = 1, D = 0$.

$$z = a_1^* a_2^* + a_1^* \bar{a}_3^*.$$

The reader can verify that the conclusions are the same as for (b).

(3) $C = 0, D = 1$.

$$z = a_1^* a_2^* + a_2^* \bar{a}_3^*.$$

The reader can verify that the conclusions are the same as for (a).

(4) $C = 1, D = 1$.

$$Z = a_1^* a_2^* + a_1^* \bar{a}_3^* + a_2^* \bar{a}_3^*.$$

This case superposes cases (c.2) and (c.3).

(5) $B = F = 1$ or $E = F = 1$. The reader can verify that a dynamic hazard cannot exist. In conclusion, there will be a dynamic hazard if the output equation can be written in one of the (6.17) forms:

$$z = a_1^* + a_2^* \bar{a}_3^*$$
$$z = a_2^* + a_1^* \bar{a}_3^*$$
$$z = a_1^* a_2^* + a_1^* \bar{a}_3^*$$
$$z = a_1^* a_2^* + a_1^* \bar{a}_3^* + a_2^* \bar{a}_3^* \tag{6.17}$$

and if the contacts $a_1^*, a_2^*, \bar{a}_3^*$ switch in a determined order. Note that, in general, the switching order of the contacts is uncertain and consequently, even with the preceding conditions, dynamic hazards are not necessarily present. The systems of Boolean Equations (6.18) must also be satisfied:

$$G = H = 0 \begin{cases} D = E = 1 & F = 0 \\ C = F = 1 & B = E = 0 \\ B = 1 & \begin{cases} C = 1 & D = 0 \\ C = 0 & D = 1 \end{cases} \\ E = F = 0 & \begin{cases} C = 1 & D = 1. \end{cases} \end{cases} \tag{6.18}$$

The reader can show that if the output function is expressed in a conjunctive form, there is the possibility of a dynamic hazard if the output equation can be brought to one of the (6.19) forms

$$z = a_1^* (a_2^* + \bar{a}_3^*)$$
$$z = a_2^* (a_1^* + \bar{a}_3^*)$$
$$z = (a_1^* + a_2^*)(a_2^* + \bar{a}_3^*)$$
$$z = (a_1^* + a_2^*)(a_1^* + \bar{a}_3^*)$$
$$z = (a_1^* + a_2^*)(a_1^* + \bar{a}_3^*)(a_2^* + \bar{a}_3^*). \tag{6.19}$$

Example. Reconsider the circuits of Figure 6.35.

$$A = 0 \quad B = 0 \quad C = b \quad D = 0 \quad E = ad \quad F = ab \quad G = a \quad H = bd.$$

From (6.18) the possible case of dynamic hazards corresponds to the system:

$$a = bd = 0 \quad b = \bar{a}b = 1 \quad ad = 0 \quad \text{hence} \quad d = 0.$$

There is one dynamic hazard possible.

6.3.3.3. *Dynamic hazard and technology*

In transistor circuits, if a variable is used more than twice in its normal and complemented form, the different delays prevent synchronization of the different signals which can cause a dynamic hazard.

There are two types of relays with two contacts: ordinary contact relays and special contact relays. The reader can verify that a static hazard corresponds to an order in the opening or closing of these contacts.

If the relays have three contacts, two of one type and one of the other, we cannot speak of ordinary or special contact relays. There can be dynamic hazards depending on the circuit's topology and the switching order of the different contacts.

6.3.3.4. *Elimination of dynamic hazards*

A circuit will be dynamic hazard free if at the point of operation under consideration, the output expression is not in the form of either (6.17) or (6.19).

THEOREM.   Every circuit having equations (with respect to each variable) which can be put in the form of (6.11) and (6.12) (taking (6.15) into account) is static and dynamic hazard-free.

The output equation of the circuit can be written:

$$z = Ea_1^* + F\bar{a}_2^* + H \qquad H \geqslant EF \qquad (6.20)$$

or

$$z = (K + a_1^*)(L + a_2^*)M \qquad M \geqslant KL. \qquad (6.21)$$

According to Section 6.3.2.5 the circuit is static hazard-free. Moreover, according to Section 6.3.2.2 it is dynamic hazard-free.

Comment. Dynamic hazards occur, if the contacts under consideration switch in a certain order. Another solution for the removal of this type of hazard is to impose conditions on the switching order. By mechanical means, the closing or opening of contacts in a certain order can in fact be realized. It is easy to see the order necessary for the elimination of the hazard. Note that in the majority of cases, we shall avoid this difficult process.

Figures 6.37(a) and (b) represent two contacts opening and closing in the order x_1, x_2. Whenever the armature A moves in the direction of the arrow, x_1 opens (case (a)) followed by x_2, or they close (case (b)).

6.3.4. *Multiple input change hazards*

We shall not study the case in which switches and relays have more

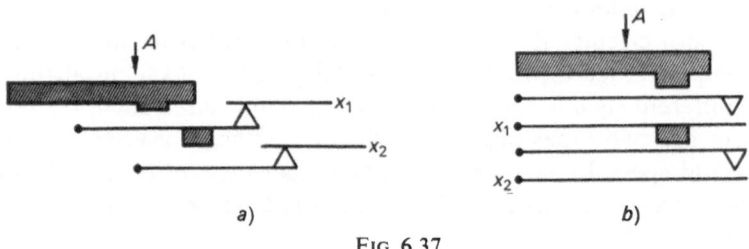

FIG. 6.37.

than three contacts of different types. The reader interested in this problem is requested to consult Moisil [15].

6.3.4.1. *Definition*

Consider the circuit defined by the Karnaugh map in Figure 6.33. It has been shown that

$$z = \bar{b}\bar{d} + bcd + \bar{a}\bar{b}\bar{e} + bde + a\bar{b}e + ade + \bar{a}d\bar{e}$$

was a static hazard-free solution. The corresponding Karnaugh map is shown in Figure 6.38. Note that $\bar{a}bd$ is the only prime implicant which

ab $\diagdown$ cd	00	01	11	10
00	1	0	0	1
01	1	1	0	0
11	1	1	1	0
10	1	0	0	1

$e = 0$

ab $\diagdown$ cd	00	01	11	10
00	1	0	0	1
01	0	1	1	1
11	0	1	1	1
10	1	0	0	1

$e = 1$

FIG. 6.38.

has not been used. If inputs $(abcde) = 0\ 1\ 0\ 1\ 0$, then $0\ 1\ 1\ 1\ 1$ are successively applied, the variables abd respectively keep the values $0, 1, 1$. The output expression is:

$$z = c + (e + \bar{e}).$$

Consequently, when c and e simultaneously go from 0 to 1, the output

z can take the value 0 during the transient. We say that the system has a multiple input change hazard or hazard (by analogy with sequential systems).

DEFINITION. If a combinational system is such that the output keeps the same value whenever at least two variables change value for the input in steady state, but not during the transient, we say that the system has a race hazard. (It is actually an extension of the static hazard.)

6.3.4.2. *Elimination of the race hazard*

In the preceding example, if the redundant term $\bar{a}bd$ had been added to the expression for the output, the function z would have remained equal to 1 during the transient. There would not have been a race hazard.

THEOREM. The necessary and sufficient condition that a circuit be free from race hazards is that its output be expressed in the form of a Boolean sum of all its disjunctive prime implicants or a Boolean product of all its conjunctive prime implicants.

In fact, let us study a circuit's transient which results from the instantaneous modification of k input variables $a_1, ..., a_k$. The state of the other input variables is $b_{k+1}^*, b_{k+2}^*, ..., b_n^*$. We assume that there are no static hazards; i.e. for the 2^{n-k} points $b_{k+1}^*, ..., b_n^*$ the function takes the value 1. The output z is a function of $a_1, \bar{a}_1, a_2, \bar{a}_2, ..., a_k, \bar{a}_k$. During the transient we can have the relations: $a_1 = \bar{a}_1 = a_2 = \bar{a}_2 = a_3 = \bar{a}_3 = \cdots = a_k = \bar{a}_k = 0$. If the term $b_{k+1}^*, ..., b_n^*$ is not contained in the expression for the output, z will become 0 during the transient. This term is either a prime implicant or is contained in a prime implicant which must figure in the expression for z.

Reciprocally, if z is the sum of all the prime implicants, there exists one which contains $b_{k+1}^*, ..., b_n^*$ or is equal to this term. In the same way, the dual result relative to the conjunctive form of z, can be proven by means of the complementary function.

6.3.5. *Superposition of static and dynamic hazards*

6.3.5.1. *Analysis*

In order to correctly analyze a combinational system, the circuit's steady state must first be studied in terms of classical Boolean algebra (cf. Sections 3.4.1 and 3.5.1). The system's truth table giving the different outputs for each input is thus obtained. To analyze the possibility of hazards, the circuit's Boolean equations are written in a different way: an index is associated with each contact of a relay or switch; the same as an index $(a_1, a_2, a_3, \dots)$ is associated with each input corresponding to a same variable (a or $\bar{a}$) in an electronic system. We shall therefore seek the Boolean output equations without applying the simplification rules of Boolean algebra.

$$(a_j \bar{a}_j \neq 0, \qquad a_i + \bar{a}_i \neq 1).$$

Consider the circuits in Figures 6.39 and 6.40. In steady state we may write:

$$z_1 = ad + a\bar{b} + cd = \bar{z}_3$$
$$z_2 = a + cd + cb = \bar{z}_4.$$

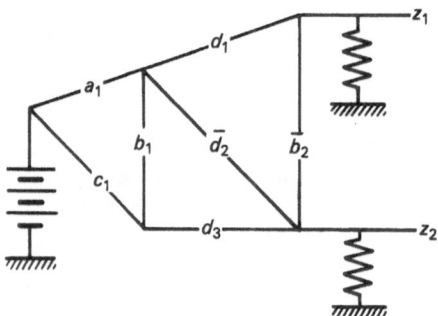

FIG. 6.39.

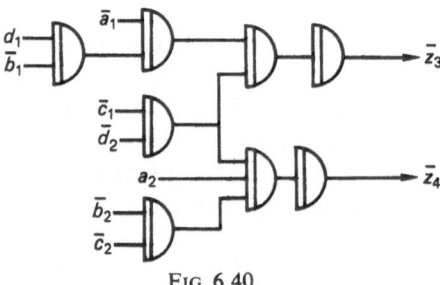

FIG. 6.40.

In order to study the transient we are obliged to give indices to the different forms of the same Boolean variables as in Figures 6.39 and 6.40.

For the circuit of Figure 6.39 the transient equations are written:

$$z_1 = a_1(d_1 + \bar{b}_2 d_2 + b_1 \bar{b}_2 d_3) + c_1(b_1 d_1 + d_3 \bar{b}_2) \qquad (6.22)$$

$$z_2 = a_1(\bar{d}_1 \bar{b}_2 + \bar{d}_2 + b_1 d_3) + c_1(d_3 + b_1 \bar{d}_2 + b_1 d_1 \bar{b}_2) \qquad (6.23)$$

For the circuit of Figure 6.10 the transient equations are written:

$$\bar{z}_3 = a_1(\bar{b}_1 + d_1) + c_1 d_2$$
$$\bar{z}_4 = a_2 + c_1 d_2 + b_2 c_2. \qquad (6.24)$$

The circuit of Figure 6.40 has neither static nor dynamic hazards (cf. Equations (6.24)). The static and dynamic hazards can be obtained from Equations (6.23); we suggest that the reader solve this problem as an exercise.

6.3.5.2. Synthesis

It is possible to cancel the static and dynamic hazards in the different output equations. This brings out the problem of circuit realization. If the different functions $z_1, z_2, \ldots, z_m$ are separately realized, there will be no risk, but in general the number of switching elements for circuit representation will be minimized (by one of the methods discussed in Chapter 3). It will be necessary to be sure that the circuit obtained is hazard-free. *There is a compromise to be made between minimization and hazard suppression.*

6.4. HAZARDS IN ASYNCHRONOUS SEQUENTIAL SYSTEMS

We shall now study the effects of operating hazards, already considered, in sequential systems. At the same time we shall see if other types of hazards, specific to these systems, exist.

6.4.1. Change-over hazards in sequential systems

This type of hazard corresponds to the transient of a Boolean variable:

$a, \bar{a} = 0, 0$ for any ordinary contact.

$a, \bar{a} = 1, 1$ for any special contact.

In a combinational system a change-over hazard modified only the circuit's transient without changing its steady state. It is the same for a sequential system if the change-over hazard concerns only the part beneath the feedback branches (part B in Figure 6.41). We know how to remove the possible change-over hazard.

If the hazard concerns the part containing the feedback branches

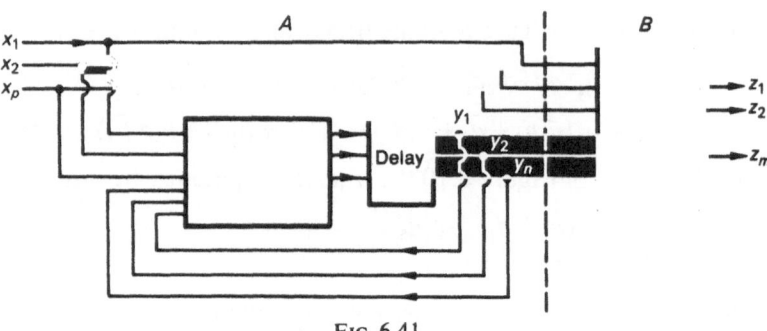

FIG. 6.41.

(part A in Figure 6.41) the Y_i will be modified and therefore the transition can differ from what it should be. This is our subject of study.

In electronic systems we can indifferently have the conditions $a\bar{a} = 1$ or $a + \bar{a} = 0$ in the same circuit.

In a relay system we have come across one or the other of these relations depending on whether we were dealing with ordinary or special contacts – but never both. We are thus led to separately study relay and electronic systems.

6.4.1.1. *Relay systems*

Notice that in relay systems the dynamic operating hazards, as defined in Section 6.3.3, present no inconveniences. The relay's inductance coil works as a filter diminishing the signal's rebound. We shall only study the hazards having the same origin as static hazards in combinational systems: they are called change-over hazards and we shall study two possible cases relative to secondary variables or primary variables.

(a) *Transient of ordinary or special contact relays supplied in series*. Suppose that a switch or relay with make- and break-contacts a and $\bar{a}$ supplies the coil X in series. This situation corresponds to the configurations in Figure 6.42.

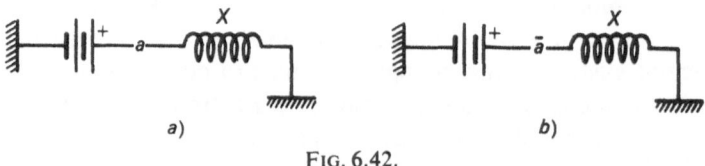

FIG. 6.42.

The corresponding Boolean equations are written:

$$X = a \quad \text{or} \quad X = \bar{a}.$$

During transient of the control switch or relay, the variables a and $\bar{a}$ satisfy the condition:

$a = \bar{a} = 0$ if a and $\bar{a}$ are ordinary contacts (break before make transfer contacts)

$a = \bar{a} = 1$ if a and $\bar{a}$ are special contacts (make before break).

The following conclusion can therefore be drawn: *a relay can never be closed during the transient of ordinary contacts and can never be released during the transient of special contacts if the supply is in series.*

We shall consider only relays supplied in series in that which follows.

(b) *Change-over hazards on secondary variables.* Consider a sequential system having its X relay excitation equation in the form:

$$X = Az + B\bar{z} \quad \text{if } z \text{ and } \bar{z} \text{ are ordinary contacts,}$$
$$X = (A + \bar{z})(B + z) \quad \text{if } z \text{ and } \bar{z} \text{ are special contacts,}$$

Z itself being a secondary relay.

In the first case, at the point of functioning $A = B = 1$, if the relay Z switches, the excitation of the X relay becomes 0 although it should remain 1.

In the second case, at the point of functioning $A = B = 0$, if the Z relay switches, the X relay excitation takes the value 1 although it should remain 0.

The signals 0 or 1 being brief (acting time of a secondary relay), the X coil will generally filter them and prevent any possible hazard in the circuit.

However, we shall show by taking the X excitation equation (cf. Section 6.3.2.5):

$$X = Az + B\bar{z} + AB = (A + \bar{z})(B + \bar{z}),$$

that, if the contacts z and $\bar{z}$ are ordinary, all possible risk of hazards is eliminated.

Suppose that the system (shown in Figure 6.43) goes from state $xyz = 101$ to state $xyz = 100$ when a goes from 0 to 1.

Z takes the value 0 instantaneously and the system reaches the

xyz $\diagdown$ a	0	1
101	(101)	100
10t		100
100		(100)

FIG. 6.43.

state 100. The presence of the term AB keeps the X relay excitation value at 1 (during the t transient of z) which prevents all hazards.

The absence of this term would imply that the excitation of X takes a 0 value therefore that the system reaches the state 0 0 0 which, if it were stable, would correspond to a hazard in the system.

In the same way it can be shown that all possible hazards are eliminated in the case in which z and $\bar{z}$ are special contacts if the X excitation equation (cf. Section 6.3.2.5) is taken as:

$$X = (A + \bar{z})(B + z)(A + B) = Az + B\bar{z}.$$

Thus, we eliminate sequential change-over hazards by eliminating static change-over hazards.

(c) *Switching hazards on primary variables.* Consider the passage of the system from an internal state M to an internal state N when the input a goes from 0 to 1. The excitation matrix is composed of two columns $a\bar{a} = 01$ and $a\bar{a} = 10$. By adding two columns corresponding to $a\bar{a} = 00$ and $a\bar{a} = 11$, the transient during the input change can be studied. The system's equations define, for $a\bar{a} = 00$ or 11 the next internal state of one of the system's states. For this, consider the circuit which has its excitation matrix represented in Figure 6.44(a).

By analogy with the case of change-over secondary variables, we consider

$$X = aA + \bar{a}B + AB$$

as the system's equation, where a is a primary variable and A and B polynomials of other variables. We shall see if hazards still occur. we have:

$$X = x\bar{y} + \bar{a}x + x\bar{z} + a\bar{y}z + \bar{a}yz$$
$$Y = a\bar{z} + ay + xy + y\bar{z}$$
$$Z = az + \bar{x}z + yz + \bar{a}xy.$$

xyz \ a	0	1
000	(000)	010
001	(001)	101
011	001	(011)
010	110	(010)
110	111	(110)
111	(111)	011
101	100	(101)
100	(100)	110

FIG. 6.44(a).

xyz \ aā	00	01	11	10
000	(000)	(000)	010	010
001	(001)	(001)	(101)	101
011	001	001	(011)	(011)
010	(010)	110	110	(010)
110	(110)	111	111	(110)
111	011	(111)	(111)	011
101	100	100	(101)	(101)
100	(100)	(100)	110	110

FIG. 6.44(b).

From these equations, an extension of the circuit's excitation matrix, which takes into account the input's transient, can be realized (Figure 6.44b). We study this matrix.

Case of aā ordinary contacts. If it is in state 000 ($a = 0$) and an input $a = 1$ is applied, the system remains in this state during the transient (column 00) and goes into state 010 at the end of the operation ($a = 1$).

The only difficulty occurs when the system is in the total state ($xyz = 0111$). If, in fact, we go to $a = 1$, the system can during transient ($a\bar{a} = 00$) attain 001 where it remains.

At the end of the input's transient the system goes to 101 instead of 011, where we wish it to be.

Case of aā special contacts. A hazard can equally appear, if starting from the total state ($xyz = 0100$), the input $a = 1$ is applied: the system can attain 011 after passing 110, 111, 011 instead of reaching 110 as we wish.

These two types of hazards are due to the input's acting time. In the light of this two categories of systems will be distinguished.

(d) *Normal input control systems.* As in the case of hazards on secondary variables, the relay's coil can prevent eventual hazards because the signals 0 or 1 (during the transient of the relay) are pulses.

In the opposite case, we shall consider an ordinary contact circuit having the X relay equation in the form:

$$X = Ha + K\bar{a},$$

where H and K are Boolean functions of the circuit's other variables and $(a, \bar{a})$ the A switch's make- and break-contacts. Suppose (Figure 6.45) that if the input goes from 0 to 1 the system goes from state $xyz = 101$ to state $xyz = 100$.

xyz \ $a\bar{a}$	01	00	10
101	(101)	100	100
100			(100)

FIG. 6.45.

We shall show that if the X excitation equation is (cf. Section 6.3.2.5)

$$X = Ha + K\bar{a} + HK = (H + \bar{a})(K + a),$$

the system does not have hazards.

First suppose that the X equation does not contain HK. During A's switching $(a = \bar{a} = 0)$ the Z relay is released (Section 6.4.1.1) as well as the X relay. The system passes state 000, which, if it is stable for $a = 1$, corresponds to a hazard.

If the X equation is corrected by adding the redundant term HK, during the switching of A, X remains closed and Z releases. The system reaches state $xyz = 100$. It can evolve further by itself because, by hypothesis, the acting times of the different technological devices of the circuit are equal. The system therefore remains in state 100 at the end of the A transient. There are no hazards.

In the same way, it can be shown that if the A contacts are special, all risks of hazards due to a relay X having its excitation equation written:

$$X = (H + \bar{a})(K + a)(H + K) = Ha + K\bar{a},$$

are eliminated.

(e) *Slow input switching systems (Joanin method)*. This is the case of ordinary contact relays in which the coil's excitation current can reach several amperes under 110 or 220 volt.

Gavrilov representation. This representation of relay system's behaviour is analogous to the sequence chart (Section 5.A.1).

Consider the relay system in Figure 6.44(a). We draw a table in which each row corresponds to a variable. Suppose that the system is initially at rest $(a = x = y = z = 0)$. This corresponds to the state $\bar{a}$, $\bar{x}$, $\bar{y}$, $\bar{z}$ of the different variables. If we let $a = 1$ in the excitation matrix, the system evolves to the state 010. In the Gavrilov representation the different phases of this action are shown (phases 1 and 2): the system starts from the total state $\bar{a}\bar{x}\bar{y}\bar{z}$, passes the total state $a\bar{x}\bar{y}\bar{z}$ (the system has not yet had the time to evolve) arriving at the total state $a\bar{x}y\bar{z}$ (Figure 6.46). The problem is to compute the expressions X, Y, Z from this representation. By comparison with the matrix in Figure 6.44(a), we see that $Z = 1$ for phases 4, 5, 6, 7, 8, 9, 10, 11 of the Gavrilov table.

	1	2	3	4	5	6	7	8	9	10	11	12	13	14	15
$\bar{a}$	a		$\bar{a}$			a		$\bar{a}$	a			$\bar{a}$		a	
$\bar{x}$				x			$\bar{x}$				x				
$\bar{y}$		y							$\bar{y}$						y
$\bar{z}$					z								$\bar{z}$		

FIG. 6.46.

If we consider the phases before the appearance of $x(n_a)$ and before its disappearance (n_d), the set of phases n_a, $(n_a + 1), \ldots, (n_d - 1)$ defines the corresponding relay excitation. We may write:

$$X = \bar{a}xy\bar{z} + \bar{a}xyz + axyz + a\bar{x}yz + \bar{a}\bar{x}yz + \bar{a}\bar{x}\bar{y}z + a\bar{x}\bar{y}z + ax\bar{y}z.$$

Causes of hazards. We assume that the static operating hazards have been eliminated and that the input change had modified the excitation state of the coil X. We seek what repercussion this has on the system's other coil Y.

From the preceding comment relative to ordinary relay transition $X = 0$ during the corresponding transient whenever the input changes value.

If Y was zero at the start, no modification is brought about by the transition. Suppose that Y was initially 1. In order that it keeps this value during transition, it is necessary that $\bar{x}y$ be in the Boolean expression of Y. We must therefore study the case in which the input change (a^* represents a or $\bar{a}$) excites the X relay, then the opposite case in which the input change unexcites it (Figures 6.47a and b).

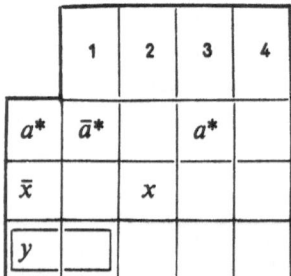 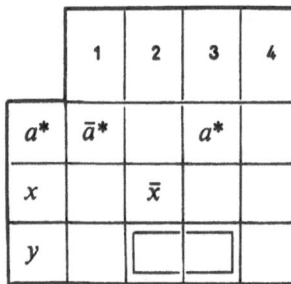

FIG. 6.47(a).   FIG. 6.47(b).

In the case of Figure 6.47(a) (X operated) there are no hazards because Y contains the term $\bar{x}y$ (marked in heavy lines in the figure). In the case of Figure 6.47(b) (X released) there are no hazards if the cell of row Y only has $\bar{y}$ in phase 4. Both cases of hazards are represented in Figures 6.48(a) and (b).

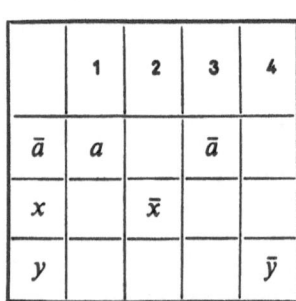

FIG. 6.48(a).   FIG. 6.48(b).

Example. Consider the table in Figure 6.46. Figure 6.49 represents phases 6, 7, 8, 9. The configuration in Figure 6.49 relative to Y and Z is that of Figure 6.48(b). There is a risk of a hazard.

	6	7	8	9
	$\bar{a}$	a		$\bar{a}$	
	x		$\bar{x}$		
	y				$\bar{y}$
	z				

FIG. 6.49.

Elimination of the hazards. (1) A simple method is to introduce a supplementary relay in such a way that Figures 6.48(a) and (b) are no longer obtained. A relay T can therefore be used so that $\bar{y}$ in phase 4 of Figures 6.47(a) and (b) is replaced by the release or locking of z (Figures 6.50a and b).

X can also be unexcited by locking the auxiliary relay T (Figures 6.51a and b). In this last case, the excitation of T occurs only at the end of the transient. During the release of X transient due to the input is no longer to be feared.

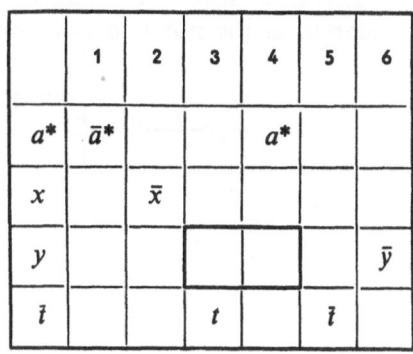

	1	2	3	4	5	6
a^*	$\bar{a}^*$		a^*			
x		$\bar{x}$				
y					$\bar{y}$	
$\bar{t}$				t		$\bar{t}$

FIG. 6.50(a).

	1	2	3	4	5	6
a^*	$\bar{a}^*$			a^*		
x		$\bar{x}$				
y						$\bar{y}$
$\bar{t}$			t		$\bar{t}$	

FIG. 6.50(b).

	1	2	3	4	5	6
a^*	$\bar{a}^*$			a^*		
x			$\bar{x}$			
y					$\bar{y}$	
t		t				$\bar{t}$

FIG. 6.51(a).

	1	2	3	4	5	6
a^*	$\bar{a}^*$			a^*		
x			$\bar{x}$			
y						$\bar{y}$
$\bar{t}$		t			$\bar{t}$	

FIG. 6.51(b).

Another solution would be to use a timed relay for X which would be locked only at the end of the transient.

(2) Since the existence of two different types of contacts in the excitation equations of the relays are the origin of the hazards, it seems logical to make only one form of the variable which corresponds to a series-parallel supply of the relay coil appear in the excitations' equations.

Suppose the excitation equation of an Y relay can be written:

$$Y = (ax\bar{z} + xy\bar{z})(\bar{a} + \bar{x}z + xy)$$
$$= x\bar{z}(a+y) \cdot (a(x+\bar{z})(\bar{x}+\bar{y})),$$

which corresponds to Figure 6.52.

However, if the two make-contacts a_1 and a_2 of switch A are considered, at the point of functioning $x = 1$, $y = z = 0$, the excitation

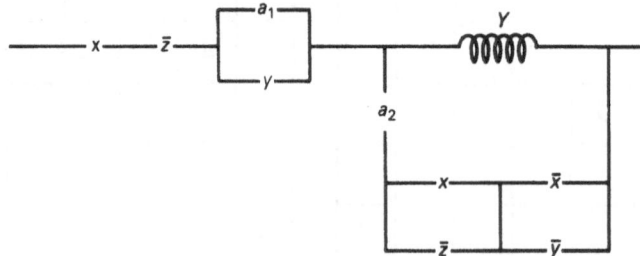

FIG. 6.52.

equation of the relay becomes:

$$Y = a_1 \bar{a}_2.$$

The make-contacts a_1 and a_2 cannot simultaneously close. Therefore if a_1 closes before a_2 when a goes from 0 to 1, there is a hazard. Thus a_2 must close before a_1 in order to avoid this hazard.

Note, however, that introduction of a resistance in the principal branch (to limit the current in the deviation branch) weakens the current running through the Y bobin and can prevent the relay from switching. The advantage of this method is that the current in the deviation branch of the X coil can therefore be limited without adding supplementary relays.

Note. (1) Consider an ordinary contact circuit and let us study the case of Figure 6.53 where a switch A controls three relays X, Y, Z.

We seek the conditions for Z not to open during the transient from phase 1 to phase 2.

1	2	3	4	5	6	7
a^*	$\overline{a^*}$		a^*		$\overline{a^*}$	
x		$\bar{x}$				
y				$\bar{y}$		
z				▨	▨	

FIG. 6.53.

Relays X and Y are opened during the transient. The Z expression should have $\bar{x}\bar{y}z$ (phases 5 and 6). Z must therefore not be opened during phase 7. This result can easily be generalized.

(2) The preceding results can be extended by duality to the case of a special contact circuit. A hazard will be caused by the inopportune excitation of a relay.

Note that there cannot be a hazard in the Y relay excitation in the case of Figure 6.54 during the transition from phase 1 to 2. For this we study the $\bar{Y}$ function.

We may write:

$$\bar{Y} = x\bar{y} + \bar{a}^*\bar{x}\bar{y}.$$

1	2	3	4	5
a^*	$\bar{a}^*$		a^*	
x		$\bar{x}$		
$\bar{y}$				y

FIG. 6.54.

During the transient period from phase 1 to 2. X is excited. Therefore, $\bar{Y}$ has a 1 value. During phase 2, $\bar{a}$ has a 1 value as well as $\bar{x}$ and $\bar{Y}$ keeps a 1 value. Therefore the Y relay remains unexcited. Both cases of hazards correspond to Figures 6.55(a) and (b).

1	2	3	4	5
a	$\bar{a}$		a	
$\bar{x}$		x		
$\bar{y}$				y

FIG. 6.55(a).

1	2	3	4	5
$\bar{a}$	a		$\bar{a}$	
$\bar{x}$		x		
$\bar{y}$				y

FIG. 6.55(b).

In fact, $\bar{Y}$ does not contain the term $x\bar{y}$ and during the transient from phases 1 to 2, $\bar{Y}$ has a 0 value: Y is inopportunely excited.

To eliminate these hazards, it is sufficient to introduce supplementary relays in a way which avoids the sequences in Figures 6.55(a) and (b).

(f) *General discussion*. The proposed methods permit the elimination of switching hazards in relay systems whenever the Boolean equations of the Y_i are independently considered. For the definitive realization of the system, a minimisation of the number of elements is generally performed. This can lead to new switching hazards in combinational systems.

Here again, there must be a compromise between minimisation and hazards. Generally, switching hazards of a given system are studied by attributing a different index to each contact of a same relay.

Consider the following equations of a circuit:

$$X = axy + b, \qquad Y = axy + \bar{b}.$$

If the input has a normal commutation, we must realize X and Y separately. In order to study the transient we need the equations:

$$X = b_1 + axy\bar{b}_2 + \bar{b}_2 b_3 b_4$$
$$Y = \bar{b}_4 + axy b_3 + b_1 \bar{b}_2 b_3$$

corresponding to the circuit of Figure 6.56.

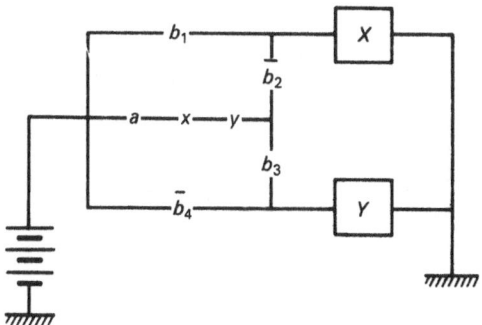

FIG. 6.56.

If the B switch is equipped with ordinary contacts, the tie-sets will have static hazards; if it is equipped with special contacts, the cut-sets will have a hazard which can be eliminated by imposing the order of closing or opening of the contacts as precedingly described. But this method is a bit too theoretical.

In conclusion, the first condition to be realized for the elimination of a relay system's switching hazards, is the suppression of all hazard risks in the Y_i equations and to be sure that hazards are not created in the circuit realization. Note that change-over hazards are the only hazards in sequential relay systems.

6.4.1.2. *Electronic systems*

In these systems hazards can appear in tie-sets $(a + \bar{a} = 0)$ as well as cut-sets $(a\bar{a} = 1)$. The acting time of the inputs is about the same as the internal variables. The process for these systems is the same as for normal command relay systems by defining the secondary variables by equations of the form:

$$Y = aA + \bar{a}B + AB$$

or

$$Y = (a+B)(\bar{a}+A)(A+B).$$

6.4.2. *Propagation hazards in electronic systems*

A sequential system can be represented as in Figure 6.57, where the different blocks $A_1, \dots, A_n$ generate the Boolean quantities $Y_1, \dots, Y_n$. We have not represented the combinational portion relative to the output circuits.

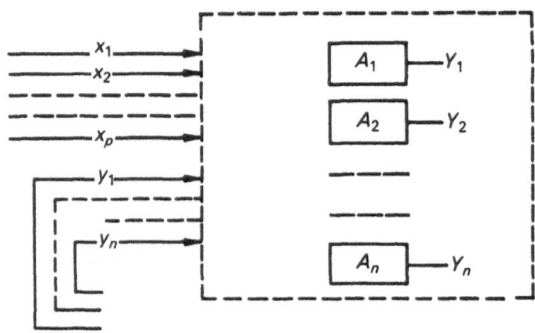

FIG. 6.57.

Suppose that the change-over hazards have been eliminated, i.e., the different forms of an input variable attacking a block A_i are synchronized.

We shall now study another possible cause for the malfunctioning of electronic sequential systems. If an input signal is imposed on two blocks A_i and A_j, there can be a time difference from one block to the other. We seek what influence this phenomenon has on the system's exterior transition.

Consider the sequential system which has its equations written:

$$\begin{aligned}
Y_1 &= \bar{b}y_1 + by_3(y_1 + \bar{y}_2) \\
Y_2 &= y_2 + by_1y_3 + \bar{b}(y_1\bar{y}_3 + \bar{y}_1y_3) \\
Y_3 &= \bar{y}_1\bar{y}_2y_3 + b(\bar{y}_1 + y_3).
\end{aligned} \qquad (6.25)$$

This system's excitation matrix is shown in Figure 6.58.

6.4.2.1. *Analysis of a sequential system by means of graphs*

Suppose that the system is initially in the total state $by_1y_2y_3 = 0000$. Let input b equal 1. The signal b is transmitted to three blocks $A_1A_2A_3$

b $y_1 y_2 y_3$	0	1
000	(000)	001
001	011	101
011	010	(011)
010	(010)	011
110	(110)	010
111	110	(111)
101	100	111
100	110	000

FIG. 6.58.

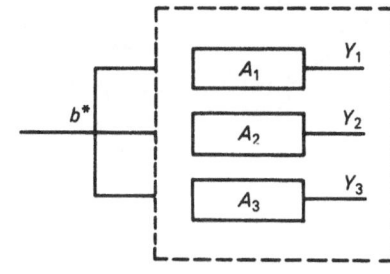

FIG. 6.59.

as in Figure 6.59. If it is transmitted instantaneously to blocks A_1 and A_2, Y_1 and Y_2 do not change and the system remains in the internal state 000 until A_3 reacts.

If the signal b instantaneously attains A_3, the system reaches the internal state 001: suppose that $b = 1$ has not yet reached blocks A_1 and A_2; to study the system's transition the excitation matrix in Figure 6.58 is used. We examine Y_1 and Y_2 in the $b = 0$ column and Y_3 in the $b = 1$ column.

Two cases can occur.

(1) Either $b = 1$ reaches A_2 before the system has had time to evolve by itself from the internal state 001. In this case Y_2 remains 0 but (Figure 6.53) Y_1 in column $b = 0$, Y_2 and Y_3 in column $b = 1$ must be considered to determine future transition.

(2) Or, $b = 1$ has not yet arrived at either A_1 or A_2. The system evolves by itself toward 011 because Y_2 takes the value 1.

In order to represent all possible transitions of the system we draw a graph as in Figure 6.60. For each of the graph's branches the block reached by the input to generate this transition is indicated; if nothing is indicated, the transition is done automatically (on the graph $y_1 y_2 y_3$ replace $A_1 A_2 A_3$).

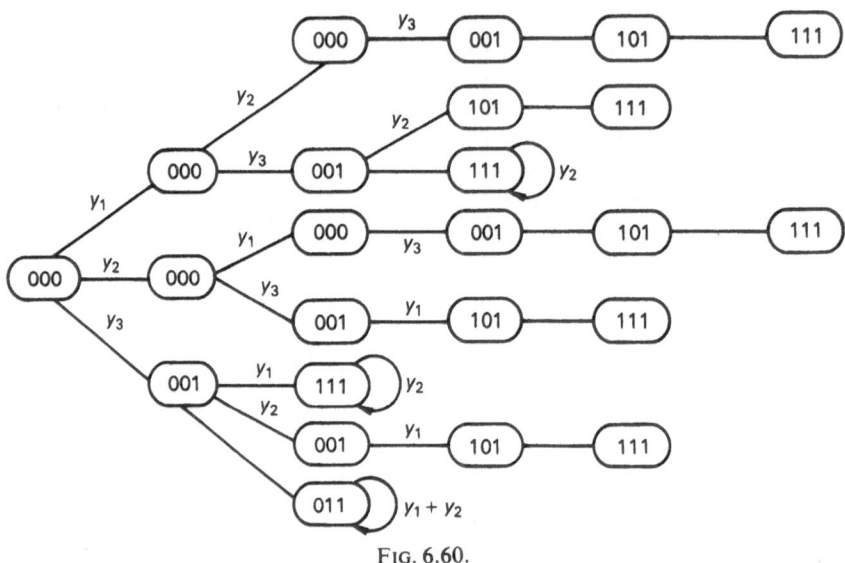

FIG. 6.60.

Comment. This discussion supposed that the only possible delay concerned the input. An identical propagation delay for the signal Y_i was not envisaged; this problem will be dealt with in Section 6.4.5.

6.4.2.2. *Definition of propagation hazards*

Whenever, under the influence of the command signal's propagation delay to the different blocks defining the internal variables, the system's transition brings it to a stable state other than the one indicated in the excitation matrix, the system is considered to have a hazard of propagation.

In the example precedingly studied the graph (Figure 6.60) shows that the system presents a risk of a propagation hazard if starting from the total state 0000, input $b = 1$ is applied (if the signal reaches A_3 before A_1 and A_2, the final state is 011).

The reader can verify that another propagation hazard risk exists if input $b = 0$ is applied, when the system is in the total state 1111.

6.4.2.3. *Elimination of the propagation hazard*

A bad input signal's wave (not straight enough) can cause its delay. Some of the A_i blocks can hence react before the input reaches its threshold while others are not at all modified. In this case, the input signal is corrected in such a way as to obtain a square wave or perfect step in order to eliminate the propagation hazards.

Another method of elimination is to introduce appropriately placed delays. In the Figure 6.58 example the reader can verify that the propagation hazards occur if Y_3 immediately changes value. The introduction of a delay at signal a's arrival of A_3, which gives the variation $A_1A_2A_3$ or $A_2A_1A_3$ of the three blocks, can therefore avoid the hazards. A delay could also be given at the A_3 output; this leads to the same result.

6.4.3. *Transient hazards in electronic circuits driven by switches and using NOR, OR operators*

6.4.3.1. *Cause of Transient hazards in electronic circuits*

The type of control switch used in digital training devices corresponds to the diagram in Figure 6.61. We study the form of signals b^* and $\bar{b}^*$ when b^* goes from 0 to 1. This transition can be performed as indicated in Figure 6.62. The problem of the transient between the first and second times is solved under the assumption that the change-over hazards have been corrected.

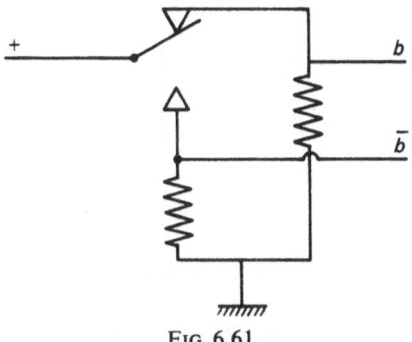

FIG. 6.61.

When b^* goes from 0 to 1, $\bar{b}^*$ changes instantaneously from 1 to 0, while the contacts' rebound causes b^* to follow 0101 before definitively stabilizing itself in 1 (Figure 6.63). This rebound can be the cause of operating hazard as we shall see.

6.4.3.2. *Analysis of hazards due to the inputs in electronic circuits*

Figures 6.64(a) and (b) show two different mountings for realizations which obtain the input signals b and $\bar{b}$. In the first case b_0 and $\bar{b}_0$ are taken directly at the terminals of the switch B. In the second case, they are taken at the terminals of the NOR circuit which complements the preceding signals. Equations (6.25) corresponding to the Figure

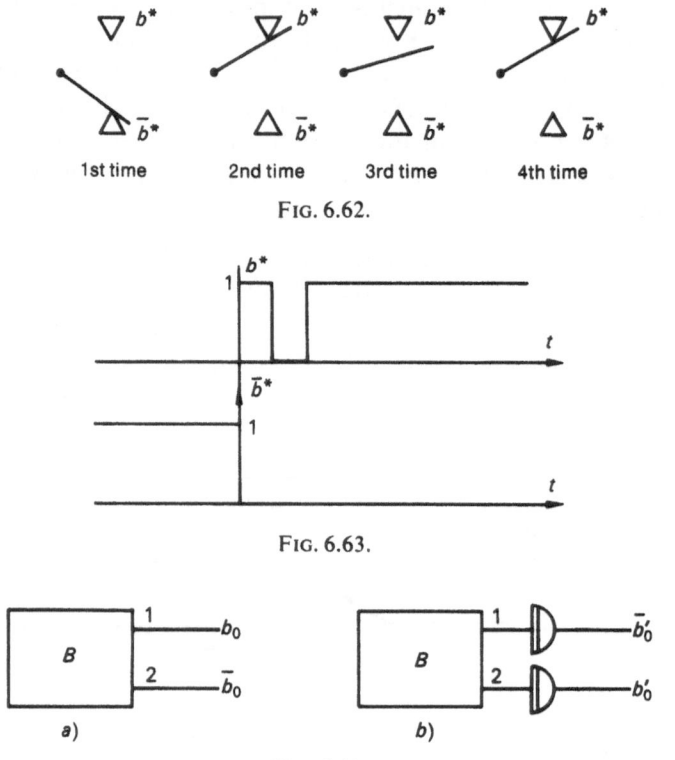

FIG. 6.62.

FIG. 6.63.

FIG. 6.64.

6.58 excitation matrix have been simulated (Figure 6.65) by successively using two types of inputs.

Inputs in Figure 6.64(a). (1) When the switch B goes from position 2 to position 1, the $\bar{b}_0$ output instantaneously becomes 0 (Figure 6.64b), b_0 instantaneously becomes 1, then 0 and definitively fixes itself at the 1 level (Figure 6.64a). But the b_0 inputs of Y_1 and Y_3 in the electrical diagram (Figure 6.65) correspond to the variable $\bar{b}$ in Equations (6.25). To study the circuit's transient, we shall admit that in Equation (6.27) $\bar{b}$ rebounds (the $\bar{b}$ inputs on Y_1 and Y_3 for the circuit in Figure 6.65 correspond to b in Equations (6.25)).

We shall assume that if the switch B goes from position 2 to position 1, its output $\bar{b}_0$ instantaneously becomes 0. This shows that b in Equations (6.25) instantaneously becomes 1.

The transient equations are obtained from (6.25) by replacing b by

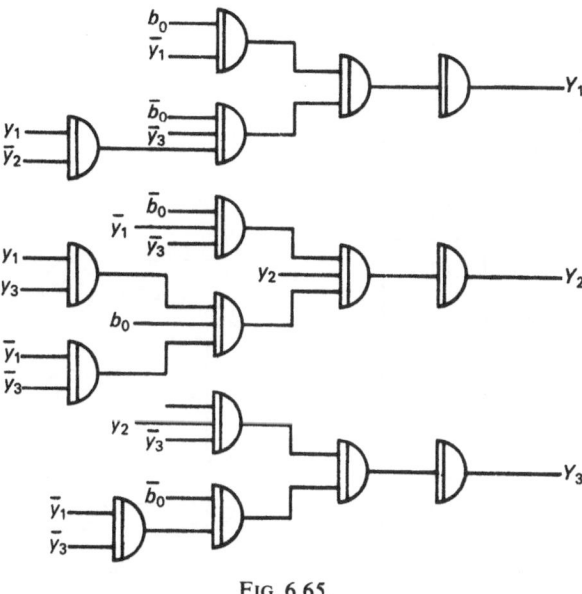

FIG. 6.65.

1, which gives:

$$Y_1 = \bar{b}y_1 + y_3(y_1 + \bar{y}_2)$$
$$Y_2 = y_2 + (y_1\bar{y}_3 + \bar{y}_1y_3)\bar{b} + y_1y_3$$
$$Y_3 = \bar{y}_1\bar{y}_2y_3 + \bar{y}_1 + y_3.$$

These equations correspond to the table in Figure 6.66. Several cases must be envisaged according to whether the time of the different phases of $\bar{b}$, before it stabilizes itself at 0, is greater than, equal to, or less than the system's response time.

The Figure 6.67 diagram shows that the stable state 011 corresponds to a critical race. As a matter of fact, b has a 0 value instaneously, the system goes to the state 001; then if the $\bar{b} = 0$ signal lasts less than the system's response time, the system should reach the stable state 111 (cf. Figure 6.58). The transition will be directed towards 011 or 101. This hazard appears in the simulation.

The transient can therefore be studied by performing three successive input variations ($\bar{b} = 0, 1, 0$) on the Figure 6.66 table.

(2) We now discuss the inverse phenomenon: b_0 takes the value 0, $\bar{b}_0$ follows the sequence 101. To analyze the evolution it is sufficient to

$y_1y_2y_3$ \ $\bar{b}$	0	1
000	001	001
001	101	111
011	(011)	(011)
010	011	011
110	010	(110)
111	(111)	(111)
101	111	111
100	000	110

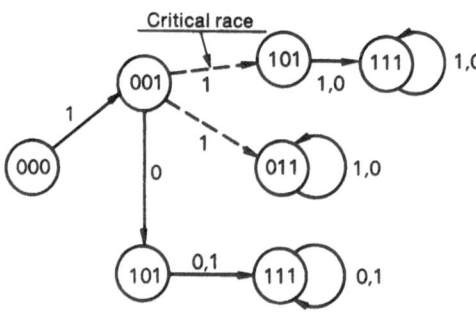

FIG. 6.66.   FIG. 6.67.

replace $\bar{b}$ with 1 in Equations (6.25). The transient equations are written:

$$Y_1 = y_1 + by_3(y_1 + \bar{y}_2)$$
$$Y_2 = y_2 + y_1\bar{y}_3 + \bar{y}_1y_3 + by_1y_3$$
$$Y_3 = \bar{y}_1\bar{y}_2y_3 + b(\bar{y}_1 + y_3).$$

Figure 6.68 represents the corresponding transition. The system goes to state 110 as in the Figure 6.53 excitation matrix. This result is confirmed by simulation.

Inputs in Figure 6.64(b). The reader can show that in this case, position 1 of the switch corresponds to the variable b in Equations (6.25) and position 2 corresponds to $\bar{b}$ in the same equations.

(1) *B goes from 2 to 1. b'* goes from 0 to 1: transient equations are obtained by letting $\bar{b} = 0$ in Equations (6.25),

$$Y_1 = by_3(y_1 + \bar{y}_2)$$
$$Y_2 = y_2 + by_1y_3$$
$$Y_3 = \bar{y}_1\bar{y}_2y_3 + b\bar{y}_1y_3.$$

These equations correspond to the table in Figure 6.69. We note that the system evolves towards the state 111. There are no hazards.

b $y_1 y_2 y_3$	0	1
000	(000)	001
001	011	111
011	010	(011)
010	(010)	011
110	(110)	(110)
111	110	(111)
101	100	111
100	110	110

FIG. 6.68.

b $y_1 y_2 y_3$	0	1
000	(000)	001
001	(001)	101
011	010	(011)
010	(010)	011
110	010	010
111	010	(111)
101	000	111
100	000	000

FIG. 6.69.

(2) *B goes from 1 to 2. b'* goes from 1 to 0: the equations showing how the system operates are obtained from (6.25) by letting $b = 0$: they correspond to Figure 6.70,

$$Y_1 = \bar{b}y_1$$
$$Y_2 = y_2 + \bar{b}(y_1\bar{y}_3 + \bar{y}_1y_3)$$
$$Y_3 = \bar{y}_1\bar{y}_2y_3.$$

There is a hazard because the system stabilizes itself in state 010 if it starts from the stable state 111 (cf. Figure 6.58 indicating the stable state 110).

Comments. (1) Note that the Figure 6.58 table foresaw two propagation hazards: the first occurs if we let $b = 1$ when in state 000; the second if we let $b = 0$ when in state 111. Notice that the hazards of digital training devices are not like propagation hazards.

(2) The memory in Figure 6.71 eliminates the contacts' rebound (cf. Section 2.7) and therefore these types of hazards. We may write:

$$A = (a+A)(\bar{a})$$
$$\overline{A} = \bar{a}\overline{A}.$$

If a goes from 0 to 1, $\bar{a}$ goes instantaneously to 1. Therefore A

$y_1y_2y_3$ \ b	0	1
000	(000)	(000)
001	011	(001)
011	010	010
010	(010)	(010)
110	(110)	010
111	110	010
101	100	000
100	1↑0	000

FIG. 6.70.

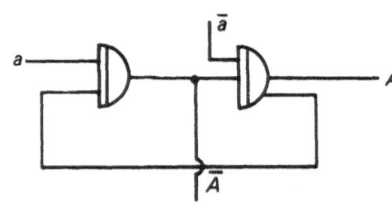

FIG. 6.71.

instantaneously takes the value 0 which it keeps while $\bar{A}$ takes the value 0. In the same way, if a goes from 1 to 0, A and $\bar{A}$ take and keep the values 0 and 1.

6.4.4. *Simulation of a propagation hazard*

The circuit in Figure 6.72(a) has been represented in simulation. The system's equations are written:

$$Y_1 = (A + y_1)\bar{H}$$
$$Y_2 = (\bar{H} + y_2)\bar{A}\bar{y}_1$$
$$Z = \bar{A}H\bar{y}_2.$$

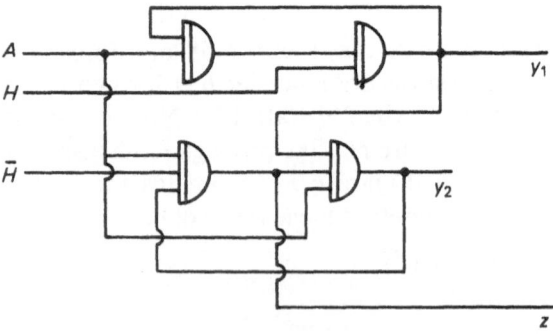

FIG. 6.72(a).

Figure 6.72(*b*) represents the system's excitation matrix. This system corresponds to a control unit. The problem is the following: given a clock *H*, a pulse *A* permits us to obtain a pulse phased with the clock and following *A* at the system's output (Figure 6.73). It is supposed that the pulse *A* is not in phase with the clock. The reader can verify that the table in Figure 6.72(*b*) represents the system sought. To do this, it is advised to start from the state $Hay_1y_2 = 0\ 0\ 0\ 1$: from this state the Figure 6.73 diagram shows that the states 01, 00, 10, 10, 00 (phases 1, 2, 3, 4, 5) are successively attained.

$y_1 y_2$ \ HA	00	01	11	10
00	01/0	10/0	(00/0)	(00/1)
01	(01/0)	10/0	00/0	(01/0)
11	10/0	10/0	00/0	00/0
10	(10/0)	(10/0)	00/0	00/1

FIG. 6.72(*b*).

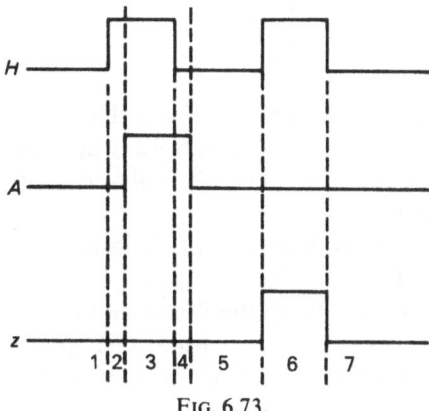

FIG. 6.73.

The simulation of this system, using a clock *H* and its complement $\bar{H}$, and a rectified input pulse *A*, shows that there is a hazard when the input 10 is applied to the system in state 10 with a 00 input. The system goes towards 01 instead of 00 where it should go.

Figure 6.66*b* shows that there is the risk of a propagation hazard as in Figure 6.74. To eliminate it, the clock's signal must arrive at the y_2 block before the y_1 block, therefore, $\bar{H}$ must be before H. But the clock's signal was obtained with the dispositive in Figure 6.75 which will be explained in Appendix 4 of Chapter 11.

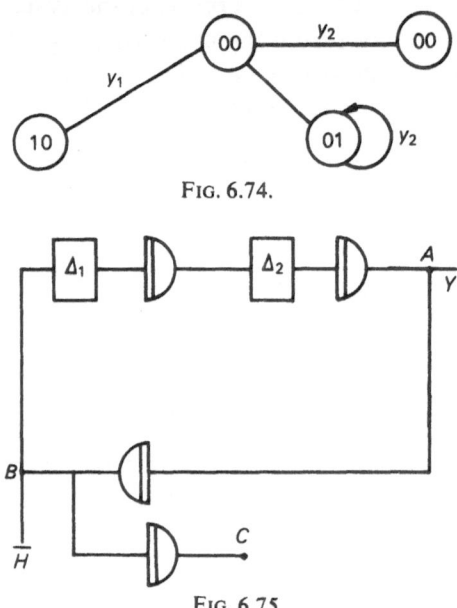

FIG. 6.74.

FIG. 6.75.

The circuit's equation is written $Y = \bar{y}$. Delays Δ_1 and Δ_2 allow for the square waves frequency and duration adjustments. Two delays are used because each one intervenes only on the rising wave (0 to 1) of the signal it attacks.

$\bar{H}$ is used in B. If H is taken at A, $\bar{H}$ is later than H. If H is taken at C, H is later than $\bar{H}$.

The simulator shows that in the first case the propagation hazard is produced while in the second case it has disappeared. A delay of only one transistor is therefore sufficient for the creation of a propagation hazard.

6.4.5. *Propagation delay in the loops*

During the study of propagation hazards we omitted the case in which the signals y_i or $\bar{y}_i$ coming from Y_i, could not reach other blocks defining the secondary variables in a perfectly synchronized way.

This case is an illustration of the appendix to Chapter 4. We have shown that the type of hazard connected with this phenomenon comes from the fact that the Boolean equations do not correspond to the real functioning of the circuit. There is, therefore, reason to modify the choice of the system's internal variables and write the new equations. Consider, for example, the sequential system described by the Boolean equations:

$$Y_1 = \bar{x}y_5$$
$$Y_5 = x\bar{y}_1$$
$$Y_8 = y_8 + y_1\bar{y}_5. \tag{6.26}$$

The representation on logical simulator is that of Figure 6.76. This system's excitation matrix is shown in Figure 6.77. We shall consider the passage from state 000 to state 010 when the input goes from 0 to 1.

The reader can verify that the transient equations (input contact's rebound) are obtained by replacing the variable x by 1 in Equations (6.26).

$$Y_1 = \bar{x}y_5$$
$$Y_5 = y_5 + \bar{y}_1$$
$$Y_8 = y_8 + y_1\bar{y}_5.$$

These equations lead to Figure 6.78.

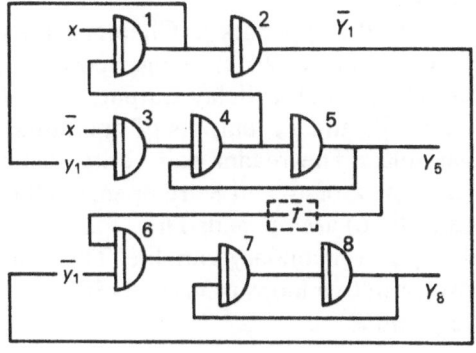

Fig. 6.76.

We notice that on the logical simulator, in agreement with the flow table of Figure 6.78, if the input goes from 0 to 1, the system goes to the stable state 010 as in the excitation matrix (Figure 6.77) in spite of the contact rebound.

x / $y_1 y_5 y_8$	0	1
000	(000)	010
001	(001)	011
011	111	(011)
010	110	(010)
110	111	011
111	(111)	011
101	001	001
100	001	001

Fig. 6.77.

$\bar{x}$ / $y_1 y_5 y_8$	1	0
000	010	010
001	011	011
011	111	(011)
010	110	(010)
110	111	011
111	(111)	011
101	001	001
100	001	001

Fig. 6.78.

Suppose that a parasitical delay exists. We simulate it by a delay in branch 5-6 (cf. Figure 6.76). In this case the system goes from 000 to 011 if the input changes from 0 to 1. If the input is corrected as in Figure 6.71, this hazard disappears. The table in Figure 6.78 cannot explain this phenomenon.

Taking into account the appendix to Chapter 4 the delay T implies that the Boolean Equations (6.26) no longer correspond to the functioning of the circuit. At the T delay output, we define an internal variable y_T. We take Y_4 and Y_8, outputs of operators 4 and 8, as the other internal variables. The reader can verify that if the branches coming from T and operators 4 and 8 are opened, all loops on the circuit's graph (Figure 6.76) are opened. The T delay which is imposed, obliges us to take y_T as a secondary variable. The other two variables correspond to two primitive loops (454) and (787).

The system's equations are:

$$Y_4 = \bar{y}_3 \bar{y}_5 = y_4(\bar{x} + y_1) = \bar{x} y_4$$
$$Y_T = \bar{y}_4$$
$$Y_8 = y_6 + y_8 = y_8 + \bar{y}_2 \bar{y}_T = y_8 + \bar{x} \bar{y}_4 \bar{y}_T. \qquad (6.27)$$

Figure 6.79 represents the excitation matrix corresponding to Equations (6.27).

$y_4 y_T y_8$ \ x	0	1
000	011	010
001	011	011
011	(011)	(011)
010	(010)	(010)
110	100	000
111	101	001
101	101	001
100	(100)	000

FIG. 6.79.

$y_4 y_T y_8$ \ $\bar{x}$	1	0
000	011	010
001	011	011
011	(011)	(011)
010	(010)	(010)
110	000	000
111	001	001
101	001	001
100	000	000

FIG. 6.80.

Note that the stable state $xy_1 y_2 y_8 = 0000$ corresponds to the stable state $xy_1 y_2 y_8 = 0100$ in the Figure 6.79 table.

We shall study the transient corresponding to the input change. We may write:

$$Y_4 = y_4(\bar{x} + y_1).$$

But $\bar{x}$ is one of the three operator inputs and instantaneously becomes 0, hence:

$$Y_4 = y_4 y_1 = y_4 \bar{x} \bar{y}_4 = 0,$$

and also

$$Y_T = \bar{y}_4, \qquad Y_8 = \bar{x} \bar{y}_4 \bar{y}_T + y_8.$$

The variable $\bar{x}$ of Y_8 comes from input x of operator 1. It will therefore take the sequence of values 010.

The table representing the functioning described by these equations appears in Figure 6.80, the transient graph is given in Figure 6.81.

There is a risk of hazard: the system can go towards 011 instead of 010.

The reader can verify as an exercise that the hazard no longer exists if Figure 6.64(b) is adopted for the input.

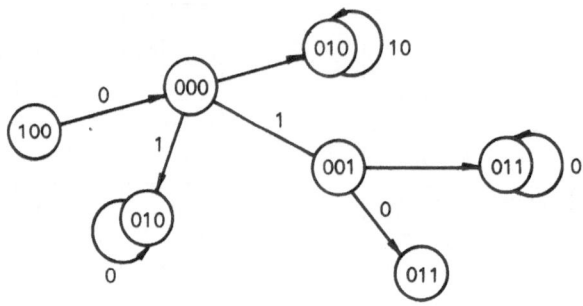

FIG. 6.81.

Interpretation of the results. Reconsider the Equations (6.26).

$$Y_1 = \bar{x}y_5$$
$$Y_5 = y_5 + x\bar{y}_1$$
$$Y_8 = y_8 + y_1\bar{y}_5.$$

We start from state $xy_1y_5y_8 = 0000$ and apply input $x = 1$. Instantaneously y_5 takes the value 1. Suppose that x is not yet 1 on the Y_1 block: Y_1 becomes 1. If during the same time, $y_5 = 1$ has not yet reached block Y_8, Y_8 takes the value 1. At the moment of the steady state, Y_1 retakes a 0 value and the system keeps the 011 state.

There are therefore two propagation hazards: one on the input variable and the other on Y_5.

In simulation, signals x and $\bar{x}$ have the form shown in Figures 6.82(a) and (b) at the input of operators 1 and 3.

In phase I, $Y_1 = 0$ and Y_5 takes the value 1. In phase II, Y_1 takes 1 and the T delay causes $Y_5 = 1$ to have not yet reached block Y_8. Y_8 therefore takes the value 1. The system stabilizes itself in state 011. If, on the contrary, signals x and $\bar{x}$ have, at the input of operators 1 and

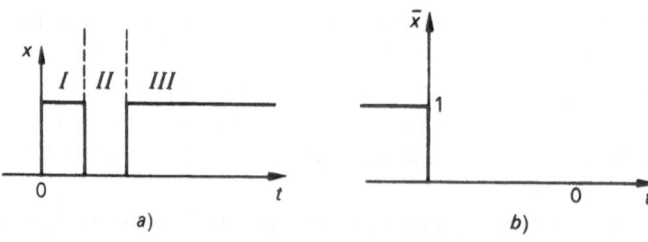

FIG. 6.82.

3, the form shown in Figures 6.83(a) and (b), neither Y_1 nor Y_8 can ever take the value 1; there are no longer any hazards.

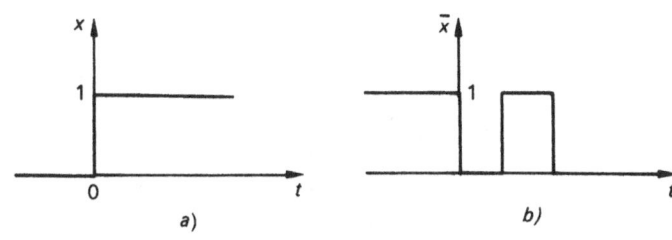

FIG. 6.83.

Conclusion. Our analysis procedure shows that this type of hazard is due to the wrong choice of the system's internal variables. In the following, we shall suppose that such dissymmetries do not exist in the realized circuit. At any rate, we are able to study such phenomena.

6.5. HAZARDS IN SYNCHRONOUS SYSTEMS

In the case of synchronous systems, the problem of hazards is linked to pulse duration, flip-flop response time, and input variation frequency.

A flip-flop is characterized by an excitation time t_e, a response time t_r, and a rise or fall time t_s. The excitation time is the time during which the input must be applied in order to obtain modification of the flip-flop's internal state. The response time is the time at the end of which the signal charges at the flip-flop's output. t_s corresponds to the fact that the square waves of the output are not perfect (Figures 6.84a and b).

The quantities characterize synchronous systems' inputs: the

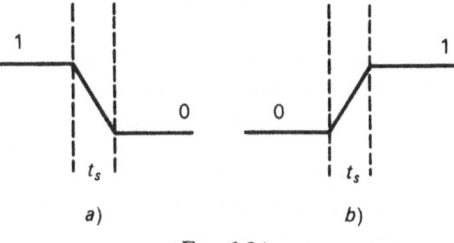

FIG. 6.84.

length of the pulse T_m and the time separating two successive pulses (T_i) as indicated in Figure 6.85. We shall study examples showing incidents which can occur in synchronous systems:

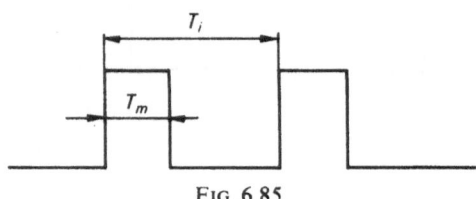

FIG. 6.85.

6.5.1. *Many input gate*

Suppose that an AND gate has two inputs: one is at the output of a flip-flop and the other a pulse.

Figure 6.86 explains the difficulties which can be encountered. In case (a), the lack of synchronization creates a hazard on the output. In case (b), the output signal is truncated and can lack enough energy to operate a flip-flop. Case (c) corresponds to good functioning.

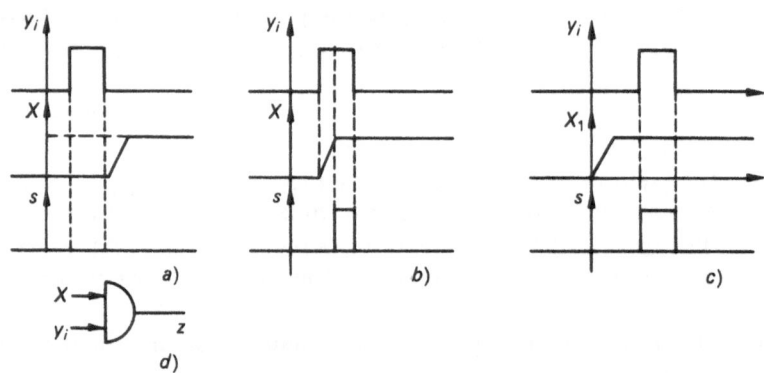

FIG. 6.86.

6.5.2. *Minimal input width*

t_e, the excitation time of the flip-flop, signifies that the incident pulse should last T_m more than t_e if the flip-flop is to react.

6.5.3. *Hazards due to pulse width*

Consider the circuit in Figure 6.87. This circuit is a two-digit binary counter. The first pulse X brings the system to state $Y_A Y_B = 10$ (initial

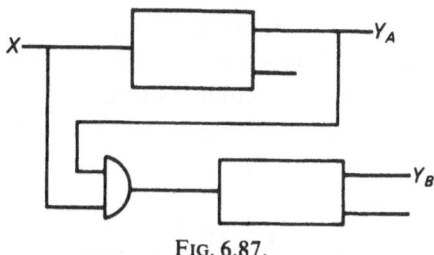

FIG. 6.87.

state 00). The second pulse X brings it to 01; the third to 11 and the fourth is a reset to 0.

If we suppose that the duration of the X pulse, T_m, is greater than the expression $t_e + t_r$ (sum of the excitation and response time of the flip-flop), then, during the first pulse X, the system goes to state 10 then state 11, because the signal X is maintained 1 at the moment of the flip-flop response. In order that the counter functions, the condition

$$T_m \leqslant t_e + t_r$$

must be realized.

6.5.4. Half-pulse hazards

We apply X_1 then X_2 to the system of Figure 6.88 in state $Y_1 Y_2 = 00$. T_i is the time interval separating X_1 and X_2. The system successively passes 10 and 11. The 1 level is reached by Y_1 after a period of time equal to $t_e + t_s$. If the time interval between pulses X_1 and X_2 is less

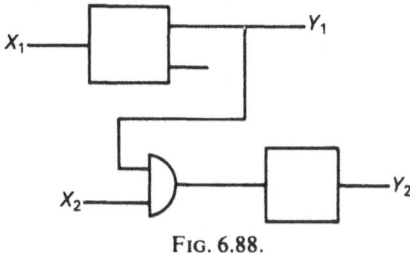

FIG. 6.88.

than $t_e + t_s$, X_2 arrives at the AND gate, when Y_1 still has the value 0. Consequently, X_2 will have on influence. There will be no hazards if the condition

$$T_s \geqslant t_e + t_s$$

is realized.

6.5.5. *Hazards at outputs*

Consider the circuit in Figure 6.89. In absence of a T delay, if the input X is applied, Y_1 takes the value 1 but the output keeps the value 0 instead of taking the value 1 as we wish because the duration of X is generally less than the sum $t_r + t_s$.

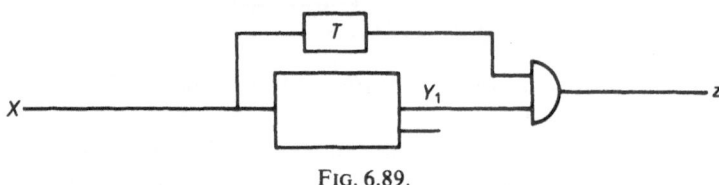

FIG. 6.89.

We shall introduce a delay T such that the condition

$$T_e + T \geq t_r + t_s$$

is realized.

Conclusion. In a synchronous sequential system a certain number of inequalities must be verified. This will impose technological conditions.

BIBLIOGRAPHY

[1] HUFFMAN, D. A., 'The Synthesis of Sequential switching Circuits', *Franklin Institute* **25J** (1954) 161–90, 275–303.

[2] CALDWELL, S. H., *Switching Circuits and Logical Design*, Wiley, New York, 1958.

[3] ROGINSKII, V. N., *The Synthesis of Relay Switching Circuits*, Van Nostrand, 1963.

[4] MALEY, G. A. AND EARLE, J., *The Logic Design of Transistor Digital Computers*, Prentice Hall, Englewood Cliff, N.J., U.S.A., 1963.

[5] FLORINE, J., *La synthèse des machines logiques et son automation*, Presses Académiques Européennes, Bruxelles, 1964.

[6] NASLIN, P., *Circuits logiques et automatismes à séquences*, Dunod, Paris, 1965.

[7] BRUNIN, J., *Logique binaire et commutation*, Dunod, Paris, 1966.

[8] IOANIN, G. H., 'Contribution à l'étude des schémas fonctionnant avec des contacts réels', présentée au Congrès de la Théorie des relais de l'I.F.A.C., Moscou, 1957.

[9] UNGER, S. H., 'Hazards and Delays in Asynchronous Sequential Switching circuits', *I.R.E. Trans.* **CT6** (1959) 12–15.

[10] NASLIN, P., 'Les aléas de continuité dans les circuits de commutation à séquences', *Automatisme* (1959) No. 6.

[11] NASLIN, P., 'Micro-analysis of Sequential Circuits – Propagation and Change-over Hazards', *Process Control Automation* **8** (1961) No. 12.

[12] McCLUSKEY, E. J., 'Transient in Combinational Logic Circuits', in *Redundancy Techniques for Computing Systems* (ed. by R. H. Wilcox and W. C. Mann), Spartan Books, 1962.

[13] WOOD, P. E., 'Hazards in Pulse Sequential Circuits', *I.E.E.E. Trans.* **E.C.13** (1964) No. 2.

[14] EICHELBERGER, E. B., 'Hazard Detection in Combinational and Sequential Switching Circuits', *I.B.M.J. Res. Development* **9** (1965) Ni. 2.

[15] MOISIL, GR., C., *Transient States in Switching Circuits and Many-valued Logic*, Academic Press, New York, 1969.

EXERCISES

6.1. Determine the phase, flow, transition tables, the excitation, output, transition matrices, and the transition graph of the relay circuit in Figure 6.90. Look for cycles and races.

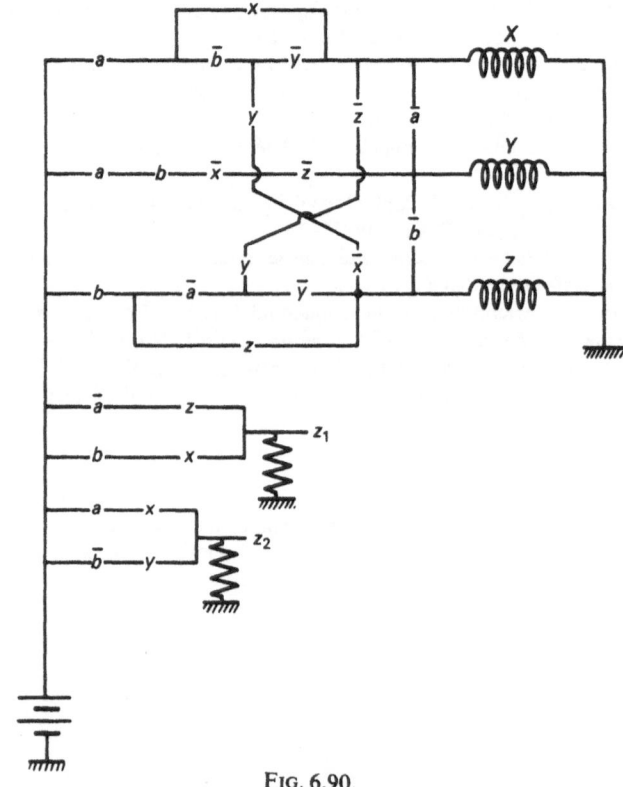

FIG. 6.90.

6.2. Consider the JK flip-flop circuit which has its equations written:

$$J_1 = X_1 \bar{y}_2 \qquad J_2 = X_2 \qquad J_3 = X_1 y_2 + X_2 \bar{y}_2$$
$$K_1 = J_2 \qquad K_2 = X_2 \qquad K_3 = X_1 + X_2 y_2$$
$$Z = \bar{y}_3 (y_1 + \bar{y}_2).$$

Represent this circuit and give its excitation matrix.

6.3. Consider the PQ flip-flop which has its equations written:

$$P_1 = X_1\bar{y}_2 \qquad P_2 = X_2 \qquad P_3 = X_1\bar{y}_3 + X_2\bar{y}_2$$
$$Q_1 = y_2 \qquad Q_2 = y_2 \qquad Q_3 = X_1\bar{y}_2 + y_3$$
$$Z = X_1 y_2 + y_1 y_3.$$

Same questions as for exercise 6.1.

6.4. Consider the RS flip-flop circuit which has its equations written:

$$R_1 = X \qquad R_2 = \bar{X}y_2 \qquad R_3 = \bar{X}\bar{y}_1 y_3$$
$$S_1 = 0 \qquad S_2 = \bar{X}\bar{y}_2 \qquad S_3 = \bar{X}\bar{y}_1 \bar{y}_3$$
$$Z = X(\bar{y}_2 + y_3).$$

Same questions as for exercise 6.1.

6.5. Consider the symmetrical flip-flop circuit which has its equations written:

$$\tau_1 = Xy_1 \qquad \tau_2 = \bar{X} \qquad \tau_3 = \bar{X}\bar{y}, \qquad Z = \bar{y}_1(y_2 + y_3).$$

Same questions as for Exercise 6.1.

6.6. Look for the hazards in the combinational circuits of Figures 6.91 and 6.92, (discuss according to the nature or order of the contacts' switching).

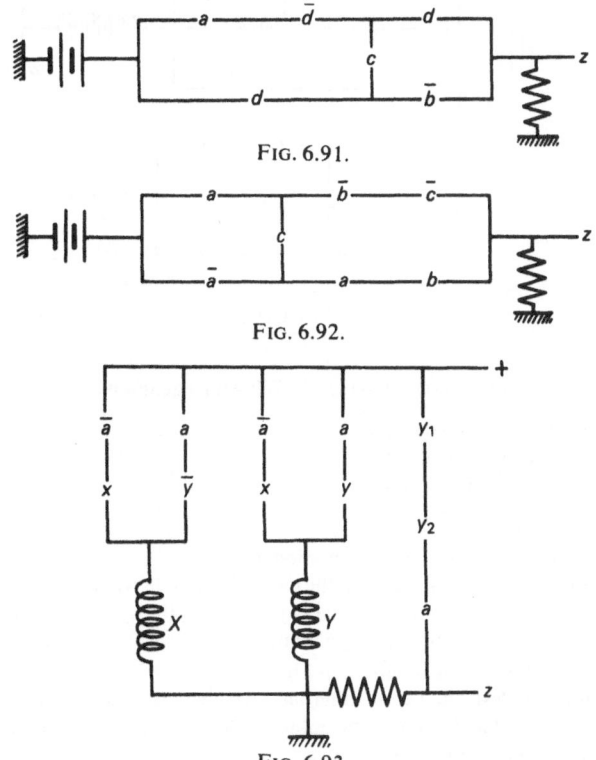

FIG. 6.91.

FIG. 6.92.

FIG. 6.93.

6.7. Consider the circuit in Figure 6.93.

(a) study its functioning;

(b) if the A switch has normal switching, look for the system's hazards and eliminate them;

(c) Assuming the hazards to be eliminated in static functioning, determine the system's hazards if A switches slowly. How can they be eliminated?

6.8. Consider the system in Figure 6.94.

(a) Determine the system's equations and give the different tables and matrices for ideal functioning.

(b) Determine the system's possible hazards in function of the nature and order of the contacts' switching.

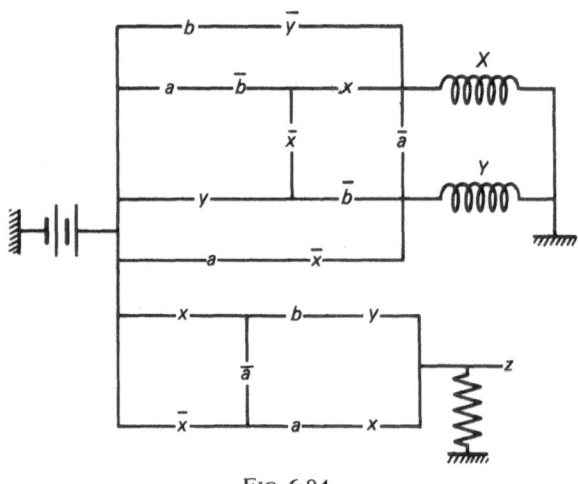

FIG. 6.94.

6.9. Consider the relay system having the following equations:

$$Y_1 = \bar{a}y_1 + y_1\bar{y}_2 + y_2y_3$$
$$Y_2 = \bar{a}y_1\bar{y}_3 + ay_2 + \bar{y}_1y_3$$
$$Y_3 = \bar{a}y_3 + a\bar{y}_1\bar{y}_2 + y_2y_3$$
$$Z = y_1\bar{y}_2 + y_2y_3.$$

Sketch the circuit and determine its excitation matrix.

(b) Look for the system's hazards in the case in which A switches slowly.

(c) In the case in which A switches slowly, look for the system's hazards and find a means of eliminating them after having eliminated the hazards in static functioning.

6.10. Consider the transistor circuit in Figure 6.95.

(a) Find the simplest choices of internal variables. Show that variables y_2 and y_4, outputs of operators 2 and 4, are sufficient to define this system. In this case, determine the excitation and output matrices.

(b) Look for races, cycles, and change-over hazards.

(c) Look for propagation hazards: deduce, from them, that the critical race on the secondary variables can be eliminated by the introduction of an appropriately placed delay.

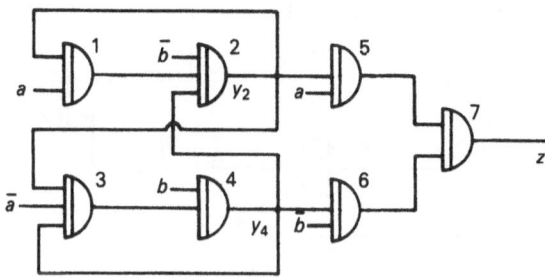

FIG. 6.95.

6.11. Consider the circuit in Figure 6.96.

(a) Analyze the system: give its excitation matrix with respect to variables y_2, y_3, y_5.

(b) Look for propagation hazards.

(c) Determine the contact rebound hazards if the signals a are supplied by a switch.

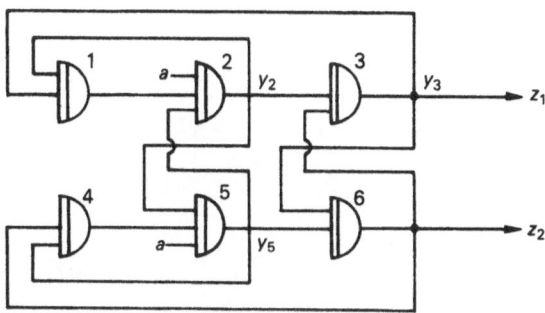

FIG. 6.96.

6.12. Consider the circuit in Figure 6.97.

(a) Show that this circuit is a three-counter by determining its excitation and output matrices.

(b) Study the propagation and contact rebound hazards.

(c) Using a supplementary secondary variable, find the circuit's evolution if a delay such as in Figure 6.97 is introduced.

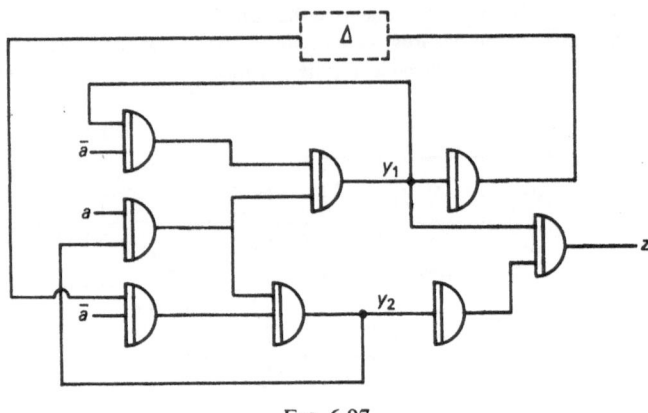

FIG. 6.97.

6.13. In the circuit of Figure 4.57 what influence does a delay placed between operators 1 and 3 have? Give the system's equations and determine the new excitation matrix.